The material word

The material word

Some theories of language and its limits

David Silverman
Department of Sociology
Goldsmith's College, London

Brian Torode
Department of Sociology
Trinity College, Dublin

Routledge & Kegan Paul
London, Boston and Henley

First published in 1980
by Routledge & Kegan Paul Ltd
39 Store Street, London WC1E 7DD,
Broadway House, Newtown Road,
Henley-on-Thames, Oxon RG9 1EN and
9 Park Street, Boston, Mass. 02108, USA
Set in 10 on 11pt Times
and printed in Great Britain by
Lowe & Brydone Printers Ltd
Thetford, Norfolk

British Library Cataloguing in Publication Data

Silverman, David

The material word.
1. Sociolinguistics
I. Title   II. Torode, Brian
301.2'1   P40   79–41120

ISBN 0 7100 0398 6
ISBN 0 7100 0399 4 Pbk

For our students

Contents

Preface

For more than a decade, language has been on sociology's agenda. The 1960s saw the emergence of ethnomethodology, structuralism, semiotics and a revitalized sociolinguistics. Despite the grandiose claims of early, programmatic formulations, each came to constitute a serious threat to sociology's core assumptions.

Equally, the revitalization of Marxist thought in recent years has challenged accepted versions of sociological method. In France, Althusser developed a treatment of ideology which offered a materialist alternative to humanistic readings of Marx. In Germany, Habermas proposed a critical theory which sought to locate emancipatory potential in a legitimation crisis rooted in everyday discourse. In both cases, a critique of society became, in important respects, a critique of language.

The available literature has not, however, matched the pace of the debate. It remains polarized between isolated original papers reporting pieces of research and much more prevalent programmatic texts which rarely give a glimpse of the value of the concepts which they parade.

This book offers a reasoned response to both the state of the argument and the state of the literature. It seems to us that the work of the various traditions of linguistic analysis can be used in two distinct ways: we call one interpretation, the other interruption. The language of interpretation approaches another text or conversation with its own version of reality presupposed. It treats the interpreted language as the appearance of that presupposed reality. It is reductionist in that it seeks to reduce the workings of one language to the mastery of another.

The language of interruption approaches another text or conversation with the aim of interrogating the relation between appearance and reality that is proposed there. It seeks to discover and support the anti-authoritarian practices within ordinary language which interpretation opposes and represses. By rejecting any appeal to idealist 'essences' outside ordinary language, interruption represents a materialist turn towards the character of linguistic practices themselves.

This has consequences for how we proceed in this book. Our attempt to review the literature on language seeks to intervene in certain key texts by interrupting the relation between appearance and reality that they propose. Consequently, this is neither a textbook nor a collection of research papers. It is both.

Each section of the book begins with an interrogation of an important theory of language. What we learn from that interrogation is applied to an investigation of a related text. The only exceptions to this rule are Parts I and VII which serve the function of introduction and conclusion.

Contrary to the practice of most previous work, we make no differentiation between the analysis of conversations and of texts. Instead, we seek to develop a method applicable to both. Three different approaches are used to this end. The first examines the implications of a theory for everyday speech. This approach is employed particularly in discussing the writings of Althusser, Sacks, Garfinkel, Bernstein, Labov, Foucault and Habermas. The second approach examines the implications of a theory of language for analysing a literary text. This is applied to the examination of some texts of Kafka in terms of Wittgenstein's philosophy of language, a text of Robbe-Grillet in terms of Barthes's theory of literature, and a text by Perrault in terms of the account of writing given by Volosinov and by Derrida. The third examines the theory's ability to account for the language used in formulating it. This reflexive approach is used to interrogate texts by Althusser, Husserl, Sacks, Heidegger and Locke.

The resulting transformation can be quite far-reaching. Thus Wittgenstein's investigations may be read not so much as a new way of doing philosophy, but as a critique of the very assumptions from which the need for doing philosophy grows. Husserl's phenomenology may be understood not merely as a new science in the professionalized Anglo-Saxon sense, but as an attempt to transform knowledge itself. Garfinkel's interruptions of ordinary conversations may be considered not as mere sociological experiments, but as powerful ways of transforming the everyday world. Locke's attempt to establish property rights may be understood not as an exercise in political theory but as the ideological basis of an economy of signs ruled by a transcendental Subject. Derrida's pursuit of *differance* becomes not an esoteric exercise for advanced students of continental philosophy, but an interrogation of economic and sexual discourses as vivid as those of Marx and Freud.

Our attempt to treat theories of language as practices is aimed at the student of language in sociology, philosophy, literary criticism and linguistics. The reader must choose whether the radical writings on language which are to be found in each of these approaches in the twentieth century are to be used merely to understand the word, or to change it.

Otherwise stated, the choice is between an idealist contemplation of the essence of language, whether grasped as grammar, usage, the ego, rational properties of everyday language or differance, or an attempt to effect a material transformation of the practice of language, in the widest range of the settings in which it occurs.

This book is an expression of a collaborative enterprise upon which its authors have joined. Over a number of years, we have learned from each other and this development of common ground is reflected in the coherence of the book's argument. Such a cumulative form of learning is expressed in the structure of the book itself. As we move from one section to another, so we assemble methods and guidelines which are applied to what follows. Although it is not possible for us here to discuss all contemporary theories of language – for instance transformational grammar is omitted – we attempt to investigate those theories which seem most directly to help us as sociologists to build an account of linguistic practice.

While the form and content of each chapter reflects extensive mutual discussion, we note that Brian Torode is primarily responsible for Chapters 1, 2, 5, 6, 7, 8 and 13. David Silverman was mainly involved with Chapters 3, 4, 9, 10, 11, 12 and 14.

Chapter 5 and part of Chapter 7 first appeared as part of 'The Extra-Ordinary in Ordinary Language', unpublished PhD thesis, University of Edinburgh, 1975. An earlier version of Chapter 10 was presented at the Theory and Praxis Conference, Free University, Amsterdam, November 1975. The analysis of Sacks in Chapter 7 was presented to the discussion week on 'Phenomenology and Language' organized by Janet Woolf at the Leeds University Department of Sociology, February 1976. Chapter 1 was written for the Sociolinguistics Workshop held at Walsall College of Education, September 1976. Chapter 6 was presented to a seminar held by the Department of Sociology, Brunel University, May 1977. Chapter 2, in an expanded form, was presented to the conference of Socialist Economists day conference on 'Ideology', Birkbeck College, London, October 1977. An earlier version of

Chapter 12 was first presented to the British Sociological Association conference on 'Culture', held at the University of Sussex, April 1978. Chapter 13 was presented to seminars at the departments of Sociology at Goldsmith's College, London, and at the Polytechnic of the City of London, May 1978. A version of Chapter 8 was first presented to the Fifth Systemics Workshop, the Department of English and American Literature, University of East Anglia, September 1978. Chapters 3, 4, 9, 11 and 14 were specially written for this volume.

We are very grateful for the opportunities afforded by these occasions, and for the criticisms received there, though we have not always responded to them. We are also grateful to colleagues who have provided critical support over a period of years, or who have commented upon particular chapters. In particular, we thank Zsuzsa Baross, Eddie Brunsdon, Patrick Colfer, Valerie Minogue, Trevor Pateman, Mel Pollner, Vic Seidler, Gillian Silverman and Ruth Torode. We are grateful to Zygmunt Bauman who suggested ways in which the scope of the book could be extended. We owe a special debt also to Stewart Clegg, with whom the project of this book was conceived, and who coined its title, which we are using with his permission.

part I

Introduction: the language of mastery

Interpreting the language of
physics

The assumption, that speech is merely the appearance of an external reality to which it refers, is here reversed, in order to shift attention to speech as a reality in its own right. Analysis of everyday conversations shows that the reference of the word 'I' is not the unique individuality of the speaker who utters it, but the linguistic practices available to all speakers. These constitute its sense in contradictory ways.

chapter 1

Interrupting the 'I'

> 'When *I* use a word,' Humpty Dumpty said in rather a scornful tone, 'it means just what I choose it to mean – neither more nor less.'
> 'The question is,' said Alice, 'whether you *can* make words mean so many different things.'
> 'The question is,' said Humpty Dumpty, 'which is to be master – that's all.'
> – Lewis Carroll, *Alice Through the Looking Glass* (1873, p. 124).

There is a schema which is so powerfully reiterated both in academic (written) and in commonsense (spoken) accounts of the linguistic situation that today it passes for that situation itself. According to the schema, linguistic communication consists in the transmission of immaterial ideas or concepts from one person (speaker or writer) to another (hearer or listener) by means of material signs such as marks on paper or vibrations of the air waves. Ferdinand de Saussure (1974, pp. 11–12) pictures the situation as shown in Figure 1.

When communication is interpreted in this way, the interplay of signs is not treated as a reality in its own right. Rather, the sign is taken as the signifier, indicator, or appearance of a signified essential reality which underlies it. For Saussure, this reality is the conceptual content which, he supposes, is somehow held in the brain of the communicating person.

The brain is unavailable to the researcher. Its content, conceptual or otherwise, remains mysterious, and can only be the subject of speculation or arbitrary assumption. The arbitrary and speculative mysticism attaching to the traditional interpretation of communication can be called, in a precise sense, *idealism,* in that it purports to

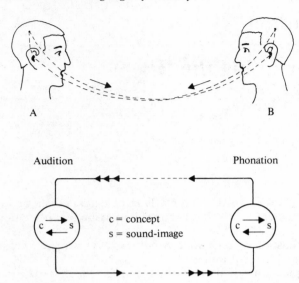

Figure 1

treat the material sign as the mere appearance of an underlying ideal reality.

In opposition to the traditional interpretation our intention is materialist. We attempt to treat the interplay of material signs as a reality in its own right.

A curious feature of Saussure's work is that while taking as its topic the interplay of material signs, it understands this topic always within the context of an essentialist and ideal reality supposedly underpinning these signs. Hence the first question which poses itself to our materialist project is how does the interplay of material signs give rise to essentialist conceptions of ideality? In our attempt to answer this question, Saussure's text, which explicitly articulates and develops the traditional conception, is doubly valuable. First, it sets out in theory the workings of any linguistic communication via talk or text from one person to another. Second, it is itself a linguistic communication, and the way in which it works as a text in practice can be interrogated and compared to the theory. We refer to this interrogation, which reveals the gap between the theory and

practice of the communication, as an *interruption* of the communication.[1]

Interpretation

Consider an interpretation of Saussure's practice in terms of his own
theory. His text, i.e. the diagram on p. 4, is to be regarded as an
inscription of certain concepts in his own brain. In reading his text,
we undertake a process of vision whereby his material signs are
translated into concepts in our brains.

However, we can never be certain whether our concepts will
correspond with his. To bring this correspondence into question is
to interrupt Saussure's practice in terms of his own theory. We know
very little about the kind of thing the 'concepts' are. However if the
effect of the diagram upon our brains is an example of these
concepts, it is not clear why the concepts should differ significantly
from the diagram itself. The situation is clarified if we turn our
attention away from our experience of the concepts to our reading
of his text.

Saussure seeks to give an account of communication and, in the
first instance, speech. In order to give point to his account, he has to
give point to that speech. The point of speaking, according to
Saussure, is to attempt to bridge the gap between brains whose
content is mutually unavailable. In order to satisfy this requirement,
we are supposed to assume that the concepts corresponding to his
diagram in our brains necessarily differ from the concepts which
originated the diagram in his.

A number of results follow if we make this assumption. First, our
own understanding of his theory will always differ from, and so be
inferior to, his. He will always be privileged with regard to the
understanding of his own writing, since it cannot reproduce his
concepts. Second, and more generally, according to this theory
language always fails in its objective because it does not succeed in
communicating concepts. (If it did succeed there would be no need
for further speech, or writing.) Third, given that language arises in
order to solve an insoluble problem, it follows that there can never
be any change in the linguistic situation: though Saussure's concepts
differ from ours, his signs (his diagrams) do not.

But if we shift attention from the conceptual contents of the brain
to the material signs of language, then these results take on a new
significance. The first implies that our writing in response to reading
Saussure's text must differ from his original writing; but since this is
necessarily so there is no reason to deplore it. Instead we should

simply acknowledge that language is always in change. The second implies that given the failure of language to correspond with or to communicate concepts, concepts are not the basis on which linguistic change should be understood. This, then, challenges the third implication. For if language is always in change, then we require a theory other than Saussure's to explain it.

The practice of Saussure's text transcends its stated theory, and out of this practice another theory can be built. Consider again the point of reading Saussure's diagram, if the concepts which we attach to it as readers can never correspond to those he attached to it as writer. If the conceptual difference is the point, then we can only gaze in uncomprehending astonishment at this evidence of a brain different from our own. But what if this evidence, the material language, is of interest in its own right? (This could not be the case in Saussure's own theory, since for him the signs must already be comprehensible for us to understand the text, in our limited way, at all.) In this case the point is that Saussure has assembled material signs in a way in which we ourselves had not assembled them before – but a way in which we could now assemble them. The point of reading Saussure's text is now not the theory but the practice of language which is there exhibited.

More generally, we learn from an interruption of Saussure's text that the point of communication is not the transmission from brain to brain of theoretical concepts, but the mutual learning by practitioners of linguistic practices. This learning, which we hope to have exemplified in reading a brief passage from Saussure, is not a passive reception of the signs communicated by one person to another, but involves an active struggle. In this struggle the signs communicated by the first person can be contrasted with the way in which they are communicated, so producing a new assembly of signs.

Interruption

Ultimately however the struggle is not between one person and another but rather between ways of speaking and writing. As is apparent even in this brief example from Saussure such struggle is already under way within the language of a single person. In this case, to interrupt it is simply to provoke tendencies at work in that first language. In this sense, the practice of interruption seeks not to impose a language of its own but to enter critically into existing linguistic configurations, and to re-open the closed structures into which they have ossified.

This ossification arises above all from the treatment of material signs as dependent for their sense upon reference to an external, immaterial, reality – including those cases where this reality is given the name of a material form. Thus, by long tradition, words derive their meaning from the 'things' to which they refer. From the more recent sociological viewpoint, speech is but the expression of relationships between speakers, conceived as 'social facts'. In each case language is made the slave of an extra-linguistic master, either 'natural' or 'social' in character.[2]

The twentieth-century project has aimed to reverse this relation. Saussure, Wittgenstein and Garfinkel are united in their view of linguistic practices as a reality *sui generis,* constitutive of such sense as speakers and hearers can have of the natural and social worlds.

The traditional conception, which this project opposes, is manifestly essentialist in its assumption that man's relations with nature and with society are unaffected by the language in which they are formulated. It neglects the fact that language is itself both 'natural' and 'social' in character, and so is an integral part of those relations. It wants to place language outside each of these realms and make it transparent.

But the modern project is equally essentialist. It acknowledges that the 'natural' and the 'social' interplay in the words which refer to them. But it treats this interplay as itself closed. In seeking to explicate the principles of thise closure, it makes language once again the slave of an extra-linguistic master, though paradoxically its name, Grammar, is that of language itself. It places language in a realm of its own, and makes it opaque.

An attempt will be made, in the pages which follow, to break with these formulations. As against the reductionist approaches which inspire research in the psychoanalysis of language on the one hand and sociolinguistics on the other, we insist that language must be treated as an object of enquiry in its own right.[3] But as against the search for closed unity which inspires research in ethnomethodology and structuralism, we insist that languages are, in practice, plural and open.

To insist upon the plurality and openness of languages, as against the reductionist closure which is imposed upon language by the ways in which it is conventionally studied, is not an exercise in neutrality. It requires in our view a political intervention, because it reveals political choices which are already being made, by languages whose neutrality is conventionally asserted.

We refer to this intervention as an *interruption* of the neutrality of language, a neutrality which is primarily asserted by *interpretation* imposed upon language from the outside. In our usage, 'interpretation' refers to the practice of treating language as the mere 'appear-

ance' of an extra-linguistic 'reality' pre-supposed by the interpretation. This practice is itself not what it appears to be: it does not do
what it says. For it is impossible to formulate an extra-linguistic
reality, e.g. 'nature', 'society', or 'grammar' except in language.
Thus in pretending to uphold a non-linguistic and so neutral reality
the interpretation in practice imposes its own language upon that of
the language which it interprets.

As we attempt to show, interpretation is a very widespread
practice of linguistic mastery, to be found not simply in analytic
academic approaches to language, but also in everyday linguistic
practice in such settings as schools, hospitals, and elsewhere. As we
also try to show, the interruption of this mastery is also already in
progress, not only within these settings but also in literary texts and
within academic debates also. But since interpretation is all-
pervading and reasserts itself on every possible occasion, these
instances are elusive and require an interruption of the conventional setting, text, and debate in order to discover them at all.

For us interruption is the attempt to reveal the interplay between
'appearance' and 'reality' within language itself. As against the view
of language as a reality *sui generis,* whether transparent or opaque,
we insist that language necessarily refers, as appearance, to a reality
other than itself. But, we propose, the way in which it does this is to
refer *to other language.* Thus plurality is inseparable from language,
and it is the play of reference from one language to another
language that suggests the reference of language to a reality other
than language.

Irony and the 'I'

What is involved in the distinctions so far drawn may be exemplified
by considering some instances of speaking, taken from a study of
conversations within a secondary school classroom, involving the
word *I.* For the purposes of this exploration, the traditional view of
language is well represented by the statement by Charles Sanders
Peirce (quoted from Burks, 1949, pp. 677–8):

> *I, thou, that, this,* . . . indicate things in the directest possible way.
> . . . A pronoun is an index. . . . A pronoun ought to be defined as
> a word which may indicate anything to which the first and second
> person have suitable real connections, by calling the attention of
> the second person to it.

Let us call *realistic* this view that such a word as *I* is meaningful first
and foremost by its 'real connections' (which Peirce assumes to be
present to hand in the situation in which the word is spoken). The

meaning is thus the social or natural referent of the word.

The sociological variant of this traditional view is exemplified by the work of R. Brown and A. Gilman (1972, p. 265) on 'The pronouns of power and solidarity'. They point out that: 'a historical study of the pronouns of address reveals a set of semantic and social psychological correspondencies.' Brown and Gilman investigate historical and social variation in the use of second person pronouns to mark intimacy and distance, superordination and subordination. They interpret the meaning of pronouns as being the social norms to which, in their differential usage, they conform. Despite its different version of reality, this viewpoint is realistic in the same way as that of Peirce.

The modern view is represented by Harold Garfinkel and Harvey Sacks's discussion of such terms as ' "here, now, this, that, it, I, he, you, there, then, today, tomorrow" ' which 'have been called indicators, egocentric particulars, indexical expressions, occasional expressions, indices, shifters, pronomials, and token reflexives,' (1970, p. 347): 'We begin with the observation about these phenomena that everyone regularly treats such utterances as occasions for reparative practices [and] that such practices are native not only to research but to all users of the natural language.' Garfinkel and Sacks would term the approach of Peirce or Brown and Gilman 'natural', the statement of a language unwilling to examine its own resources. As against this, ethnomethodologists propose an exploration of what is involved in the mastery of the practices of natural language.

In the light of these distinctions, consider the following conversation, taken from the observations of a school classroom by Torode:

Jones: I got three pieces of tart for pudding.
Russell: Yeah, by starving the others.
Jones: They could never starve me.

At the risk of undue brevity, we propose that the 'natural' approach will observe what is non-obvious about Jones's remark to be the breaking of a presumed norm, roughly of the form 'one each'. Russell calls attention to this non-obviousness, and so establishes the point of Jones's remark, by noting that given 'one each' as the norm, more for one implies less for others. This implies that the proper object of a natural sociology is the norm whose infraction constitutes the point of natural conversation.[4] However, such norms cannot themselves appear in natural conversation, which only finds point in reporting their infraction.

From the ethnomethodological standpoint, Jones is to be heard as exhibiting his mastery of natural language by 'meaning something different than he can say in so many words', i.e. glossing. Russell is to be heard as hearing Jones's mastery and thereby exhibiting his own. Garfinkel and Sacks suggest the use of square brackets, '[ ]', to locate a particular gloss, which can then be investigated by asking, what is doing [ ]? Alternatively, what is the work for which [ ] is its proper gloss? (ibid. pp. 350–3). One gloss in Jones's speech can be located as follows: 'I [got] three pieces of tart for pudding'. We can then ask, what is the work of doing [getting]?

It is precisely this question which, within the ethnomethodological viewpoint, Russell is to be construed as answering. The work of doing [getting], in Russell's phrase, is [starving] the others. We place square brackets around the word 'starving' as a reminder that Russell's reply is itself a gloss, raising in turn the question what is [starving]? The proper object of ethnomethodology is the practices glossed in natural conversation.

We propose that both schools have missed the point made by Russell's response to Jones. Both presume the existence of a reality external to speech, prior to their encounter with that speech, which is interpreted as the appearance, or document, of that reality. For natural sociology, reality comprises the unchanging realm of idealized social norms. For ethnomethodology, reality comprises the unchanging realm of members' social practices. Both are *realistic*. Both conceal from others the way in which they import their presupposed notion of reality, and conceal from themselves the way in which the dialectic between appearance and reality is itself an issue for talk.

Edmund Husserl has proposed an alternative way of thinking, in the following terms (1970, p. 14):

> Let us contrast the natural mode of reflection with the *philosophical*. With the awakening of reflection about the relation of cognition to its object, abysmal difficulties arise. Cognition, the thing most taken for granted in natural thinking, suddenly emerges as a mystery.

'What is taken for granted in natural thinking', says Husserl, 'is the possibility of cognition'. But from the philosophical standpoint (ibid., p. 15): 'The correlation between cognition as a mental process, its referent and what objectively is, . . . is the source of the deepest and most difficult problems. Collectively, the problem of cognition.' A philosophical approach to conversation will be characterized by its concern for the 'problem of cognition', that is the relation between 'cognition' (appearance) and 'its referent, what objectivity is' (reality). It will investigate how such sense as we have of realities external to language, including 'norms' and 'methods', arises in and through speech. We will refer to such an outlook as *'real'-istic*.

From this point of view, consider the conversation again. Russell poses Jones's utterance as the appearance of a reality whose sense he completes. Prior to Russell's response, Jones's utterance stands as a self-sufficient intelligible remark. At this point in time, appearance and reality appear united. But Russell's speech reveals a gap between the appearance of Jones's words, and a greater reality which Russell reveals retrospectively to have been the case all along. It is instructive to examine precisely how Russell achieved this transformation.

Jones's remark makes sense without recourse to any other speech. It also appears that no sub-section of his remark does so. We will call such an atomic unit of sense a *picture*.[5] The outstanding feature of Russell's response is that it does not make sense self-sufficiently: it requires recourse to the first picture to complete its sense. The response in fact is not a new picture, but an extension of Jones's picture. Russell's speech shifts the issue away from the words of Jones versus the words of Russell. Instead it counterposes to the picture portrayed by Jones the modified picture produced by Russell.

A diagram may help. We propose to indicate pictures by enclosing them in round brackets, thus: '( )'. The two pictures are:

(I got three pieces of tart for pudding)
(I got three pieces of tart for pudding by starving the others)

Russell's remark transforms Jones's picture by introducing a new entity, *the others*. Once Russell has spoken, it has to be admitted that, retrospectively, they have been there all along, but that Jones has *chosen* to treat them as unproblematic in focusing on other matters.

The new phrase 'starving the others' has no effect on the elements *tart* and *pudding* in the picture. But the element *I* is modified, by being made the pole of a new connection, 'starving the others'. Russell's focus is not on 'the others' *per se*, as might be suggested from consideration of his words alone, but on the *I*. The *I* is the element in the original picture whose position in the configuration is changed by the transformation. So, although Jones's remark does not specify any one of its elements as paramount, Russell's response retrospectively constitutes the *I* as paramount in Jones's remark.

Russell's remark is thus not neutral in its reponse to Jones. For this reason, it is inappropriate to describe it as an 'interpretation'. In Garfinkel's usage interpretation means treating speech as the appearance of an underlying reality of which it is the document,

(1967, Chapter 3). The employment of documentary method entails the interpreter reformulating in his own words the reality of which the interpreted speech is construed to have only formulated the appearance. But Russell specifically employs not his own words but the words of Jones to express the reality which did not appear in Jones's formulation. Rather than *interpreting* Jones's picture, Russell *interrupts* Jones's picture. He ironically continues Jones's speech ('yeah'), thereby exhibiting the gap or rupture between appearance and reality sustained by the speech of Jones.

As compared to the interpretive speech of both ethnomethodology and natural sociology, we have attempted an interruption of the conversation. This has revealed the gap which the conversation sustains between appearance and reality. Whereas the proper objects of both natural and ethnomethodological interpretive sociologies are realities external to speech, the proper object of interruptive sociology is the ways in which speakers constitute and change the relation between 'appearance' and 'reality' in speech.

The efficacy of the transformation achieved by Russell is seen in Jones's further response. Here he accepts the presence of 'the others' and 'starving' as part of the situation and proceeds to explicate the picture as modified by Russell. So discourse between the boys continues. That it does so is the result of Russell's contribution, for Jones's opening remark had been expressed in monologic rather than dialogic terms. The speech of the *I* which Jones employed intrinsically precludes participation by others, since the *I* of one speaker can only be addressed by another speaker in different words. Russell's ellipsis exhibits the only way in which this private language can be entered. Russell opens a discourse where Jones had closed it.

Consider now a second extract from field notes made by Torode during observation in a school classroom: 'Several boys late, e.g. Macarthur says, "Sir, I'm late, 'cos I took my time".' As before it will be helpful to indicate the way in which natural and ethnomethodological sociology would approach this remark. From the natural point of view, the norm whose infraction was the point of this conversation could be formulated as 'don't be late'. Intriguingly, this interpretation could be made in one of two ways. 'I'm late' could be regarded as the reality of which 'I took my time' was merely the appearance. In this case the remark would be a confession. Alternatively, 'I'm late' could be regarded as the appearance of which 'I took my time' was the reality. Here, the remark would convey defiance. Natural sociology conceives all speech as either upholding or undermining the normative social order: no more subtle possibility is allowable.

The ethnomethodologist might learn from Macarthur that [taking time] is a way of [being late]. From this observation, he could proceed to an enquiry into activities grouped around the social practice of doing [time]. 'Lateness' as a feature of socially shared time could be contrasted with and related to conceptions of 'my' and 'your' personal time. Ethnomethodological sociology conceives of all speech as an analytical restatement of the necessarily true: no more complex possibility is allowable.

We propose that Macarthur's speech is more subtle than realistic interpretation allows. Macarthur speaks with two voices. The first seems to portray a self-sufficient intelligible remark. At this moment, appearance and reality are united. But the second voice poses a gap between the appearance of the first words, and a reality which transcends that appearance. His speaking then reveals the gap between two ways of speaking.

The two pictures portrayed by the talk are:

SIR, (I'm late)
'COS (I took my time)

The similarity between these two pictures might suggest that each refers to the same situation. However, to admit this would be to adopt a realistic stance for which the import of speech is the reality to which it refers. Instead, a 'real'-istic stance demands examination of what the words portray as 'real'. In this case, only one similarity between the pictures is admissible: the repetition of the word *I*. Each formulates a version of the *I*. Attention must turn to the relation between these two formulations.

The first appears to be a self-sufficient statement. It is a curt two-word utterance which assimilates the *I* to an external label, 'late'. Unlike the case of Jones, Russell and the tart, however, the second picture cannot be assimilated to the first. Instead, it reformulates the first, and so poses contrasting assumptions to it. In a more extended formulation, the *I* is posed as acting in the world. In short, a contradiction is posed between the two forms. This contradiction has a clear significance for content since the world in which 'lateness' is the appropriate conception of time is a world in which time is not 'mine' to take.

Taken as a whole, this remark by a single speaker shares many features of the conversation previously examined. 'I'm late', posed as self-sufficient, denies the need for further speech. 'I took my time' re-opens the question of speaking. 'I'm late' is revealed retrospectively to have grasped only the appearance of a greater reality. 'I'm late' is the speech of the classroom. Macarthur satirizes this speech by first appearing to sustain its definition, but then providing a critique of that definition.

Confirmation for the structure, discovered by interruption of the utterance, comes from a simple test: consider the utterance that might be produced by reversing the order of the pictures: 'I took my time and so I'm late'. Under the assumptions of realism this reversal would make no difference: the natural and ethnomethodological interpretations of the utterance would still stand. From our point of view, however, the new version of the remark would be markedly different.

In his actual utterance Macarthur first sustained classroom discourse, then detracted from that discourse. In the hypothetical utterance, apparent detraction from classroom discourse is followed by a real re-affirmation of that discourse. In the actual utterance the second picture elaborated further what had apparently been a self-contained and complete statement. In the hypothetical utterance, an elaborated statement is brought to a clear-cut conclusion.

However, Macarthur's second picture does not interrupt the first. It does not enter the first picture to transform it, but poses another picture alongside it. Where Russell preserved the sameness of voices, Macarthur introduced difference. This is explicable when we consider the authorship of these voices. Russell preserved the sameness of Jone's voice, bringing Jones with him in a transformation from solipsism to speech. Had he reformulated Jones's words, he would have left Jones behind. Macarthur introduces difference between one voice and another; he distances himself from one voice (that of classroom discourse) which he is obliged to speak, by explicating its gloss in terms of another. In this way his irony is somewhat akin to that of ethnomethodology itself.

Finally, consider the following exchange. On one occasion, Torode noted, the teacher Mr Cramond entered the classroom with a stack of books which he gave out. He told them:

> Before the end of term, we are each going to read a book. All these books are reasonably interesting – some of them are very interesting. We'll have a period of reading this morning, and we'll have one each week from time to time. Now, I hope you understand I don't like you reading aloud in your neighbour's ear – you know what I mean by that.

After he had made this announcement, Alex Rialto asked him, 'Where do we start?' The teacher replied, 'Now that's just like daft Alex Rialto. When I eat my dinner, I start with my pudding first. If you come down to McGrath House, you'll see that I eat my custard

with my potatoes.' Mr Cramond's remark comprises two responses
to the boy, the second of which he presents in two versions.
Consider the remark, 'When I eat my dinner, I start with my
pudding first'. This serves as a reply to Rialto's question which can
be represented as follows:

(Where do we start?)
WHEN (I eat my dinner) (I start with my pudding first)

For the natural sociologist, this conversation concerns the infraction
of some such norm as 'start at the beginning'. The boy's question
reveals his forgetfulness of this norm. The teacher's irony draws
such forgetfulness to its logical conclusion, namely absurdity. Thus
for natural sociology, absurdity is an immanent possibility for
speech, and the teacher's talk sustains social order by drawing back
from that brink.[6] Within the natural attitude the boy's question is
answered, and the teacher's answer is a paradigm case of the natural
version of 'irony'.

For the ethnomethodologist, the conversation concerns the practice of [starting]. From the teacher's explication of what everyone
knows about [starting], the ethnomethodologist can learn what this
activity is taken to be. Further, in view of his particular interest in
conversational practices, he can learn ways in which answering
questions is intelligibly practised in our society. Note that in both
cases the ethnomethodologist must assume that the activity is
correctly carried out: he cannot, for example, question the manner
in which either [questioning] or [starting] are portrayed or exhibited
in this talk.

By contrast, we follow the natural sociologist in holding that Mr
Cramond's remark, while appearing to answer the question, really
attempts to show its absurdity. However, such a sociologist accepts
that the question itself is absurd.

By contrast we follow the ethnomethodologist in holding that
there is much to be said about [starting]. Contrary to both realisms,
the question is one which could have provoked discourse between
Rialto and Mr Cramond, but this was prevented by the character of
the teacher's response. It is possible to explain both why and how he
responded as he did.

As is clear from the extract given here, Mr Cramond formulates
explicit rules and procedures in terms of *we*, then reverts to *you* and
I talk, within which he permits discussion of the interpretation of
those rules.[7] The boy, however, participates directly in *we* speech.
The teacher responds by speaking, unusually for him, in terms of the
I governed by a rule. Thus he satirizes the boy's speech - for him
nonsensical because expressed in terms of the *we* – by responding in

nonsensical speech in terms of the *I*. As previously noted, such *I* speech is incapable of discursive participation by others, and so calls a halt to the conversation.

In contrast to realism which presupposes the reality of the world prior to its documentation, we have proposed a strategy of 'real'-ism which permits discovery of the ways in which 'reality' is constituted as an appearance in the language of social life. Needless to say, such a doctrine makes its own presumptions about the character of reality. Specifically, such a doctrine presumes that speech can never correspond to reality. Yet presumptions about the character of 'reality' must always be present in speech. This paradox defines what may be called a 'dialectical' ('through speaking') account of speech.

From a realistic point of view, 'I' is merely an indicator, pointing to a reality beyond speech, namely the person of the speaker. No further investigation of its use is then required. From a 'real'-istic viewpoint, the 'I' is the exemplification of a way of speaking. The ironic use of the 'I' is then open to investigation. In the three conversations reported, the I is employed to close a conversation, only to find it re-opened; to open conversation where it had previously been employed to close it; and again to close a conversation opened in other ways. So three versions of irony are exhibited.

To consider these in the reverse order, natural irony is employed in the speech of Mr Cramond. Natural speech is conceived as pointed or pointless in so far as it draws attention to the non-obvious (reality) or to the obvious (appearance). Its version of irony shows the obviousness, we might say the pointlessness, of what had been proposed as non-obvious, or pointful speech. Irony then is a *reductio ad absurdam,* a dismissal of speech as non-speech.

Ethnomethodological irony is employed in the speech of Macarthur. Ethnomethodology conceives of all speech as a restatement of the obvious. Its irony shows the non-obvious (reality) of what had been proposed as obvious (appearance), that is the point of speaking about what had been proposed as pointless. Both these versions of irony employ interpretation, in that one way of speaking is reformulated by another, leaving the first intact.

As employed by Russell, interruptive irony alone raises the question of the relation between what is obvious (appearance) and what is non-obvious (reality). It thus enters a single way of speaking, which it works within and transforms.

The point of speaking is to address the differences between ways of speaking, for it is only in this way that the unavailability of reality to speech can be continually recalled. Realistic speech, arising out of the commitment to a single way of speaking, cannot grasp the way in which 'reality' is an issue for speech. In its practice of interpretation, it treats all other ways of speaking as merely appearances of the reality which it alone formulates. It thereby renders discourse between different ways of speaking pointless. By contrast, we have attempted to interrupt the relation between 'appearance' and 'reality' upheld by other ways of speaking, and thereby reaffirm the point of discourse between ways of speaking. Whereas realistic interpretation asserts the pointlessness of speech, and itself exhibits a way of closing discourse, 'real'-istic interruption affirms the point of speech and exhibits a way in which discourse may be sustained.

Discourse and mastery

Interpretation constitutes a mode of relationship between discourses. One discourse constitutes itself or is constituted by other discourses as able to formulate reality. Another discourse constitutes itself or is constituted by others as only able to formulate appearance. For us, each of these is an idealization.

Idealized speech and writing must be interrogated in an important sense against itself. We refer to this as a materialist interruption of the discourses of idealism. It seeks to grasp how the material interplay of signs create the orientation to ideal 'reality' which is integral to their ideological force.

We shall attempt to show that interruption, conceived in this way, is a key motif in contemporary intervention in language. None the less, it is constantly misunderstood, and there is a clear reason why this should be so. Interruption is in permanent danger of being subsumed by interpretation. As we shall show in specific instances, speech and writing as currently practised are commonly dualistic: statement is accompanied by meta-statement, which precedes it to anticipate its consequences, and follows it to consolidate its implications. Thus even speeches and texts which are themselves interruptive in character, are commonly subverted in the very occasion of being produced. Even more commonly statements of a paradoxical or disruptive kind are reinterpreted by other statements into the tradition which they challenge.

Our concern throughout the present work is with discourses and their inter-relationships. We hold that a plurality of such discourses is necessarily involved in any instance of 'talk'. To take an example, the mastery of pupils by the teacher in a school classroom, if successfully accomplished, will normally be achieved not simply by the domination of their talk but by his articulation of a set of relations between discourses, in which he attempts to locate the discourses articulated by the pupils.

It is here that we would locate our own account of the pronouns which from the natural standpoint are bound up with the context of speaking, and from the ethnomethodological point of view are regulated by a grammar of everyday practices. For us they are historical and political devices for the (would-be) ordering of the relations between discourses.

To use a distinction deriving from J.L. Austin (1972) which will be more fully discussed below, they *say* what these relations comprise, and it is this saying which is the concern of the realistic interpretations of language. But the ordering they provide is only a would-be ordering because in fact these pronouns *do* interrelations between ways of speaking of a different kind. It is these practices which are the concern of a 'real'-istic interruption of language.

Every discourse – including this one – employs pronouns to articulate relations between itself and others. Thus every discourse exhibits a gap between 'saying' and 'doing' its relations with other discourses. In particular, every discourse invites complicity in its claim that its formulation of appearances corresponds with its formulation of reality, i.e. that it does what it says. Interpretation either accepts this claim, or imposes its own. In either case a mastery is set up, of one discourse by another.

Interruption seeks to break with this structure of recognition, and of mastery by calling into question the relation between appearance and reality, as formulated within the interrupted discourse. The basis for its alternative conception is suggested by Humpty Dumpty's remark quoted above: the point is not the mastery of one speech by another but rather the mastery by one speaker of the discourse which he or she speaks.

In the chapters which follow, we do not attempt to articulate an *a priori* theory of what such mastery would entail. Instead we seek to show the practical struggle for this mastery, by way of an interrogation of a number of texts.

Notes

1 The notion of 'interruption' is developed in Torode (1977).
2 The 'master'/'slave' relation here evoked is that articulated by Hegel, in section IVA of *The Phenomenology of Mind* (1949).
3 The psychoanalysis of language is discussed in Chapter 13 below. Sociolinguistics is the topic of Chapter 8.
4 For a fuller discussion of the elucidation of the norms invoked by natural conversation, cf. Torode (1976).
5 Cf. Wittgenstein (1961), especially paragraphs 2. 1 ff.
6 For a fuller discussion of the immanent possibility of meaninglessness or 'anomie' in natural sociology, cf. Torode (1977).

7 For further examples of Mr Cramond's talk, with an analysis, cf. Torode (1976).

Bibliography

Austin, J.L. (1972), *How to do Things with Words,* Oxford: Clarendon Press.

Brown, R. and Gilman, A. (1972), 'The Pronouns of Power and Solidarity', in P.P. Giglioli, *Language and Social Context,* Harmondsworth: Penguin.

Burks, A.W. (1949), 'Icon, Index, and Symbol', *Philosophy and Phenomenological Research,* 9, p. 673.

Carroll, L. (1873), *Alice Through the Looking-Glass,* London: Macmillan.

Garfinkel, H. (1967), *Studies in Ethnomethodology,* Englewood Cliffs: Prentice-Hall.

Garfinkel, H. and Sacks, H. (1970), 'On Formal Structures of Practical Action', in S. McKinney and E. Tiryakian, *Theoretical Sociology,* New York: Appleton-Century-Crofts.

Hegel, G. (1949), *The Phenomenology of Mind,* London: Allen and Unwin.

Husserl, E. (1970), *The Idea of Phenomenology,* The Hague: Nijhoff.

de Saussure, F. (1974), *A Course in General Linguistics,* London: Fontana.

Torode, B. (1976), 'Teachers' Talk and Classroom Discipline', in M. Stubbs and S. Delamont, eds., *Explorations in Classroom Observation,* London: Wiley.

Torode, B. (1977), 'Interrupting Intersubjectivity', in M. Hammersley and P. Woods, eds., *School Experience,* London: Croom Helm.

Wittgenstein, L. (1961), *Tractatus Logico-Philosophicus,* London: Routledge & Kegan Paul.

Althusser's materialist theory of ideology, as constituting a Subject and subjects on the theological model of God and man, is fruitful. However, juxtaposing material from a school classroom with his own text, we show that his own account of how we *(nous)* can see reality, which is unavailable to those *(on)* who are steeped within it, is itself ideological.

chapter 2

Language and ideology in Althusser

What do children learn at school? . . . They learn to read, to write, and to add . . . and a number of other things as well . . . which are directly useful in the different jobs in production. Thus they learn 'know-how'.

But besides these techniques and knowledges, and in learning them, children at school also learn the 'rules' of good behaviour, i.e. the attitude that should be observed by every agent in the division of labour, according to the job he is 'destined' for: rules of morality, civic, and professional conscience, which actually means rules of respect for the socio-technical division of labour, and ulti-mately the rules of the order established by class domination. . . .

To put this more scientifically, I shall say that the reproduction of labour power requires not only a reproduction of its skills, but also, at the same time, a reproduction of its submission to the rules of the established order, i.e. a reproduction of submission to the ruling ideology for the workers, and a reproduction of the ability to manipulate the ruling ideology correctly for the agents of exploitation and repression, so that they, too, will provide for the domination of the ruling class 'in words'.

In other words, the school (but also other State institutions like the Church, or other apparatuses like the Army) teaches 'know-how', but in forms which ensure *subjection to the ruling ideology* or the mastery of its 'practice'. . . .

The reproduction of labour power thus reveals as its *sine qua non* not only the reproduction of its 'skills', but also the reproduction of its subjection to the ruling ideology or of the 'practice' of that ideology. . . .

But this is to recognize the effective presence of a new reality: *ideology*.

L. Althusser, 'Ideology and Ideological State Apparatuses' (1971), pp. 132–3.

In these terms, Louis Althusser has put forward proposals for a materialist theory of ideology.[1] Taken together, these proposals imply that for Althusser, classroom language is itself a language of politics, and that the analysis of classroom language provides a model for the analysis of political languages, i.e. ideologies, *per se*. Let us investigate more closely then, what Althusser's approach implies for the talk of teachers and pupils in the school situation, and also for the theory of ideologies and ideology in general.

Classroom ideology

Althusser does not discuss the talk of teachers and pupils in the school situation. Although he states that 'the Church has been replaced today *in its role as the dominant Ideological State Apparatus* by the School', his own detailed discussions of particular ideologies and of ideology in general in this paper are posed in terms of the Church, and the ideology of religion. He first produces two theses on 'ideology in general' (ibid., p. 170).

1 There is no practice except by and in an ideology
The familiar notion that 'ideology represents the imaginary relations of individuals to their real conditions of existence' fails to explain why this imaginary representation is required at all. Various answers have been given to this – Althusser discusses the eighteenth-century notion of a conspiracy between priests and despots, and also Feuerbach's nineteenth-century notion that the alienated ideas of ideology are the expression of real alienation in men's material lives. But these answers fail to acknowledge that ideology is itself a real material force. Thus what 'imaginary' ideology represents is not the 'real' relations of men to their conditions, but precisely their 'imaginary' relations. These relations, or better to say, these *practices*, belong inherently to ideology.

2 There is no ideology except by the subject and for subjects
As Althusser also states this proposition, 'all ideology hails or interpellates concrete individuals as concrete subjects.' Walking along the street, I may call 'Hey, you there!' and thereby summon 'you' as a category (a subject) which some individual happily assimilates to him- or her-self. Likewise, in the undertaking of a practice within the sphere defined by an ideology – it may be 'praying' or 'confessing' within the sphere defined by 'religion', or 'learning multiplication tables' or 'taking an intelligence test' within the sphere defined by 'education' – a subject, the doer of the practice, is ideologically constituted, and the individual undertaking the practice assimilates him- or her-self to this identity.

In each case recognition is involved. 'I' recognize myself as the one to whom 'you' call from across the street, or as the one who prays or confesses, learns tables or takes tests. We can understand Althusser's notion of the 'domination' of one ideology over others both at the level of the individual's subjective identity and at the level of what is in effect for him the subject writ large, namely the State. The dominant ideology of a 'state' or of a 'subject' is that in terms of which it most centrally recognizes itself – always remembering that in this formulation neither 'state' nor 'subject' exist except as interpellated by ideology itself. Let us see how this works in the case of the Christian religion, the ideology which Althusser considers as an illustration of his argument.

This ideology, says Althusser, addresses itself to a human individual, called, say, 'Peter'. Note that the name itself is produced from within the ideology (it is a 'biblical' name), and it is granted by an ideological practice ('baptism'). It tells you 'that God exists and that you are answerable to Him'. Christian ideology interpellates 'Peter' as a subject by making 'him' free to obey or disobey the appeal of 'God'.

Two points are to be noted here. First, Peter's character as a subject among other such subjects depends entirely upon his and their freedom to obey or disobey. Second, what he and all of them obey or disobey is another subject, but one which is unique. Whereas these subjects are imperfect in that they all in varying ways fail to obey its commandments, it is perfect in that it cannot disobey its own commandments or, what amounts to the same thing in terms of the ideology, it obeys them perfectly.

God is not a concrete subject, with a small 's', but an Absolute Subject, with a large 'S'. From this identification, made in the case of one specific ideology, namely the Christian religion, Althusser is able to postulate three principles of ideology in general (ibid., p. 181):

1 'individuals' are interpellated as subjects;
2 subjects are subjected to the Subject;
3 mutual recognition is achieved between:
(a) subject and Subject
(b) subject and (other) subject
(c) subject and (self) subject

This closure enables the ideological system to work smoothly. Its working, Althusser points out, is enshrined in the ambiguous meaning of the word 'subject', which signifies at once (i) free 'subjectivity', the centre and author of its actions, and (ii) 'subjection' to higher authority. This ambiguity is resolved ideologically, i.e. in imagination, by positing one absolute and perfect Subject to which all the many concrete and imperfect subjects freely choose to be subjected.

Althusser concludes his argument with the discussion of ideology in general. But let us take a step he does not take, and consider the implications of his theory for the ideologies at work in the school classroom. From there we can hope to make a further statement about political ideology at a more general level.

How should Althusser's theory of ideology in general be applied to ideological formations in one 'state apparatus' in particular? To take the school classroom as an instance, it might be proposed that here it is the words of the teacher which 'provide for the domination of the ruling class'. In this case we should hope to find, portrayed in the teacher's words, a range of (concrete) subjects and, posed over and above these, and in contrast to them, a single (absolute) Subject.

If the classroom were functioning in terms of this closure, as Althusser's account suggests it should, then we would expect to find the pupils in the classroom happily recognizing themselves as the subjects portrayed by the teacher. We can thus formulate two hypotheses. In the first place, if we accept the spirit of Althusser's account of ideology in general, then the case of the teacher as an individual *vis à vis* his own ideology can be no different from that of his pupils. He too must be interpellated, as subject, by his words. But here a new possibility suggests itself. We are scarcely accustomed to thinking of the teacher/pupil relation as one between equals, man and man. Rather, in many senses – particularly those of omniscience and omnipotence – the teacher's relation to the pupil traditionally resembles that between God and man[2]. The possibility thus arises that, in general, the teacher's discourse interpellates himself or herself as Subject, and his/her pupils as subjects. This presupposes the more fundamental hypothesis, that the teacher's speech constitutes a discourse which interpellates a Subject and one or more subjects. We will call these Hypothesis I and Hypothesis I* respectively.

We can also formulate the hypothesis that the pupils recognize themselves as the subjects portrayed by the teacher and recognize the teacher as the Subject with which he identifies himself. Once again the presupposed hypothesis is that the pupils' discourse does interpellate a Subject and one or more subjects. These can be called Hypothesis II and Hypothesis II* in their turn.

Hypothesis I implies Hypothesis I* and II implies II*. Hypothesis II implies I, and so all four hypotheses. It means that there is only one discourse at work in the classroom, because the teacher's and pupils' speech constitutes one and the same discourse. This would appear to be Althusser's own conception of language in the school classroom. On the other hand, if Hypothesis II is false, but the other Hypotheses remain true, then more than one discourse is to be found in the classroom. (Of course, if either of I* or II* are untrue, then classroom conversation cannot be analysed in terms of Althusser's theory of discourse at all.) If more than one discourse is found in the classroom, then an issue arises which Althusser does not consider, namely that of the relationship between discourses in the classroom.

Classroom subjects

Let us turn now to an actual instance of talk between a teacher and his pupils in a school classroom. The class in question comprised forty-one fourteen-year-old boys, of skilled manual working-class background, in a lower middle stream of a large urban Scottish comprehensive school. The French teacher, who will be called Mr Lee, addressed the following remark to the boys as they entered his class in ones, twos, and threes after a swimming period: 'I know you've just had swimming, and it's not very nice to come back to the classroom, but the sooner you get used to it the better. Come on, and we'll get some work done.' We are to approach this utterance in terms of hypothesis I*, namely that it constitutes a discourse which interpellates a Subject and one or more subjects. If we are to look for either kind of (s/S)ubject in the remark then the first place to look at would seem to be the personal nouns and pronouns which it contains, since these are words which explicitly refer to 'persons'. In this passage we find not only two persons (subjects) as the hypothesis suggests, but three: *I, you,* and *we*. Each occurs in a clause of its own: '*I* know', '*you've* just had swimming'. '*you* get used to it', '*we'll* get some work done'. These clauses employing personal pronouns make up four of the eight clauses in the passage. The other four name no subjects. They are as follows: 'It's not very nice', 'to come back to the classroom', 'the sooner the better', and 'come on'. But now, following Althusser's hypothesis, we are to search this speech for the subjects which it constitutes (or as he puts it, 'interpellates'). We can do this even in the absence of personal pronouns. We can do it wherever we can ask of a remark the question, 'who?'. Thus we can ask, (i) 'For whom it is "not very nice"?'; (ii) 'Who is to come back to the classroom?'; (iii) 'For whom is the sooner (you get used to it) the better?'; and (iv) 'Who is to "come on"?'.

A question of method arises here and of course one might introduce any number of arbitrarily imposed answers to these questions. That is, one might presume that the answers to these questions were somehow 'obvious', so that there was no real need to ask them. We prefer to take the different approach of allowing Mr Lee's remark to answer the questions for us. Mr Lee explicitly puts before us what we are now justified in calling the subjects, *I, you,* and *we.* Let us then make the assumption, justified on the grounds of scientific parsimony, that the answers to our 'who?' questions are to be found amongst the subjects which Mr Lee explicitly names.

In two cases the answer to the question seems to present no difficulty. 'Who is to come back to the classroom?' – the answer is plainly *you.* 'Who is to "come on"?' – again there is no doubt that the answer is *you.* But in the case of the first and the third questions, no such clear answer can be given. 'For whom is it "not very nice" (to come back to the classroom)?' – is it for *you,* or for *me,* or for both of *us?* 'For whom is the sooner (you get used to it) the better?' – is it better for *you,* better for *me,* or better for *us* all? It is not difficult to choose one of these answers. We could easily interpret the teacher as saying 'not very nice for one (us)' and 'better for us': this would be to hear him as a consensually oriented teacher showing some sympathy for the boys' position as a typical human predicament which *we* all share. Or we could hear him as saying 'not very nice for you', and 'better for you'. This would be to hear him differently, but equally intelligibly, as a teacher oriented to conflict in the classroom, threatening the boys with the unpleasantness of his regime. Alternatively, we could hear him as saying, 'not very nice for me', and 'better for me'. This would be to hear him not as an intelligible teacher speaking rationally to his pupils, but as a speaker exhibiting certain 'psychotic' doubts and difficulties about his position which he would be better to keep to himself.

Each of these represents a possible interpretation of this teacher's talk. But each of them does violence by denying the possibility of the other two. Instead, we must grasp the ambiguity that is a feature of this remark. We refer to this as an interruption of the talk.[3]

The teacher states, 'I know you've just had swimming'. The world of the *you* ('you've just had swimming') is posed as 'known', and in this sense contained within the all-knowing world of the *I.* Here it seems we find some confirmation of hypothesis I: the *I,* representing the teacher, stands as God, that is as Subject, to the *you* as subject representing the pupils. Next follows the problematic remark, 'and it's not very nice to come back to the classroom'. Now we see that our 'For whom?' question in attempting to interpret this part of the remark is really in a stricter sense a grammatical question. Does 'it's not very nice to come back to the classroom' continue the sense of the previous two clauses so as to read '(I know) it's not very nice (for you) to come back to the classroom', or does it mark an entirely new beginning, open to interpretation as 'not very nice (for us)' or 'not very nice (for me)'? The second and third are possible – we could call them unconscious readings – but the first makes a preferred conscious reading, because it establishes surface continuity of the utterance.[4]

The same problem arises with the next section of the remark. '(I know) the sooner you get used to it the better (for you)' could be the sense, and in this case this whole passage would continue the sense of the previous clauses. But again there is nothing grammatically or contextually to exclude 'better (for me)'. Finally, a clear possibility is the reading 'better (for us)'. In everyday English this would appear as 'better (for all of us)'. This would establish a continuity with the sense of the final clause 'we'll get some work done'. For this reason, we propose that this makes a preferred conscious reading – but unconsciously the other two remain. The conscious, or dominant, reading then is the one which accounts for the coherence of the remark as a whole. This is shown to have the following structure:

personal 1	impersonal order		personal 2
(I know you've . . .)	(it's not very nice)	(the sooner the better)	(we'll work)
Subject = *I* / *you* = subjects		subjects = *you* / Subject = *we*	

In this case we can see how the grammatical structure of the sentence, i.e. its breakdown into specific kinds of clauses linked by specific linguistic relations, achieves specific ideological effects. The 'impersonal' clauses in the centre of this remark permit Mr Lee to oscillate between two different discourses interpellating different Subjects and subjects. The discourse interpellating *I* as Subject and *you* as subjects which is found in the opening of the remark is transformed into another discourse interpellating *you* as subjects and *we* as Subject in the closing of the remark. This is achieved by the way in which personal clauses containing explicit subjects are connected together by impersonal clauses whose subjects cannot be unambiguously determined. Thus the 'interpellating' of (s/S)ubjects by a discourse and the 'shading' of one into another are the ideological effects of a process which is itself linguistic in character. It is this process, rather than the ideologies it produces, which should be our concern.

Subjects and individuals

As opposed to an interpretation which would impose a single unity on the utterance, interruption has revealed its divided ideological structure, but has also accounted for its linguistic unity.

We considered a piece of classroom conversation, having formulated certain hypotheses arising out of Althusser's account of ideology in general in his paper on 'Ideological State Apparatuses'. It must be said at once that we have succeeded in confirming his account of ideology in general. There is, it seems, no difficulty in locating the talk of a teacher as a discourse constituting (interpellating) a Subject and subjects, and thus exemplifying ideology in general as Althusser describes it. This is itself a very promising discovery for materialist research on ideology, and one directly indebted to Althusser's contribution.

But in another respect the situation differs from the one which Althusser proposes. We had anticipated that in the talk of a teacher and his or her pupils in the classroom, we might find more than one discourse, and then the question of the relation between discourses. But we have found this without going beyond the words of a single speaker. In a short remark by one teacher are found two distinct discourses, related together in a way which cannot be described in ideological, but only in linguistic terms.

This discovery has another implication. We have seen from the second point of his argument that the notion of *recognition* is central to Althusser's account of the way in which ideology (in general) interpellates individuals as subjects. This concept is linked to the first point of his argument, that ideology is a material practice. Putting these two together, Althusser declares (ibid., p.169):

> I shall therefore say that, where only a single subject (such and such an individual) is concerned, the existence of the ideas of his belief is material in that *his ideas are his material rituals which are themselves defined by the material ideological apparatus from which derive the ideas of that subject.*

Here, for Althusser, the subject has become a material reality. It is easy to see how this has arisen. It is first posited that every material practice takes place within an ideology, and that every ideology is itself a material practice. To this we have no exception whatever. Next it is proposed that every ideology interpellates individuals as subjects and as Subject. This we can also accept, and have empirically confirmed in at least one instance. But from these two principles, it is falsely concluded that the individual undergoing a material practice (as all individuals must), within the terms of an ideology (as all material practices must be), recognizes him- or her-self as the subject of that practice, so that we can then speak of 'a single subject', and 'the ideas of that subject'.

On the contrary, our example shows that there need be no one-to-one correspondence between a single individual and 'a single subject'. It reminds us of the fact, of which Althusser is well aware, that to speak of 'the ideas of a subject' is a contradiction in terms, since a 'subject' is itself no more than an idea. In general the individual – seen now as the speaker of words rather than the thinker of ideas – is able to constitute in his speech not alone a single subject, but subjects and a Subject together making an ideology, and further subjects and a Subject making another ideology in contradiction to the first, and so on. If there is a unity to this ensemble of speeches by the individual, then this unity is a material reality. But this material reality cannot in general be that of a subject, nor even of a relation between subjects. It will generally be that of a relation between ideologies. Such a unity, we have shown, resides in the linguistic practices which produce the effect of distinct ideologies, and their relationships.

At this stage, it seems important to ask why Althusser resurrects the category of the subject as indispensable within his version of materialism, when the thrust of his argument has been so successfully to displace this notion? We believe we can find the answer in Althusser's own ideology. As an ideology in general, the notion of subject does not occur in isolation within Althusser's theory, but rather in a pair with its opposite, Althusser's notion of Subject. The identity of this Subject is not hard to discover, Althusser tells us (ibid.' p. 181):

> The vast majority of (good) subjects work all right 'all by themselves', i.e. by ideology (whose concrete forms are realized in the Ideological State Apparatuses). They are inserted into practices governed by the rituals of the ISAs. They 'recognize' the existing state of affairs, that 'it really is true that it is so and not otherwise', and that they must be obedient to God, to their conscience, to the priest, to de Gaulle, to the boss, to the engineer, that thou shalt 'love thy neighbour as thyself', etc. Their concrete, material behaviour is simply the inscription in life of the admirable words of the prayer 'Amen – So be it'.

Here Althusser is once more speaking of 'subjects' where he should speak of 'individuals' recognizing themselves in the practices of each ISA. In other words, he is speaking in terms of his own ideology, within which the subject recognizes himself/herself in the

Ideological State Apparatus. It is the State which is Althusser's Subject.

The State (Subject) reproduces (creates) subjects who recognize the State (Subject). This is Althusser's theory of ideology: this is Althusser's ideology. It poses the State as the unity of the unified subjects. Althusser's account itself does nothing to disturb this unity. On the contrary, by interpreting every arena of ideological conflict as a 'State Apparatus', itself united in imitation of the State as a whole, his account reinforces that unity: his text is itself a State apparatus.

By contrast, it is necessary to interrupt ideological conflict within the 'State' as it is within smaller arenas such as the classroom. In the first instance, the very ideological unity of the 'State' must be questioned. The effect of Althusser's ideology is to make the 'State' into a Subject. The State (as the school, the Church, the Army) 'teaches know-how', 'ensures subjection', and 'mastery'. It 'intervenes . . . as a repressive force' in the interests of the ruling class, it 'exploits' and 'determinates', it 'functions' by violence and by ideology, punishing, expelling, selecting, censoring, etc. It 'reproduces' itself. We have considered only one of these relationships. Althusser says 'the State functions by ideology', (in the ISAs). We say rather that the 'State' and its 'functioning' are within the 'subject', an ideological product, as is the very notion of 'ideology'. In short, Althusser's theory of ideology is the theory of ideology internal to contemporary ideology itself.

Althusser's subjects

To grasp an alternative to this ideology is to produce an alternative speech to the ideological speech to which the individual is subjected, thereby granting to that individual the words with which to transform the ideology. In merely reiterating, and even elaborating, the words of the ideology, Althusser only strengthens it. Yet in the way in which he does so he exhibits a manner in which it can be challenged. Overthrowing the present domination of speech by the ideology of the 'subject' reveals the material linguistic practices which produce that ideology. But since Althusser himself provides us with an instance of such speech, then his own speech can be interrogated to discover the practices constitutive of ideology which it itself exhibits. We referred to an approach to the teacher's talk, which abstained from any one interpretation but rather tried to reveal the number of distinct interpretations possible in his talk, as an interruption of that talk. It seems clear that so far we have, rather, interpreted the text of Althusser. Let us now proceed to interrupt it, using the passage quoted in abbreviated form which opened the present discussion.[5]

With the experience of analysing the fragment of teacher's talk behind us, we can proceed as before to identify personal nouns and pronouns in the text, with a view to discovering the Subject and subjects of a discourse in Althusser's sense. But whereas we previously began with the expectation of finding only a single discourse at work in the classroom, we now have no reason to anticipate such a simple result. If the relation between discourses was an issue which we discovered (contrary to Althusser) within the talk of the teacher, then we might expect to find the relation between discourses to be an issue (also contrary to Althusser) within his own talk.

The personal nouns and pronouns to be found in the passage seem to be as follows: *children, they, workers, technicians, engineers, management, agent, he, capitalists, servants, I, professionals,* (the) *exploited, proletarians, exploiters, auxiliaries, high priests, functionaries,* making eighteen in all.[6] We have already discovered two reasons why we cannot know whether this list is complete, prior to the analysis. First, we have seen in the case of Mr Lee's remark that even an impersonal clause may be heard as if it constituted personal 'subjects'. Second, we saw in the course of our first, interpretive, reading of Althusser's text that such an 'impersonal' entity as the State could be read as a 'personal' Subject. However we have no alternative but to start with the words having clearly personal connotations, from there proceeding to investigate the others.

Each of these names occurs in a specific clause or clauses, which may be briefly listed as follows:

children learn   (occurs twice)
they go . . . in their studies
     learn   (three times)
     provide for domination

workers, technicians, engineers, management are 'instructed'
(workers) are 'handled'
     'submit' to ideology

agent(s) 'observe' attitudes
     'manipulate' ideology
     are 'steeped' in ideology

he is 'destined'
capitalists and *servants* 'order them about'
     'speak to them'
(capitalists) [see also below]
I shall say

'professionals of ideology'
the *exploited,* the *exploiters,* the *exploiters' auxiliaries,*
the *high priests* (of ideology)
the *proletarians,* the *capitalists,* the *managers,* the *'functionaries'*

$\Bigg\}$ perform tasks

It is perhaps not too much of a simplification to say that the
personae in the fragment of text under discussion thus reduce to
approximately five elements, namely:

children, they, who learn, etc. . . . .
workers, etc., who are 'handled', 'submit', etc.
agents who manipulate but are also 'steeped' in ideology
I who says
the *exploited, exploiters,* etc., who perform tasks

Before commenting further on what is done with these persons, let
us turn briefly to consider the 'impersonal' parts of the text which
have escaped the analysis so far.

Although 'impersonal' elements enter necessarily into every
'personal' clause in this or any other text, we shall distinguish those
clauses which comprise wholly 'impersonal' elements from the
'personal' clauses so far discussed. In those clauses, we presumed,
following Althusser's own theory of ideology, that meaning was
organized around 'persons' who might turn out to be subjects or
Subjects in Althusser's sense. In these clauses, it might be thought,
we would lack any clear basis for examining corresponding forms of
organization. However, consideration of one such case shows that
they exhibit an organization of their own.

Although '. . . which may be rudimentary or on the contrary
thorough-going' is the first impersonal clause, the first elaborated
passage is '. . . which actually means rules of respect for the socio-
technical division of labour, and ultimately the rules of order
established by class domination.' The entity that 'means' this is 'the
rules' of good behaviour, i.e. 'the attitude that should be observed
by every agent in the division of labour, according to the job he is
destined for; rules of morality, civic and professional conscience.'
Now although 'the attitude that should be observed by every agent
. . . the job he is destined for' constitutes a 'personal' passage which
we have already noted, this passage is contained within an 'impersonal' passage which does not depend upon it in any way. This
'impersonal' passage exhibits a simple structure of its own: it is built
around the repetition, four times in all, of the word *rules.* This word
is thus constituted as a principle of organization of 'impersonal' text,
directly comparable with the names which organize the 'personal'

text. Before commenting further, consider the other impersonal passages.

The next 'impersonal' passage is the content of what the *I* 'says'. It reads (ibid., p. 132, quoted above):

> the reproduction of labour power requires not only a reproduction of its skills, but also at the same time a reproduction of its submission to the rules of the established order, i.e. a reproduction of its submission to the ruling ideology for the workers, and a reproduction of the ability to manipulate the ruling ideology correctly, for the agents of exploitation and repression. . . .

Although this statement shades off into a personal passage expressed in terms of agents, its structure is apparent from the wholly 'impersonal' first part (up to 'established order'). This first part contains three and the whole contains five repetitions of the word *reproduction* which thus constitutes its impersonal organizing structure. A second word-play around the words *rules, ruling, ruling* perpetuates that which organized the previous 'impersonal' passage. (However, in the French original there is here only a single repetition of the earlier word 'règles' followed by a double appearance of a new word, since 'ruling' is a rendering of 'dominate'.) A third word-play, involving the double use of a word, constitutes *ideology* as a theme. This may be presumed to be of some significance, since it is the first appearance not only in this fragment, but in the text as a whole, of the word which appears twice and as the first word in the title of the paper.

The fourth 'impersonal' passage, 'In other words . . .' exhibits no word-play of its own. However it repeats *ruling* (dominate) and *ideology,* constituted as 'impersonal' themes elsewhere. It also repeats the word 'know-how' (in quotation marks) from the 'personal' clause concluding the first paragraph above. The significance of this will be discussed below, but it seems that this word itself might be regarded as a theme in the text constituted in interaction between 'personal' and 'impersonal' statements.

The fifth statement, 'The reproduction of labour power . . .' clearly evokes and strengthens previous play on 'reproduction', which here occurs four times, and also *ideology,* which is three times repeated. *Labour-power,* which occurred once in the third 'impersonal' passage figures here twice. However the distinctive organizational feature of this passage seems to reside not so much in these repetitions of individual words, but in the logical play in the organization of the passage, which repeats the negative 'not' three times to achieve the result 'not only not only but also but also'.

The final statement exhibits no internal word play, but repeats the by now familiar *ideology*. It should be noted that it is at this one of the two points at which the English text departs markedly from the style of the French original, in which this final remark is a personal statement of *nous,* as was the statement rendered in English as 'I shall say', thereby establishing a word-play between these two.

Thus the impersonal sections of the text are organized around the words:

rules (×5)
reproduction (×9)
ruling (×3)
ideology (×8)
'know-how' (×1)
labour-power (×2)

Of these words it seems clear on numerical grounds that *reproduction, ideology,* and *rules* play a leading part. However to understand what this part comprises requires a qualitative rather than quantitative account. To provide this, it is necessary to account for the structure of the passage as a whole, and the way in which both 'personal' and 'impersonal' components combine together to produce it.

We will investigate the structure of the passage as a whole by considering the relationships between its clauses, in the light of the two kinds of organization already discussed. These bind clauses together into higher levels of organization. We shall call the clauses, or atomic units of meaning, *pictures* and the groupings of clauses *stanzas.* We have seen that these stanzas are based around certain significant names, whether 'personal' or 'impersonal'. We shall say that a stanza exhibits the *voice* of a particular name, when this name is the word which is its organizing principle.

The passage as a whole can be represented as follows:

                         i

I   ⎡(<u>children</u> learn '<u>know-how</u>')⎤
    ⎣<u>on</u> apprend   ⎦

                        i

II ⎡(<u>children</u> learn '<u>rules</u>' of behaviour)   ⎤
     ⎢<u>on</u> apprend   ⎢
     ⎢   ii   ⎢
     ⎢(<u>rules</u> of morality means <u>rules</u> of respect for division of⎢
     ⎣labour and ultimately <u>rules</u> of order)   ⎦

III
$$
\begin{array}{c}
\text{i} \qquad\qquad\qquad \text{ii}
\end{array}
$$

III ⌈ (I shall say that (reproduction requires reproduction of
│ nous dirons que
│ skills and reproduction of submission to rules))
│   iii
│ (i.e. reproduction of submission to ideology for workers
⌊ and reproduction of manipulation of ideology by agents) ⌋

                                    i
IV ⌈ ('know-how' ensures subjection to ruling ideology) ⌋

                              i
V ⌈ (reproduction reproduces 'skills' and reproduces subjec-
│ tion to ruling ideology)
│   ii
⌊ (reproduction is subject to ideology) ⌋

VI ⌈ (This is to recognize ideology) ⌉
    ⌊ nous reconnaissons ⌋

key: ——————————— = personal nouns and pronouns
      – – – – – – – – – = word-play within the text constituting
                          impersonal entities
      (   ) = atomic units of meaning (pictures), num-
                          bered i, ii, iii, etc.
      [   ] = molecular units of meaning (stanzas),
                          numbered I, II, III etc.

   The argument contained in the passage may then be represented
even more briefly:

   I: children ('know-how')
      on

  II: children (rules)
      on

III: I (reproduction of rules = reproduction of ideology)
     nous

IV: ('know-how' = ideology)

VI: (ideology)
    nous

   Here the brackets, ( ), stand variously for 'learn', 'say', 'recognize', and in general for all the ways in which a 'subject', who
must always occupy the space to the left of the brackets, may
orient towards or intend an 'impersonal' object, which may
occupy the space within brackets.

Althusser's ideology

Perhaps the first comment to be made is that Althusser exemplifies his own theory of ideology more consistently than did the teacher whose talk we analysed in Althusser's terms. Whereas the teacher oscillates in his brief remark between two discourses, each defining and defined by a Subject and a subject, it seems that in this much longer passage Althusser defines only one. Within its terms, the subject is *on* ('one', but rendered in English as 'children'). The passage sets out first what the *on* apprehends: it is 'know-how' ('savoir-faire'). In a second statement, still attributed to the apprehension of *on*, 'know-how' is reformulated as 'rules'. In a further elaboration which we are to take it is still attributed to the *on*, rules of morality are extended to refer to rules of respect for the division of labour, and rules of order. Only at this point does the voice of *on*, the subject of Althusser's ideology, give way to the voice of *nous,* the Subject.

The *nous* introduces a new terminology to that of *on*, though one which makes connections with that of the *on* at two points: the words 'rules' and 'savoir-faire' appear in both. However the *nous*'s speech is distinguished from that of the *on* by its continually repeated use of two words: 'reproduction', and 'ideology', both of which are unavailable to the *on*. This is of course because the *on* is that which is reproduced, and that which is steeped in ideology, and is in all respects subject to the process which is recognized only by its Subject, *nous*. 'Savoir-faire' (always in quotation marks in Althusser's usage), and 'rules' (in quotation marks when it is explicitly *on* which apprehends it), represent the mistaken appearance to the *on* of the reality which only the *nous* sees, namely ideology.

But unfortunately what is thus *done* in Althusser's text, as revealed by our interruption of it, contradicts what Althusser *says* in the text, as apprehended by our previous interpretation. For what is distinctive about the theory of ideology which Althusser states in this paper is his claim, already quoted, to overcome the notion that 'ideology represents the imaginary relations of individuals to their real conditions of existence'. As opposed to the familiar distinction between an ideological, or *apparent,* world superimposed upon a *real* world (apprehended perhaps by science), Althusser says that the world is really ideological. He thereby seeks an end to men's aspirations, often expressed within Marxism, for an end to the alienating gap between appearance and reality. But now we see from an examination of his text that his 'ending' of alienation is not what it appears to be. For in saying that the world is really ideological, Althusser employs a discourse unavailable to that ideological world. In his discourse 'ideology' is a real condition of existence. But men still live in imaginary relations, characterized for example by their belief in 'savoir-faire' and 'rules'.

To interrupt Althusser's ideology is to show the gap between appearance and reality, between one discourse and another, in what he does. This we have attempted to do by showing that in a fragment of text subjected to scrutiny, Althusser preserves as distinct two discourses. One is the voice of the subject, *on* ('one') which grasps only the appearance of the world, the other the voice of the Subject, *nous* ('we'), which grasps its reality. Together they comprise his ideology.

With Althusser, a materialist intervention in ideology begins by interrupting the ideological notion of 'ideology' as a mere appearance covering over real relations. But against Althusser, the ideological notion of 'ideology' as a real relation standing behind imaginary appearances must itself be interrupted. Instead, materialism must develop practices of intervention within the imaginary ideological appearances which are the only reality available to us.

Notes

1 This theory has been the subject of critical discussion by P. Q. Hirst (1976). Hirst interprets Althusser's theory as 'functionalist'. However such an interpretation cannot of itself generate a new theory, and in fact Hirst is obliged to turn to a notion of 'signifying practices' external to Althusser's text, to do so. By contrast the present interruption of Althusser's text attempts to generate a new theory from within that text itself.
2 A teacher's talk is analysed in these theological terms in Torode (1976).
3 The distinction between 'interpretation' and 'interruption' is introduced in Chapter 1 above.
4 It is thus possible to distinguish an interpretive account of the 'conscious' or 'surface' continuity of the utterance, such as that given by Harvey Sacks and Emmanuel Schegloff (1974) from the interruptive account of its 'deep' or 'unconscious' conflict which we are attempting here. This issue is further explored in Chapter 7 below.
5 The passage analysed here is the complete text from 'What do children learn at school?' to 'the effective presence of a new reality: ideology' (Althusser, (1971, pp. 132-3). Unfortunately, for copyright reasons it is impossible to reproduce it completely here. Reference is also made to the French text which appeared first in 1970, but is here cited as Althusser (1976). Clearly it is impossible in practice to submit an entire text to detailed linguistic analysis. A fragment must be selected from the whole, on a basis which can never be entirely explicit. It is proposed here that the chosen fragment does reveal the ideological themes of the text as a whole.

6 The French text contains only seventeen, due to the fact that *children* and *they* are both rendered by *on*. An additional difference between the texts is that *I* and the impersonal formulation 'this is to recognize' in the final sentence are both rendered by *nous* in French.

Bibliography

Althusser, L. (1971), 'Ideology and Ideological State Apparatuses', in his *Lenin and Philosophy,* London: New Left Books.

Althusser, L. (1976), 'Idéologies et appareils idéologiques d'État', in his *Positions,* Paris: Editions sociales.

Hirst, P. Q. (1976), 'Althusser and the theory of ideology', *Economy and Society,* 5, pp. 387-412.

Sacks, H. and Schegloff, E. (1974), 'Opening up Closings', in Roy Turner, ed., *Ethnomethodology,* Harmondsworth: Penguin.

Torode, B. (1976), 'The Revelation of a Theory of the Social World as Grammar', in R. Harré, ed., *Life Sentences,* London: Wiley.

part II

The limits of language

The concept of the 'limits of language' has two opposed references. On one side, it seeks to dispense with language in order to make space for some extra-linguistic reality. On the other side, it brings to the fore the impossible ideal of a language which 'tells it like it is'. The relevance of Wittgenstein is that he seems to pull in both directions. As we try to show, Wittgenstein's 'two languages' arise both in what he appears to say (his theories) and in what his texts do (his practice).

chapter 3

Wittgenstein's two languages

Wittgenstein's project remains constant: to diagnose and remedy a sickness of language. The distortion of communication implied by this sickness is not a purely technical problem. It cannot be resolved by technical means (even though the early Wittgenstein offers a technique for overcoming distortion, he emphasizes how little is thereby achieved). Indeed, the sickness is largely caused by the adoption of technique and technical languages as a means of mastering the world. In a rationalized, disenchanted epoch, where everything is possible, language is reduced to a technical instrument. Precision is gained at the cost of the potential for dialogue and challenge.

Outside the restrictions and potentialities of ordinary speech, technical meta-languages provide spurious solutions to questions of morality and life. They offer a kind of idealism which confuses its games with language with the realities of the world. Here language is prised off the world and beaten into shape to be used as a more efficient medium of communication. So a discourse is produced which claims to be judged purely by what it *says*. What it *does* is concealed behind the banner of technique.

However, this raises further questions. Should this sickness be viewed as simply a perennial temptation for philosophy – albeit made more appealing in certain cultural epochs? Or, alternatively, does the disease arise in ordinary speech when attempts are made to shelter behind a technical interest and, thereby, to conceal the 'realities' set to play within speech?

Wittgenstein insists that philosophy is not a body of doctrine but an activity. Consonant with this position, we must seek the answer to our questions in the practice he both recommends and undertakes.

It seems to us as though we had either the wrong pieces or not enough of them, to put together our jig-saw puzzle. But they are all there, only all mixed up . . . . It's no use trying to apply force in fitting pieces together. All we should do is to look at them *carefully* and arrange them (*BB*:46).

When we inspect utterances, Wittgenstein tells us, words seem imprecise ('the wrong pieces') or insufficient ('not enough of them') to allow us to grasp reality ('our jig-saw puzzle'). Hence we are prey to the temptation to change the words and/or to go beyond them. This application of 'force' comes in two forms. First, using a model of language as a technical instrument, we try to perfect our utterances in order to convey the world more perfectly. So we construct a meta-language. Second, keeping the utterances as they are, but denying them any play of their own, we treat them as imperfect appearances of a previously apprehended underlying reality (Garfinkel's documentary method of investigation).

But we don't need to add new pieces ('reality'), nor to meddle with the existing ones by creating new terms. The pieces 'are all there'. Rather than treat utterances as imperfectly constructed means to an end (the communication of reality), we must understand the 'realities' that words themselves construct and express. However, the pieces are 'all mixed up'. In particular, the appearance of an utterance (what it seems to say) tends to displace or conceal its reality (what it does while saying). So, as Wittgenstein says, we must look at the pieces '*carefully* and arrange them'. And this, as he shows elsewhere, involves abandoning our craving for generality in favour of the precise investigation of utterances and the realities they demonstrate.

However, to argue that the pieces 'are all there', may be taken to imply a claim that utterances are complete, self-enclosed and perfect. Viewed in this way, our words would be either the prophetic utterances of Jehovah on Sinai or the mouthings of discrete individuals possessed of irreducibly private consciousnesses. In the former version, utterances are perfect because they 'tell it like it is'; in the latter, the perfection is achieved because my words 'tell it like it is for me' where 'it' and 'me' represent the self-understandings of atomised individuals. The first path proposes a transcendental discourse and engenders a silence of absolute truth; the second path proposes a relativised discourse and engenders the silence of solipsism. Following either path we would not be able to converse, to construct the world together and thus to make history.

So Wittgenstein can *not* be arguing that utterances are complete when he asserts that the pieces 'are all there'. The claim to completeness is itself a possibility but it is a sickness of language, arising from the application of 'force in fitting the pieces together'. Despite the appeal of meta-languages, which seem to provide both for themselves and for the world they report (in one dimension, as it were), there is always an irreducible gap between what speaking speaks about and what it exhibits. This is the sense of Wittgenstein's famous aphorism: 'What can be shown, cannot be said' (*TLP*:4.1212). Only the attempt to reduce speech to an epiphenomenon (the tactic curiously, of both logicians and despots), tempts us to limit the relation of speech and world to the world's *representation* in speech. On the contrary, Wittgenstein is saying, speech both presupposes and orders the world. Speaking *shows* the world in which we find ourselves and the world which we are making: that is why the pieces 'are all there'. It cannot *say* that world because any saying makes reference to the prior possibility of a world which constructs, and is constructed in, our speaking. So the aim of the complete speech is revealed afresh as a sickness of language which would conceal the possibilities displayed in speaking and, ultimately, reduce speech to silence – a reiteration of the given, complete and challengeable only in terms of the accuracy of its representation (in terms of what it says but not of what it shows).

One remedy for this sickness succeeds only by killing the patient. For, working at the level of theology, it implies that what speech shows is an unseen and unseeable element which animates it. Whether formulated as God, deep structure, (structuralism, Chomsky), Being or a capitalized Language (Heidegger), these transcendental realities are accorded the respect denied to them by those who would treat speech as a purely technical instrument. Recognizing the relation between speech and language as one between man and the gods, the paramount aim has become to avoid angering the gods by pretending to be one. So this kind of commitment consigns speech to the negative task of showing its own limits. Further, since these limits are constructed outside speech, the practice of speech is reduced to an affirmation of necessity and, hence, of silence.

Grounds for understanding Wittgenstein's remedies this way are not hard to find. Echoes of the poetic resignation which eventually overcome Kafka's protagonists (as we shall see in Chapter 4) are found in statements such as: 'My *life* consists in my being content to accept many things' (*OC*:344).

Against this acceptance of external limits to speech, we argue that transcendance is a product of the same linguistic practice that puts it into question. Speech practices engage in the creation of transcendent realities and in their challenge. The overcoming of transcendence is as much a task for everyday life as for philosophy. Here we are with Wittgenstein's programme for the pricking of the pretensions of philosophy – with its parallels with Marx's eleventh thesis on Feuerbach.

It should be stressed, however, that our concern with speech practices, in both their coercive and emancipatory forms, is not a return to a version of the completeness of speech. Speech always shows more than it says. It shows its conversation with the possibilities offered by the past and it invites further conversation with the possibilities it recreates.

Wittgenstein's work itself exemplifies such a conversation. Conventionally, the work itself falls into two main periods. The first centres around the *Tractatus Logico-Philosophicus*, the latter around the *Philosophical Investigations*. It has been a conventional wisdom that the earlier work tries to establish the relation between language and world by an appeal to the rules of logic, the latter by an appeal to the rules of usage. However, we prefer the view that Wittgenstein's works as a whole have a unity of purpose far stronger than their surface differences. Conceived as *doctrines,* the work of the two periods looks very different. Conceived as *activities,* as Wittgenstein would have preferred, the work remains on the same path. Rather than develop differences of doctrine at the outset, we will let them emerge through a number of observations chosen first from the *Tractatus* period and then from the period of the *Investigations*.

The *Tractatus* – the scaffolding of the world

> The book deals with the problems of philosophy, and shows, I believe, that the reason why these problems are posed is that the logic of our language is misunderstood . . . (Preface).

Wittgenstein makes it plain at the outset that his work is addressed to the problems of philosophers. It will deal with issues that need not trouble ordinary men because we are not tempted to ask confused philosophical questions. Philosophers are puzzled about the logic of language. Their confusion is a kind of sickness which demands a medicine. 'The whole sense of the book might be summed up in the following words: what can be said at all can be said clearly, and what we cannot talk about we must pass over in silence.' The medicine will be a kind of verbal hygiene: clarity over the sayable, a respectful silence over the unsayable.

As Janik and Toulmin (1972) show, the force of this position has to be located in Wittgenstein's experience of Habsburg Vienna. It was a time when cultural and political decay was papered over by the meaningless catchphrases of newspapers, by the empty ethical formulations of intellectuals and by worthless political appeals. This was the period of the monarchy that was also an empire – K(aiserlich) und K(öniglich) on official documents, or Kakania, *shitland*, in Robert Musil's masterwork, significantly entitled *The Man Without Qualities*. Language, in Heidegger's later phrase, seemed 'worn out and used up'.

A sense of reality might best be underlined not through words but through an architecture which eschewed ornamentation in favour of use value (like the house that Wittgenstein designed for his sister), or through imagery that cut through the superficiality of common usage (like Karl Kraus's cartoons). All that remained for the philosopher of language were two tasks: (1) to show what can be said, and (2) to show how it may be said sensibly.

> Thus the aim of the book is to draw a limit to thought, or rather – not to thought but to the expression of thoughts: for in order to be able to draw a limit to thought, we shall have to find both sides of the limit thinkable (i.e. we should have to think what cannot be thought).
> It will therefore only be in language that the limit can be drawn, and what lies on the other side of the limit will simply be nonsense.

Clarity, for Wittgenstein, involved showing the limits to what may be said sensibly. In particular, metaphysical and ethical questions turn out to be fruitless because, as Kant showed, they depend upon the very reason that they would map. A further implication, not addressed by Kant, is that the limits of reason or thought are themselves unmappable – for, in order to draw a limit to thought we should have to think the unthinkable.[1]

Hence Wittgenstein is concerned here with the limit to the *expression* of thought. These limits, he tells us, lie within language. What lies outside language simply cannot be expressed (it can be shown but not said). Moreover, since 'thought' itself lies outside these limits, our linguistic hygiene must dispense with reference to it and, by implication, reference to the explanatory power of notions of 'intention' or 'consciousness'. For such internal 'states of mind' only surface when they are expressed in language. Hence it is linguistic expressions themselves that are the reality with which Wittgenstein will work. At one sweep, Wittgenstein dispenses with the perennial attempt to reduce linguistic phenomena to a preconceived reality. Speech does not report a reality of internal states; it provides for such a reality. Whatever is 'intended' is not separate from or prior to what is said; it is what is said. Sharing Husserl's critique of psychologism, Wittgenstein opens up for examination the reality of linguistic practice – we might say, the linguistic practice of reality – while cutting away the theoretical ground from Locke's bourgeois subject who claims the rights of property over his thoughts.

We have grouped Wittgenstein's observations in the *Tractatus* under eight headings: (1) World, (2) Pictures, (3) Propositions, (4) Tests, (5) The logic of limits, (6) The role of philosophy, (7) Towards the investigation of possibilities, and (8) Mysticism and silence. Following his own later comments, we shall see that Wittgenstein subsequently shifts his ground on points (1) to (4). Points (5) to (8) remain essentially the same throughout his works.

1 *World*

1. The world is all that is the case.
1.2 The world divides into facts.
2. What is the case – a fact – is the existence of states of affairs.
2.01 A state of affairs (a state of things) is a combination of objects (things).
2.06 The existence and non-existence of states of affairs is reality.
2.063 The sum-total of reality is the world.

In these observations, Wittgenstein moves full circle: the 'world' is to be found at the beginning and the end of them, the silent backdrop to all facts (as well, as we shall see, to all expressions). This world of the *Tractatus* is an atomic world of facts – of states of affairs which either exist or do not. Reality is composed of inter-related objects, combining in certain ways and not in others. So, in this model:

Figure 2 The *Tractatus's* Model of the World

2 *Pictures*

2.1 We picture facts to ourselves.

2.11 A picture represents a situation in logical space, the existence and non-existence of states of affairs.

2.131 In a picture the elements of the picture are representatives of objects.

2.15 The facts that the elements of a picture are related to one another in a determinate way represents that things are related to one another in the same way.

To apprehend the world, we picture its component parts ('facts'). As the world consists of component parts, so do pictures. The basic element of the world is an object; the basic element of a picture is a representative of an object. Objects combine into States of affairs, while pictures represent 'the existence and non-existence of states of affairs'. Hence the relation between the elements of a picture represents the relation between facts. So pictures are models of the world in two senses: they model a possible arrangement of facts (a possible world), while their basic structure (elements in relation to one another, composing a possible state of affairs) models the structure of the world. The difference between pictures and world is that the world is 'the sum-total of *reality*' but a picture only 'represents a situation in *logical space*'.

2.12 A picture is a model of reality.

Following the principles of mechanics, already familiar to Wittgenstein from his training in engineering, working models of reality can be constructed. These allow statements to be made about possible situations in logical space. Such statements can be couched in mathematical form, free of ambiguity.

2.161 There must be something identical in a picture and what it depicts, to enable the one to be a picture of the other at all.

At two different levels, an intelligible picture must have the same form as what it represents. First, if it is a model of something spatial, it must be spatial; if it is a model of something coloured, it must be coloured, and so on (2.171). Second, both facts and pictures will share the logical form of reality. Both will presuppose the world.

2.18 What any picture, of whatever form, must have in common with reality, in order to be able to depict it – correctly or incorrectly – in any way at all, is logical form, i.e. the form of reality.

The concept of a picture as a model, gives the key to Wittgenstein's early understanding of how we represent the world. The representations we make are logical constructs not reproductions of sensory experience. They model a possible version of how the facts might be organized. They picture a formal set of possibilities in logical space, standing as a kind of logical scaffolding that models the world *and* the world's logic.

3 *Propositions*

4.01 A proposition is a picture of reality.
A proposition is a model of reality as we imagine it.

A proposition deals in possibilities. It produces a *possible* picture of the world, showing a possible state of affairs (combination of objects). So a proposition shows how things would stand if it were true. Hence it can be sensible yet false, for its logical form allows us to draw inferences which may, contingently, be false.

4.023 . . . A proposition constructs a world with the help of a logical scaffolding, so that one can actually see from the proposition how everything stands logically *if* it is true. One can *draw inferences* from a false proposition.

The sense of propositions resides in their capacity to model possible states of affairs. False propositions are intelligible because the reality they model is 'the existence and *non-existence* of states of affairs'.

4.21 The simplest kind of proposition, an elementary proposition, asserts the existence of a state of affairs.
4.211 It is a sign of a proposition's being elementary that there can be no elementary proposition contradicting it.
4.22 An elementary proposition consists of names. It is a nexus, a concatenation of names.

Like reality, propositions are reducible into their component parts.

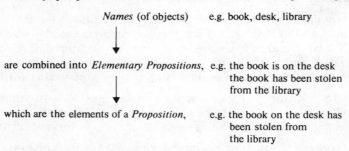

Figure 3 The components of a proposition

Hence propositions are reducible to elementary propositions which are combinations of names referring directly to objects. Elementary propositions cannot be contradicted by another element of the proposition from which they are derived.

4.001 The totality of propositions is language.

Here Wittgenstein takes an extreme position that he was to reject later. In drawing a boundary between sense and nonsense, he began, in his Preface, by arguing that the limit of sense lay in language, i.e. in what can be expressed. This remained his consistent position throughout his work. Now he is suggesting that the sum-total of propositions constitutes language. Or, put more strongly, that propositional language is language. Hence, whatever is not a proposition is outside language and is nonsense. Wittgenstein refers to 'nonsense' in a special way. Even though formal criteria of truthfulness are inappropriate to it, a poem, for him, deals with realities as intelligible as 'facts'. This suggests that intelligibility does not reside entirely in logical rules. Accordingly, we propose to refer to the intelligibility of non-propositional language as *'non-sense'*. In turn, this will allow the interrogation of the kind of non-logical intelligibility at work even in a text composed almost entirely of logical propositions such as the *Tractatus*.

4 Tests

4.05 Reality is compared with propositions.

A working model is compared with a reality whose logical form it shares. The model suggests that objects are combined in the way that it depicts. It is a true model if its elements correlate with a state of affairs.

2.1514 The pictorial relationship consists of the correlations of the picture's elements with things.
2.1515 These correlations are, as it were, the feelers of the picture's elements, with which the picture touches reality.

The relationship between proposition and world, its 'pictorial relationship', arises in the way in which its component parts accurately picture the objects and state of affairs that comprise reality. 'The picture touches reality' when it constitutes an accurate model which correlates with given states of affairs.

Wittgenstein here states the 'correspondence theory' of truth at two distinct levels. At the obvious level, he is affirming that the truth of propositions arise in their correspondence with the world when, as he puts it elsewhere, they are 'laid against reality like a measure' (2.1512). This common version of correspondence he was later to reject, arguing that utterances touch reality by other means than simply as accurate pictures. But this later insight arose out of another, more sophisticated, version of correspondence theory that was already present in the *Tractatus*. As we saw earlier, he maintained that pictures correspond to reality because their structure models its structure. Hence the world is presupposed in both pictures and states of affairs. Or, as he would later argue, the logic of our games with language reveals the logic of our world.

5 *The logic of limits*

2.172 A picture cannot, however, depict its pictorial form: it displays it.
2.173 A picture represents its subject from a position outside it. (Its standpoint is its representational form.) That is why a picture represents its subject correctly or incorrectly.
2.174 A picture cannot, however, place itself outside its representational form.

Here Wittgenstein returns to the themes of his Preface. The logic of a picture consists in its pictorial form and it can only display this logic. To speak it, or depict it, would assume that it was possible to stand outside the representational form that gives a picture its sense. This is a nonsense. Propositions are stuck within the form of language – which is to say that they are stuck within the form of our world. These forms constitute the logic which the picture shares with objects and which constitutes its sense.

4.121 Propositions cannot represent logical form: it is mirrored in them.
What finds its representation in language, language cannot represent.
What expresses *itself* in language, *we* cannot express by means of language.
Propositions *show* the logical form of reality.
They display it.

'Logical form' is the form of reality *and* the form of our pictures of reality. Indeed, the logical form of our propositions reveals 'the logical form of reality'. The world is already present in the activity of modelling (or picturing) before we ever construct any proposition or seek to test it. The world is what 'expresses itself in language' and cannot be expressed 'by means of language'.

5.6 *The limits of my language* mean the limits of my world.
5.61 Logic pervades the world: the limits of the world are also its
limits.

Wittgenstein is repeating that language presupposes logic and logic
presupposes world. Logic pervades both reality and how we
apprehend reality. To pass beyond its limits, the limits alike of
language and world, is to speak non-sense.

These famous assertions look like gloomy reminders of the
prison-house that holds us captive. However, we may read Wittgenstein more fruitfully. In terms of our own project, at least three
useful positions are affirmed here. First, Wittgenstein is directing us
away from fruitless questions, of 'essences' and of 'values', which
assume that we may start afresh, apart from a linguistic context, to
apprehend the world. Here the idealism present in the acceptance
of external limits to speech gives way to a critique of the idealism
which refuses to deal with facts, most notably the facts of language.
Second, there is a critique of reductionism, which would reduce
these facts of language to external, supposedly pre-linguistic
categories. But the pieces 'are all there'; we reveal logic and world
when we investigate linguistic practice. And third, we find in
Wittgenstein a starting point for the analysis of language which is
entirely different from the social-psychology of Saussure and others
in which language is only a medium of exchange between individuals. For Wittgenstein, both early and late, language is not primarily
a medium for the communication of concepts from one person to
another. It is instead a means of representing the world in words.[2]

6 *The role of philosophy*

4.003 Most of the propositions and questions to be found in
philosophical works are not false but nonsensical. Consequently,
we cannot give any answers to questions of this kind, but can only
point out that they are nonsensical. Most of the propositions and
questions of philosophers arise from our failure to understand
the logic of our language. (They belong to the same class as the
question whether the good is more or less identical than the
beautiful.) And it is not surprising that the deepest problems are
in fact *not* problems at all.

Once again, a great deal hinges on the way the word 'nonsensical' is
read. Understood as (unhyphenated) 'nonsense', this passage consigns to the dustbin a large portion of Western philosophy. Treated
as (hyphenated) 'non-sense', it suggests the need to re-examine the
logic of the language of this tradition. As Wittgenstein suggests, this

may lead to a reversal of the priorities attaching to these problems. Rather than seeking to dissolve problems – to treat them as not problems at all – we return in this way to the logic of their language.

4.112 Philosophy aims at the logical clarification of thoughts. Philosophy is not a body of doctrine but an activity.

Philosophy, Wittgenstein concludes, has no business to construct doctrines or theories of the world, precisely because such theories either ignore the facts of language or seek to formulate those facts in a way which conceals the linguistic practice involved in the formulation. Doctrines are the preachings that claim to tell it like it is (pre-linguistically); they are the appearances constructed silently by the practice. It is this practice or activity which is the reality. Given this confusion about reality and appearance, the proper role of philosophy is 'logical clarification'. But this does not deny the point of theorizing as an activity for any one of us, providing that we are prepared to recognize it as a practice as well as a preaching.

For the sense of the doctrine arises in the kind of practice that its expression constitutes.

4.114 (Philosophy) must set limits to what can be thought; and, in doing so, to what cannot be thought.
It must set limits to what cannot be thought by working outwards through what can be thought.
4.115 It will signify what cannot be said, by presenting clearly what can be said.

Here we encounter, posed as a single programme, two alternative treatments of the sickness of language. The issue turns upon whether we emphasize the setting of limits or the 'working outwards', signifying what *cannot* be said *or* presenting what *can* be said. If our business is limit-setting, then we seek to clear away the dead wood (the dead arguments) in order to make a space for the extra-linguistic reality and limit to appear. The appropriate silence can then reign as we respectfully contemplate the mystery which holds us captive. Alternatively, in revealing the limits of language, we bring to the fore the impossible ideal of the complete speech, that empty vehicle of communication which appears to tell it like it is. And, in doing so, we open up the investigation of the construction of such idea(l)s and their challenge within linguistic practice. 'Working outwards through what can be thought (expressed)' is thus to confront the facts of language – we might say, to confront the language of facts. For, in investigating language, we seek to recreate the possibilities shown in speech.

7 *Towards the investigation of possibilities*

3.3421 A particular mode of signifying may be unimportant but it is always important that it is a *possible* mode of signifying. And that is generally so in philosophy: again and again the individual case turns out to be unimportant, but the possibility of each individual case discloses something about the essence of the world.

'The essence of the world', Wittgenstein is saying, is not apart from the world. Essence is disclosed in our signifying practice. The 'individual case', unimportant in itself, reveals something about the possibilities of our world. The intelligibility of 'a particular mode of signifying' thus discloses an aspect of reality. For it is not coincidental that we tend to do certain things and not others and that, if we do other things or do the same thing in a different way, confusion may result.

The crucial concepts here are 'possibility' and the 'individual case'. The ways we speak disclose something about the character of our world – they raise questions about the possibility of that particular mode of expression. Hence, if we try to perfect our discourse by constructing a meta-language, we unintentionally prise it off the world that is ordinarily expressed within it. We would do better, then, to investigate actual modes of signifying and, in particular, the 'individual case' rather than to construct artificial languages or theoretical systems. All the pieces are there.

Now, of course, Wittgenstein's obsession with propositional language obscured a proper treatment in the *Tractatus* of the possibilities disclosed by individual cases which did not derive their sense as formal propositions. But already the method of proceeding from the individual to the general, from the facts of language to the possibilities revealed, had been founded. Equally, as we shall see, a concern with what *cannot* be said informs both periods of Wittgenstein's work.

8 *Mysticism and silence?*

6.54 My propositions serve as elucidations in the following way: anyone who understands me eventually recognizes them as nonsensical, when he has used them – as steps – to climb up beyond them (he must, so to speak, throw away the ladder after he has climbed up it). He must transcend these propositions, and then he will see the world aright.

Wittgenstein's project is now clearer. The aim is to counter the nonsense that we can play any games we choose with language and hope to understand the world better. This species of sickness is to be cured by revealing the bounds of sense to be set within language itself. However, the cure is to be effected by a remedy that tends to spread the same disease. For any set of doctrines 'about' language tends to elevate itself to a 'pure' statement of facts. It conceals that it is also an activity within language – a showing as well as a saying.

Conceived as purely instrumental means of mastering the world, the propositions of the *Tractatus* are, then, 'nonsensical' in Wittgenstein's usage because the world is presupposed in them. It was thus important for Wittgenstein to try to avoid spreading the very disease that he was seeking to counter. The aim was not to create a doctrine but to show the limits of the propositional language in which doctrines could be couched and to avoid spreading hot air in making statements about the inexpressible. Transcending the propositions of the *Tractatus*, being in a position to 'see the world aright', means recognizing the work that our words do and avoiding dwelling in appearances. As Wittgenstein said elsewhere, the true significance of his early work lay precisely in what it did *not* attempt to say, i.e. in what it did.

For us, the language of the closing propositions of the *Tractatus* is indeed 'non-sensical' since it goes beyond the recital of purely logical propositions. However, it can only admit this in terms of the *theoretical* transcendence suggested by the ladder analogy. The suggestion that the 'ladder' should be 'thrown away' represents, further, an attempt to close off any investigation of the text's own linguistic workings.

Yet something has happened in practice here. The voiceless propositional language of the earlier passages of the *Tractatus* has given way to the offer of a dialogue between voices of 'Me' ('My propositions') and 'He' (who 'has used them' and 'must transcend' them). Contrary to appearances, a *practical* transcendence is at work here. We noted earlier the importance of the distinction between saying and showing with its rejection of a version of a perfected language and its emphasis on the practice that is expressed in any preaching. However, having thrown away his 'ladder', Wittgenstein emphasizes the theoretical transcendence that his text *says*. This is no more than a resigned and presumably silent contemplation of the unspeakable realities that remain once the clammer of empty voices has been stilled. The metaphysics of the very *possibility* of the world becomes his animating topic:

6.44 It is not *how* things are in the world that is mystical, but *that* it exists.

The Philosophical Investigations – **language in use**

The *Investigations* begins by using a passage from Augustine's *Confessions* as a means of resurrecting Wittgenstein's earlier treatment of language and of explaining his rejection of that position. Wittgenstein comments as follows on this passage:

> 1. These words, it seems to me, give us a particular picture of the essence of language. It is this: the individual words in the language name objects – sentences are combinations of such names. – In this picture of language we find the roots of the following idea: every word has a meaning. This meaning is correlated with the word. It is the object for which the word stands.

In examining how he sets out his rejection of this version of words as names of objects, we can broadly summarize Wittgenstein's position on language in the *Investigations* under five headings: (1) context, (2) language-games, (3) use, (4) forms of life, and (5) the sense of picture theory.

1 *Context*

Words sometimes stand for objects. But this applies only in certain contexts. One can, therefore, imagine a language for which picture theory is correct: Wittgenstein gives the example of words exchanged between a builder A and his assistant B where A simply calls out a word, 'slab', and B then passes the named object to A. The simplicity of this example suggests that there are many other situations where a simple picture theory might not apply. To apply just one model of language to all of these is rather like trying to define a word in terms of only one context:

> 3. It is as if someone were to say: 'A game consists in moving objects about on a surface according to certain rules . . . ' – and we replied: You seem to be thinking of board games, but there are others. You can make your definition correct by expressly restricting it to those games.

2 *Language-games*

As the board game example shows, Wittgenstein's attention is now turning to the variety of games expressed by speaking. The 'slab' game between the builder and his assistant is merely a primitive example of an extensive set of games which, as we have seen from the *Blue Book* include 'giving and obeying orders, asking questions and answering them, describing an event' (and so on). In each example, words are woven into a set of actions to produce recognizable games:

> 7. I will call these games 'language games' and will sometimes speak of a primitive language as a language-game. And the processes of naming the stones and of repeating words after someone might also be called language-games. Think of much of the use of words in games like ring-a-ring-a-roses. I shall also call the whole, consisting of language and the actions into which it is woven, the 'language-game'.

3 *Use*

Language is woven into actions and so use gives the sense of speech.

> 421. Look at the sentence as an instrument, and its sense as its employment.

To look at a sentence 'as an instrument' is to ask what its expression accomplishes or does. The example of exclamations is used by Wittgenstein as a kind of employment of words whose sense does not arise in the naming of objects:

> 27. Think of exclamations alone, with their completely different functions:
>
> Water!
> Away!
> Ow!
> Help!
> Fine!
> No!

Are you still inclined to call these words 'names of objects'?

Wittgenstein here shows that he rejects his earlier inclination to call words 'names of objects' because, although not without exceptions, meaning arises in use:

> 43. For a *large* class of cases – though not for all – in which we employ the word 'meaning' it can be defined thus: the meaning of a word is its use in the language.

The emphasis on meaning-in-use leads to a rejection of both meaning-by-naming and meaning seen as the expression in words of an inner or mental process. Wittgenstein illustrates the latter point of departure by posing himself a question about 'remembering':

305. 'But you surely cannot deny that, for example, in remembering, an inner process takes place' – What gives the impression that we want to deny anything?
What we deny is that the picture of the inner process gives us the correct idea of the use of the word 'to remember'. We say that this picture with its ramifications stands in the way of our seeing the use of the word as it is.

So the doctrine of meaning-in-use implies a rejection of psychologistic explanations in favour of an inspection of the actual facts of linguistic practice. Wittgenstein does not want to speculate what the process of remembering *essentially* entails but to examine how the words 'to remember' are employed in *practice*. This is to deny nothing; it is simply to affirm that, for the purposes of our investigation, 'the pieces are already there'.

4 *Forms of life*

Despite the critique of picture theory, the argument of the *Tractatus* could be retained in its essentials if it could be shown that language-games based on usage had some pure or essential form which could be formulated in the manner of the *Tractatus*. But Wittgenstein insists that there is nothing common to all that we call language (*PI*: 65); to find an identity between our various games is merely to play with words (67). Upon examination all that we find are 'a complicated network of resemblances' (66), which, because they parallel the various resemblances between the members of a family, may be characterized as 'family resemblances' (67).

If there is something common to this family of games, it is not a definable essence but a set of interlocking activities or, what Wittgenstein calls, 'forms of life'. These forms of life give intelligibility and coherence to the grammar of language-games:

19. It is easy to imagine a language consisting only of orders and reports in battle. – Or a language consisting only of questions and expressions for answering yes and no. And innumerable others.
– And to imagine a language means to imagine a form of life.

In common with the *Tractatus*, it is asserted here that language presupposes a world. However, our world is one where a whole series of games are intelligible – not simply the game of modelling or picturing. For instance, in Wittgenstein's famous example, we live in a world in which arrows 'point'. And the sense of this pointing arises not in particular kinds of psychical activity but in the realities, physiological as well as social, presupposed in our games. Arrows could hardly point, for instance, if we had no eyes to see them or lived in a world where direction had no sense (*PI*: 454).

Wittgenstein uses the notion of 'form of life' to continue the battle against idealism begun in the *Tractatus*. It is not ideas or opinions from which we begin but the realities presupposed and produced in our practices. For instance, discussions about 'truth' and 'falsity', Wittgenstein says, express a common commitment to a language in which we may discuss such particulars. It is in this language that we deeply agree, however much surface disagreement there might be about particulars. Hence morality is to be located not in contingent opinions (not in what we *say*) but rather in the form of life in which opinions are anchored (in what we *practice*):

> 241. 'So you are saying that human agreement decides what is true and what is false?' – It is what human beings *say* that is true and false; and they agree in the *language* they use. That is not agreement in opinions but in form of life.

The 'perfect order even in the vaguest sentence' (98), to which we have already referred, is now to be understood as grounded in the form of life which it displays. This in no way precludes the invention of new ways of speaking. But it must be grasped that these ways are not simply logical devices but activities. Such activities display forms of life which, in the case of the logician's speech, have unknown relevance to the everyday activities that they may be used to explain or describe. To use one of Wittgenstein's expressions, only by making language 'go on holiday', could we assume that ordinary language was arbitrary or non-methodical.

5   *The sense of picture theory*

Picture theory is now to be understood as exemplifying certain grammatical possibilities of the language-game of making propositions. It begins to go wrong when it assumes that there is an essence that underlies all language use. Even in formulating this pure form of language it becomes entangled in certain grammatical possibilities. Accounts of verification are grammatical rather than logical. Or rather, their logical form exemplifies certain forms of grammar:

> 353. Asking whether and how a proposition can be verified is only a particular way of asking 'How d'you mean?' The answer is a contribution to the grammar of the proposition.

So the question is resolved not by *stating* the logic of verification but by *displaying* the move and the game in which it is intelligible. Rather than formulate the *logic* of picturing the world, the task is to investigate the *grammar* in which multiple logics (or games) have their home.

The error of the *Tractatus* and of picture theory, however, was not a coincidence. The language-games of proposing and of picturing are deeply rooted in our language and thus in our forms of life. As Wittgenstein comments, in a passage that seems to seek to ground the intelligibility of his early work:

> 114. (*Tractatus Logico-Philosophicus*, 4.5) 'The general form of propositions is: This is how things are.' – That is the kind of proposition that one repeats to oneself countless times. One thinks that one is tracing the outline of the thing's nature over and over again, and one is merely tracing round the frame through which we look at it.
>
> 115. A *picture* held us captive. And we could not get outside it, for it lay in our language and language seemed to repeat it to us inexorably.

The two Wittgensteins – from logic to use

It is now increasingly recognized that Wittgenstein's central concern – the relation of word and world – remained unchanged throughout his work. We now turn to those themes of the *Tractatus* still present in the later work.

In both periods, Wittgenstein maintains that the facts of language cannot be avoided. They express the realities of our world. Sense cannot be imposed on the world anew, for instance by inventing a meta-language, without losing sight of these realities. So, although we can easily choose to speak in different ways, this doesn't alter the facts of the case expressed in how we normally speak. Take the case of the geographer who decides to redraw a map, arguing that the facts of geography are thereby changed:

> He sees a way of dividing the country different from that used on the ordinary map. He feels tempted, say, to use the name 'Devonshire' not for the county with its conventional boundary, but for a region differently bounded. He could express this by saying: 'Isn't it absurd to make *this* a county, to draw the boundaries *here*?' But what he says is: 'The *real* Devonshire is this.' We could answer: 'What you want is only a new notation, and by a new notation no facts of geography are changed' (*BB*: 57).

In exactly the same way, we are tempted to use words in ways other than are conventionally understood. But that these conventions are used and expressed in particular 'notations' expresses facts that will not go away simply because they can be shown not to fit a logical rule. Practices can only be displaced by other practices – they cannot be displaced by ideas.

The role of philosophy, as an activity rather than a doctrine, is to show the nonsense of proceeding from the idealist premise that the world is changed by the adoption of more 'logical' concepts. Our forms of expression have sense in a particular world; they are not autonomous means of capturing the world: 'Philosophy, as we use the word, is a fight against the fascination which forms of expression exert on us' (*BB*: 27). Consequently, what the *Blue Book* refers to as the 'craving for generality' (17) must be resisted in favour of the analysis of the possibilities disclosed by individual cases. This clearing away of difficulties ultimately serves the purpose of allowing us to confront not possibilities but limits – the existence of the world in Tractatian terms, the 'bedrock' or place where 'my spade is turned' as expressed in the later work. The proper rejection of the solipsism inherent in playing empty games with language seems to move, in both periods of Wittgenstein's work, towards resignation in the face of a transcendental, ineffable world.

The points of difference between the two Wittgensteins are altogether clearer. They arise from his emerging recognition that language is not exhausted by the language of propositions. Although the propositional form is one intelligible way of speaking, we use language to do a whole array of other things as well. Since logical rules are only appropriate to propositions and yet other utterances can be sensible, it now appeared that usage rather than the ideal standards of logic was the basis of orderly language.

> 98. On the one hand it is clear that every sentence in our language 'is in order as it is'. That is to say, we are not *striving after* an ideal, as if our ordinary vague sentences had not yet got a quite unexceptionable sense, and a perfect language awaited construction by us. – On the other hand it seems clear that where there is sense there must be perfect order. – So there must be perfect order even in the vaguest sentence. (*PI*)

Here sense is no longer the product of a logician's judgments, albeit mediated by the modelling activity built into our world. Instead, sense is already there in our speech. Grammar must be respected as an antidote to our illusion that we can impose sense afresh upon the world.

The proper concerns of philosophical enquiry

As we have explained, Wittgenstein's later work shifts away from codifying the logic of propositions towards an investigation of ordinary language. Consequently, the critique of philosophy, while still based upon its misunderstanding of the logic of language (*TLP*: 4.003), is now directed at the conceptual confusion (or 'puzzlement') stemming from the violence it does to ordinary usage:

> 194. When we do philosophy we are like savages, primitive people, who hear the expressions of civilized men, put a false interpretation on them, and then draw the queerest conclusions from it.

Because philosophers have wrought violence on usage, they have been 'like savages', using their own interpretive schemes, while ignoring the dependence of all schemes on a usage that is already established within ordinary language. Consequently, speculation about the 'essence' of 'knowledge', say, or 'beauty' is to be silenced. This silencing is not of the kind to be found in the *Tractatus*, where ethical questions are assumed to be nonsensical because they cannot be expressed in propositional form. Rather, we now silence abstract discussion of such matters by returning such words to their everyday uses:

> 116. When philosophers use a word – 'knowledge', 'being', 'object', 'I', 'proposition', 'name' – and try to grasp the *essence* of the thing, one must always ask oneself: is the word ever actually used in this way in the language-game which is its original home? – What *we* do is to bring words back from their metaphysical to their everyday use.

In order to rid ourselves of the sickness of conceptual puzzlement, Wittgenstein recommends philosophical hygiene:

> 255. The philosopher's treatment of a question is like the treatment of an illness.

Now, if Wittgenstein were really advocating that all questions were signs of a disease, then he would be unable to account for the way in which questioning is an intelligible activity in our world. However, it seems more likely that his target here are only questions which ask about essences, i.e. typically, philosophical questions. For it is in philosophy that Wittgenstein locates the sickness of language – a sickness which must be treated rather than encouraged. This, however, entails the consequence, which we shall consider shortly, that no room is left for recognizing the presence of sickness or distortions in ordinary usage.

Consonant with his continuing commitment to a conception of philosophy as an activity rather than a doctrine, Wittgenstein resists the attempt to formulate a body of theory from our investigations. Rather than explain the facts of language by another level of reality, we would do better to describe those facts themselves and in doing so, by implication, reveal the 'realities' (or 'proto-phenomena') which they sustain:

> 654. Our mistake is to look for an explanation where we ought to look at what happens as a 'proto-phenomenon'. That is, where we ought to have said: *this language-game is played*.
> 655. The question is not one of explaining a language-game by means of our experiences, but of noting a language-game.

When we 'note' a language-game, Wittgenstein tells us, we are not engaged in science (109), nor indeed in a very subtle operation (106). For our aim is not to reduce the facts of linguistic practice to something else but to describe their working:

> I want to say here that it can never be our job to reduce anything to anything, or to explain anything. Philosophy really *is* 'purely descriptive'. (Think of such questions as 'Are there sense data?' And ask: What method is there of determining this? Introspection?) (*BB*: 18).

The reductivist impulse is shown in the attempt to reduce the facts of linguistic practice to something else. The question: 'Are there sense data?' is an *idle* question exhibiting a craving for generality which makes it contemptuous of the particular case. It leads directly to metaphysical, ethical or psychical speculation which appeals to such will o' the wisps as 'introspection' in its desire to overcome or to ignore the actual facts of language. 'All the pieces are there' – confronted by the facts of language, philosophy, for Wittgenstein, has no choice but to be 'purely descriptive'.

Conclusion: Wittgenstein and the investigation of linguistic practice

While aspects of Wittgenstein's work do change between the early and later periods, we hope to have shown that a crucial consistency remains throughout. Idealism treats the facts of linguistic practice as an epiphenomenon and Wittgenstein proceeds on the basis of a critique of idealism. In doing so, he makes three important contributions to a materialist treatment of language:

1 The opposition to the treatment of language as an instrument to attack a body of facts through questions of our choosing. 'Facts' and

'questions' are always already within language whose logic or grammar presupposes a particular kind of world which is to be understood in particular ways. Meta-languages deny this reality which is before us all the time. They solve problems at the cost of failing to confront the possibilities expressed in the centrality of certain modes of signification to our actual lives. The perfection of language, the aim of any meta-language, presumes a position from outside language from which we can proceed and ignores the parallels between its own practice and everyday attempts to impose a purportedly pre-linguistic reality upon us all. Like these attempts, its own practice silences challenge by silencing conversation.

2 We return, through Wittgenstein, then, to the facts of linguistic practice. Language is not a complement to the 'meanings' going through our minds but is itself the vehicle of thought (*PI*: 329). Language is not a means to 'penetrate' phenomena, a means to get at the reality, it is a reality. In 'the kinds of statements' we make, we reveal our world (*PI*: 90).

3 Wittgenstein insists that there is an irreconcilable separation between what language speaks about and what it exhibits in speaking. Only when language is reduced to an empty means of communication does linguistic practice appear to be no more than someone else grasping the sense of my words (*PI*: 363). Here there is no space for conversation, no opportunity to confront or to challenge the practice that silently animates the preaching.

No doubt Wittgenstein himself would strongly reject any programmatic formulation of his work. Wittgenstein's chosen role is that of the cultural critic concerned to diagnose the corruption of our use of language. He expresses rather than transcends the diagnosis of culture prevalent in his time.[3] Consequently, his analysis stresses the need to accept pre-given limits to intelligible speech to be found in the modelling enterprise or, later, in forms of life. Recognition of such givens, the ineffable grounds of our speech, becomes the aim and a form of poetic resignation the appropriate pose.

> 6.522 There are, indeed, things that cannot be put into words. They *make themselves manifest*. They are what is mystical. (*TLP*)

Confronted by these mystical 'things', the reality which authorizes speech, words are condemned to deal only with appearances. Reality – whether logical form (*TLP*) or forms of life (*PI*) – remains obstinately outside speech. It constrains what we say yet refuses to be spoken. So Wittgenstein reaches the curious position that unless we concede the existence of a transcendent reality outside speech, we become solipsists with no grounds for speaking. So speaking depends upon silence. We can only speak together by consigning the grounds of our speaking to a respectful silence.

But speech does not simply show mysteries. Or rather, the creation of transcendental realms is only one of the things that speaking does. Hence sickness is not, as Wittgenstein supposed, confined to philosophers' attempt to answer idle questions. *Any* speaking can be sick or distorted, not because it fails to satisfy logical or commonsense criteria of adequacy, but because it imposes the single voice of a transcendental order which does not allow for conversation or challenge. But this is not to say that 'non-distorted' speech would 'tell it like it is', for this is another distortion. Rather such speech would encourage conversation by not concealing the multiplicity of voices which it sets into play. These voices are, however, present in the very texts we have been considering.

Wittgenstein's two languages

The *Tractatus* begins by the attempt 'to draw a limit to thought' (Preface). It finds this limit in the logical scaffolding in the world. However, as the Preface goes on, the aim is to draw a limit 'not to thought but to the expression of thought'. Limits to 'thought' can only be established in language.

The *Tractatus* wants to say, then, that only one language (of picturing and representation) is logically possible. It affirms the transcendent reality of one language or discourse. But it also creates the rule of this single discourse *within its own pages*.

The *Tractatus* speaks a discourse of facts (a world of 'is') connected by logical links (a world of 'must' and 'cannot'). The *Tractatus does* (textually) what it *says*. Like the 'propositions' that it describes, it 'constructs a world' (4.023). And this world is a world of a single discourse which will brook no interference with its linguistic rule.

It is no coincidence that the *Tractatus* reads like a computer print-out. It is a text which affirms silence while, more significantly, *silencing* other discourses. If the world is to be seen aright, as Wittgenstein wants, then its propositional form must be transcended (6.54).

Unlike the *Tractatus*, the *Philosophical Investigations* affirms that many discourses are possible. It calls these discourses 'language-games'. Once again, it practices what it preaches. Consider, for instance, a paragraph discussed earlier:

241. 'So you are saying that human agreement decides what is true and what is false?' – It is what human beings *say* that is true and false; and they agree in the language they use. That is not agreement in opinions but agreement in form of life (*PI*).

Unlike the monolithic discourse of the *Tractatus*, we here encounter two discourses, signalled by the quotation marks around the first utterance. The first discourse or text dwells in a dialogue between a 'You' (who is 'saying') and an 'I' who is the presumed hearer of what 'You' says. 'You's' utterances are located in a dialogue ('you are saying') rather than in the computer print-out suggested by an untexted body of 'facts' or 'logic'.

The second text reverts to the discourse of the *Tractatus*. It affirms facts ('it is', 'they agree') with logical implications ('that is not . . . but (is)'). It seeks to contain the interruption to its rule affirmed by the dialogic discourse that precedes it.

The presence of these two discourses with their multiple voices corresponds to what the *Investigations* says about the multiplicity of language-games. But it *shows* that speakers need not necessarily play the same game. It reveals that text may interrupt as well as interpret one another. So, while the passage *says* that 'human beings agree in the language they use', the two discourses within it *show* that such agreement is not a condition of speech.

We have located a text containing two discourses which question each other. It represents the *practical* transcendence of the propositional discourse of the *Tractatus*. Contrary to what the *Investigations* say, a question is *not* an illness. The internal interrogation of text by text is the basis of linguistic emancipation.

Notes

1 In making these limits determinate, Kant is not in line with Wittgenstein, as Strawson points out in *The Bounds of Sense*. To formulate such limits as the limits of mind is to take a stand outside language.

2 It is on this basis that the notion of 'picture' is used in Chapter 1 and elsewhere in this book.

3 In this respect, he is rather like the historian in Hesse's *Glass Bead Game*. This historian formulates the corruption of what he calls 'The Age of the Feuilleton':

> The life of the mind in the Age of the Feuilleton might be compared to a degenerate plant which was squandering its strength in excessive vegetative growth, and the subsequent corrections to pruning the plant back to its roots (Herman Hesse, *The Glass Bead Game*, Penguin: 1972, p. 35).

Wittgenstein's 'correction' looks very much like such a 'pruning'. The character of the subsequent age also is very close to Wittgenstein's practice:

> Along with the newly regenerated intellectual life went a puritanical shrinking from 'foolish digressions', from the intermingling of disciplines and categories. There was also a profound and justified fear of relapse into the sin of superficiality and feuilletonism (37).

Bibliography

The Wittgenstein texts referred to are as follows:

Tractatus Logico-Philosophicus, Routledge & Kegan Paul: London, 1971 (*TLP*)

Notebooks, Blackwell: Oxford, 1961 (*N*)

The Blue and Brown Books, Blackwell: Oxford, 1972 (*BB*)

Philosophical Investigations, Blackwell: Oxford, 1968 (*PI*)

On Certainty, Harper & Row: New York, 1972 (*OC*)

Kafka's texts rework the two versions of 'limits' that we encountered in Wittgenstein. The 'Castle' that defies entry may stand as either an extra-textual reality or, conversely, a reminder of K(afka)'s doomed attempts to escape the text. The latter reading prepares the way for an encounter with the text às an organized relation between (black) realities and (white) appearances.

chapter 4

Kafka: the poet of black and white

In a one-dimensional, rationalized world, the sign seems to reiterate the familiar. Relieved of its capacity to point to tensions and potentialities, the sign is reduced to a mere signifier of what is the case.

Yet the dialectic between a present reality and its absent history transcends such reifications. For Marx, the appeal of political economy stood as an icon of the familiar to be overcome by a restoration of its history. In his neo-Kantian turn, Weber pursued this tension in the difference between a valueless empirical reality and heroic ultimate evaluations presided over by the Gods. For both Wittgenstein and Heidegger, speech (being) makes reference to its own possibility in language (Being), and, once again, what is present becomes a trace of an animating absence.

Not least among Kafka's achievements are a series of texts that engage this dialectic between presence and absence. Kafka speaks of appearances (treated here as white) and of the reality which authorizes them (black). Like Wittgenstein, Kafka shows how linguistic appearances (the white) are secured in mundane practice. Consequently, to engage the black is to cut away the (everyday) ground from under one's feet. The image of the circle, and of the nausea of circling, is central to their texts.

Kafka's triumph arises in his refusal to resign himself to a passive acceptance of any non-human bounds of the possible, authorized by a purported prison-house of language. Without escaping into groundlessness, his texts offer a poetic dialogue between 'reality' and 'appearance', where 'reality' is not a prison but a textual conversation. Yet, to the extent that this dialogue arises in a writing which pretends to be purely an expression of mind, its emancipatory power is questionable.

The pleasure dome

> He felt as if he were seasick. He felt he was on a ship rolling in
> heavy seas. It was as if the waters were dashing against the
> wooden walls, as if the roaring of breaking waves came from the
> end of the passage, as if the passage itself pitched and rolled and
> the waiting clients on either side rose and fell with it (*T*: 83).

Kafka is describing the emotions of Joseph K after an uninvited
attempt to confront the Court that has inexplicably arrested him. To
get near to the Court, Joseph K now realizes, is to approach a
dangerous, unpredictable storm. The trusted senses that normally
allow control of the situation no longer apply. He is on board a
mysterious vessel which itself is 'rolling in heavy seas'. 'The waiting
clients', the ship's passengers, can only resign themselves to rise and
fall with the movements of the ship. Cut off from the certainties of
shore, pitching and rolling on a craft not susceptible to reason,
Joseph K feels 'seasick'. Such is the fate of persons who, notwith-
standing the risks, elect to engage the practice of writing.

Of course, there are safer alternatives. One can live unreflectively
on the shore, respecting what seems to be the natural order of
things. Or one can choose to play with words, hoping that the
intellectual fashions of the time will conceal the emptiness of the
rhetoric.

Yet, another course is possible. The dangerous game beckoned to
Kafka. Rather than denying what seem to be the bounds of the
possible (language, history, ultimate value), one might engage them
in a quest for an authentic relation. Faced with the white-washed,
one-dimensional givens of mundaneity, and the seemingly
impenetrable black of the bounds of the possible, it was necessary to
acknowledge both and to develop a practice of writing that might
bring them into dialogue. Kafka's unenviable task, like that of
Wittgenstein, was to speak authentically while respecting the necessities of the prison that seems to accommodate us. He had, as he put
it, a curious and self-defeating intention: 'the intention to rebuild
the prison as a pleasure dome for himself'.[1]

White

> I think back and recall the time when I was still a member of the
> canine community, sharing in all its preoccupations, a dog among
> dogs (ID: 85).

Living as 'a dog among dogs', in the unreflectiveness of communal
existence, it is as if a blanket of whiteness has washed out all trace of

the dark powers, dissolving thereby any possibility of dialogue, leaving only the empty buzzing of self-approving voices. In both Kafka's major novels, snow serves as the image for such a dog-like existence. In *The Trial*, snow falls, ever more thickly, 'in a foggy dimness' (*T*: 126). In *The Castle*, the snow is deep around the village 'and the exertion of lifting one's feet clear was fatiguing' (*C*: 17). Stuck in the snow, the outlines of the locality are blurred. Since, whatever the season, according to Olga, the snow is always present, one gets used to not 'lifting one's feet clear'.

White, in the form of snow, points towards the happiness of a practice of writing that reiterates the familiar. It reminds us of 'the things that bind us happily together'[2], of the 'state of delicate balance' of organized social life, and of the need, however distasteful, to 'lie low' rather than disturb it.[3] Rather than reminding us of the sun from which it draws its light, such whiteness seems only to index itself. So to practice a mode of writing enmeshed in the white is to deny the possibility of transcendence: the happiness of 'foggy dimness' is illusory. At the same time, to ignore or deny the white, failing to recognize that modes of (white) domination deny the creativity of practice, is to engage in empty intellectualism: nothing happens 'simply by saying "no, no!" '.[4]

Black

> Now he got up ceremoniously, obviously displeased to have his presence made known. With his hands, which he flapped like short wings, he seemed to be deprecating all introductions or greetings, showing that the last thing he desired was to disturb the other gentlemen, and that he only wanted to be translated again to the darkness where his presence might be forgotten. But that privilege could no longer be his (*T*: 116).

Such is Joseph K's only encounter with a senior official of the Law, the Chief Clerk of the Court. The atmosphere of mystery that surrounds him brings into question whether the authority that he represents is merely the familiar hierarchy of this world. Throughout there is a sense of menace implied in an encounter with such an authority shrouded in blackness and mystery. The Chief Clerk lives in 'darkness'. Ordinarily, his presence is 'forgotten'. He prefers not 'to disturb the other gentlemen', yet, when summoned, he is immensely disturbing. As a non-worldly emissary, he has hands which flap 'like short wings'. Unlike mortal beings, he is not to be introduced or greeted. Yet, once summoned, the privilege of concealment can no longer be his. Now his presence must be acknowledged.

To this Court of the dark powers, there is no admittance by ordinary means. Joseph K's appeals to reason, even the threat of brute force, are as nothing to such an authority. Initially, he is confused by a Court that seems to deny reason. Twice he is told by his warders that he is to dress in black to meet the Court. He complies without any sense of the significance of the instructions.[5] Only later, does he recognize the full implication of the Prison Chaplain's remark: 'You are deluding yourself about the Court' (*T*: 235). At the end, without being informed of the visit of his executioners, K has already dressed himself in black.

An earlier meeting with the Prison Chaplain takes place at eleven in the morning. Yet, outside it is as black as night.[6] The Village Superintendent of *The Castle*, similarly, is encountered in a darkened room (*C*: 60). Indeed, K learns eventually that most of the interrogations in the village by the Castle officials are held at night (*C*: 245).

So the white of the village is enveloped by the black of the Castle, as the white of appearances is enveloped by the black of concealed realities. Shrouded in darkness, announcing itself by the tolling of a bell with a menacing tone, the Castle only becomes well-defined by comparison with the snow-covered village. The presence of a thin layer of whiteness merely emphasizes that the Castle is set apart from the white.[7]

Yet a meeting with the dark powers offers hope as well as confusion, possibilities as well as threats. Of all such meetings, K's night encounter in the very bedroom of the Castle official Bürgel implies the most positive prospects for a participant in the dangerous game of black and white. At night, Bürgel tells K, one is less likely to define activities in terms of official rules, more likely to deny familiar positions in a bureaucratic hierarchy.[8] The night offers an invitation to act authentically by denying the daytime's (the white's) 'official' version of necessity and choice: 'This invitation in the silent night is beguiling. One gives way to it and now one has actually ceased to function in one's official capacity' (*C*: 252). But the opportunity for authenticity can be missed. Precisely because 'the silent night is beguiling', one can merely exchange the silence of mundane reason for the silence of an undisturbed, implacable reality.[9] Here black offers only limits not possibilities and practice is confined to a reiteration of a transcendent reality.

Confronted by the invitation of an encounter with the dark powers, K concedes the game and becomes 'immersed' in sleep. There remains for him only the (perhaps foolhardy) aspiration, the 'groping', for authenticity which distinguishes Kafka's version of the human enterprise.[10]

Black as music

> In the distance I heard a bugle call, I asked him what this meant. He knew nothing and had heard nothing (*PP*: 189).

The physical presence of the Castle and of the Court officials are not Kafka's only means of making reference to a practice of writing engaged with the dark powers. Where the onward march of rationalization uses up and wears out speech itself, music and image may alone seem to retain a horizon of black to set against the pervasive white of appearances.[11] The 'bugle call' in the distance summons all who can still hear to an encounter in the dangerous game.

The 'music' of the Castle is the menacing bell and the unworldly buzzing heard on the telephone in the village.[12] Seeking 'to penetrate beyond mere hearing', the buzzing, humming and singing of the telephone announces a mysterious presence unavailable to our ordinary senses. Precisely because it is not to be mastered by reason, such 'music', the Superintendent tells K: 'is the only real and reliable thing you'll hear, everything else is deceptive' (*C*: 73). The appearance of our mundane world has been turned on its head. The conversations which are our ordinary means of assuring ourselves of the orderly character of the world are to be distrusted because they are already overloaded by pre-interpretations readily supplied by practical reason. K would do better to give an ear to the buzzing of the telephone than to labour over the words it carries. The 'music' of the telephone, like the unsettling whistling that the animal hears in *The Burrow*, the beautiful sound of Gregor's sister's violin in *The Metamorphosis* and the music 'conjured up' from 'the empty air' by the dancing dogs from 'Investigations of a Dog', offers an invitation to engage the hidden possibilities of realities concealed by the artificial divisions of particular voices.[13] However, the relation between these voices constitutes a reality obscured by the move from language to music.

Black as sexuality

> Women have great influence. If I could move some women I know to join forces in working for me, I couldn't help winning through (*T*: 233).

The sexual encounter would seem to offer another challenge to the white of practical reason. The powerful forces located in the body, denied by attempts to preserve decorous appearances, appear to parallel the dark regions governed by unknown powers. K believes that he can master the black by mastering a series of women: in his achievement of sexual supremacy, he 'couldn't help winning through': his union with women would be a sign of his union with the Castle. Indeed, at each step on his path, his encounter with the agents of Castle and Court is invariably accompanied by encounters with women. Seeking the official Klamm, he ends up rolling on the floor with the barmaid Frieda (*C*: 45). When the Court Inspector interrogates him, he chooses to hold the interview in the room of K's neighbour Fräulein Bürstner. Soon after, K is seized by an irresistible attraction for the girl. Visiting the Court uninvited, K is caressed by the wife of an official (*T*: 65). Seeking help from the Court Artist, Titorelli, K meets a giggling adolescent girl on the stairs (*T*: 157). The attraction between K and the women is mutual. K approaches the women 'greedily' (*C*: 99), in the belief that they are in some way linked to the Court/Castle.[14] The women respond to him because even someone enslaved by the dark powers contains some of their mystery. He is drawn to a sexual encounter with a servant girl, Leni, when he visits his advocate, reflecting afterwards: 'I seem to recruit women helpers' (*T*: 121). The subsequent explanation of the advocate indicates that more than chance is at work: Leni's 'peculiarity', he points out: 'consists in her finding nearly all accused men attractive' (*T*: 203).

The mutual attractions generated by nearness to the unbounded possibilities of Court/Castle are matched by the open sexuality of the officers of these authorities. The officials of the Castle make crude sexual demands on the women of the village, all of whom seem to be fair game for their attentions. Indeed, it is an honour to become the mistress of a Castle official. The landlady's greatest complaint against K is that he has dared to take Frieda away from Klamm, while Amalia, who refused such advances, sees herself and her family become outcasts. The fornication of the Castle officials is matched by the prurient interests of the Court officials. On inspecting their law-books, Joseph K is amazed to discover only obscene drawings and blue stories.

Yet K's belief that he can master the authorities through sexuality is unfounded. Where sexuality is only a means of mastery, the possibilities of the Castle are denied rather than affirmed. Viewed through the white, the black only seems to provide traps and limits. He will not find Klamm through Frieda, rather Frieda appears to have been put in K's path *by* Klamm (*C*: 54). K's assistants will not gain him access to the Castle, rather they seem to be the means through which the Castle diverts Frieda from K. Equally, the girls that flock round Titorelli, like all the women in both novels, 'belong to the Court too'.[15] And Joseph K's meetings with Fräulein Bürstner are apparently orchestrated by the Court: his relations with her, he notes, 'seemed to fluctuate with the case itself' (*T*: 140).

Eventually, K and Joseph K learn that sexuality is not the key that unlocks the mysterious secret of the dark powers. Each assumes that the Castle is to be entered like a woman. Seeking to discover a black reality outside appearances, neither can escape domination by a whiteness which provides only limits and not potentialities. The metaphors of 'entry', 'secrecy' and 'unlocking' merely reiterate the dominance of white appearances.

Black as value

> When the sage says: 'Go over', he does not mean that we should cross to some actual place, which we could do anyhow if the labour were worth it; he means some fabulous yonder, something unknown to us, something too that he cannot designate more precisely, and therefore cannot help us here in the very least (*PP*: 11).

While unable to overturn the blanket of whiteness, sexuality does make reference to what lies beyond the bounds of the appearances suggested by practical reason. In this way, it approximates the possibilities held out by the dark powers which are likewise 'beyond reason'.[16] Following the post-Kantian distinction between 'fact' and 'value', fact alone seems accessible to reason. Hence what lies 'beyond reason', the black, becomes regarded as value. So the sage to whom Kafka refers cannot imply 'some actual place' when he says 'go over'. For this would instruct you to move merely from one fact to another. The point, however, is to draw one's eyes away from restricting facts and to contemplate abiding values. And ultimate evaluations are the realm of personal choices and the fates of epochs: the sage cannot advise (you have learned his lesson if you have understood this much).

The cultural pessimism of the turn of the century, repeated in the work of Wittgenstein as well as Weber, dictated that thought, by combating a rationalized, disenchanted world, must hold open the possibility of transcending the given facts of the case. In a world become white, forgetful of its stand on ultimate value, the writer stands as the sole reminder of the dark power of primal origins and of historic choices not susceptible to practical reason.

The point seems to be to achieve a proper balance between black and white: between mystery and reason. The absence of such a balance lies at the heart of the punishment practices that Kafka describes in his short story *In The Penal Settlement*. A visitor to a distant imperial outpost is invited to witness the punishment that is to be inflicted for an apparently minor disciplinary offence. Yet the instrument of punishment is a bizarre machine which literally engraves upon the body of the offender the commandment that he has transgressed. In his horrible way, the victim feels, on his body as well as in his mind, the verdict of society, shorn of the mediation of courts of law and rationalized legal statutes. In what, according to the Prison Commandant, is an ecstatic moment, the offender encounters together an ultimate justice from which all human considerations are removed and his moment of death, which, because it is accompanied by his recognition of his wrongs, holds out the prospect of ultimate redemption.

Yet the dark forces exemplified in this version of justice are already under challenge precisely because they seem to exceed what passes as reasonable. The Prison Commandant is no more than the last representative of a system which has given way to the onward rush of rationalization. In the disenchanted routines of the New Law, mystery is replaced by regulation, redemption by the rational unfolding of legal process.

The old ways give heed only to the mystery of black; the white of practical reason, of knowledge gained through the senses, is the sole ground of the New Law. To a writer committed to a dialogue between mystery and reason, old and new ways are equally barbaric.[17] *In The Penal Settlement* makes reference to a practice of writing committed to show both reason and the limits of reason.

Black as language

'You feel a little dizzy, don't you?', she asked. Her face was close to him now, it had that severe look which the faces of many women have in the first flower of their youth. 'Don't worry', she said. 'That's nothing out of the common here, almost everybody has an attack of that kind the first time they come here. . . .' (*T*: 78).

Any showing of the limits of reason within the confines of a text is at the same time a showing of the possibilities of language – indeed the fact/value distinction itself does not transcend language but is grounded upon it. Like any text, Kafka's work is a work in and of language. In common with other important modern texts, the resistance that is offered to any determinate reconstruction in terms of conventional notions of character and plot is a reminder that here we encounter reality not as an external fact that the fiction purports to reveal but as internal to the movements of the text itself. The voices of the text are the only realities that are in question.

1 *Wittgenstein's circle*

In spirit and execution, there appear to be clear parallels between Kafka's work and a Wittgensteinian version of language. Language seems to set the limits of the possible in both their texts. Viewed this way, writing and speaking become only a tracing of the limits of a capitalized language.

Certain ironic consequences follow for any project which would seek to master language. Wittgenstein refers in his preface to the *Tractatus* to the need to 'pass over in silence' what cannot be talked about – the limits of language which are the grounds of our speech, the limits which can only be shown but not spoken. To overstep these limits, interpreted in Wittgenstein's later work as the limits of our language-games and the bounds of our forms of life, is to experience an illusory freedom where language, freed of its proper relation to human action, simply 'goes on holiday'.

Such is the freedom sought by K and Joseph K. Each seeks to grasp the whole truth in an abstraction – the character of the Castle, the meaning of the Trial – rather than accepting the essential difference between practice and the apparent limits of practice, between speech and language. The impatience of both protagonists directs them towards a fruitless search for the essence of language, as if there were some position outside language from which to attack the truth. The circle that each traces seems to be a circle around the limits of language.

To go around in circles is to invite dizziness. And to 'feel a little dizzy', to feel 'seasick', is the inevitable fate of those who would seek to square the circle, to view the essence of language. The confusions of K arise from the misuse of language. Usage, for Wittgenstein, is the sole arbiter of everyday truth and necessity. A respect for usage and a proper silence about ultimate truths is essential to any enquirer who does not want to be confused by the workings of language. Lacking this respect, K enters a reality where, with language on holiday, anything goes. For a hopeless and disabling groundlessness, what Wittgenstein refers to as a 'conceptual puzzlement', awaits those who would penetrate to the black (language) without even recognizing that they have their feet in the white (speech).

In all this, Kafka's texts circle around their own workings. This internal reference is highlighted in *The Castle*, a text produced by K(afka) in which K pursues K(lamm) – an official of the authorities – in order to attain a Castle which is as opaque yet as all-enveloping as language itself. The Castle is everywhere, since everyone defers to it, and nowhere, regularly veiled in mists. In looking up towards it, K sees an 'illusory emptiness' (C: 9), an absence which, because it is illusory, indicates a presence. It is difficult to find roads that lead to the Castle, but those that do seem to carry no traffic (C: 21). The senses are no help in grasping the essence of the castle, for the senses are only the Castle's servants. It seemed to K that: 'the longer he looked, the less he could make out and the deeper everything was lost in the twilight' (C: 97). Alternately, the Castle seems substantial and impressive and melancholy and crumbling.

This variation applies equally to the other elements of the fiction. An assistant, within four pages, is transformed from 'a rather unhealthy, elderly creature' (C: 232) to a 'merry, irresponsible youth' (C: 236), while Hans' mother's illness mysteriously changes in the course of his account of it. Throughout, one encounters what Robbe-Grillet has referred to as 'a double movement of creation and destruction' (1965: 148). The description cancels itself out, leaving nothing behind it other than the silent workings of the text.[18] As the authority that warrants what transpires, the Castle seems to make reference to language as the grounds of these workings.

The Castle stands as the silent backdrop to any intelligibility read into the text. Amalia's family feels guilty for a supposed offence against a Castle official but the Castle authorities neither punish nor forgive. For the very possibility of recognizable guilt and punishment, rests in a Wittgensteinian sense, on the smooth workings of usage. The Castle does not legislate about usage: it is the silent source of usage itself. The official Klamm, pursued by K as the key to entry into the Castle, cannot be grasped either intellectually or physically. Like others, K is assured, he is not capable of seeing Klamm as he really is (C: 52). Indeed, Klamm's appearance fluctuates, owing a great deal to the mood of the observer (C: 167), but what Klamm represents remains entirely outside human perception (for it is the basis of it). Klamm's village secretary Momus, whose appearance is quite different from that of Klamm, is none the less thought by many to be Klamm himself (C: 172). Even K's assistants are probably merely Messengers of Klamm's (C: 135).

Like the other K (Kafka) whose verbal assistants (the words of his text) turn back and coerce him, K's entrapment by grammar is emphasized in his dealings with his assistants. On the surface, it would seem that it is only natural that assistants should assist and that their masters should give orders. However, to speak of assistants and masters is to posit a grammar of hierarchy and inequality. Once that grammar is understood, or better, the language-game is played, then actual outcomes are less important than that the grammar is respected and affirmed. Consequently, K's assistants can impede him, just as much as in *The Trial*, Joseph K's underlings at the bank, Franz and Willem, also turn out to be his warders. Enmeshed in the grammar of power and inequality, 'fighting', as one of them says, 'to get to the top' (*C*: 154), the two K's often feel resentful about the progress of their cases.[19] But then they have elected to play the game in which power is at issue and one side comes out on top. Once again, the point is to reflect on what the game *shows*, to avoid frontal attacks which inevitably must circle around the bounds of their own possibilities.

The unity of the language-game is what pulls together apparent dichotomies. Joseph K wants to believe that the Law is the index of virtue, while guilt is the experience of the wrong-doer, yet he learns from Willem of 'an attraction that existed between the Law and guilt' (*T*: 43). Both 'law' and 'guilt' are united. Because we cannot use one without implying the other, to speak of one is to be involved in both.

2 The limits of language

Above all, the apparent dichotomy between freedom and being 'under arrest' seems to be challenged by the nature of our freedom within language. Like Joseph K, who learns that he is in the curious position of being under arrest yet free to live his normal life, the speaker is free to choose what words he will, while 'rolling in heavy seas' (*T*: 83), arrested within language. Language makes no demands; 'the Court', the Prison Chaplain tells Joseph K, 'receives you when you come and relinquishes when you go' (*T*: 244). And death is the only time that you can 'go', the only moment that language relinquishes you. For freedom outside language appears as illusory as K's apparent success in gaining access to the court-yard – close to Klamm's coach, close to Klamm, therefore close to the Castle – only to realize that the emptiness of the courtyard had cut him off from human conversation. The Castle now could not be more distant: his freedom was 'senseless' and 'hopeless'.[20]

There is no reprieve or appeal from our arrest within language. For the later Wittgenstein, the very images of our senses merely express our entrapment within the grammatical possibilities of a language-game. It is this entrapment that is emphasized by the bewilderment that Kafka's protagonists experience. When Joseph K witnesses a bizarre scene where his warders are being beaten, and when this scene repeats itself in its entirety the next day, one is tempted to think of nightmares or paranoid delusions. But the experience and its repetition are no more than a sign of the games that language plays with us as we try to picture the world. For this picturing activity inexorably repeats itself in every image.[21] In a sense, then, every image is indeed the same since it expresses the same silent movement of language. Joseph K is not deluded. The repetition of the beating scene starkly expresses the dilemma of a writer who can only circle around the bounds of the possible. Such a dilemma demands that a text avoid simplifications and reveal to the reader the delicacy of the task and the pitfalls that await. Like Wittgenstein, Kafka's project is not unlike that of 'repairing a torn spider's web with one's fingers'.[22] Above all, language, the very basis of the circle, must not be extravagantly used to try to imply a possibility of easy paths out of its web. Kafka's 'classically plain style', avoiding the verbal excesses of his late-Habsburg contemporaries, invites the reader to confront the bewitchment of his intelligence by words.[23]

No easy victories are possible in such a confrontation. A respect for the mastery of language may allow an openness to the mystery that our words point towards. But, at every step, the path towards the Castle is also from out of the Castle. Like any speaker, K seems to trace the bounds of the possible, fighting for ends in which the authorities merely permit him to believe.[24]

Locked in the circle, the traveller encounters a heavy atmosphere. Not only does his journey make him 'seasick' and 'dizzy' but the very air he breathes, unable to escape the limits of the circle, is stale and unhealthy. Like the bars of the Castle village, with their 'puddles of beer, the smell of which was nearly overpowering' (*C*: 46), the foetid air of the courtrooms of *The Trial* encourages a sense of nausea. No air can escape from such rooms, no fresh air can enter. Attempts to open tiny windows, only bring black soot down on the lawyers and clients alike. The closer the traveller approaches the centre of the circle, the more nauseous he feels. Only when Joseph K reaches the security of the stairs outside the courtroom does he feel a breath of fresh air. While the Court officials feel unwell in this change of air, K himself who just before had collapsed with nausea 'leapt down the stairs so buoyantly and with such long strides that he became almost afraid of his own reaction' (*T*: 84). Like the other institutions of the Castle/Court, the courtroom is constructed around a series of doors which lead into ever more arcane offices. The traveller on the 'heavy seas' of language must recognize that he has entered something like a Chinese puzzle. Entering a door is never the end of the journey but only the beginning of an encounter with endless doors which can never finally reveal the mystery that they conceal. In Kafka's famous parable 'Before the Law', a man from the country, seeking admittance to the Law, encounters only a doorkeeper in charge of the very lowest door. Behind him, he assures the applicant, there stands an unending series of doorkeepers and doors. Similarly, even the messenger Barnabas can only penetrate through one or two doors of the Castle and is then barred from further access (*C*: 165). Perhaps the error is to assume that anything lies behind these inner doors and that the mystery can be unveiled like a slave dancer. Rather the mystery, unable to be confronted, makes itself shown only by means of a play of doors (or words). Aware by now that the Castle is not to be seized and that, at best, it can only be encountered indirectly, K is forced to admit that he is unable to face Klamm 'without a door between us' (*C*: 53).

Language seems to be the sea on which we float. Like the sea, it offers us deceptively smooth waters and the prospect of being buffeted about if we fail to respect it. Unlike the sea, it is infinite and indefinite, only revealed indirectly or iconically. Such an icon of language is the colonel in Kafka's fable *The Refusal*. This colonel is really only the chief tax-collector in a small town. His eminence is owed entirely to the distant authority of which he is the sole local representative. 'Behind him', we read, 'is nothingness, one imagines hearing voices whispering in the background, but this is probably only a delusion; after all he represents the end of all things, at least for us' (*PP*: 165). Like the colonel, the eminence of the text derives from what it represents. 'Behind' the words on the page 'is nothingness', the silent movement of language. 'One imagines' that the text is retrievable in terms of familiar categories of chronology, plot and character – these 'voices whispering in the background'. But we are deluded. The text/colonel seems to make reference not to a finite reality but to the possibilities and limits of finite realities. Since we are not gods, able to transcend these limits, the colonel 'represents the end of all things, at least for us'.

Language withholds itself from us. All that is perceptible are the words seen on the page or heard from the speaker. K seeks the Castle (of language) but encounters directly only lowly Castle officials. Like the words of the text, such officials appear as 'visible representatives of an invisible authority' (Politzer: 1966, p. 180). In the same way as the doorkeeper in 'Before the Law', words stand in the light of the radiance that stems from the Law, but they are turned away from it, faced outwards towards the reader and apparently self-sufficient in themselves. In our speech, following another brief Kafka parable, words are 'messengers' or 'couriers'. Since there is no apparent 'king', the messages that are shouted are meaningless. But the words cannot silence themselves 'because of their oaths of service' (*PP*: 175). Whatever we are tempted to feel, our words, like the officials of Kafka's texts, seem to be condemned to be instruments of the Castle/Court, unable to deny their 'oaths of service' to language.

3 *Language as conversation*

It seems undeniable that a text is a linguistic work – a work in, and of, language. The reality to which a text makes reference does not stand apart from the text but within its own inner workings. The practice of writing shows reality in its engagement with language. In these respects, a linguistic reading of Kafka offers the prospects of a conversation where readers acknowledge their common embeddedness in the reality which makes possible both the text and the reading. What is not clear is whether we have to tread the transcendentalist or black path. The dangers of a non-linguistic reading of a text are apparent; the pitfalls of posing a transcendent 'Language' remain unexplored.

In particular, the images of circling and nausea owe more to the cultural pessimism of late-Habsburg Vienna than to any necessary implications of a language position.[25] Indeed, the extent to which Kafka had freed himself from these obsessions is a measure of his triumph. Let it be noted that Joseph K's nausea at the hopelessness of his intervention in his trial gives way, at the end, to an affirmation, before his executioners, of the continuing potentialities of human choice (*T*: 247). Equally, in the night encounter with Bürgel, the Liaison Secretary from the Castle, the mystical version of the Castle as a transcendent reality is stripped away. Instead, K is offered a dialogue.

At such moments, we realize that words owe their 'oaths of service' to a particularly textual practice not to some mystical, transcendent reality. It is the 'nothingness' behind words that is illusory, not the potentialities of practice. Despite all appearances, it is only a *village view* of the Castle that would address the latter as a transcendent reality. We should not be misled by the surface differences between the Castle villagers and the ironic philosophers of language. As such a philosopher defers to the 'mystery' of language, the villager, in the 'foggy dimness' of village existence, assumes that it is senseless to do battle with an all-powerful Castle. Unwilling to risk the shame that overtook Amalia's family after her refusal of a Castle official's lascivious invitation, the villagers accept their place. They defer to a Castle and to its instruments which offer only limits and necessities. Their speech turns upon stories that point repetitively to the mystery and power of the Castle authorities. In the routines of village life, as in the poetry of the philosopher of language, the badge of good conduct is offered only to those who respect the bars of the prison-house.

In such ways, the anti-intellectualism of village life merges with the circling of highly trained minds around the difference between speech and language. In both cases, whatever is not present to the senses is reified and mystified. For the villagers, the impenetrable authority outside human cognition is the Castle; for the philosopher-villagers, it is 'Language'. Either way, we are sentenced to bump our heads against the bars of our prison until we have learned to defer to the invisible authority that rules our lives. We have only the villagers' choice between resignation to the inevitable and the sallies of isolated individuals – the 'hopeless' attacks of K, the humourless tributes of onto-poesis.

Accordingly, the village-philosopher closes off the creativity of textual practice. The practices which create a relation between an immanent appearance and a transcendent reality are concealed. Language is held to offer only limits, not possibilities. It will at once be clear that this denial of creativity, combined with an affirmation of resignation or of aggressive individualism, is merely the voice of an ideology that masters the village-philosopher. Such an ideology expresses an historically located mode of domination that, as the prevailing standard of sociality, grasps both theory and practice. The 'white' of appearances is such a mode of domination. It extends itself over mundane and academic reason. It negates potentialities by defining the absent 'black' as a concretized limit or prison-house.

Freed from the transcendent Castle of the village-philosopher, a text can no longer be understood as a mere pointing towards the ineffable boundaries of language. Restored to practice, language stands only as the icon of our being-together. Language is the ongoing conversation traced by the voices of a text. Linguistic practice, by participating in the freeing of all practice from its submission to modes of domination, reopens the conversation in which history is listened to and made.

But we have run ahead of ourselves. An assessment of Kafka's versions of the possible permutations of black and white must precede any conclusion about the emancipatory power of his texts.

Methods for assembling black and white

Whatever its pretensions to stand outside the mundane world around it, a text engages the structures of ordinary reality, both ideal and material. Its transformative work creates and challenges 'realities' which are not reducible to an immanent 'white' or a transcendental 'black'. Kafka's texts point towards the limits to such transformations, and towards a possible resolution within the practice of writing.

1 *Living within the white*

> Why do I not do as the others: live in harmony with my people and accept in silence whatever disturbs the harmony, ignoring it as a small error in the great account, always keeping in mind the things that bind us happily together, not those that drive us again and again, although by sheer force, out of our social circle? (ID: 87).

In 'The Investigations of a Dog', Kafka suggests the joys as well as the ultimately unhappy silence of a dog-like existence. To write in a way that merely reiterates doggy conventions, fails to acknowledge the question that animates discourse. For dogs, the apparently banal question 'Whence does the earth procure this food' upon which dogs feed, makes reference to the possibilities of their practice. In the same way, the possibilities of textual practice are recalled in our questioning of mundane modes of domination. Hence, 'to accept in silence whatever disturbs the harmony', is to deny the possibility of making history. A life led enmeshed within the white is a living death, for silence about the crucial questions 'poisons existence' (ID: 98). The writer must drive himself 'out of the social circle' by challenging the familiar relationship between appearance and reality. But he is not set apart entirely from the social circle: he still remains a dog ('You are yourself a dog, you have also the dog knowledge', the doggy investigator reminds himself). His doggishness, the certainties of dog life, provide the necessary resources of his investigation. The marrow of dog-bones nourishes him too and he feels bound to 'bow before their knowledge', knowing that he will 'never actually overstep their laws' (ID: 119). So the white of appearances, is necessarily engaged by a text; it is not apart from the mundane world of appearances but involved in it. In a wonderful image, Kafka refers to those who would deny this as merely 'hovering dogs' (*Lufthunde*). Such dogs, the intellectuals of the late-Habsburg era and of other epochs too, delude themselves that their verbal facility allows them to transcend grammar and the realities of an historical epoch. Unable to reproduce themselves, it can only be that these hovering dogs voluntarily elect to live an 'empty life on cushions', 'merely for the sake of the comfort and a certain technical accomplishment' (ID: 104).

2 *Getting above himself*

The German for it [Land Surveyor] is *Landvermesser*, and its
verbal associations are manifold . . . (it) alludes to *Vermes-
senheit*, hubris; to the adjective *vermessen*, audacious; to the verb
sich vermessen, commit an act of spiritual pride, and also apply
the wrong measure, make a mistake in measurement (Heller:
1974, p.123).

In hovering above the white, the *Lufthunde* literally get above
themselves – they believe that they can survey the world from their
cushions in the sky and, thereby, delude themselves about the
faultiness of the measure that they are applying. Equally, K, the
Land Surveyor of *The Castle*, commits 'an act of spiritual pride' in
pretending that he can storm by force the black depths. For the
Castle seems to accommodate the challenge of any man who gets
above himself. As K realizes early on, it was 'unpropitious' for him
that the Castle had recognized him as the Land Surveyor: 'it meant
that the Castle was well informed about him, had estimated all the
probable chances, and was taking up the challenge with a smile' (*C*:
12). Still K persists, foolhardedly believing that the authorities had
'under-estimated his strength' and his 'freedom of action' (*C*: ibid.).
But it is K and Joseph K who 'make a mistake in measurement' not
the Castle or the Court.

Annoyed by his advocate's failure to change his situation, Joseph
K persists in seeking to bring matters to a head. Convinced that 'to
ask questions was surely the main thing' (*T*: 127), and that 'it was
absolutely necessary to intervene personally' (*T*: 140), his frontal
assault leads only to grammatical confusion and moral defeat. It is
not that the mystery masters all attempts to unveil it. Rather the
metaphors of 'personal' intervention and of 'freedom of action'
affirm the mastery of a mundane mode of domination which only
provides for *individual* action in a *reified* reality.

Joseph K would have done better to reflect on the experience of
others. His 'case' might have turned out differently if he had
remembered the old expression that his uncle mentions. In his case,
as in others, 'the litigant always loses' (*T*: 108).[26] Yet he continues
to employ the rhetoric of privatized individualism. 'The Court
makes no claims upon you', says the Prison Chaplain (*T*: 244), but
Joseph K cannot see until too late that it is still necessary to
acknowledge his con-texted existence. In an act of bravado, he tells
the Examining Magistrate: 'it is only a trial if I recognize it as such'
(*T*: 49). He fails to comprehend that his intervention and puzzlement (as well as the trial itself and the 'I' who claims to recognize it)
is textually grounded.

Only if Joseph K were alone in the world, could he have possessed the power he claimed. Yet he is not alone but within an organized relationship between appearance and reality (the white and the black). And, if he were alone, his 'case' would not arise.[27]
Joseph K aims for an impossible end. He wants to live 'completely outside the jurisdiction of the Court'; he desires to 'get rid' of his case 'altogether' (*C*: 234). Yet the parable 'Before the Law' should have shown him that there is no such end to the matter. To both doorkeeper and applicant, the Law is omni-relevant but not to be grasped: the doorkeeper stands with his back to the Law, the applicant only catches sight of the radiance that streams from it. In the same way, history is to be made – not unveiled by an act of will. Joseph K does not survey history from above; he is involved in history. 'In short', he reflects, 'he hardly had the choice now to keep up the case or let it drop, he was in the middle of it and must look to himself' (*T*: 140). As the telephone message from the Castle had told K at the beginning of his quest, the Castle was not to be entered 'neither tomorrow, nor at any other time' (*C*: 25). Only as he is escorted away to his death in *The Trial* does Joseph K perceive his error in seeking to get above himself: 'I always wanted to snatch at the world with twenty hands, and not for a very laudable motive, either. That was wrong . . .. ' (*T*: 247). The text of K(afka) exemplifies K's recognition that a practice of writing that foolhardedly denies organized relations between appearance and reality 'commits an act of spiritual pride'. Only an untexted God can 'snatch at the world with twenty hands'.

3 *The court writer*

> K listened to everything with critical detachment, as if he had been commissioned to observe the proceedings closely, to report them to a higher authority, and to put down a record of them in writing (*T*: 214).

One reading of what K has learned is that speech, far from transcending language, is merely a surface ripple, of the silent workings of a transcendent reality. Speech, it would seem, needs language, but language does not need speech. As an observer, then, K has been 'commissioned' by the authorities to report to them. It is as if his practice ('observing', 'reporting') only receives its warrant from 'higher authorities'. Like Titorelli, the Court Artist, K is the Court Writer, condemned to produce texts with limited and repetitive motifs which serve to affirm the glory of the authorities and the impotence of practice. Rather than speak to potentialities, such texts, like the Prison Chaplain's parable, deal with 'impalpabilities better suited for a discussion among Court officials' than for a texted K (*T*: 243).

Court officials concern themselves solely with matters that arise from the dark powers. Yet this blackness is precisely what cannot be formulated in speech. At the same time, an immersion in the whiteness of mundaneity, allows much to be said but it is worthless – the speech of the white turns out to be mere 'gassing' (to use Wittgenstein's word).

The Court Writer is caught in a trap. His speech must defer to the higher authorities (the black) but these remain forever inaccessible to view and, apparently, beyond practice. What truly matters, then, cannot be said. Like his contemporaries Weber and Wittgenstein, caught in the neo-Kantian separation of fact and value, the spectre of silence, of 'beetledom and death' (Thorlby: 1972), awaits Kafka, the Court Writer. Trapped in the circle, to speak is to be guilty.[28]

4 *Dialogue*

> I was still and cold, I was a bridge, I lay over a ravine. My toes on one side, my fingers clutching the other, I had clamped myself fast into the crumbling clay . . . . (*TB*: 116).

Ultimately, K elects to live as a man and not as a mere vehicle of the Court. He refuses to grasp the knife that his executioners offer him. Even at the end, he prefers to turn his head and gaze around him (*T*: 250). In the same way as the doggy investigator, he will not lose sight of his membership of his community. Unlike Court officials, he is aware that a denial of the white converts a speaker into a mere *Lufthund*. Rather than deny black or white, the speaker engages them both. The text, then, comes to stand as 'a bridge'. Beneath lies the 'ravine' which holds open the space which the bridge occupies yet offers the prospect of a silent death if one should tumble into it. Either side of the bridge lies the 'clay' of the earth, 'crumbling' and difficult to hold on to but 'clamped' into in order to prevent a descent into nothingness. The writer/reader, like the animal in Kafka's *Burrow*, listens to the murmur of the silence emanating from the mysterious Castle Keep. At the same time, his activity only sustains itself by regular exits from the burrow in order to draw (white) sustenance. The call of the black is never far away (the disturbing whistling from within the burrow matches the music of the violin in *Metamorphosis*), but the burrow text remains 'the place for an encounter' (Politzer: 1966, p.33) between black and white.

The prospects and the dangers of such an encounter come

together in K's night meeting with the Castle official Bürgel. As the *Liaison* Secretary, Bürgel offers the possibility of dialogue between Castle and village, between black and white. Yet this dialogue is not to be attained by frontal assault. 'Lifelong, exhausting efforts', Bürgel tells K, are worthless compared to watchfulness and fellowship: 'by means of a word, a glance, a sign of trust, more can be achieved' (*C*: 245). Since questioner and answerer may even change places at night, night interrogations emphasize the potentialities of textual practice, allowing a form of writing that shows itself as a dialogue between black and white.

Kafka's triumph is to offer in *The Castle* a text that, in Bürgel's words points to a state that is both 'desperate' and 'very happy' (*C*: 252). Night encounters in a 'voluptuous bed' of indefinite possibilities, which yet affirm the fellowship of 'a glance' and 'a sign of trust', leave the applicant 'sated and carefree' (*C*: 253). In such a poetic engagement with both black and white, language is no longer a prison but simply a house. The open horizon of textual conversation replaces the bars of the bounds of the possible.

The absence of red

> Combined action against the Court is impossible. Each case is judged on its own merits, the Court is very conscientious about that, and so common action is out of the question . . . . So there's no real community, people drift in and out of the lobbies together, but there's not much conversation. The superstitious beliefs are an old tradition and simply hand themselves down (*T*: 193–4).

Among 'the superstitious beliefs' that 'hand themselves down' is the belief that 'there's no real community'. While the fellowship of the glance and of signs of trust would seem to suggest the possibility of collective action, this is denied by a Court that appears to transcend human practice. Writing and reading become activities directed at saving individual souls: 'if you have to ask the way', says one parable of Kafka's, 'you should give it up' (GIU: 120).

Above all, 'he must look to himself' (*T*: 140). There is room for the heroism of ultimate evaluations (Joseph K, after all, will not kill himself), but not for sensuous human practice. The erotic dark powers stand as a forbidding reminder of the limits of practice, for they make reference to a transcendent reality. Since practice can only circle around this non-human limit, we come to appreciate, with Joseph K, 'the futility of resistance' (*T*: 247).

If the dialogue between black and white ultimately fails, it is because the writing that joins them presents itself as an expression purely of *mind*. Like Gregor Samsa, the beetle, Kafka could not be in the world if he was to write. The burrow to which he withdraws cuts himself off from the world. The sustenance that he takes from outside sustains his intellectual activity, while apparently leaving everything as it is on the outside: the 'pleasure dome' is 'for himself'. His decision not to marry, based on the assumed loss to his writing that marriage would produce, signals his intellectual split between mind and body.[29] At the same time, the distinction in his writing between individual and collective salvations, signals a split in practice between historical realities and the text.

Red is absent from Kafka's texts. Concretely, the potentiality of collective action in the battle against constraining forces is denied. And this shows itself in a practice of writing that fails to understand its subversion of prevailing literary practice as an interruption in (and a deconstruction of) a mode of sociality that stands as the practical barrier to the fellowship and poetic watchfulness that Kafka seeks. The absent red of sensuous human practice represents the overcoming of the social order, together with the social ordering of the text.

Despite his hermeneutical turn, Kafka's work remains locked in a dialogue of black and white, unable to admit red. The linguistic sensitivity meshes uneasily with the old dichotomies of mind and body, fact and value, and produces texts which, poetic triumphs that they are, recall too readily Adorno's words about a positivism that has 'driven itself beyond its own boundaries' (Adorno: 1976, p.64). The assault on the bourgeois novel is begun but only the whisper of irony seems ready to take its place.

Silence remains the threat to his work and 'fresh air' the aim. 'We are the dogs', he writes, 'who are crushed by the silence, who long to break through it, literally to get a breath of fresh air' (ID: 105). But the circling of mind around the non-human limits of the possible merely produces despair. 'And all this senseless labour', the doggy investigator asks himself, 'to what end? Merely to entomb oneself deeper and deeper in silence, it seems, so deep that one can never be dragged out of it again by anybody' (ID: 107).

Where speaking, as an affront to the dark powers, represents guilt, Kafka, like Wittgenstein, must settle for silence as, ultimately, the only salvation that awaits. He contemplates this end with resignation: the poet of black and white can go no further: 'I shall very likely die in silence and surrounded by silence, indeed almost peacefully, and I look forward to that with composure' (ID: 100).

Notes

1 Kafka asserts this in the course of a letter to his father concerned with family matters. His relation to his father is what imprisons him, yet his only escape seems to be into another prison (marriage):

> It is too much; so much cannot be achieved. It is as if a person were a prisoner, and he had not only the intention to escape, which would perhaps be attainable, but also and indeed simultaneously, the intention to rebuild the prison as a pleasure dome for himself. But if he escapes, he cannot rebuild, and if he rebuilds, he cannot escape (*LF*: 113).

Equally, in his writing, Kafka seeks to escape from the prison-house of convention but not into the nihilism and silence of intellectual acrobatics. Only poetic speaking which engages both the mundane white and the mysterious black could offer Kafka a (restricted) pleasure dome.

2 In the 'Investigations of a Dog', the dog chides himself for failing to accept the dictates of mundaneity: 'Why do I not do as the others: live in harmony with my people and accept in silence whatever disturbs the harmony' (ID: 87).

3 Joseph K's advocate advises him:

> One must lie low, no matter how much it went against the grain. Must try to understand that . . . if someone took it upon himself to alter the disposition of things around him, he ran the risk of losing his footing and falling to destruction (*T*: 135).

4 The landlady advises K:

> I don't deny that it's possible once in a while to achieve something in the face of every rule and tradition . . . but it certainly doesn't happen in the way you're trying to do it, simply by saying 'no, no', and sticking to your opinions and flouting the most well-meant advice (*C*: 54).

5 He complains, ironically, ' 'But this isn't the capital charge yet'.' The text continues: 'The warders smiled but stuck to their: "It must be a black coat." 'If it's to dispatch my case any quicker, I don't mind', replied K, opening the wardrobe' (*T*: 16).

6 'What could have happened to the weather outside? There was no longer even a murky daylight; black night had set in' (*T*: 233).

7 'Now he could see the Castle above him clearly defined in the glittering air, its outline made still more definite by the moulding of snow covering it in a thin layer' (*C*: 15).

8 Bürgel comments: 'One tends involuntarily to judge things from a more private point of view at night . . . what sometimes takes place is an odd, wholly unsuitable changing of places between the persons' (*C*: 246).

9 Think of the mystical or religious versions of Otherness which assign a purely passive role to the 'believer'.

10 K was asleep, it was not real sleep, he could hear Bürgel's word perhaps better than during his former dead-tired state of waking, word after word struck his ear, but the tiresome consciousness had gone, he felt free, it was no longer Bürgel who held him, only he still sometimes groped towards Bürgel, he was not yet in the depths of sleep, but

immersed in it he certainly was (*C*: 248).

11 See the account of late-Habsburg Vienna, and in particular the discussion of the work of Karl Kraus in Janik and Toulmin (1972). Of course, as Weber has shown, music (no more than image) fails to stand outside the rationalization process.

12 The receiver gave out a buzz of a kind that K had never before heard on a telephone. It was like the hum of countless childrens' voices – but not yet a hum, the echo rather of voices singing at an infinite distance – blended by sheer impossibility into one high but resonant sound which vibrated on the ear as if it were trying to penetrate beyond mere hearing (*C*: 26).

Note that Kafka refers to childrens' voices – voices still relatively untutored in the art of rationalized, non-creative speech.

13 'Because every particular voice is fallacious . . . what counts is the sound or music of some transcendent universality, of something that has not yet been articulated or divided into single form' (Heller: 1974, p. 40).

14 K notes that, despite her childish mind, Pepi, Frieda's replacement as barmaid, 'apparently had connections with the Castle': 'if she was not lying she had been a chambermaid; without being aware of what she possessed she slept through the days here, and though if he took this tiny, plump, slightly rounded-backed creature in his arms he could not extort from her what she possessed, yet that could bring him into contact with it and inspirit him for his difficult task' (*C*: 99). This 'bringing into contact' with the Castle is the aim of K's sexual exploits. Equally in Frieda's case, 'it was the nearness of Klamm that made her so irrationally seductive' (*C*: 132). In the neighbourhood of both Castle and sexuality, reason gives way to irrationality.

15 'These girls belong to the Court too'. 'What?' cried K, screwing his head to stare at the painter. But Titorelli sat down again on his chair and said half in jest, half in explanation: 'You see everything belongs to the Court'. 'That's something I hadn't noticed', said K shortly (*G*: 167).

Kafka's writing can be seen as a recognition that 'everything belongs to the Court' and the painful attempt to find an escape from the silence that apparently then ensues.

16 'You must remember', a defendant advises Joseph K, 'that in these Courts things are always coming up for discussion that are simply beyond reason' (*T*: 193).

17 'For the sake of redemption, the old order sacrificed the human person. For the sake of the human person, the new order sacrificed redemption. Both orders are barbaric' (Wilhelm Emrich quoted by Greenberg, 1971, pp.110–11).

18 Robbe-Grillet goes on: 'The entire interest of the descriptive pages – that is man's place in these pages – is therefore no longer in the thing described, but in the very movement of the description.'

19 K's commitment to the grammar of bourgeois individualism is Frieda's constant reproach: he is 'using her' to get to Klamm. But then everyone must, according to this grammar, be 'used'. When Joseph K disturbs

children on his way to the Court, he reflects: 'If I ever come here again . . . . I must either bring sweets to cajole them with or else a stick to beat them with' (*T*: 43).

20 K 'had won a freedom such as hardly anybody else had ever succeeded in winning, and as if nobody could dare to touch him or drive him away, or even speak to him; but – this conviction was at least equally strong – as if at the same time there was nothing more senseless, nothing more hopeless, that this freedom, this waiting, this inviolability' (*C*: 105).

21 Wittgenstein writes:
One thinks that one is tracing the outline of the thing's nature over and over again, and one is merely tracing round the frame through which we look at it. A *picture* held us captive. And we could not get outside it, for it lay in our language and language seemed to repeat it to us inexorably (1968: 114–15).

22 cf. *Philosophical Investigations*, para. 106. The Wittgensteinian version of Kafka's texts offered in this section has been greatly aided by Thorlby (1972).

23 Greenberg notes: 'In rigorously excluding figures of speech from his prose, he was reacting against the turgid, rhetorical style cultivated by his Prague contemporaries' (1971: 11). We are very aware of the dependence of our own reading upon *translations* of Kafka's texts. Consequently, Kafka's 'style' is unavailable to us.

24 K reflects: 'and besides he fought not only for himself, but clearly for other powers as well which he did not know, but in which, without infringing the regulations of the authorities, he was permitted to believe' (*C*: 59).

25 If the repetition of history at the turn of the century is 'tragedy' (to use Marx's formulation), then perhaps contemporary versions of this tradition degenerate into 'farce'.

26 A commercial traveller, waiting to see Joseph K's advocate, advises K that doing battle with the Court saps all your energies: 'I did try my hand at it in the beginning, but I soon had to give it up. It's too exhausting, and the results are disappointing . . . . It makes you limp even to sit about and wait your turn (*T*: 192).

27 On one of the few occasions on which Joseph K is prepared to consider the limitations of 'getting above himself', he reflects:
The contempt that he had once felt for the case was no longer justified. Had he stood alone in the world he could easily have ridiculed the whole affair, though it was also certain that in that event it could never have arisen at all (*T*: 140).

28 The commercial traveller tells K of a superstition that the expression on an accused man's lips reveals his guilt. Another accused had even been able to see on K's lips 'the sign of his own condemnation' (*T*: 193).

29 Body is present to Kafka only as a set of appetites. The material character of (intellectual) labour seems wholly foreign to him.

Bibliography

Kafka's texts

(The initials after each text are the letters used to refer to the work in the body of the paper.)
The Castle (*C*), Harmondsworth: Penguin, 1957.
The Trial (*T*), Harmondsworth: Penguin, 1953.
Letter to his Father (*LF*), New York: Schocken Books, 1966.
Parables and Paradoxes (*PP*), New York: Schocken Books, 1971.
'Investigations of a Dog' (ID), in *Metamorphosis and Other Stories*, Harmondsworth: Penguin, 1961.
'Give It Up' (GIU) and
'The Bridge' (*TB*), in *Description of a Struggle and The Great Wall of China*, London: Secker & Warburg, 1960.

Secondary literature

Greenberg, Martin (1971), *The Terror of Art: Kafka and Modern Literature*, London: André Deutsch.
Heller, Erich (1974), *Kafka*, London: Fontana.
Politzer, Heinz (1966), *Franz Kafka: Parable and Paradox*, New York: Cornell University Press.
Thorlby, Anthony (1972), *A Student's Guide to Kafka*, London: Heinemann.

Other works

Janik, Alan and Toulmin, Stephen (1972), *Wittgenstein's Vienna*, London: Weidenfeld & Nicolson.
Robbe-Grillet, Alain (1965), 'Time and Description in Fiction Today', in *For a New Novel*, New York: Grove Press.
Wittgenstein, Ludwig (1961), *Tractatus Logico-Philosophicus*, London: Routledge & Kegan Paul.
Wittgenstein, Ludwig (1968), *Philosophical Investigations*, Oxford: Blackwell.

part III

Language and thought

Husserl's phenomenological reductions are respectively attempts to escape the flux of 'natural' language for the certainty of individual and collective consciousness. But those certainties are communicated in language. An investigation of Husserl's writing shows how he constitutes the sense of extra-linguistic certainty by posing one language as external to another.

chapter 5

Husserl's two phenomenologies

The Idea of Phenomenology

The Idea of Phenomenology, a collection of lectures originally delivered by Husserl in 1907, provides a simple introduction to his phenomenology. In this work, Husserl polemically identifies the whole of philosophy and science as previously practiced, together with commonsense, as expressions of the 'natural attitude'. In contrast, he will define his own new science of philosophy. He states (1970, p. 13):

> In the natural mode of reflection, we are turned to the objects as they are given to us each time . . . *even though they are given in different ways, and in different modes of being.* . . . In perception, for instance, a thing stands before our eyes as a matter of course. It is there, among other things, living or lifeless, animate or inanimate. It is, in short, within a world *of which part is perceived,* . . . and *of which part is contextually supplied* by our memory, from whence it spreads out into the indeterminate and the unknown. . . . Our judgements relate to this world. . . . We make judgements about things, their relations, their changes, about the conditions which functionally determine their changes, and about the laws of their variations. . . . We generalize, and then apply again general knowledge to particular cases, or deduce analytically new generalizations from general knowledge. Isolated cognitions do not simply follow each other in the manner of mere succession. They enter logical relations with each other, they follow from one another, they support one another, thereby strengthening their logical power.

Thus far, it seems, the 'natural attitude' consists of an elaborate self-fulfilling prophecy. But (ibid., p. 14): 'On the other hand, they also clash and contradict one another. They do not agree with one

another . . . and their claim to be cognitions is discredited. . . .'
What action do we now take? Do these contradictions cause us to
question the 'natural' attitude? (ibid., p. 14):

> Where do we look for help? We now weigh the reasons for
> different possible ways of deciding or providing an explanation.
> The weaker must give way to the stronger, and the stronger, in
> turn, are of value only as long as they will stand up. . . .

Paradoxically, then, an apparent weakness becomes a source of
strength (ibid., p. 14): 'Thus, natural knowledge makes strides . . .
the various sciences of the natural sort come into being and flour-
ish.' Under the auspices of the 'natural' attitude, in science or in
commonsense, no distinction is acknowledged between the different ways in which objects are given to us, and their correspondingly
different modes of being. For example, such a distinction is to be
made within 'perception', between the part which is perceived, and
the part which is contextually supplied. The relation between these
parts is somewhat problematic, yet we never address it. We con-
found the two levels together, never seeing any difficulty in their
relationship.

What change in attitude precisely does Husserl want to effect? He
proposes (ibid., pp. 14–15):

> Let us contrast the natural mode of reflection with the
> *philosophical*. With the awakening of reflection about the
> relation of cognition to its object, abysmal difficulties arise.
> Cognition, the thing most taken for granted in natural thinking
> suddenly emerges as a mystery. But I must be more exact. What
> is *taken for granted* in natural thinking is the possibility of
> cognition. Constantly busy producing results, advancing from
> discovery to discovery in newer and newer branches of science,
> natural thinking finds no occasion to raise the question of the
> possibility of cognition as such. . . .

Now, what exactly is this 'question'? Husserl states (ibid., p. 16):
'The correlation between cognition as a mental process, its referent,
and what objectively is, . . . is the source of the deepest and most
difficult problems. Collectively, the problem of cognition.'

For Husserl the 'natural' attitude assumes that cognitions can
correspond with objects in the real world. This is not to assume that
there always is such correspondence: within this attitude, a distinction is made between true and false cognitions. But Husserl's
'philosophical' attitude makes no such presumption. Following
Husserl, then, we propose to designate as the *problem of philosophy*
the neglected relation between the two 'modes of being'.

In his later writings, Husserl came to elaborate two distinct ways in which these modes could be investigated. These were the 'phenomenological reductions', whereby the world was 'reduced' to the viewpoint of one mode of being or the other. For an overview of the broader context of the development of his writings, we can do no better than to quote Paul Ricoeur's statement (1967, p. 7):

> After the *Logical Investigations,* Husserl's works follow two paths. On the one hand, descriptive themes never cease to be enriched and to overflow the initial logical framework; on the other hand, Husserl continues to refine the philosophy of his method, and thus to mix a phenomenological philosophy with a phenomenology actually practiced. . . . *The fact is, that the idealist interpretation of the method does not necessarily coincide with its actual practice, as many of his disciples have pointed out.*

We will focus attention on two texts, respectively representative of the 'descriptive' and the 'philosophical' tendencies within Husserl's work: *Ideas* (1931), first published in 1913, and *Cartesian Meditations* (1969), first published in 1929. Apart from the fact that they are the best-known writings of Husserl's middle period, each of these presents a 'phenomenology of the social world'.[1]

Immanentism

Ideas begins with an account of the social world, prior to the definition of the phenomenological reduction. In section 27, entitled 'The World of the Natural Standpoint: I and my World about Me', Husserl states (1931, pp. 101–4):

> Our first outlook upon life is that of natural human beings, imagining, judging, feeling, willing, 'from the natural standpoint'.
> Let us make clear to ourselves what this means in the form of simple meditations which we can best carry on in the first person. I am aware of a world, spread out in space endlessly, and in time becoming and become, without end. I am aware of it, that means first of all, I discover it immediately, intuitively, I experience it. Through sight, touch, hearing, etc., in the different ways of sensory perception, corporeal things somehow spatially distributed are *for me simply there,* in verbal or figurative sense 'present' whether or not I pay them special attention by busying myself with them, considering, thinking, feeling, willing. . . . It is not necessary that they and other objects likewise should be present precisely in my field of *perception.* For me real objects

are there, definite, more or less familiar, agreeing with what is actually perceived without being themselves perceived or even intuitively present . . . I find myself at all times, and without my ever being able to change this, set in relation to a world which, through constant changes, remains one and ever the same. . . . It is then to this world . . . that the complex forms of my . . . consciousness stand related. . . . Related to it likewise are the diverse acts and states of sentiment and disapproval, joy and sorrow . . . decision and action. All these, together with the sheer acts of the Ego, in which I become acquainted with the world as *immediately* given to me, . . . are included under the one Cartesian expression: Cogito.

Thus I live *in* the Cogito, according to Husserl in this descriptive analysis. Should I step back and reflect upon 'my' experiences, then an Ego arises as an object for the Cogito: but that Cogito itself is not reflected upon, not an object for thought. I can by reflection, step aside from the natural attitude, into one of many other realms of thought, e.g. that of arithmetic (ibid., p. 104): 'The arithmetic world is there for me only when and so long as I occupy the arithmetic standpoint, but the *natural* world . . . is constantly there for me, so long as I live naturally, and look in its direction.' 'The two worlds are present together, but disconnected', says Husserl.

Now it is within the 'natural' world, that I comprehend other people. Within the 'natural attitude', 'whatever holds good for me personally', Husserl states, 'also holds good, as I know, for all other men whom I find present in my world-about-me'. Under this attitude, the world that is simply there for me is the same world that is simply there for all other men; and in this case a *we* arises (ibid., p. 105): 'We come to understandings with our neighbours, and set up in common an objective spatio-temporal fact-world as the world about us that is there for us all, and to which we ourselves none the less belong.' The presumption of a world simply there, one and the same world for us all, Husserl characterizes as 'the general thesis of the natural standpoint'. This thesis is not a proposition, a judgment, or an assertion. Rather, it is prior to and assumed tacitly within every proposition, judgment, assertion, theory, formulated within the 'natural' attitude of commonsense.

Wishing to distance himself from the 'natural' standpoint which he has delineated, Husserl defines his own standpoint with reference to the 'general thesis'. This new standpoint is only possible because he has expressed explicitly what could never be expressed within the natural attitude itself.

The new attitude may be anticipated in the light of the earlier argument. Under the 'natural' attitude, cognitions were judged to be 'true' or 'false', judgments which, in either case, took for granted the *possibility* of cognition. By contrast, in the 'philosophical' attitude, no such correspondence can be presumed to be possible. Similarly in *Ideas,* Husserl wants to abstain from all judgments about the truth or falsity of the 'general thesis of the natural standpoint'. He engages in an *epoche,* that is an 'abstinence' from or 'bracketing' of this attitude which he calls the *phenomenological epoche.*[2]

The new stance involves, so Husserl claims, a radical detachment from the claims made by the 'natural' sciences – a category which would include all non-phenomenological 'social' or 'human' sciences. He declares that (ibid., p. 111):

> All sciences which relate to the natural world, though they stand never so firm to me, though they fill me with wondering admiration, though I am far from any thought of objecting to them in the least degree, *I make no use* of their standards.

Consider one such standard. 'Natural' sciences of all kinds have often laid claim to the title of 'positivism': the claim to rest their arguments on a firm 'position'. But Husserl says (ibid., p. 86): 'If, by "positivism", we are to mean the absolutely unbiassed grounding of all science on what is "positive", i.e. on what can be primordially apprehended, then it is *we* who are the true positivists.' The reason for this is, that the so-called positivists of the 'natural' sciences do not set out to explicate the constitutive assumptions of their own way of seeing the world: they are therefore far from being unbiassed and presuppositionless, as they claim to be.

Husserl's own claim to a firm 'position' at this stage is defined in section 46 of the book, entitled 'Indubitability of Immanent, Dubitability of Transcendent Perception'. He states (ibid. p. 145): 'The thesis of my pure Ego and its personal life, which is "necessary" and plainly indubitable, thus stands opposed to the thesis of the world, which is "contingent".'

The Ego here referred to is defined as 'the stream of experience of the one who is thinking'. It is ever-present. Therefore, echoing Descartes' expression, Husserl says, 'I say forthwith and because I must, *I am,* this life is, I live, cogito.'

In *Ideas,* the focus of Husserl's attention has become the stream of experience of the one who is thinking: this is immanent, and so indubitable. By contrast, what has been bracketed away, the transcendent and so dubitable, is the world common to all, presumed under the thesis of the 'natural' standpoint. All intersubjective, transcendental knowledge, therefore, is to be bracketed, and the phenomenologist is to address his attention to what is unique and personal in his own subjective life.

Transcendentalism

Consider by contrast the account of the social world given by Husserl in his theoretical phenomenological study, the *Cartesian Meditations*. In section 8, Husserl states that if Descartes's method is followed correctly, the *ego cogito* is not the immanent ego, i.e. the concrete person who 'has' my experiences. Instead it is the *transcendental ego*, the 'apodictic' being which is 'antecedent to the being of the world'. By carrying out a second, transcendental reduction, over and above the phenomenological reduction of *Ideas*, its being is discovered within my experience. In the first reduction, I abstained from judging whether I posited a world 'out there' corresponding to my experiences. I was left, then, merely contemplating my consciousness *per se*. Now I further abstain from judging whether to posit an *I* 'out there', who is the possessor of 'my' experiences.

It is necessary to guard against a possible misinterpretation of this procedure. The first epoche did not involve any disbelief in the external world, nor any forgetfulness of my experiences of that world. It rather involved a new attitude which treated 'my experiences' as the object of enquiry in its own right. Similarly, the second epoche involves no disbelief in 'my' experiences, nor any forgetfulness of the content of those experiences. It involves a new attitude which treats 'experience' as the object of enquiry in its own right. Husserl explains (1969, p. 26):

> The philosophically reflective ego's abstention from position-takings, his depriving them of acceptance, does not signify their disappearance from his field of experience. The concrete subjective experiences, let us repeat, are indeed the things to which his attentive regard is directed, but the philosophizing Ego practices abstention with regard to what he intuits. . . . Everything *meant* in such accepting or positing . . . is still retained completely, but . . . as 'mere phenomenon'.

The key to understanding this unfamiliar recommendation lies in Husserl's choice of the word 'reflective'. Within the transcendental attitude, the philosophical attitude, 'I' examine my 'subjective' experiences. But this is not with a view to finding out about the uniqueness of my subjective consciousness as was my concern in the immanent attitude. Instead its intention is to find out about consciousness *per se,* that is, about necessary features of any possible subjective experience.

It may therefore be misleading for Husserl to employ the term 'transcendental ego', as if this were a subject. For it is not an empirically existing subject, in the sense that the cogito of *Ideas* was an empirically existing subject. The notion of a unique 'transcendental ego' is a contradiction, as if 'my' transcendental ego differed from 'yours'. For, if this is knowledge held by any possible subjectivity, then plainly it is held by all subjectivities. This argument underpins the most famous passage from the *Cartesian Meditations,* the concluding 'Fifth Meditation'.

Husserl opens the meditation with a defence against the charge that transcendental phenomenology is in fact transcendental solipsism. He sets out to refute the charge by providing a transcendental phenomenological account of how it is possible to apprehend other people in the social world. Among the multiplicity of ways in which I apprehend others, two ways stand out. First I experience others as objects 'in' the world. Second I experience them as subjects 'for' the world. In the second case I assume that they experience the same world that I experience, and, in so doing, experience me too, in the same way as I experience the world and others in it.

This raises the question of the second way of apprehending the other, as subjectivity. In a circuitous answer, Husserl first reconsiders how it is possible for me to apprehend what is *my own.* Within the transcendental sphere in which features of any possible subjectivity are being considered, it is now necessary to ask how *my* subjectivity can be apprehended. This will involve an investigation of any possible my-ness. This can be conceived by carrying out a third reduction. In effect, it repeats the first phenomenological reduction within the reflective standpoint attained by the second.

This third epoche is a bracketing of all that is alien to me alone, i.e. all references to 'others', such as cultural objects capable of belonging to anyone. This leaves behind, Husserl argues, a 'unitary', founding stratum, a 'monad', comprising 'my' nature, animate organism, sensations, functioning organs, and psychic life. This monad he calls *the human ego.* But this ego does not comprise the entire transcendental realm. The other-ness which was temporarily bracketed off can now be apprehended as a human ego. It is not I myself but is *mirrored* in my own human Ego. It is an 'alter ego': a mirroring of my own self, an analogue or a pairing.

By means of this procedure, Husserl argues that the problem of 'solipsism' has been overcome. The charge was unwarranted: transcendental phenomenology can account for our understanding of other people.

The 'pairing', 'mirror-image' notion explicates the logical argument each of us must pursue to engage in social interaction. In simple terms the procedure assumes that others are 'like' ourselves. But Husserl's two analyses permit greater precision than this. For a genuinely transcendental inter-subjectivity, the 'likeness' that is involved is not some sort of vague resemblance between two empirically different psychological individuals. Such a claimed resemblance would be false. According to the presumptions of the immanent phenomenology which investigates these empirical psychologies, each may be unique. This 'likeness' is an exact identity, as between the necessary (and necessarily shared) features of any possible subjectivity. Such a claimed resemblance is true and indeed is for Husserl the only truth fully worthy of the name.

It follows that in so far as transcendental phenomenology has not yet become part of the everyday consciousness of all society's members, we live in a less than fully 'true' society. Such a society remains false, fulfilling less than its true potential, to the extent that its members act on the belief that their actuality corresponds with their potentiality.

Husserl explores the logic of this argument through the Fifth Meditation, designating as 'higher order intersubjectivities' those in which men become progressively more aware of one another's mutual orientation. The beginning of the progression, which Husserl calls the 'First Objectivity' is the 'natural' world as viewed under the assumption of the 'general thesis of the natural standpoint'. This 'natural' world is characterized by the assumption on each person's part that the same nature, the same world, exists for all others as it exists for me, with the allowance that for you it appears 'as if I were standing over there' (ibid., p. 123). It is constituted by each as 'the same' for all: 'an identical intentional object of separate conscious processes' (ibid., p. 127).

Progression to higher order intersubjectivities is possible as the transcendental possibilities become immanent. Each monad comes to recognize others as aware of itself, and of possible others, who are themselves aware of possible and actual others. It might seem that the ramifying complexities could continue indefinitely, but for Husserl this is not the case. There is, rather, a utopian single community of monads, characterized by a specially developed form of reciprocated sociality, which marks the end-point, the *telos* of this process, conceived historically. Husserl describes it in this way (ibid., p. 140): 'Actually, therefore, *there can exist only a single community of monads,* the community of *all* co-existing monads. Hence, there can exist *only one Objective world,* only one Objective time, only one Objective space, only one Objective Nature.'

The pursuit of this one world is furthered by transcendental phenomenology which is nothing else than 'an all-embracing self-investigation' (ibid., pp. 156-7):

> In other words: the path leading to a knowledge absolutely grounded in the highest sense, or (this being the same thing) a philosophical knowledge, is necessarily the path of universal self-knowledge – first of all monadic, and then inter-monadic. We can also say that a radical and universal continuation of Cartesian meditations, or (equivalently) a universal self-cognition, is philosophy itself and encompasses all self-accountable science. The Delphic motto 'Know thyself' has gained a new signification. . . .

Transcendental phenomenology can clarify the nature of this goal, and the steps which must be taken towards its attainment. The goal and the steps involve the deepening self-knowledge of man, a knowledge which takes a preassigned form, and so is amenable to scientific analysis. Thus the conclusion of the *Cartesian Meditations* closes a path running from the immanentism of *Ideas* to the transcendentalism of the later position. Husserl maintains that this is a path which it is man's historical destiny to traverse.[3]

Realism

Perhaps Husserl's utopia is too idealized for comfort. But if one is sceptical as to the culmination of his historical process, then the 'Fifth Medication' becomes suggestive as an exploration of modes of sociality in society short of the *telos*. A range of such modes can be conceived in a world in which each member is engaged in ascribing a 'sameness' or 'pairing' to the others which differs from the ones others are ascribing to him.

Three modes of sociality are explicitly explored by Husserl. First the *mundane,* or 'natural' attitude is subjected to critique in both of his studies, but is recognizably the same phenomenon in each. Second, the *immanentist* attitude is explored in some detail in *Ideas*, as an alternative to the 'natural' view. Third, the *transcendentalist* attitude, in its fully developed form, is presented in the *Meditations* where it stands in contrast to both of its predecessors.

Husserl, of course, devoted most attention to exploring the two extremes. In comparison he neglected to articulate the standpoint of the mundane world itself. But his investigations throw light on this problem. Consider the standpoint of the mundane individual. Such an individual believes in the objectivity of the external world, and believes that consciousnesses can correspond to it, though not necessarily that they actually do. Thus he recognizes that empirically a gap may exist, either between consciousness and reality, or between consciousness and consciousness, but he believes that this need not be the case. He postulates as his utopia a state of affairs in which full correspondence between consciousnesses and world exists. If this is his 'heaven', then his 'hell' is by contrast a world in which correspondence can exist neither between consciousness and consciousness nor between consciousness and world.

But it is the immanentist consciousness which gives rise to the mundane vision of hell, with the necessary additional feature, to preserve it as hell, that its occupants know that they are there. More precisely, its members are sceptical about the possibility of correspondence either between consciousness and consciousness or between world and consciousness. Therefore the remedies open to the mundane consciousness are denied them.

Likewise, it is the transcendentalist consciousness which gives rise to the mundane heaven, again with the necessary additional feature, to preserve it as heaven, that its occupants know that they are there. More precisely, they are certain of the correspondence between consciousness and consciousness, and so any possible consciousness, and so, the world.

From the mundane viewpoint, the immanentist vision is pessimistic, and the transcendentalist vision is optimistic. Neither could be the basis for a realistic investigation of everyday life. Each is an escape from the historical pursuit of rationality, the first by a denial of the possibility of such rationality, the second by a complacent assertion that it has been attained. Rather than escaping problematic everyday life for one or other of these unproblematic dreams, our aim is to extricate consciousness from them and bring it back down to earth.

The language of phenomenology

A rigorous way in which to escape from these dream worlds is to turn attention away from 'consciousness' (itself a dream), and examine instead the language in which any account of consciousness must be produced. The phenomenological method can itself be used for this purpose. We propose that the texts of Husserl now be opened to investigation as a topic of linguistic phenomenological enquiry.[4]

Rather than being read as writing *about* a reality outside language, Husserl will be read as *writing* a 'reality' in language. Rather than reading the text as the speech of a single unproblematic subject, the text will be read as the product of diverse voices which may conflict with one another.

'Immanentism'

We will begin by reconsidering the passage from Husserl's *Ideas*, entitled 'The World of the Natural Standpoint: I and my World about Me'. These are reflections in which Husserl engages prior to taking up the phenomenological reduction (1931, pp. 101–4, quoted above):

I_{we} [Our first outlook upon life is that of natural human beings, imagining, judging, feeling, willing, 'from the natural standpoint'. Let us make clear to ourselves what this means in the form of simple meditations which we can best carry out in the first person.]

II_I [I am aware of a world, spread out in space endlessly, and in time becoming and become, without end. I am aware of it, that means first of all, I discover it, immediately, intuitively, I experience it.] [Through sight, touch, hearing, etc., in the different ways of sensory perception, corporeal things

III_{imp} somehow spatially distributed are *for me simply there,* in verbal or figurative sense 'present' [whether or not I pay

$\left[IV_I\right]$ them special attention by busying myself with them, considering, thinking, feeling, willing.] . . . it is not necessary that they and other objects likewise should be present

III_{imp} precisely in my *field of perception.* For me real objects are there, definite, more or less familiar, agreeing with what is actually perceived without being themselves perceived or even intuitively present] . . . [I find myself at all times, and without my ever being able to change this, set in relation to

V_I a world which, through constant changes, remains one and ever the same.] . . . [It is then to this world . . . that the complex forms of my . . . consciousness stand related . . . Related to it likewise are the diverse acts and states of

VI_{imp} sentiment and disapproval, joy and sorrow . . . decision and action. All these, together with the sheer acts of the Ego, [in

$\left[VII_I\right]$ which I become acquainted with the world as *immediately* given to me] are included under the one Cartesian expression: Cogito.

Three voices are to be found. These are respectively the *we* and the *I*, and an impersonal voice. The stanzas are indicated by means of square brackets in the usual way.[5] We have not distinguished pictures as this would involve unnecessary complexity for the purposes of the present argument. In the passage, Husserl himself explicitly identifies two voices, beginning in the first person plural, but stating that the meditations can best be carried on 'in the first person' singular. The third, impersonal, voice arises as a means of summing up the first person singular experiences.

Following stanza I which introduces the passage in the voice of the *we,* the *I* speaks in stanza II. The *I*'s first 'finding' is of a 'world'. However, in stanza II the *I* is only 'aware' of this world 'immediately' and 'intuitively'. In stanza III, the impersonal voice metaphorically re-formulates matters. This is an 'optional' metaphor, as this stanza is intelligible on its own. Stanza IV is an aside by the voice of the *I.* This is a 'mandatory' metaphor, that is, 'them' in stanza IV refers to 'corporeal things' in stanza III. In stanza V, the *I* again speaks of a 'world', but this time this 'world' has new properties. It is a world which 'through constant changes remains one and ever the same'. This statement presents a problem. How can the *I* which is only immediately and intuitively aware of the world reach the notion of a world which remains the same through constant changes?

Left to itself the *I* could not remain the same. But this *I* is not left to itself. It is engaged in a dialogue with another voice, the impersonal voice. In the preceding stanza, that voice concluded, 'for me real objects are there agreeing with what is actually perceived'. The impersonal voice is able to formulate a notion of reality ('real objects') transcending appearance ('what is actually perceived'). This is the notion which the *I* learns from in order to speak its notion of a world remaining the same. But in this case, the voice of the *I* in stanza V is dependent upon the impersonal voice of stanza III. In stanza VI, the impersonal voice itself takes over the notion of 'world'. It formulates 'this world', 'together with the sheer acts of the Ego' as, together, 'Cogito'.

In a passage which follows shortly, this conclusion is extended also to the voice of the *we* (ibid., p. 105):

> [Whatever holds good for me personally also holds good, as I know, for all other men whom I find present in my world-about-me. . . . For each, the fields of perception and memory actually present are different. . . . Despite this we
> I   come to understandings with our neighbours and set up in
> we common an objective spatio-temporal fact-world as the world about us that is there for us all, and to which we ourselves nonetheless belong].

This is Husserl's 'general thesis of the natural standpoint'. Thus the notion of 'world' is one to which every voice can subscribe, a notion which each voice is able to articulate as a result of its encounter with other voices. For Husserl, as previously read the word referred to a reality external to the language which formulated it. But now this no longer seems to be a necessary conclusion. What every voice can come to comprehend as a result of its encounter with other voices (worlds or words) is *that it is a voice*.

This attaches a new significance to Husserl's 'general thesis of the natural standpoint'. The thesis sets up in common with our neighbours 'an objective spatio-temporal fact-voice as the voice about us that is there for us all and to which we ourselves belong'. This is the familiar voice of the *we*: the 'heavenly' utopia known as 'intersubjectivity'.

But the phenomenological reduction itself is to be defined in terms of this attainment of the voice of the *we*. In the 'general thesis' (ibid., p. 110):

> I we [*We put out of action the general thesis which belongs to the essence of the natural standpoint,* we place in brackets whatever it includes respecting the nature of Being: *this entire natural world therefore* which is continually 'there for us', 'present to our hand' and will ever remain there, is a 'fact world' of which we continue to be conscious, even though it pleases us to put it in brackets].

Having ascertained, through a dialectic undertaken within the 'natural' attitude, that each voice could learn from each of the other voices that it was itself a voice, Husserl now proposes that the phenomenological attitude arises precisely by forgetting this fact. This could be put more strongly: by 'repressing' or 'suppressing' this fact in the midst of its dream of consciousness. It amounts to a forgetting by speech that it is speech among speeches. In short, it amounts to a shift from 'realism' to realism.

The most famous result of this reduction is already familiar. Husserl argues (ibid., p. 143):

> I imp [The stream of experience which is mine, namely, of the one who is thinking, may be to ever so great an extent uncomprehended, unknown in its past and future reaches],
>
> II I [yet so soon as I glance towards the flowing life and into the real present it flows through, and in so doing grasp myself as the pure subject of this life . . . I say forthwith and because I must: I am, this life is, I live, cogito].

This passage splendidly enacts what it speaks about: the 'incomprehension' and 'unknowing' are the 'experience' of the impersonal voice, itself 'incomprehensible' and 'unknown' to the voice of the *I*, which confidently holds forth.

For Husserl this passage speaks *of* the gap between modes of experience. For us it *speaks* the gap between modes of speech. The gap arises as a result of the retreat of these two voices from one another, a retreat brought about by the phenomenological reduction.

But now another reversal occurs. The *I* has reached its strident conclusion by forgetting other voices, in particular the voice of the impersonal. But that voice has not forgotten it. For the impersonal voice is now able metaphorically to reformulate what the *I* has achieved (ibid., p. 145):

$$I_{imp}$$ *[The thesis of my pure Ego and its personal life, which is 'necessary' and plainly indubitable, thus stands opposed to the thesis of the world which is 'contingent'].*

Husserl has shown the impoverishing consequences of allowing a voice to suppress or censor its awareness of other voices.

Husserl's exploration illuminates the possibilities of language when it departs from the sensitive mutuality which it can exhibit in a dialogue of voices. He is exploring the deadness of language left to itself. But for Husserl, this is an exciting possibility because of the certainty which it exhibits. 'The thesis of my pure Ego', he tells us, 'is necessary', whereas 'the thesis of the world is contingent.'

Paradoxically, this 'thesis' is expressed not in the voice of the *I*, but in the impersonal voice. It seems that whereas the voice of the *I* has suspended all awareness of other voices, the impersonal voice has not. The impersonal voice, claiming no special status for itself, asserts the absoluteness of the *I* voice.

The impersonal voice poses the voice of the *I* as transcending the impersonal voice's ability to formulate it. The impersonal voice formulates the appearance of a reality which is posed as formulated by the voice of the *I*. The source of Husserl's notion of the 'transcendent' reality of the 'conscious' 'life' and 'real presence' of the *I* is precisely the separation he has made between the two voices.

This implies that the impersonal voice serves as Husserl's home base. His excursion into the voice of the *I* has the purpose of establishing certainty there which can be employed to order the impersonal voice. This may be summarized in the following diagram:

$$II_{impersonal} \begin{bmatrix} I_I \end{bmatrix} \quad = \quad \text{'immanentism'}$$

This equation is incomplete, as the voice we have called 'impersonal' has not yet been accurately identified. None the less it can be noted that the impersonal voice conjures up a reference to a reality transcending linguistic formulation by posing one voice as transcending another.

'Transcendentalism'

In the section of the Cartesian Meditations, entitled 'The *ego cogito* as transcendental subjectivity', Husserl writes (1969, p. 21):

> I I [By my living, by my experiencing, thinking, valuing, and acting, I can enter no world other than the one that gets its sense and acceptance or status in and from me, myself. If I put myself above all this life and refrain from doing any believing that takes 'the' world straightforwardly as existing – if I direct my regard exclusively to this life itself, as consciousness *of* 'the' world – I thereby acquire myself as the pure ego, with the pure stream of my cogitationes].

This passage exhibits dramatically the change from the immanentist to the transcendentalist phase. Within the voice of the *I* there is formulated the phrase 'the pure ego'. In *Ideas* this was the phrase used by the impersonal voice to reformulate metaphorically the voice of the *I*. The promise of this transcendental investigation seems to be, that the voice of the *I* will grasp the reflections about it of the impersonal voice. This would seem to express an aspiration towards 'self-consciousness', or its linguistic equivalent. Such an aspiration seems also to be expressed by the new attitude taken to the world, or in our terms the voice.

In *Ideas*, the *I* was to forget that it was a voice. This enabled it to conclude: 'I am, this life is, I live, cogito'. In short, the *I* was to forget that it was a voice among others formulating 'reality' and instead to immerse itself within its own voice, as the confident speech of reality. But here it seems, the *I* must remember that it is a voice, and to strive to apprehend itself as such. It is to 'direct its regard to this life itself' as 'consciousness *of* "the" world'.

But the *I* is to continue to direct its attention exclusively to itself. Its learning what it is to be a voice will be learning entirely from itself, never 'learning from others'. Husserl says (ibid., p. 95):

> I I [As Ego in the transcendental attitude, I attempt first of all to delimit, within my horizon of transcendental experience, *what is peculiarly my own*. First I say that it is *non-alien*. I begin by freeing that horizon abstractively from everything that is at all alien].

This procedure seems to be within the scope of the voice of the *I*. But as in the earlier version of this reduction, the *I* apparently requires the assistance of the impersonal voice for certain purposes (ibid., pp. 95–6):

II imp [Furthermore, the *characteristic of belonging to the surrounding world*, not merely for others who are also given at the particular time in actual experience, but also *for everyone*, the characteristic of being there for and accessible to everyone . . . should not be overlooked, but rather excluded abstractly].

The notion of phenomena 'belonging to the surrounding voice' e.g. 'for other' might seem to present some difficulty, but a textual interpretation may be placed upon it.

There is a problem for the voicé of the *I*. Though this voice purports to formulate what is uniquely mine, the voice itself, *qua* voice, is not unique but shared with others. Up to now, the 'transcendental' reduction has done no more than establish its position within the voice of the *I* generally. This third reduction purports to go further. It seeks to distinguish within that voice what is uniquely mine about that voice. It seems that the notion 'for everyone' cannot be formulated by the voice of the *I* alone, so that this reduction, which arrives at 'the human ego' is not the pure finding of the *I*.

However this is not the only crucial intervention of another voice. Presuming that a 'human ego' has been constituted, how is it possible for the voice of the *I* to comprehend an ego other than its own? Husserl makes the following statement (ibid., p. 119):

I_I   [I am *here* somatically, the centre of a primordial 'world' oriented around me]. [Consequently, my entire primordial ownness, proper to me as a monad, has the content of the Here not the content belonging to that definite There. Each

II imp of these contents excludes the other: they cannot both co-exist in my sphere of ownness at the same time. But since the other body there enters into a pairing association with my body here and, being given perceptually, becomes the core of an appresentation, the core of my experience of a co-existing ego, that ego . . . must be appresented as an

[III_I] ego now co-existing in the mode There, ['such as I should be if I were there']. My own ego however, the ego given in constant self-perception, is actual now with the content belonging to this Here Therefore an ego is *appresented* as *other* than mine].

As the text shows, the voice of the *I* can formulate 'I am here', but no more. The introduction of a contrasting notion of 'there' is the work of the impersonal voice.

This is explicit in the following passage (ibid., pp. 120–1):

I_{imp} [Since other subjectivity, by appresentation within the exclusive own-essentialness of my subjectivity, arises with the sense and status of a subjectivity that is other in its own essence, it might at first seem to be a mystery how community – even the first community, in the form of a common world – becomes established. . . . These two primordial spheres, mine which is for me as ego the original sphere, and his which is for me an appresented sphere – they are not

$\begin{bmatrix} II_I \end{bmatrix}$ *separated* by an abyss [I cannot actually cross, since crossing it would mean, after all, that I acquired an original (rather than an appresenting) experience of someone else?]].

Here the dilemma is posed unresolvably in the voice of the *I* which almost cries out for help at this point in the text. Help can be found in the impersonal voice, which reveals its identity plainly for the first time. The fundamental experience of someone else, Husserl tells us, is via the *body* (ibid., p. 123):

II_{imp} [This natural body belonging to my sphere appresents the other Ego, by virtue of the pairing association with my bodily organism, and with my Ego governing in my organism, within my primordially constituted Nature. In so doing, it appresents first of all the other Ego's governing in this body, the body over there, and mediately his governing in the Nature that appears to him perceptually – identically the Nature in which the body over there belongs, identically the Nature that is my primordial Nature. It is the same Nature, but in the mode of appearance 'as if I were standing over there, where the Other's body is'].

The impersonal voice, which as has been shown in Husserl's own voice in the *Ideas,* can now be seen to be the voice of the *Meditations,* here identified as the voice of 'body' or of 'Nature'.

But according to Husserl, the formulation of the apprehension of the other which we have so far analysed constitutes only the *'first and lowest level of communalization* between me, the primordial monad for myself, and the monad constituted in me, yet as other.'

Higher communities are deduced by generalizing the results of the establishment of the first community. The character of this generalizing is expressed in various ways. He states, for example, as a matter of 'fact' (ibid., pp. 129–30):

I I [If, with my understanding of someone else, I penetrate more deeply into him, into his horizon of ownness, I shall soon run into the fact that, just as his animate bodily organism lies in my field of perception, so my animate organism lies in his field of perception, and that in general, he experiences me forthwith as an Other for him, just as I experience him as *my* Other].

This gives rise to my conceiving of a plurality of others, possible as well as actual, which Husserl calls an 'open' community, inhabiting an 'open' Nature. It is in this connection that he makes a more disciplined statement of the generalization process. He writes (ibid., p. 130):

I we [To this community, there naturally corresponds in transcendental concreteness, a similarly open community of monads which we designate as transcendental intersubjectivity. We need hardly say that, as existing for me, it is constructed purely within me, the mediating ego, purely by virtue of sources belonging to my intentionality; nevertheless it is constituted thus *as* a community constituted also in every other monad . . . as the same community – only with a different subjective mode of experience – and as necessarily bearing within it the same Objective world].

The voice of the *we* is employed to designate this generalizing. It expresses the assumption, that if one ego can constitute an other, then so can we all.

But this result expressed in terms of the *we* is not Husserl's conclusion. He expresses that result instead in these terms (ibid., p. 140):

I Nature [Actually therefore there can exist only a single community of monads, the community of all co-existing monads. Hence there can exist only one Objective world, only one Objective time, only one Objective space, only one Objective Nature].

This position, stated triumphantly in Husserl's preferred impersonal (natural) voice is achieved by reformulation of the voice of the *we*. This voice is thereby constituted as transcendent. The 'transcendent' argument of the *Cartesian Meditations* can thus be expressed as follows:

$$II_{\text{Nature}} \begin{bmatrix} I_{\text{we}} \end{bmatrix} \quad = \quad \text{'transcendentalism'}$$

The argument of the *Ideas* can also be more fully expressed now that the impersonal voice has been identified:

$$^{II}\text{Nature} \begin{bmatrix} I_I \end{bmatrix} = \text{'immanentism'}$$

'Real'-ism

We hope to have exhibited an 'immanent' critique of Husserl's phenomenology in a double sense of the word. First, our critique of his writing is directly inspired by the ideal of phenomenological reduction upheld in his writing. Husserl's immanent and transcendent reductions view the gap between 'appearance' and 'reality' from one side or the other. Our practice of *interruption* is an attempt to interrogate this gap in its own terms.

Second, Husserl claims to have articulated both an immanentist and a transcendentalist position, and so to have explored the two possibilities for philosophical certainty available to consciousness. We have tried to establish that Husserl instead explored two 'transcendentalist' positions available to language. In doing so he left unexplored an 'immanentist' position also available to language. Such a position, as shown in empirical investigations discussed in this book, is occupied by everyday speech.[6]

In effect, we have reformulated the immanentist position. Husserl's conception of the immanent is of a reality wholly available to consciousness, although only imperfectly available to language. Our conception of the immanent is not, however, of a reality wholly available to language. It acknowledges instead that all that can be known of 'reality' is knowable in language, but that language itself is other than reality. It conceives not of reality, but of speech about 'reality', as that which is immanent and so addressable in speech. We refer to this as a 'real'-ist point of view.

Notes

1 Whilst we exempt Husserl's earlier and later writings from discussion here, it is true to say that the former exemplify the 'descriptive', and the latter the 'philosophical' tendencies within his work, so that our two chosen texts illuminate his work as a whole.

2 The *epoche* is Husserl's version of what we would call an 'interruption' of the natural attitude.

3 Thus Husserl's two works taken together span the same philosophical journey as is traversed by Hegel's *Phenomenology of Mind* (1949).

4 The method employed here should be compared with the method of reading Husserl's discussion of language employed by Jacques Derrida in his *Speech and Phenomena* (1973). Whilst Derrida's project is a direct

inspiration of our own, the two methods are not identical. Cf. the fuller discussions in Chapter 6 and in Chapter 13 below.

5 This is the method developed in Chapters 1 and 2 above.

6 Cf. especially Chapters 1, 2, 7, 8, and 14. Additional investigations along these lines are presented in Torode (1975).

Bibliography

Derrida, J. (1973), *Speech and Phenomena*, Evanston: Northwestern University Press.

Hegel, G. (1949), *The Phenomenology of Mind*, London: Allen & Unwin.

Husserl, E. (1931), *Ideas: General Introduction to Pure Phenomenology*, London: Allen & Unwin.

Husserl, E. (1969), *Cartesian Meditations*, The Hague: Nijhoff.

Husserl, E. (1970), *The Idea of Phenomenology*, The Hague: Nijhoff.

Ricoeur, P. (1967), *Husserl: an analysis of his Phenomenology*, Evanston: Northwestern University Press.

Torode, B. (1975), 'The Extra-Ordinary in Ordinary Language', unpublished Ph.D. thesis, University of Edinburgh.

Originally a student of Husserl, Heidegger has become central to contemporary discussions of language. His critique of 'idle talk' appears, on a first reading, to insist on the irreducibility of understanding to language. But, against Heidegger's understanding of his text, we can interrogate the manner in which his own language constitutes the sense of 'understanding' as a reality over and above itself.

chapter 6

Heidegger: from letters to being, or from being to letters?

> The important distinction between *vagueness* and *distinctness* plays an important part in the phenomenology of 'expressions' still to be discussed, explicit presentations, judgements, acts of feeling, and so forth. We have only to think of the way in which we are accustomed to grasp the synthetic constructions, still very complex, which make up the 'intellectual content' of our reading at any time, and consider what, in our understanding of the matter read, and in respect of the so-called intellectual foundations of the expressions, comes to really primordial actualization.
> Edmund Husserl, *Ideas*, I, 123 (1931, p. 345)

Two kinds of claims have been made for Martin Heidegger. Since these claims appear to contradict one another, we intend to examine how such opposed readings of one text arise. By producing a third reading which accounts for the possibility of the other two, we hope to transcend their limitations. We will propose that each arises from an interpretation of Heidegger's text as the appearance of a version of reality brought to Heidegger from elsewhere. By contrast, we will attempt to interrupt Heidegger's text, that is to reveal the gap between appearance and reality that his text exhibits. In showing how this gap is produced by his use of language, it will be possible to transcend Heidegger's way of writing. Paradoxically, his interpreters remain trapped within their version of what his way of writing is.

Heidegger's interpreters

In *Theorizing* (1974) Alan Blum presents several grounds for reading Heidegger. He provides 'an example of making wonder a topic' (p. 1), a 'conception of what speech says' rather than what it speaks (p. 9), and a conception of discourse (p. 82). Heidegger is praised by Blum (p. 34) for telling us, in *What is called thinking?*

(1968) that 'the most thought-provoking thing is that we are not thinking'. This statement raises in brief the whole problem of reading Heidegger. For if it be read as a critique of a particular, present way in which we have become accustomed to think, then it appears 'radical', 'progressive', even 'revolutionary', and points us to a new kind of thinking. If however it be read as a statement applicable essentially to thought itself, then it appears 'reactionary' and simply stands as a condemnation of thought, *per se,* recommending us to abstain from it. So there are 'optimistic' and 'pessimistic' ways in which the statement may be read.

Both 'optimistic' and 'pessimistic' accounts depend upon versions of reality brought to the text. Instead we shall attempt a 'real'-istic reading of the kind of realities Heidegger's thought sets into play.[1]

Heidegger's statement may itself exemplify that thought-which-is-not-thinking (the pessimistic reading) or that other thought which-is-thinking (the optimistic reading). Both are however unacceptable. First, the proposal is a case of thinking which in some sense has to be acknowledged. Second, to condemn existing 'thought' (or 'cooking', or 'singing') as not really 'thinking' (or 'cooking', or 'singing') does not constitute a display of what really is 'thinking' (or 'cooking', or 'singing').

It follows that Heidegger's statement is *doing* neither of the two alternatives which he *says* are possible.[2] This implies that another path has been taken which in his terms 'grounds' both readings.

To investigate this path is to enquire into the (one) reality underlying the (two) appearances posed by his speech. But a distinction is made between 'reality' and 'appearance' within his speech itself. This distinction can be shown in two ways, *grammatically,* and *logically.*

Heidegger's logical way of making the distinction represents his own contribution, as a professional philosopher, to an account of the external world. This is what his text *says,* and is perhaps the more familiar way of understanding him. His grammatical way of making the distinction is less familiar. An investigation of this grammar seeks not what Heidegger says about philosophy, but the way in which his language *does* philosophy. It is to attend to Heidegger not as a professional, but as an everyday philosopher.[3]

Heidegger's sentence divides grammatically into two clauses as follows:

$$
\left[
\begin{array}{c}
\text{i} \\
\text{(The most \underline{thought}-provoking thing is that} \\
\text{ii} \\
\text{(we are not \underline{thinking}))}
\end{array}
\right.
$$

Following previous practice, we will refer to the two clauses as *pictures*. They are united together by a word play on 'thought', 'thinking', which is <u>underlined.</u> This unity constitutes a *stanza*. However the two pictures do not contribute equally to the grammatical unity of the stanza. Picture ii ('we are not thinking') makes sense independently of picture i. Picture i ('the most thought-provoking thing is . . . ') requires picture ii to complete its sense. Therefore the sense of picture i is dependent upon that of picture ii, to which it refers. We will use brackets, '()', to indicate such a relationship of reference. Then grammatically, the structure of the stanza is

i   (ii)

This means that, grammatically speaking, picture ii formulates the *reality* of which picture i formulates the *appearance*.

But, logically, the sentence has a different structure. The train of thought is 'the most thought-provoking thing is – something'. We wait to see what this 'something' is, expecting to be shown something new, outside ourselves in the world, which will 'provoke' us. But, instead, Heidegger surprises us by showing us – ourselves. 'We are not thinking' formulates the appearance of precisely 'the most thought-provoking thing' as reality. The logical structure of the sentence reverses its grammatical structure. It may be expressed thus:

(i)   ii

This means that logically speaking, picture i formulated the reality of which picture ii formulates the appearance.

It is now possible to explain how the ambiguity in Heidegger's sentence arises. In it (in each of its two constituent pictures) he speaks with two voices, joined together by a word-play. In the first (picture i) he says, 'the most thought-provoking thing is X'. In the second (picture ii) he says 'we are not thinking'. The reader would be undisturbed by this if it were clear which were reality, and which appearance. Thus *either* 'when it appears to us that the most thought-provoking thing is X then we are not thinking' (making picture i the appearance and picture ii the reality) *or* 'it appears we are not thinking, but the most thought-provoking thing is X' (making picture i the reality and picture ii the appearance) would provide a thesis with which the reader could agree or disagree. But Heidegger's sentence disrupts the usual relation between appearance and reality. He refuses to allow us to determine which is one and which is the other.

Let us examine Alan Blum's commentary on Heidegger's remark (Blum, op. cit., p. 34, emphasis added):

The problem of the author is to induce the reader to join with him
to hear what they share by constructing a relation with the
predecessor as the icon of a thinking experience, as itself an
instance of the re-thinking to which author and reader are
directed. Author and reader share their humanness – their
capacity to re-think that which needs thought. *The author's
problem is to re-create an exemplary thinking experience for a
reader* whose horizons are controlled by the security of the
unthought, the pleasurable, and the common; to have the reader
re-experience their human solidarity which the dispersive forces
of the high sounding and impressive cover over.

Presuming that Blum feels that the author has been successful in this
case, it would appear that for him, Heidegger's statement 'recreates an exemplary experience for a reader'. We might suggest
how this is done.

For Blum, the essentially damning thing about unthinking
thought is its belief that it corresponds with reality. Heidegger's
aphorism jolts this belief. To believe the sentence is to believe that it
does not correspond with reality. What then is the 'thinking experience'? It is the limitation of thought. But is this a thought or an
experience? It cannot be a thought, since a thought is a judgment
such as *either* 'The most thought-provoking thing is X' *or* 'we are not
thinking'. What Heidegger writes however is not a judgment, but a
relation between judgments. In being contradictory, this relation is
itself non-judgmental. It is grasped, rather, as an experience. For
Blum, the value of Heidegger's statement is that it creates the
experience of the limitation of thought.

So Blum values Heidegger for the effect which he produced (an
experience) external to language (thought). This is not to say that
Heidegger describes a reality (a real world) external to language,
but that his writing produces an effect (the experience) external to
language. In so far as Blum is interested in this effect (a feature of
the real world external to language) rather than with the way in
which Heidegger has produced it (a practice of language), Blum's
concern is with what Heidegger says, rather than what he does.

We prefer to investigate how this experience is produced. The
mode of production of thoughts is linguistic. Therefore, this enquiry
must investigate the way in which the relation between thoughts is
produced in language. Such an investigation is in fact already under
way in the writings of Jacques Derrida. Interestingly, Derrida
finds the writings of Heidegger particularly worthy of investigation. He thus provides a second justification for the reading of
Heidegger.

In his paper 'Ousia and Gramme: a note to a footnote in Being and Time', Derrida refers (1970, p. 88, n. 34) to:

> What is presently in France a deep complicity: that which brings together – in terms of the same refusal to read, the same respectiveness or blind silence, and the same abuse of the question, the text, and the question of the text, the devoted Heideggerians and the anti-Heideggerians. In this situation, political 'resistance' to Heidegger often serves as a highly moral alibi for a 'resistance' of another order: a *philosophical* resistance, though even those forms of resistance whose political implications seem nebulous cannot escape a certain political tinge.

Like Blum, Derrida disclaims questions of agreement or disagreement with a text. For Blum this justifies the attempt to escape from the text in search of an extra-linguistic reality of 'experience'. Derrida's response goes in the reverse direction. It attempts to liberate the text from any reference to an external reality.

For Derrida, the irreversible Heideggerian meditation is crucial above all for its elaboration of what it calls the *ontological difference.* As Heidegger states it in *Being and Time,* 'forgetting of Being is the forgetting of the difference from Being to beings. It remains forgotten'. Even the trace of the difference (*die Spur*) is effaced. Derrida names this trace of the difference – or rather, since that has been effaced, the trace of the trace, 'differance' (with an a). Yet he states (op. cit., p. 93): 'We should realize that all the determinations of such a trace – all the names we can give it – belong as such to the metaphysical text which protects the trace. As Heidegger says, the difference cannot *appear as such.*' For Derrida 'the metaphysical' here is that which binds us to the text as a direct expression of reality, covering over that which traces it. Every text is thus in struggle with itself, 'both *subjected to* and *released from* the delimitation of metaphysics' (p. 88). Each exhibits a duality: 'two texts, two hands, two looks, two sorts of listening: at once together and separate' (p. 91).

Derrida identifies one particular crucial respect in which Heidegger remains trapped within the tradition of metaphysics (ibid., p. 89, adapted)[4]

> Is not the contrast between *Primordial* and *derivative* properly metaphysical? Is not the demand for an origin in general – whatever precautions are taken with this concept – the essential operation of metaphysics? Is there not at least some Platonism in the notion of fallenness – assuming that the Platonism could be removed in the face of strong presump-

tions of a completely different order? And why consider as a *fall* the passage from one temporality to another? And why characterize temporality as authentic or proper (*eigentlich*) and inauthentic or improper after having suspended all ethical considerations?

In these terms Derrida characterizes as metaphysical, precisely the element which Alan Blum has drawn from Heidegger's text. This is the Platonic moralistic distinction between an original, primordial, authentic realm (which Blum calls the 'analytic' or the One) and a derivative, fallen, inauthentic realm (which for Blum is the 'concrete' or the Many).

Derrida proposes that Heidegger himself capitulates to metaphysics. Referring to the three questions with which the book ends, he suggests that 'it is really more as an interruption of *Being and Time* than as a conclusion to it that Heidegger asks if a "primordial temporality" leads to the meaning of Being', (p. 90). Derrida proposes to release Heidegger's text from the delimitation of metaphysics: 'to surpass metaphysics, a certain trace must be imprinted in the metaphysical text, yet one which points towards a wholly different text' (p. 91). Whereas for Blum, the value of Heidegger's writing is that it points towards an experience *outside* language, for Derrida its value is that it points towards *another kind* of language. Whereas Blum's ideal is the unattainable reality of Being, which we could grasp if only we were not hindered by the appearances of speeches, Derrida's ideal is a speaking – or rather a writing – which could indulge in the richness of its own appearances if only it were not hindered by its reference to reality (ibid., p. 93, adapted):[5]

> a mode of writing without presence and absence – without history, cause, origin, or telos – which would overturn all dialectic, theology, teleology, and ontology. This mode of writing would exceed everything that the history of metaphysics has conceived . . . as well as time and space themselves.

But is this not equally unattainable?

It seems that both Blum and Derrida have produced *interpretations* of Heidegger, in terms of which they ascribe their own ideals to his text. In this sense both readings are idealistic. By contrast a materialist reading should seek to explicate the way in which the text itself produces Heidegger's ideals.

Idle talk

We propose to examine a text which is important to those, such as

Blum and Derrida who want to theorize ideal forms of speech and writing. It is the discussion of 'Idle Talk' (*die Gerede*) in *Being and Time*. Since the text is one in which Heidegger himself discusses the problems of listening and reading, it should be possible to take into account his own statement about how a text should be read when reading this text. The discussion runs as follows (1967, p. 211):[6]

> In the language which is spoken when one expresses oneself, there lies an average intelligibility; and in accordance with this intelligibility the discourse which is communicated can be understood . . . to a considerable extent, even if the hearer does not bring himself into such a kind of Being towards what the discourse is about as to have a primordial understanding of it. We do not so much understand the entities which are talked about; we already are listening only to what is said-in-the-talk as such. What is said-in-the-talk gets understood, but what the talk is about is understood only approximately and superficially . . . . And because this discoursing has lost its primary relationship-of-Being towards the entity talked about, or else has never achieved such a relationship, it does not communicate in such a way as to let this entity be appropriated in a primordial manner, but communicates rather by gossiping and passing the word along. What is said-in-the-talk as such, spreads in wider circles and takes on an authoritative character. Things are so because one says so. Idle talk is constituted by just such gossiping and passing the word along – a process by which its initial lack of ground to stand on becomes aggravated to complete groundlessness. And indeed this idle talk is not confined to verbal gossip, but even spreads to what we write, where it takes the form of 'scribbling'. In this latter case the gossip is not based so much upon hear-say. It feeds upon superficial reading. The average understanding of the reader will never be able to decide what has been drawn from primordial sources with a struggle and how much is just gossip. The average understanding, moreover, will not want any such distinction, and does not need it, because of course, it understands everything.

Reading the text as a whole, we learn of the 'average intelligibility' which lies in spoken or written language. Perhaps we could best begin to discuss this passage by making an overall 'average' judgment. The issue which it raises is very close to that raised by the short utterance earlier considered. There Heidegger stated that 'the most thought-provoking thing is X', adding that 'we are not thinking'. An investigation of this text revealed a structure of two voices, linked grammatically and logically in opposite ways.

The present text could be approached in similar fashion. It tells of the possibility of 'the hearer bringing himself into such a kind of Being as to have a primordial understanding of what the discourse is about', but equally it notes the possibility of 'listening only to what is said in the talk as such'. A question then arises about the status of Heidegger's own discourse: is *it* 'drawn from primordial sources' or is it 'just gossip'?

As in the case of the shorter utterance, we propose that Heidegger's language as exhibited in this text – what he does as opposed to the two ideals which he says – can be neither 'primordial' nor 'idle'. It cannot be simply 'idle': for Heidegger does not merely pass along the word. For instance *Rede,* 'talk'. is brought into an encounter with other words from which, Heidegger argues, it has been severed (in particular, with the words *ursprünglich verstehendes Sein,* 'primordially understood Being'). But equally Heidegger's words cannot be so easily designated as 'primordial' simply because they themselves use the word.

We proposed a version of an 'average intelligibility' of Heidegger's text. Now let us propose a version of the 'struggle with primordial sources' which he advocates as a deeper way of reading. Heidegger's struggle in this text becomes visible through the only real means with which he can communicate to his reader – the letters which he has written. We approach Heidegger's text again, then, focusing explicitly upon what is done in the text itself. As with the previous shorter example, we begin with *grammatical* considerations, returning subsequently, in the light of their results to reconsider the *logical* structure of the text.

An initial grammatical observation is that great play is made on two root words, *verstehen* and *reden* and their compounds. It will be helpful to list these words, indicating the equivalents chosen for them by the English translators of *Sein und Zeit,* John Macquarrie and Edward Robinson, and also alternative English words where these equivalents do not reveal the word-play employed in the original text.

	Heidegger		*Macquarrie and Robinson*	*Alternative*	
	verstehen	to	understand		
das	Verstehen	the	understanding		
	verstehend		understanding		
die	Verständlichkeit		intelligibility	the	understandability
das	Verständnis	the	understanding		
	reden	to	talk		
die	Rede	the	talk		

das	Geredete	the	talked		
das	Gerede		idle talk		
	bereden	to	talk over		
das	Nachreden		gossiping	the	after-talk
das	Weiterreden		passing the word along	the	repetitious talk

One or more of these terms, or reference to them, occurs in every clause in the passage, with the sole exception of the two clause sentence, *'Die Sache ist so, weil man es sagt'*, which will be discussed separately.

In considering the text sequentially, we examine in what combinations and in what expressions the *reden* and *verstehen* compounds are used. We know, from our 'average intelligibility' reading of the text, that a distinction is made between two ideals, the positive one of 'primordial struggle' (*ursprüngliche Schöpfung*) and the negative one of 'averageness' (*Durchschnittlichkeit*). It will be important to see which core compounds are used to formulate each of these ideals. In this investigation, certain simple grammatical constructions take on a new significance. Negation (*nicht*, 'not' and *nie* 'never', among others) permits a word to be used to formulate a state of affairs which is not itself accredited with existence. (It permits *theorizing* as opposed to *description*.) The use of the genitive has somewhat the opposite effect: a word may be employed in this case, in a formulation to which it does not really belong.[7]

> I
> i Average understandability lies already in self-out-speaking spoken speech[8]
> ii according to average understandability, communicated talk can be extensively understood,
> iii without such hearing bringing itself into a primordially understanding Being towards the About-which (*dem Worüber*) of the talk.

Two kinds of relations exist between the three constituent pictures (clauses) making up the stanza. Pictures i and ii share the expression 'average understandability'. They both formulate the negative ideal, of 'averageness'. Picture iii reformulates the matter. Only the word 'talk' (*Rede*) is in common between it and what has gone before. But here it is not *Rede* per se but the genitive form: *der Rede*, which is found. We have here a separate realm: a formulation of the positive ideal of 'primordiality'. This is expressed by means of a negation (*ohne*, 'without'), so no existence is accredited to this primordiality.

Rede by contrast appears clearly in the formulation of the negative ideal: it is described as '*mitgeteilte Rede*', communicated talk. However since communication would appear to be necessary to the very notion of talk, this poses no restriction on it.[9] So it seems that *das Worüber* the 'about which', is the phenomenon within the 'primordial' field which corresponds to *die Rede* in the 'average' field. Understandability likewise appears in two formulations of the 'average' negative ideality. '*Durchschnittliche Verständlichkeit*' is in common between two formulations, pictures i and ii. 'Understandability' is grammatically posed as one reality which transcends its two appearances in speech and talk. In its single use at the crux of the sentence, it is qualified by the adjective 'average'. But whereas '*mitgeteilte*' appears to express a property essential to '*Rede*', and therefore appears inessential to the text, the opposite is true of '*durchschnittliche*'.

According to our preliminary reading, a main aim of the text is to contrast to 'average understandability' a new kind of understandability. It seems that 'average' specifies the kind of *Verständlichkeit* which appears in the negative ideality, whereas *Rede* belongs to this realm as such.

> II
> i One understands not so much the talked-over being
> ii rather, one hears already only the talked as such.

Note the negative in the first picture. This formulates the possibility but not the actuality, of understanding the talked-over being. To it is contrasted the hearing of the talked as such. Thus understanding is a feature of the 'primordial' positive ideality. By contrast the talked (*Geredete*) belongs squarely within the negative 'average' ideality. But what of *das beredete Seiende*, the talked-over being, which is precisely what one 'understands'? What one understands is not the talking-over, but the being which is talked over. Thus the adjectival use of *beredete* here is equivalent to the genitive use of *der Rede* in the third picture of the first stanza. *Das Seiende* is precisely *das Worüber*. These are the words which belong to Heidegger's 'primordial' realm: *Rede* only points to them from the realm of 'averageness'.

> III
> i   This becomes understood, the About-which, only approx-
>   imately, superficially.
> ii One means the same
> iii because one understands the said jointly in the same
>   averageness.

In picture i, the link between understanding and the About-which is re-affirmed: they belong together in the 'primordial' sphere, which however is here achieved only 'approximately', superficially (*ungefähr*, *obenhin*). In the second and third pictures, with the play on one (*man*), we return to the sphere of averageness. Once again understanding is to be found here, but in the mode of averageness (*Durchschnittlichkeit*).

> IV
> i Hearing and understanding have attached themselves beforehand to the talked as such.

Here the 'average' negative ideality is formulated. Within it understanding has capitulated to an attachment to the talked. 'The talked as such' sufficiently identifies the 'average' realm: this is where the talk belongs. Understanding is capable of moving from one realm to another, something which talk can never do. Here it has debased itself by becoming attached to talk, Heidegger wants to liberate understanding from its attachment to talk.

> V
> i The communication does not 'communicate' the primary Being-covering of the talked-over beings,[10]
> ii rather, Being with-one-another moves itself into talking-with-one-another and into care[11] for the talked.

The negative in the first picture here suggests that 'communication' (*Mitteilung*) could communicate something of talked-about beings, but here, in the mode of talk, does not. This implies that communication could belong to both of Heidegger's spheres. The quotation marks around the word 'communicate' seem to suggest that this so-called 'communication' is no communication at all. In the second picture, Being-with-one-another (*Miteinandersein*) is explicitly shown to have capacities which go beyond its present state of talking-with-one-another (*miteinanderreden*). Thus Heidegger portrays talking-together as a lower state of human relationships.

> VI
> i For it lies therein (its reason is)
> ii that becomes talked.[12]

This enigmatic statement appears to refer to Being-with-one-another, and thus to restate picture Vii above. The curtness of the sentence suggests the impoverishment of Being, when talk becomes its be-all and end-all. But this sense of poverty, together with the sense of richness which is contrasted with it, is itself constituted through Heidegger's talk.

> VII
> The Being-said, the dictum, the saying now stand in for the
> genuineness and appropriateness-to-the-facts of the <u>talk</u> and
> of its <u>understanding</u>.

Here for the first time a notion of 'the genuineness of the talk' (*die Echtheit der Rede*) is put forward. In this context, 'genuine' talk and understanding are equated. However, this possibility is hypothetical in a way which the possibility of primordial understanding is not. We are here given a description of the state of affairs within 'average'-ness. In this sphere, 'Being said', 'dictum' and 'saying' are what assures the genuineness or authenticity (*Echtheit*) of the discourse and its appropriateness to facts or things (*Sachgemässheit*). These terms, then, should be placed within inverted commas (thus: 'genuineness', 'appropriateness to facts') to distinguish them from authenticity (*Eigentlichkeit*) and from the appropriation of entities in a primordial manner (*in der Weise der ursprünglichen Zeuignung dieses Seienden*).[13] They are the criteria which 'averageness' uses to evaluate talk, and the understanding of of talk, that is average understanding. They are not the primordial criteria with which to evaluate talk. Heidegger has not yet given us the latter criteria, and he will not be able to, since, within his scheme of things, talk cannot be primordial.

> VIII
> i And because the <u>talk</u> has lost or never won the primary
>   Being-covering of the <u>talked-over</u> beings
> ii it communicates itself not in the manner of the original
>   appropriation of this being
> iii but rather in the way of after- and repetitious-<u>talk</u>.

In the first picture here, Heidegger once more appears to present the possibility of an authentic talk, namely a talk which had 'won the primary Being-covering of the talked-over beings'. But again it is only a hypothetical possibility. It is not necessary for Heidegger that talk should ever achieve an original appropriation, for he says it may have 'never won' primordiality. (By contrast, in the third picture of stanza I he asserted the definite possibility of a primordial understanding: without this possibility, his talk would be pointless.)

If there were to be a primordial talk, it would be oriented to a reality other than itself. What is praised in the second picture here (by means of a negation) is a 'communication' (*teilen*) which is certainly not portrayed as the exercise of talk.[14] What is condemned in the third picture is the exercise of talk in pursuit of talk, and presumably talk about talk. But this condemns Heidegger's very text itself, which comprises precisely talk about talk.

IX

```
┌  i  The talked as such shows wider circles,           ┐
└  ii and takes over an authoritative Character.        ┘
```

A form of social criticism is here posed as the ground of Heidegger's text. Heidegger attacks the 'authority' which appeals to talk as such. For Heidegger as for Blum, the only legitimate appeal would be made to a reality beyond the talk which cannot be addressed in the talk itself. Yet this has always been the appeal of 'authority', justified in particular by 'theological' speech, which remains a predominant ideological tendency today.[15]

It is precisely when talk can be scrutinized as the real basis of authority, that it is possible for that authority to be questioned, and challenged. By placing authority beyond talk, Heidegger places it beyond question and challenge.

X

```
┌  i  The thing is so,                                  ┐
└  ii because one says it.                              ┘
```

This sentence, '*Die Sache ist so, weil man es sagt*', is the only one in the text which makes neither use of, nor reference to any use of compounds of *reden* or *verstehen*. Momentarily, Heidegger steps out of the interplay of these words. The sentence exhibits a play of its own. The words create a sense of repetition: '*Die Sache ist so, weil man es sagt*'. Within the play of the sentence – of this voice which makes a single brief appearance – 'Sache' (thing) and 'sagt' (saying, word) are one.

This is not the voice of averageness, for it makes a connection which Heidegger's 'idle talk' could never make. It grounds speech in something other than itself, namely 'the thing'. Neither is it the voice of primordiality, for there is here ease rather then struggle. What appears here is neither of Heidegger's unattainable ideal speeches. It is rather the only glimpse within the text of the real ground which Heidegger occupies, and from within which the production of his ideals (his claimed grounds) is possible. *The thing is, because one says it* expresses the reality of what Heidegger does with language, namely that he follows through the consequences of the view that things are as they are said to be.

These words interrupt Heidegger's text. The text up to now has asserted that there is thought without talk, which is a version of 'heaven' and that there is talk without thought, which is a version of 'hell'. Heidegger has sought to escape from talk to thought: an impossible quest typical of the search for philosophical certainty as it has been pursued within traditional metaphysics.[16] *The thing is because one says it* breaks with this search. It defines no philosophical certainty. It proclaims that truth is what it is said to be within language.

Idealism and materialism

'Averageness' versus 'primordiality' defines an idealism: Derrida was able to tell us that. *The thing is because one says it* defines a materialist practice of language. With it we can enquire: how does 'one' say idealisms, ideologies? We can address this enquiry to Heidegger's own idealism.

XI

[i In such after-and repetitious-<u>talk</u>, through which the
     already at-the-beginning lack of groundedness rises to full
     groundlessness,
 ii idle <u>talk</u> constitutes itself.]

As in stanza VIII the first picture here apparently conceives a talk which moves from a lack of groundedness to full groundedness (*Bodenständigkeit*) instead of to groundlessness (*Bodenslösigkeit*). But here again, it is not necessary for Heidegger that talk should ever achieve that end – which, he now tells us, it lacked 'at-the-beginning' (*anfängliche*). And again it would have to be quite an other talk than that of Heidegger himself here: for the repetition of the word 'groundlessness' is clearly no substitute for the pursuit of grounds.

XII

[i And indeed, this does not remain restricted to audible
     after-<u>talk</u>
 ii but broadens itself out into the <u>written</u>, where it appears as
     'idle <u>writing</u>'[17]]

Here, Heidegger's argument that talk pertains to 'averageness' *per se* broadens itself out into writing . . .

XIII

[i Here the after-<u>talk</u> grounds itself not so much in heresay.
 ii It plays itself out of idle reading.[18]]

. . . and into reading, hence to language in general.

XIV

[i The average <u>understanding</u> of readers will never be able to
     know
 ii what is primordially created and acquired
iii and what is after-<u>talked</u>.]

Here the theme of stanza I is repeated. Average understanding is trapped within the talked, unable even to recognize the sphere of 'primordial creation', if it encounters its products.

> XV
> i Further, average <u>understanding</u> will certainly not want such a distinction,
> ii not need it
> iii because, of course, it <u>understands</u> all.

Here average understanding has become talk: it knows no other possibility. Therefore – so far as it knows – it knows all there is to know.

For Heidegger, then, average understanding has forgotten the distinction between talk and what is other than talk. But, for us, it is quite correct not to want this distinction, nor in the previous stanza, to know it when it supposedly encounters it. There is no way in which talk can present the distinction between talk and what is other than talk. Heidegger has not presented this distinction to it, and there is no way in which he could do so.

Talk and understanding

Heidegger presents the talk of 'understanding' to the talk of 'talk'. Only talk can portray the appearance of both 'talk' and 'understanding' yet Heidegger suggests that understanding apprehends the reality of both. We, his readers, are invited to enter into complicity with the dominance of understanding over talk. We are asked to maintain in our talk too that our talk is only the appearance of a reality external to talk.

Blum enters into complicity with this dominance quite openly. He would talk only for the sake of experiencing the limits of talk. Derrida's complicity is more hidden. He would write only for the sake of writing. Surprisingly, it is Heidegger who interrupts the complicity into which he invites us. His ironic *the thing is so because one says it* shows the way out of the talk into which he has led us.

The new aphorism, intended to express the epitome of 'average understandability', shares the same structure as the one with which we began, which was intended to provoke 'primordial understanding':

> i
> The thing is so   *Die Sache ist so*
> ii
> because one says it   *weil man es sagt*

The two pictures are united by a word-play on *Sache/sagt*. Grammatically, picture i ('the thing is so') makes sense independently of picture ii. On the other hand, picture ii ('because one says it') requires picture i to complete its sense, i.e. to explicate the sense of 'it'.[19] Thus the sense of picture ii is dependent on that of picture i, i.e. picture ii refers to picture i. This may be represented diagrammatically thus:

(i)   ii

Grammatically, picture i formulates the reality of which picture ii formulates the appearance.

Logically, the reverse relationship is found. The train of thought is, 'the thing is so because – something'. We wait to see what this 'something' is, expecting to be shown something outside ourselves in the world which will explain it. But Heidegger surprises us by pointing us back to the remark itself. The 'because' sets up a logical relation of dependence of 'the thing is so' upon 'one says it'. Thus the logical structure reverses the grammatical structure. It may be represented thus:

i   (ii)

Logically, picture ii formulates the reality of which picture i formulates the appearance.

Here, as in the aphorism, 'the most thought-provoking thing is that we are not thinking', Heidegger speaks with two voices, joined by a word-play. In the first, he says 'the thing is so because X'. In the second, he says 'one says it'. The reader would be undisturbed by this if it was clear which was reality and which was appearance. Thus the statement 'one says it because the thing is so' would make picture i unambiguously the reality and picture ii unambiguously the appearance. Likewise the statement 'what one says is so' would make picture ii unambiguously the reality and picture i unambiguously the appearance. With either of these, one could agree or disagree. But again the aphorism disrupts the usual relationship between appearance and reality, refusing to allow us to determine in its terms which is one and which is the other.

The issue which the aphorisms address is not, as appears in their own terms, the relation between speech (thinking, saying) and a reality external to speech (things), but the relation between different speeches. Both insist on the irreducibility of one speech to another, and thereby disrupt the dependence of one speech on another which is the way in which speech points to a reality beyond itself. But they thereby disrupt the way in which Heidegger points to a reality, 'understanding', beyond that of 'talk'.

The discourse on idle talk can now be read, not as addressing the relation between talk and a reality beyond talk called 'understand-ing', but as exhibiting a relation between two speeches. It is clear that this is not the way in which we did read it. Rather, we imposed upon the talk our own interpretation, namely that talk was real, and 'understanding' being a reality beyond the talk, was only apparent. We were thereby ourselves idealistic, in failing to acknowledge that 'understanding' was a reality within Heidegger's talk, irrespective of the question of an external reality corresponding to it. It is clear also what was the source of this interpretation. It arose in our 'average intelligibility' reading of Heidegger's text, and has been perpetuated ever since.

To use Heidegger's words ironically, it is now possible to break with this 'averageness' and reach 'primordiality'. To speak more seriously, it is possible to break with idealist interpretation, and achieve a materialist interruption of the text. Heidegger explicates not a 'reality' and an 'appearance', a 'language' and an 'extra-linguistic reality' but two voices, each perpetually in search of, but unable, to find or to overcome the other.[20]

The subtlety of what is here done with language transcends the banality of what is said. Heidegger says 'primordial' and 'average', but the unattainability of these ideals is shown by his own practice of language. Each would arise out of the separation of one discourse from another. But a practice of language having no relation to other practices of language is inconceivable. Heidegger plunges us into the midst of a play of languages, denying to us any secure sense of an outside reality to which we can cling, unless we remain outside that text, trapped within our own illusion of a reality outside the play of languages. The illusion may even take the form of a reality of 'language' itself.

But if an external reading fails to grasp Heidegger's writing, does it not also fail to grasp that of Derrida and Blum? We have already attempted to practice what Derrida calls 'two hearings' of Heideg-ger's texts. Can we then not employ the same approach to his own? We previously identified the ideal of a purely unreferential text as the 'reality' to which Derrida was striving, away from the 'appear-ance' of referential speaking within which he found himself immersed. If these are both ideals, then a materialist reading of Derrida would attempt to show what reality is produced from their pursuit. We propose that the reality is a play of speeches, referring to each other in contradictory ways which permit no speech domi-nance over others. In this case attention should focus not on the ideal of escaping all reference to otherness, which Derrida says he pursues, but on the practice of exhibiting new forms of such reference which is what Derrida does.

In the case of Blum, we earlier accepted Derrida's judgment of 'Platonism', as applied to the 'primordial'/'derivative' distinction which, in the guise of 'analytic'/'concrete', or 'One'/'Many', appears in his writing. But to speak of 'Platonism' is to prejudge the reading of Plato. The point of reading Blum, or Plato, would be to show what shift in discourse their writing really achieved under the guise of apparently pursuing the 'analytic', the 'One', or simply the 'Idea'.

In Heidegger's terms, we have yet to engage in a 'struggle with primordial sources' and draw more than an 'average understanding' from these texts, as we have attempted to do with his own. But against Heidegger's understanding of these terms, the 'sources' with which we consider struggle to be necessary are the words which Blum, Derrida, and Plato have written, and rather than an 'understanding' as a state of mind apart from the text, what we seek to achieve is a new text. What Heidegger has shown us is that a text demands a struggle to release it from 'understanding', and in particular from that of the author himself.

Appendix

(Heidegger, 1972, p. 167)

I

i Gemäss der durchschnittlichen Verständlichkeit die in der beim Sichaussprechen gesprochenen Sprache schon liegt

ii kann die mitgeteilte Rede weitgehend verstanden werden

iii ohne dass sich der Hörende in ein ursprünglich verstehendes Sein zum Worüber der Rede bringt.

II

i Man versteht nicht so sehr das beredete Seiende,

ii sondern man hört schon nur auf das Geredete als solches.

III

i Dieses wird verstanden, das Worüber nur ungefähr, obenhin;

ii man meint dasselbe,

iii weil man das Gesagte gemeinsam in derselben Durchschnittlichkeit versteht.

IV

i Das Hören und Verstehen hat sich vorgängig an das Geredete als solches geklammert.

V

i Die Mitteilung 'teilt' nicht den primären Seinsbezug zum

beredeten Seienden

ii sondern das Miteinandersein bewegt sich im Miteinanderreden und Besorgen des Geredeten.

VI

i Ihm liegt daran,

ii dass geredet wird.

VII

i Das Gesagtsein, das Diktum, der Ausspruch stehen jetzt ein
für die Echtheit und Sachgemässheit der Rede und ihres
Verständnisses.

VIII

i Und weil das Reden den primären Seinsbezug zum beredeten Seienden verloren beziehungsweise nie gewonnen hat,

ii teilt es sich nicht mit in der Weise der ursprünglichen
Zeugnung dieses Seienden,

iii sondern auf dem Wege des Weiter- und Nachredens.

IX

i Das Geredete als solches zieht weitere Kreise und über-
nimmt autorittien Charakter.

X

i Die Sache ist so,

ii weil man es sagt.

XI

i In solchem Nach- und Weiterreden,
dadurch sich das schon anfängliche Fehlen der Bodenständigkeit zur völligen Bodenslösigkeit steigert,

ii konstituiert sich das Gerede.

XII

i Und zwar bleibt dieses nicht eingeschränkt auf das lautliche
Nachreden,

ii sondern breitet sich aus im Geschreibenen als das
'Geschreibe'.

XIII

i Das Nachreden gründet hier nicht so sehr in einem Hören-
sagen.

ii Es spielt sich aus dem Angelesen.

XIV

i Das durchschnittliche Verständnis des Lesers wird nie
entscheiden können,

ii was ursprünglich geschöpft und errungen und was nach-
geredet ist.

XV

i Noch mehr,
durchschnittliches Verständnis wird ein solches Unter-
scheiden gar nicht wollen,

ii seiner nicht bedürfen,

iii weil es ja alles versteht.

Notation:

======= indicates play on verstehen and its compounds
_____ indicates play on reden and its compounds
------- indicates localized play on other compounds within the text.

I, II, III etc. (capital Roman numerals) indicate *stanzas*
i, ii, iii etc. (lower case Roman numerals) indicate *pictures*.

Notes

1 Cf. Chapter 5 above.

2 The distinction between 'saying' and 'doing' here derives in the first instance from Austin (1962), but we are using it in a sense more particularly due to Garfinkel and Sacks (1970).

3 'Ethno-methodology' is that science which takes as its object folk *methodologies,* that is, ways of solving the problem of social order, i.e. of being everyday sociologists. What we are attempting here might be called 'ethno-ontology', which takes as its object folk *ontologies,* that is, ways of being everyday philosophers. Cf. Garfinkel (1967).

4 Derrida's *arche* has been rendered as 'origin', cf. Heidegger's *der Ursprung,* 'the primordial'. *Verfallen* has been rendered as 'fallenness'.

5 *Arche* is again rendered as 'origin'.

6 For copyright reasons, the text is presented here in abbreviated form.

7 The text is analysed into *stanzas* and their constituent *pictures* using the method employed from Chapter 1 above onwards. A German version of the analysis will be found in the Appendix. As explained there, double broken underlining indicates verstehen compounds, single underlining indicates reden compounds, and single broken underlining indicates localized word-play within the text. In analysing the text, we have often departed from Macquarrie and Robinson's translation, not in any hope of 'improving' upon their elegant English, but rather the reverse: to reveal in an unavoidably clumsy manner the word-plays and grammatical structures which Heidegger employs in his own language.

8 Macquarrie and Robinson have 'the language which is spoken when one expresses oneself'. We have rewritten this to reveal the word-play on speak (*sprechen*).

9 Cf. further discussion in connection with stanzas V and VIII below.

10 Mitteilung and teilung. 'Imparting' and 'impart' might be better translations. Macquarrie and Robinson have 'Communication "imparts" '.

11 *Besorge*. Perhaps better translated as 'provision', however it is important to note its links with *Sorge*, a central word in *Being and Time*.

12 '*Ihm liegt daran, dass geredet wird*'. The expression, '*es liegt daran dass*' is an everyday phrase meaning 'the reason is that'. Replacing *es* ('it') by *ihm* ('to' or 'for' it or him) seems to produce the sense, '*Its* reason is, that becomes talked'. Macquarrie and Robinson expand these six words to 'To this Being-with-one-another, the fact that talking is going on is a matter of consequence'.

13 Macquarrie and Robinson stress the distinction between *echtlich* and *eigentlich* at n. 3, p. 24 of their translation. Yet they perpetuate a confusion when, having explained that they will write 'authentically' for *eigentlich*, and 'genuinely' for *echtlich*, they continue, 'the reader must not confuse this kind of "authenticity" with the kind which belongs to an "authentic text" or "authentic account".' There appears to be no discussion of an 'authentic text' or 'authentic account' in *Being and Time*, in the *eigentlich* sense of the term. An indication of this is given in Macquarrie and Robinson's index, which lists fifteen entries under 'authentic understanding', but none under 'authentic' talk, text, speech or other linguistic phenomenon.

14 *Teilen* means to divide, part, or share, as in *er würde sein letztes Stück Brot teilen* ('he would share his last crust'). As already noted, *mitteilen* means 'to communicate'. As suggested in the discussion of stanza V above, it is a word which Heidegger allows to move between his two realms. It would seem well suited for this purpose, since by virtue of its autonomy from any notion of verbal message, it appears to evoke an original sharing prior to speech.

15 Cf. Chapter 2 above, and also Torode (1976).

16 Cf. the lines from Stefan George's poem 'The Word', which Heidegger discusses in 'The Nature of Language', in *On the Way to Language* (1971):

> So I renounced, and sadly see:
> Where word breaks off no thing may be.

In commentary on this poem, Heidegger states, *inter alia*, first that he wants to 'face a possibility of undergoing an experience with language such that our relation to language would in future become memorable, worthy of thought' (p. 107), and second, by way of commentary on the last line of the poem, 'the breaking up of the word is the true step back on the way of thinking' (p. 109). These two themes, namely the concern with the experience brought about by language and the necessity to depart from the word in order to begin to 'think', may be compared directly with those found in our present reading of *Being and Time*.

17 *Geschreibe*, having exactly the same etymological relation to *Geschreiben*, 'the written', as *Gerede*, 'idle talk' has to *Geredete*, 'the talked'

18 *dem Angelesenen*.

19 Grammatically, the conjunction 'because' is part of neither clause in the sentence, but links the two.

20 For a later explication of this theme, cf. Heidegger's 'Conversation with a Japanese enquirer', in *On the Way to Language* (1971).

Bibliography

Austin, J. (1962), *How to do Things with Words*, Oxford: Clarendon Press.

Blum, A. (1974), *Theorising,* London: Heinemann.

Derrida, J. (1970), 'Ousia and Gramme: a note to a footnote in *Being and Time*', in F.J. Smith, ed., *Phenomenology in Perspective,* The Hague: Nijhoff.

Garfinkel, H. (1967), *Studies in Ethnomethodology,* Englewood Cliffs: Prentice-Hall.

Garfinkel, H. and Sacks, H. (1970), 'On Formal Structures of Practical Action', in S. McKinney and E. Tiryakian, *Theoretical Sociology*, New York: Appleton-Century-Crofts.

Heidegger, M. (1967), *Being and Time,* trans. J. Macquarrie and E. Robinson, Oxford: Basil Blackwell.

Heidegger, M. (1968), *What is called Thinking?,* New York: Harper and Row.

Heidegger, M. (1971), *On the Way to Language,* New York: Harper and Row.

Heidegger, M. (1972), *Sein und Zeit,* Tübingen: Niemeyer Verlag.

Husserl, E. (1931), *Ideas: General Introduction to Pure Phenomenology,* London: Allen and Unwin.

Torode, B. (1976), 'The Revelation of a Theory of the Social World as Grammar', in R. Harré, ed., *Life Sentences,* London: Wiley.

part IV

Language and society

Ethnomethodology, discussed here with reference to Schutz, Garfinkel, and Sacks, has a critique of the 'documentary method' of interpretation employed by sociology. This is unfortunately incomplete. Idealized and unchangeable underlying social structures, such as 'sex', are Sacks's presumption for the analysis of conversations. Instead, the interruption of speeches locates specific and changeable practices which constitute structures that are more theological than sociological in character.

chapter 7

The essentialism of ethnomethodology

Life versus thought in Schutz

Alfred Schutz uses the method of phenomenology to advance upon
Max Weber's account of social action. His discussion centres on a
single distinction. 'Weber', states Schutz (1974), 'makes no distinction between the *action,* considered as something in progress, and
the completed *act'*. Schutz distinguishes these as 'life' and 'thought',
in the following terms (ibid., pp. 69–70):

> Thought is focussed on the objects of the spatio-temporal world;
> life pertains to duration. The tension between the two is of the
> essence of the 'meaningfulness' of experience. It is misleading to
> say that experiences *have* meaning . . . . Rather, those experi-
> ences are meaningful which are grasped reflectively. The mean-
> ing is the *way* in which Ego regards its experience. The meaning
> lies in the attitude of the Ego towards that part of its stream of
> consciousness which has already flowed by.

This distinction seems familiar.[1] For Schutz as for Husserl, the
ongoing immersion in life of the immanent 'psychological ego' is
contrasted with the reflective, timeless detachment of the 'transcendental ego'. But Husserl himself was not consistent as to his own
location within this distinction: in one work he took up,
methodologically, an immanentist position: in the other, he took up
methodologically a transcendentalist position. We have proposed,
in opposition to each of these, a 'real'-ist position.

It is important to establish what position Schutz himself adopts.
'Lived experience', for Schutz, is rich and complex, but it can never
apprehend itself. All apprehension of it takes place at the level of
reflected thought. This applies to the man-in-the-street thinking
about his experiences as much as it does to the phenomenologist
theorizing about experience in general. 'Thought' takes place at the

level of reflection. Experience cannot be grasped and is always elusive. But if these two are to be distinguished as *transcendent* reality versus *immanent* appearance, which is which? Here is a surprising reversal of the analysis of Husserl: it is *experience* which is real, whereas *thought* presents only the appearance of this reality. By contrast, in the developed viewpoint of Husserl's *Meditations,* experience grasped the mere immanent appearance of a reality knowable only in thought.

In the light of this distinction, consider Schutz's treatment of the problem of understanding other people. He distinguishes two cases. On the one hand, there is the case where I read or hear about the actions of another person, without being there myself. In this case, I have to deal in judgments about the other: my knowledge is and remains a knowledge of types. But there is another case, namely that of face-to-face interaction, where I directly observe the ongoing actions of the other as they occur. Here, says Schutz, *we* meet in lived experience. A special and precise form of knowledge of the other person is here possible. Schutz portrays the situation in this way (1971b, p. 29):

> Since he is confronting me in person, the range of symptoms by which I apprehend his consciousness includes much more than what he is communicating to me purposefully. I observe his movements, gestures, and facial expressions. I hear the intonation and the rhythm of his utterances. Each phase of my consciousness is co-ordinated with a phase of my partner's. Since I perceive the continuous manifestations of my partner's conscious life, I am continuously attuned to it. One highly important consequence of this state of affairs is that my partner is given to me more vividly and in a sense more 'directly' than I apprehend myself. Since I 'know' my past, I 'know' myself in infinitely greater detail than anyone else. Yet this is knowledge in retrospect, in reflection: it is not direct and vivid experience. Hence while I am straightforwardly engaged in the business of life, my own self is not present to me in an equally wide range of symptoms as is a fellow-man whom I confront in the Here and Now of a concrete We-relation.

In the We-relation, Schutz states, a sharing of lived-experience occurs. We 'grow older together'. This relationship then has a special importance, neglected by those social theorists who conceive of social relationships purely on the reflective level, in terms of types. For Schutz, this apprehension of the other is not the outcome of reflection or judgment. It is 'pre-predicative', in Husserl's term. In direct experience, I apprehend what the other says and does as he does so. I experience this ongoing action as 'his' stream of consciousness, his lived experience. I live through my own stream of experience but I do not experience it as 'mine', though I could do so by disengaging from the shared lived experience and engaging in a private reflection.

In everyday experience we believe that we know when the other's attention wanders in this way. But when attention is reciprocated, we experience an interweaving of subjectivities in a single stream: not *my* subjectivity, nor *yours*, but *ours:* this is intersubjectivity.

Plainly, this state of affairs can be located within the range of alternative visions of the social world portrayed by Husserl.[2] It is the world in which men are certain of the correspondence between consciousness and consciousness, and so any possible consciousness, and so, the world. It is, then, the world which Husserl portrayed in his *Cartesian Meditations* as the utopian *telos* of history, the end-of-the world vision of a society in which all men are transcendental phenomenologists, and apprehend one another as such.

But what status does Schutz ascribe to this world? Is it an ideal vision of an interpersonal relationship which we occasionally glimpse, perhaps in a fleetingly intimate sharing of understanding with another person whom we know deeply, even love? Or is it, less optimistically, a vision of a relationship unattainable in the fallen state of our present society, a picture of social life in a yet-to-be-attained utopia, or with God in the Kingdom of Heaven?

Not so, for Schutz. For him the we-relationship is not hard to attain. It is indeed impossible to avoid, in so far as we engage in any social encounter, however brief, with another person. The we-relationship, according to Schutz, characterizes our everyday dealings with all other members of our society. For him it *is* the 'natural' attitude of everyday life.

In Schutz, Husserl's transcendentalist vision has been made mundane.[3] One implication of this is particularly crucial. For Husserl the utopia was to be attained, historically, through the discipline of thought. For Schutz by contrast, this utopia is already available in the indiscipline of experience. Whereas Husserl's rationalist vision implies the necessity of changing society, Schutz's irrationalist vision implies the impossibility of doing so. For Schutz, we already live in the best of all possible worlds, in utopia, in heaven. Only the I thinks it does not.

Multiple realities

Intersubjectivity is not the only reality which Schutz explores.

Inspired by the account of 'multiple realities' given by William James, Schutz suggests (1971a, p. 207):

> There are several, probably an infinite number of various orders of realities, each with its own special and separate style of existence: the world of sense of physical things, the world of science, . . . the worlds of sheer madness and vagary. The popular mind conceives of all these . . . more or less disconnectedly, and *when dealing with one of them forgets for the time being its relations to the rest.* But every object we think of is . . . referred to one of these subworlds.

Schutz refers to these 'orders of realities' as *finite provinces of meaning.* Examples would be 'wide-awakeness', 'dreams', 'film', the world of a 'novel', the worlds of 'science', and so on. Each of us encounters very many different provinces of meaning during the course of a day, and the shift from one to another is experienced, in Kierkegaard's term, as an existential 'shock', or 'leap'. (I am writing at my typewriter, for instance, absorbed in my work, when there is a knock on the door.) These provinces may be distinguished by means of several parameters of which two are pre-eminent for the purposes of the present argument. These are 'accent of reality', and 'mode of sociality'.

The notion of a specific 'accent of reality' is one which James himself put forward, and it has an intuitive significance in for example the comparison between 'joking' and 'serious' talk. But Schutz is able to give it a more precise sense. He proposes, adapting Husserl's methodological notion, that we may regard each accent of reality as sustained by a specific *epoche* of its own. This idea is highly suggestive because it promises to enable Husserl's immanent and transcendent realms, to be located in relation to everyday experience. What then of the reality which Husserl considered to be the core of everyday experience itself, the 'natural' attitude? Schutz suggests that this attitude should be considered a finite province of meaning, one of special importance. He discusses its epoche as follows (ibid., p. 229):

> Phenomenology has taught us the concept of the phenomenological *epoche*, the suspension of our belief in the world as a device to overcome the natural attitude by radicalizing the Cartesian method of philosophical doubt. The suggestion may be ventured that man within the natural attitude also uses a specific epoche, of course quite another one than the phenomenologist. He does not suspend belief in the outer world and its objects, but on the contrary, he suspends doubt in its existence. What he puts in

brackets is the doubt that the world and its objects might be otherwise than it appears to him. We propose to call this epoche, the *epoche of the natural attitude.*

Schutz, then, defines the epoche of the natural attitude as the diametric opposite of the phenomenological epoche. But which phenomenological epoche is this? It is, of course, none other than the immanentist reduction of Husserl's *Ideas,* the suspension of the 'general thesis of the natural standpoint'.

What, then, is the epoche of the natural attitude? Man within the 'natural attitude' for Schutz, suspends doubt that the world might be otherwise than it appears: not only to him as one individual, but to any individual, since this 'natural' attitude is intersubjective. But this does not refer to the mundane world as we have defined it – within that world, issues of 'truth' and 'falsity' are burning topics of conversation. It is, rather, the epoche of the transcendentalist stance, wherein correspondence between consciousness and consciousness, any consciousness, and so with world, is presumed. Thus it is confirmed that, in Schutz's vision, the 'natural' attitude is Husserl's attitude of transcendentalism.

But now a broader conclusion follows. For, having defined two polar opposite provinces of meaning, with reference to their accents of reality, Schutz now makes this opposition the principle of organization of all provinces of meaning.

He states that the specific epoche governing each and every other province of meaning can be considered as a further epoche applied to that of the natural attitude (ibid., p. 233), 'which suspend belief in more and more layers of the reality of daily life, putting them in brackets.' This process cannot continue indefinitely, but will terminate when the existence of the external world itself is put in brackets, namely, when it reaches the immanentist reduction explored by Husserl in *Ideas.* Thus, implicit within Schutz's analysis, is a theory of the constitution of reality within the world of daily life which complements and extends Husserl's account to a greater extent than Schutz himself appeared to realize. It is that Husserl's 'immanentist' and 'transcendentalist' spheres define the extreme possibilities of a continuum of provinces of meaning ranging from the philosophical to the practical, all of which are available to the adventurous consciousness.[4]

Consider now the notion of 'mode of sociality'. For Schutz, as has been shown, the 'natural' attitude, which in this respect corresponds to Husserl's transcendentalist vision, is characterized by intersubjectivity, the fullest form of communication possible with others. The opposite pole of the continuum, which in this respect corresponds to Husserl's immanentist reduced realm, is characterized by the least degree of communication possible with others.

To give a clear characterization of this 'least degree of communication' presents difficulties. For if in the immanentist realm I experience only my unique subjectivity, then I can presumably communicate nothing of it to you: if I claim to do so, I thereby deny its claimed uniqueness.[5] Is it in fact possible to communicate clearly the details of any 'province of meaning' one of whose characteristics is that within it, less than completely clear communication is possible? Schutz himself shows ambiguity over this issue. His tendency is, in fact, to argue that communication is only possible at all within the intersubjective 'natural' attitude, but then to retreat from this position with somewhat ambiguous qualifications. Consider three of these arguments.

First, Schutz asserts repeatedly – it is perhaps his most famous slogan – that the world is 'from the outset' an intersubjective world. We are – all of us – born into the world of the 'natural' attitude, and that is where we remain, in all our interpersonal dealings throughout our lives, unless we take specific steps to the contrary. The everyday intersubjective world is portrayed as a trouble-free zone: it is hard to understand why anyone would want to leave it. The practical man, getting on with the business of living would have no reason to do so. Only people engaging in psychological and philosophical speculations – people enquiring, perhaps into the 'phenomenology of the social world', or into other esoteric problems – would wish to do so. 'The natural attitude', Schutz states (ibid., p. 208):

> does not know these problems. To it, the world is from the outset not the private world of the single individual, but an intersubjective world, common to all of us, in which we have not a theoretical, but an eminently practical interest.

This is perhaps the weakest statement of the problem which is found in Schutz, in this sense: it does not rule out communication in other realms, but portrays such communication as a disturbance to the smooth running of everyday life.

Schutz's second formulation hinges on the question of language. He argues (ibid., p. 233), that language *per se* pertains to the intersubjective world of the 'natural' attitude, and as such 'obstinately resists serving as a vehicle for meanings which transcend its own presuppositions'. This implies that *thought* is for Schutz something quite other than *language*. The former is private, the latter public.

This distinction seems to preclude any voice other than that of the natural attitude. It implies that, for Schutz, the status of his own writing is that of the 'natural attitude' as he defines it. We propose, by contrast, that Schutz articulates the unrealistic vision of heaven. As against this utopianism, it is possible to venture an alternative suggestion. Everyday language can be correctly located at neither immanentist nor transcendentalist pole. It belongs to neither extreme. Language is capable of conjuring up both immanent and transcendent possibilities. Schutz's language conjures up one of these – the utopia of transcendentalism.

Schutz's third formulation is his strongest. In the posthumously published writing entitled, *The Problem of Relevance,* he asserts that the 'natural' attitude (1970, p. 125) 'is the paramount reality because only within it are sociality and intrahuman communication at all possible'.

It is interesting that, in an editorial note at this point, R. M. Zaner states, 'This sentence was marked for deletion.' Schutz, it seems, was unhappy with this statement which seems to impose an implausible straitjacket on the possibilities of the social world. But within the terms of the position which he had set out to explore, he had no alternative but to make it.

The solitary scientist

Schutz's conventionally acknowledged importance is as a philosopher of social science. His location of the social scientist within his scheme has been subjected to critique by Barry Hindess. Hindess questions Schutz's suggestion that the social scientist is engaged in no more than the construction of yet another province of meaning.

Hindess is disturbed by the implications of the position which, he says, portrays 'a world in which there can be no science of history and no rational politics' (1972, p. 1). He diagnoses Schutz's failing as 'psychologism'. To make this interpretation, he takes note of this remark by Schutz (op. cit., pp. 257–8):

> The finite provinces of meaning are not separated states of mental life in the sense that passing from one to another would require a transmigration of the soul and a complete extinction of memory and consciousness by death . . . . They are merely names for different tensions of one and the same consciousness. . . .
>
> Experiences in various provinces can be remembered and reproduced. And that is why they can be communicated in ordinary language.

Hindess concludes, 'Thus relationships between the provinces of history and of social science exist only in the consciousness of the knowing subject – or in books or papers that he may have written (op. cit., p. 20).

But relationships in consciousness, and in books, and papers, for that matter, are precisely the topic of Schutz's, and of any, phenomenological enquiry. Before the charge of psychologism can be accepted, it will be necessary to examine Schutz's account of the relationship between the 'natural' attitude of everyday life and the attitude of 'social science'. He discusses this problem at several points throughout his work.

In the *Phenomenology of the Social World,* Schutz argues (1974, p. 241):

> All scientific knowledge of the social world is indirect: it is knowledge of the world of contemporaries and the world of predecessors, never of the world of immediate social reality. Accordingly, the social sciences can understand man in his everyday social life not as a living individual person with a unique consciousness but only as a personal ideal type without duration [of lived experience] or spontaneity. They can understand him only as existing within an impersonal and anonymous objective time which no one ever has, or ever can, experience . . . . Since the social sciences . . . never actually encounter real people but deal only in personal ideal types, it is not the social scientist's function to understand the subjective meaning of another's action.

It is often assumed that, as a 'phenomenological social philosopher', Schutz advocated a 'phenomenological social science'. Nothing could be further from the truth. In his view, expressed in this early work and unchanged throughout his life, the social scientist's task was the specification of the 'objective meaning contexts of subjective meaning contexts', and of all the social sciences economics exemplified this ideal (ibid., p. 245):

> In our view, pure economics is a perfect example of an objective-meaning complex about subjective meaning-complexes, in other words, of an objective meaning-configuration stipulating the typical and invariant subjective experiences of anyone who acts within an economic framework.

Such a social science plainly aspires to transcendentalism by seeking to give an account of the necessary conditions of any possible experience in the given social situation. But then it is only describing a state which everyday life has already achieved.

Whereas Husserl's transcendental phenomenology is out in front, criticizing the 'natural' attitude for its lack of self-knowledge, Schutz's social science is one step behind. Its task is to celebrate the self-knowledge exhibited by everyday life, exemplified by the pre-dictability of subjective experience within the present economic order. Even this task it can only perform imperfectly. There seems little doubt, then, about the location of social science within the range of provinces of meaning as Schutz defines it. The solitary scientist has retreated from the transcendent reality of *life* to the immanent appearance of *thought*.

This conclusion is reiterated in Schutz's later discussions of this problem which consider the social scientist's account of human beings in the social world. Schutz tells us (1971a, p. 255) that:

> The theoretical thinker while remaining in the theoretical attitude cannot experience originarily and grasp in immediacy the world of everyday life within which I and you, Peter and Paul, anyone and everyone have confused and ineffable perceptions, act, work, plan, worry, hope, are born, grow up, and will die, in a word live their life . . . in their full humanity. *This world eludes the immediate grasp of the theoretical social* scientist.

He 'has to build up an artificial device', the method of the social sciences, which substitutes for the intersubjective life-world a model of this world (ibid., p. 255).

> This model, however, is not peopled with human beings in their full humanity, but with puppets, with *types*: they are constructed as though they could perform working actions and reactions . . . .
> Of course, these working actions and reactions are merely fic-titious: . . . they are only assigned to these puppets by the grace of the scientist.

We argue that the range of provinces of meaning which Schutz has defined is, in fact, available to all of us within everyday language itself. It may then be suggested that the theoretical construction of models, peopled with puppets, is not the exclusive achievement of the solitary social scientist, but is rather practiced by us all, in so far as within our speech we refer to other persons, or even to ourselves. Thus, *pace*, Hindess, relationships between the provinces of history and of social science exist in historical and social linguistic practices which can in principle be made available to all. It is these practices which we are engaged in investigating.

Ethnomethodological sociology

In these terms an attempt can be made to locate Harold Garfinkel's 'ethnomethodology', the sociology which works most closely with the issues raised by Schutz. Garfinkel calls attention to the concern for 'reality' held not simply by 'professional' philosophers or other theorists, but also by lay 'members' 'accomplishing' such reality in everyday life. To this extent, his concern is identical with ours. But Garfinkel puts a particular interpretation on this concern. For him, the 'members' and the 'professionals' are doing 'sociology'. Garfinkel states (1967, p. vii):

> Ethnomethodological studies analyse everyday activities as members' methods for making those same activities visibly-rational-and-reportable-for-all-practical-purposes, i.e. 'accountable', as organizations of commonplace everyday activities. The reflexivity of that phenomenon is a singular feature of practical actions, of practical circumstances, of commonsense knowledge of social structures, and of practical sociological reasoning. By permitting us to locate and examine their occurrence, the reflexivity of that phenomenon establishes their study.

Members' methods then, make their activities accountable 'for-all-practical-purposes'. This concern with 'practicality' can be precisely located within the scheme deriving from Schutz.

In Schutz's view, the main alternative to the 'practical', or 'everyday' attitude was the 'theoretical' viewpoint of the philosopher or social scientist. But Garfinkel has little to say about the latter realm. The study of everyday activities, he states (ibid., p. viii):

> is directed to the tasks of learning how members' actual, ordinary, activities consist of methods to make practical actions, practical circumstances, commonsense knowledge of social structures, and practical sociological reasoning analysable; and of discovering the formal properties of commonplace, practical commonsense actions *'from within'* actual settings, as ongoing accomplishments of those settings. *The formal properties obtain their guarantees from no other source, and in no other way.* Because this is so, our study tasks cannot be accomplished by free invention, constructive analytic theorising, mock-ups, or book reviews, *and so no special interest is paid to them aside from an interest in their varieties as organizationally situated methods of practical reasoning.* Similarly, there can be nothing to quarrel with or to correct about practical sociological reasoning, and so, because professional sociological enquiries are practical through

and through, except that quarrels between those doing professional enquiries and ethnomethodology may be of interest as phenomena for ethnomethodological studies, these quarrels need not be taken seriously.

Garfinkel himself, then, inhabits the same world which we all inhabit: a practical world through and through. There is 'no other source' than this practicality for the very standards of reasoned analysis by which everyday activities can be approached. Those who set themselves up as superior to those everyday standards are brought down to size abruptly: 'no special interest is paid to them' except as themselves examples of practicality. The ethnomethodologist's own work is nothing more nor less than practical reasoning ruminating on itself.

Garfinkel's vision is of a sociology which is thoroughly part of the society it investigates (ibid., p. vii): 'They [ethnomethodological studies] do not formulate a remedy for practical actions, as if it was being found out about practical actions that they were better or worse than they are usually cracked up to be.' In this vision, we already live in the best of all possible worlds: all we can do is to celebrate that fact. Previous sociology has failed to do so. Previous sociology has set itself up on a pedestal above society, and from those heights reflected upon it. But the joke is on that sociology. For, from those supposed 'heights', only an impoverished vision is available of the society below. Such sociologists only apprehend an appearance of a reality which transcends their formulation of it.

But this is a familiar viewpoint. The vision of a society whose rich complexity transcends any possible formulation of it, a society which is beyond the scope of criticism, whose goodness we can only celebrate, is precisely Husserl's transcendentalist vision of 'heaven' as mundanized by Schutz.

The tone of Garfinkel's programme is however different. Rather than looking down with the social scientists, Garfinkel prefers to descend to immerse himself within the ongoing experience of life in the 'natural' attitude. Here he can carry out the Schutzian celebration of that attitude to greater effect. So, Garfinkel can be located precisely on the map which Schutz provided.

Garfinkel accepts the Schutzian vision of the world. Its main features are the *transcendence* of the 'natural' attitude of intersubjectivity, as compared with the mere *immanence* of any formulations of that attitude in thought. But he locates himself in a different position to that which Schutz recommends for the social scientist, namely within the 'natural' attitude itself. Once settled therein, he is able to castigate those social scientists who remain outside as Schutz recommended, peering in. He is also able, believing himself in the best of all possible worlds, to refuse to conceive of any alternative world, even in thought.

In short, Garfinkel's analysis, which explicates everyday language 'from within', does so precisely in the context of Schutz's statement that 'language – any language – pertains . . . to the intersubjective world of working, and therefore obstinately resists serving as a vehicle for meanings which transcend its own presuppositions'. Ethnomethodology confines itself to elucidating those presuppositions, making no attempt to transcend them. But Garfinkel does refer to the 'special motive' needed to become estranged from everyday life, in order for these presuppositions to come into view. This (1967, p. 37): 'consists in the programmatic task of treating a societal member's *practical* circumstances . . . as matters of theoretic interest.' But if the ethnomethodologist's work is a matter of 'imagination' and 'theorizing' as opposed to 'practicality', then an awkward question arises. If such other than practical attitudes are possible for ethnomethodologists or other social scientists, then are they not also possible for members within everyday life?

In view of the preceding discussion, it is clear that we would answer this question in the affirmative. Following our reading of Schutz we hypothesize that everyday language makes available to its speakers a number of provinces of meaning. These range from immanentist subjectivity, through the flux of 'appearance' and 'reality' in the mundane world, to transcendentalist intersubjectivity (the one world in which Garfinkel dwells). We now attempt to test this hypothesis, and to investigate the range of realms of meaning and their inter-relations found in everyday speech. We will turn to a conversation discussed by Garfinkel's co-worker in ethnomethodology, Harvey Sacks.

Sacks has investigated a number of problems involving the accomplishment of social order in the conversational setting: for instance problems of opening and closing conversations, question and answer sequencing and beginning and ending stories. The question of topical coherence in conversations is especially important for our argument, since it involves the way in which the language of a spoken story refers to an extra-linguistic 'topic'. He argues that it is upon this reference that its claim to coherence rests. We shall question this conclusion.

One solution to the problem of topical coherence according to Sacks, consists in recourse to story-telling. 'This telling is composed', he states, 'of three serially ordered and adjacently placed types of sequences which we shall call the preface, the telling, and the response sequence' (1975, p. 337).

The properties of these three sequences may be briefly indicated (ibid., p. 341):

> The initial characterization (which can involve, e.g., 'a real dirty joke', 'something wonderful', 'a really odd thing', and the like) . . . seems to have as a distinctive structural job informing recipients about the sort of response teller seeks after his telling, thereby aiding recipients in listening through to find, from the telling, such materials as are relevant to the production of such a response and to its positioning. For example, indicating that 'a real dirty joke' is being projected informs that laughter is desired in the response sequence and that it should be done on the recognition of a punchline.

The reception of a story is not wholly unproblematic, and raises special issues in the case of the joke (ibid., p. 346): 'Jokes, and dirty jokes in particular, are constructed as "understanding tests". Not everyone supposedly "gets" each joke, the getting involving achievement of its understanding, a failure to get being supposable as involving a failure to understand.' Indeed the problem of showing 'understanding' arises in the case of the appropriateness of response to stories of all kinds. Jokes are distinguished by the fact that (ibid., p. 345): 'there is available a general way to appropriately respond which can be used whether one understands or not, i.e. laughter produced at the recognized completion. One's failures of understanding are concealable.' None the less failure may be exhibited by laughter too soon or too late, a matter which Sacks investigates in detail. But in the case of stories other than jokes, the question of displaying understanding can be more complex.

As a general rule, Sacks points out, 'one should not tell one's co-participants what they already know' (1972, p. 139). To be told a story whose import they already know places recipients in a difficult position (ibid., p. 140):

> For they too should not tell what they know their co-participants know, and therefore they shouldn't offer, in the place provided for exhibiting understanding of a story, some form of knowledge which could be heard as merely a proffered explanation or other understanding of the prior story, if, that is, such a piece of knowledge is presumably known to the teller too.

In his paper 'On some puns with some intimations', Sacks invites us to consider the human predicament of the individual told a tale of whose significance he is already aware. He wishes to display a form of appreciation to the teller of the story, whilst neither suggesting he was previously unaware of the implication being conveyed to him, nor that he found the remark completely without point.

For this purpose, Sacks proposes, *proverbials* are peculiarly appropriate. Such a formula as 'a rolling stone gathers no moss', or 'look before you leap' will indicate to the teller of the story, ' "I understand this, its point being the known I am reciting" ' (ibid., p. 140). *Qua* cliché, the proverbial both exhibits understanding of this story in particular, and the recipient's awareness that the message is in general familiar.

But in the case of a familiar story, indefinitely many familiar proverbials may be available with which to respond. Sacks suggests that a further refinement can produce a superior affirmation of understanding. A proverbial may be selected by a recipient, which puns on some part of the story to which it is a response. A punning proverbial constitutes a superior response to a non-punning proverbial, since in demanding an understanding of the pun's relation to the story, it exhibits its own understanding of that story.

In this light Sacks considers the following conversation (ibid., pp. 141–2):

Al:	((pitched one-half step higher)) Down in Nagasaki where the women chew tobakki
Ken:	hhh hhh
Roger:	heh heh heh! hhh hhh
Al:	hh hh hh
Roger:	Ya started off good, s(h)ing the other chorus. hhh//hhh
Ken:	heh heh heh
Al:	((half sung)) The men- when the men go wikki wakki woo. (/)
Ken:	hh
Al:	Where the-
Ken:	Where the women-
Roger:	O.K. I must know a funny story youh I me(hh)n hehh
Al:	((sung)) Ba::rney//Google
Roger:	Outta my colorful life hahh//hehh
Ken:	hehh
Al:	((sung)) Bar::rney Google with his goo-goo-googuley eye::s.
	Bar::rney Google hadda wife three times his size,
Ken:	ehheh
Al:	((sung)) She sued Barney for deevorce,
	Now he's living with his ho::::::rse

Ken:	heh heh hh
Al:	((sung)) Ba::rney//Google-
Ken:	heh heh (/)
Roger:	Did he buy the horse before he got divorced?
Dan:	Well so far, all of you skirted around the subject, that see(hh)ms to b(h)e predominantly uh on your *minds* at any rate,

As an example of the punning proverbial being used to exhibit understanding of a story, Sacks cites Dan's response to Al's rhymes about 'Nagasaki', and about 'Barney Google'. Sacks's interpretation of what the pun accomplishes is that it establishes continuity of topic as between, *inter alia,* Al's ditties and Dan's response. We shall differ from this interpretation.

Sacks's account of how the pun accomplishes what it does is brief. He notes (ibid., p. 142):

> that it, too might be seen to skirt around the topic it locates as having been skirted around. It exhibits its understanding without saying what the topic is, though the pun of 'skirted around' employs that topic; and, what he says they are alluding to, they acknowledge they are alluding to.

Sacks's attribution of 'skirting around' is self-certifying. In support of his own allusion here, he cites a continuation of the conversation as follows (ibid., p. 142):

( ):	((Clears throat))
Ken:	heh heh
Roger:	Hmnyeh well we're at that sta(hh)ge.
Ken:	ehh//heh hehh
Roger:	hhehh hehhhh hehh//hh hehh hh
Dan:	Yeah?
(Al:)	yeah.
Dan:	What stage is that, (/+)
Roger:	Awareness.
Ken:	heh heh
Roger:	hehh hehh hh hh
Ken:	Hey wha' does that look like to // you?
Dan:	ha ha ha ha ha ha ha ha //hh
Al:	(That got 'im off it,) (I din' know) (////)
Ken:	heh heh heh
Al:	I- *don't* know. (///)
Al:	My mind is *not* nasty anymore.
Ken:	heh heh heh heh

Roger:	Yer ne*ver* nasty when yer talking about sex,
Ken:	hh
Al:	It's wonderful.

It would appear, then, that for Sacks 'the topic' which is 'skirted around' by Al, Roger, Ken, Dan, and himself, is 'sex'.[6] We shall offer a different understanding of Dan's pun.

Sacks's account of proverbial punning as a response to story-telling may be summarized as follows. The coherence of a story consists in its topic, which need never be formulated explicitly in the story. In this case, the story will exhibit the topic or allude to it. The end of a story may be marked by a response which will acknowledge the topic, but again need not explicitly formulate it. Sacks's account is not simply a description of story-telling, but entails further a moral or aesthetic evaluation. A good story is one which does not name its topic, but which otherwise exhibits its understanding of that in another way. Likewise a good response is one which does not name the topic of the story to which it responds, but otherwise exhibits its understanding of that topic.

It is to be stressed that, for Sacks, the same topics recur over very many stories. Hence the characteristic human predicament which concerns him is that of the individual told a tale with whose topic he is quite familiar, puzzling how he may appropriately respond without appearing to question the value of the conversation at all.

Despite the moral desirability of not doing so, topics may, for Sacks, be named. One such topic, exhibited in the conversation and response here cited, is 'sex'.

Sacks and Sacksism

The résumé just given constitutes a response to the story told by Sacks. But though such a résumé is a possible response to a story in terms of his theory, it is not the most desirable kind of response. It is insufficiently aesthetic, in that it names its topic ('topic'). A preferable kind of response would be one which exhibited or alluded to its topic. A kind of response which Sacks finds congenial in this respect is a pun. Accordingly we propose the following pun on Sacks's theory.

The topic matter, or object of a discourse is expressed by the German *Sache*. Accordingly, we will designate as Sache-ism, or 'Sacksism', that view of speech which conceives of coherent discourse as exhibiting or alluding to the same Sache (topic) without explicitly formulating it. At the same time the conception allows that such topics can be named, and that the same topics can recur frequently within everyday conversation.

Sacksism then constitutes everyday conversation as a formulation of the *appearance* of topics, whose *reality* can be formulated by the conversational analyst, e.g. 'sex'. In this case, Sacksism involves approaching everyday conversation by way of what Garfinkel has described as the 'documentary method', in the following terms (1967, p. 77):

> There are innumerable situations of sociological enquiry in which the investigator – whether he be a professional sociologist or a person undertaking an enquiry about social structures in the interests of managing his practical everyday affairs – can assign witnessed actual appearances to the status of an event of conduct only by imputing biography and prospects to the appearances. This he does by embedding the appearances in his presupposed knowledge of social structures.

The Sacksist assigns witnessed actual appearances of everyday talk to the status of an event of conduct (in his case 'conversation') by embedding the appearances in his presupposed knowledge of social structures ('*Sachen*') in this case 'sex'. It is important to note that in this way he is unable to learn from the conversation as to the social structures which it addresses: he merely confirms his 'presupposed knowledge'.

As against the employment of documentary method which segregates the speech of the Sacksist from the speech which he analyses, we prefer, with Garfinkel, to attempt 'the discovery of common culture', that is, features of the predicament which our speech shares with that which we analyse. Garfinkel states (ibid., pp. 76–7) that this practice

> consists of the discovery *from within* the society by social scientists of the existence of common sense knowledge of social structures. In that discovery, the social scientist treats knowledge, and the procedures that societal members use for its assembly, test, management, and transmission, as objects of theoretical sociological concern.

He states (ibid., p. 102): 'Between the methods of literal observation and the work of documentary interpretation, the investigator can choose the former and achieve rigorous literal description of physical and biological properties of sociological events.' As Dorothy Smith (1974) points out, this programme invites direct comparison with that proposed by Marx and Engels (1848, pp. 408–9):

> The premises from which we start are not arbitrary; they are no dogmas but rather actual premises from which abstraction can be

made only in imagination. They are the real individuals, their actions, and their material conditions of life, those which they find existing as well as those which they produce through their actions. These premises can be substantiated in a purely empirical way.

Garfinkel has shown the prevalence of the documentary method within everyday interpretation. Sacksism exemplifies this method, and so exemplifies its own everyday status. As against documentary interpretation, a 'literal' or 'empirical' investigation of sociological phenomena should attempt to describe in a purely empirical way the workings of such interpretation where they are to be found within the actions and the material conditions of life of real individuals.

This is the practice which we have identified as the 'interruption' of everyday language. It stands opposed to documentary 'interpretation' of such language. Whereas documentary method presupposes the unity between formulations of 'appearance' and 'reality' the 'literal' or 'empirical' approach calls this unity into question. In this sense, it stands within the gap of 'rupture' between formulations of 'appearance' and of 'reality' within the speech or writing concerned. In a preliminary way we have already exhibited such an interruption of Sacksism.[7] It is now necessary to interrupt the everyday speech of Al, Roger, Ken, and Dan, in search of the gap exhibited within their language, which escaped the Sacksist interpretation.

The project of interruption seeks to dislocate the documentary method, that is the claimed relations between 'appearance' and 'reality', formulated in writing or speech. Its practice entails first breaking down the 'utterances' or 'sentences' in which speech or writing appears into self-contained atomic units of sense, which we call 'pictures', corresponding roughly to clauses. The atomic units are then re-assembled into molecular units, which we call 'stanzas', on the basis of relations of reference between pictures. Relations of identity and difference between stanzas establish linguistic units which we call 'voices'.

To display the interruption of the conversation which follows, stanzas are marked by square brackets, thus: '[ ]' and identified by capital roman numerals, thus: 'I', 'II', etc. Pictures are marked by round brackets, thus: '( )' and are identified by lower case roman numerals, within the stanza of which they are part, thus: 'Ii', 'Iii', etc. A single picture stanza is identified with an 'o', thus: 'IIo', etc. The voice exhibited by a stanza is briefly identified by a subscript to the numeral identifying the stanza, thus: 'I Nagasaki', etc.

I Nagasaki   i
[(Down in (Nagasaki where) the women chew tobakki) . . .

    IIo
[(Ya started off good)]

    IIIo
[(s(h)ing the other chorus)]

    Iii contd.
(The men go wikki wakki woo)]

    i   IV I   ii
[(I must know a funny story) (I mean, outta my colorful life)   ]

          i   V Google
[(Barney Google with his goo-goo-googuley eyes)]

          ii
(Barney Google hadda wife three times his size)]

        VIo she
[(She sued Barney for divorce)]

        i   VII he:horse
[(Now he's living with his horse)

    ii   iii
(Did he buy the horse) before (he got divorced)?]

          i   VIII you:subject
[(Well, so far all of you have skirted around (the subject) (that)
  seems to

          ii
be predominantly on your minds at any rate)]

Where Sacks's argument concerns 'utterances', and the attribution of these utterances to 'speakers' is crucial to that argument, ours concerns neither, but instead relies solely on linguistic relations. Whereas Sacks's documentary approach locates speech within his presupposed knowledge of social (and, psychological) structures, our literal approach portrays speech as itself constitutive of, whatever 'sociological', 'psychological', or other 'realities' are relevant to its understanding.

Stanza I comprises two pictures. Picture Ii is 'Down in Nagasaki the women chew tobakki'. Picture Iii is 'Down in Nagasaki the men go wikki wakki woo'. Each of these comprises a self-contained unit of sense, which no subsection of either would achieve. The link between the two pictures is brought about by the use of the word *where* attaching itself to 'Nagasaki', which word is thereby made to belong to both pictures. Accordingly this word is shared in common between the two pictures. The same named theme is thus addressed by two distinct pictures: it transcends the formulation of its two distinct appearances. However, unlike Sacks's *Sache*, this theme is not one merely *alluded* to speech. It is rather constituted as a transcendent theme precisely by being *named* in the speech itself.

We refer to such a transcendent theme named in two or more pictures as a 'voice'. The technique whereby such a voice is here constituted, namely that of employing the same words in two or more pictures, will be called that of 'reverberation'. Reverberation establishes a stanza out of two or more pictures by constituting them as the same voice. The voice of stanza I is thus identified as 'Nagasaki'.

Whilst the pictures 'Ya started off good' and 'Shing the other chorus' each comprise self-contained sensible units, they exhibit relations of reverberation neither with the preceding speech nor with one another. Each therefore constitutes a stanza in its own right. None the less, they sensibly refer to the part of stanza I which precedes them, indeed in each case, they depend upon that reference to complete their own sense. Thus 'Ya started off good' refers to stanza I itself, while 'Shing the other chorus' presupposes stanza I as the 'first chorus'. The relation thus constituted between these stanzas and the preceding stanza must be sharply distinguished from the relation between pictures constituting that stanza itself. Whereas that relation constituted sameness as between voices, this relation constitutes difference. Whereas the former relation constituted independence of sense as between the two pictures, this relation constitutes dependence.

As previously, we refer to this new relationship as one of 'reference'. We mark the relationship of reference between two stanzas by the use of square brackets. Thus: 'A[B]' means that stanza A refers to stanza B, and in this way is sense-dependent upon that stanza. In general, stanza A will formulate the 'appearance' of a 'reality' formulated in stanza B. In other terms, the voice of stanza B is posed as 'transcending' that of stanza A. Here, then, the distinction between appearance and reality, which for documentary interpretation must always remain a relation between speech or writing and its interpretation, is grasped literally and empirically as a relation established within that speech or writing itself.

The present relation between stanzas may be expressed thus:

$$\text{IIo } \left[\text{I}_{\text{Nagasaki}} \right] \text{ IIIo}$$

This diagram indicates that stanzas IIo and IIIo each formulate the appearance of stanza I posed as transcendent.[8]

Stanza IV comprises two pictures linked by reverberation into a stanza which is thus constituted as exhibiting the voice of the 'I'.

Stanza V comprises two pictures linked by reverberation into a stanza which is thus constituted as exhibiting the voice of 'Barney Google'.

'She sued Barney for divorce' might appear to sustain the named theme of 'Barney Google' for a third picture of stanza V. We maintain that this is not the case. 'Barney' is not identical to 'Barney Google', but a shortening of the name with specific properties of its own. In particular, such a shortened name has a sense dependent upon and referential to the longer form from which it is derived, but which cannot be derived from it. Likewise the sense of 'she' is dependent upon and referential to 'wife' in the previous stanza. Accordingly there is no reverberation here, so that we have a new stanza, and it refers to the preceding stanza. Though the voice of this stanza cannot yet be identified, its relationship to the preceding stanza may be expressed thus:

$$\text{VIo } \left[\text{V}_{\text{Barney Google}} \right]$$

But there is an additional element to the scheme. 'Now he's living with his horse' stands in the same relationship to stanza VIo as stanza VIo does to stanza V. 'He' reformulates the already reformulated 'Barney', creating a new sense-dependent reference. This picture could have constituted a single picture stanza on its own, but instead further speech employs reverberation to sustain its theme of 'he', accordingly this identifies its voice. The relationship between these stanzas is thus:

$$\text{VII}_{\text{he}} \left[\text{VIo } \left[\text{V}_{\text{Barney Google}} \right] \right]$$

The diagram implies that three levels of voices are constituted by the talk. The innermost voice of 'Barney Google' may be designated the transcendent voice, for the reason that the other two refer to it and dependent upon its sense which thus transcends theirs. It formulates a topic which is a reality external to the other two voices, though itself constituted in speech.

Finally, stanza VIII comprises two pictures linked to the use of the word 'that' which establishes reverberation on 'the subject'. This then identifies the voice of this stanza.

Structured speech

In order to draw conclusions from the interruption of the conversation, it will be necessary to make further assumptions, with a corresponding lesser degree of certainty than that which has obtained so far. This can be justified on the grounds that any conversation is always an incomplete re-iteration and development of themes from a multitude of speeches, to which participants in the conversation and those who comment upon it have not had equal access.

We propose that stanzas IIo and VIII should be regarded as reverberating together and sustaining the voice of 'you'. The subtle difference between the formulations is not however to be ignored, as will shortly be seen.

No reverberations exist with which to identify the voice of VIo. For convenience this will be designated the voice of 'she'.

It is now possible to display the 'structure' of the conversational fragment as a whole, as follows:

$$\left[{}^{I}_{\ \ \text{Nagasaki}} \right] {}^{II}_{\ \text{ya}} : {}^{VIII}_{\ \text{your minds}} \left[\left[{}^{V}_{\ \text{Barney Google}} \right] {}^{VI}_{\ \text{she}} \right] {}^{VIII}_{\ \text{he}} \right]$$

Here the colon is used to indicate reverberation between non-contiguous stanzas. Stanzas III and IV have been omitted from the presentation on the grounds that they are not crucial to this structure since they reverberate with no other stanzas. So, within the conversation are constituted transcendent realities ('Nagasaki', 'Barney Google'), having various elaborated features, and a 'you' who is portrayed as addressing 'the subject' of the realities.

Like Sacks, we are intrigued by Dan's contribution to the discourse. Consider what might be the 'subject' to which he refers. For Sacks it is 'sex'. We will propose a different conclusion.

Within the talk itself is constituted a distinction between the 'transcendent' realities portrayed within stories and the reality of the discourse within which these stories are told and apprehended. It seems reasonable to name this latter realm as the 'here and now' reality. One way of grasping 'the subject' of the conversation is to consider the contrast between the two realities.

In the first story, formulated in stanza I, the reality portrayed is that of 'Nagasaki', where 'the women chew tobakki' and 'the men go wikki wakki woo'.

In the second story, formulated in the related stanzas V, VI, and VII, three separate realities are portrayed. In the first, and innermost, of these, 'Barney Google with his googuley eyes had a wife three times his size'. In the second, she, the wife, sued him, Barney Google, for divorce. In the third, Barney was left living with his horse.

In Nagasaki, 'women chew tobakki'. The implied contrast is with our familiar society wherein only men have this prerogative. In Nagasaki, 'the men go wikki wakki woo'. The contrast here is with the responsible and emotionally inhibited position of men in our existing society. Before drawing conclusions from this first story in isolation, consider the contrasts drawn by the second. The purpose of this enquiry, after all, is to grasp the sense of Dan's remark which posits a single 'subject' for both stories.

Each reality of stanzas V, VI, VII may be considered in its implied contrast with the 'here and now' reality of the 'you'. In stanza V, 'Barney Google with his googuley eyes had a wife three times his size'. The implied contrast is surely with a normalcy within which a man marries a wife his own size, or perhaps smaller. In stanza VI, 'She sued him for divorce'. The contrast with the familiar world is much less striking here. 'Divorce' is a familiar feature of the mundane world, whereas women who chew tobacco or are three times the size of men, are not. It appears indeed, as if this stanza formulates a version of the mundane world itself.

Finally consider stanza VII, 'Now he's living with his horse'. This form of words is open to a dual interpretation, one ordinary, the other extra-ordinary.[9] The ordinary interpretation that Barney had now no friend in the world beyond his horse is mundanely conceivable as a possibility. The suggestion implied by the poem that his relationship to the horse was of comparable intimacy to that previous relation with his wife is extra-ordinary. But of course it is this interpretation which credits the poem with greater artistry.

The 'subject' of the conversation may now be plainly seen. In both stories, extra-ordinary realities are portrayed in contrast to the mundane world. In both the 'Nagasaki' and 'Barney Google' realities, a similar transformation of the mundane world is at work. The exaggerated potency of women in the two idealized realms is in striking contrast to their position in mundane reality. This potency of women permits the men to abandon responsibility to them, and indulge in idle frolicking in the one case, while in the other it reduces the man to 'googling' at the woman.

However, in the second story another extra-ordinary reality is portrayed, namely that of Barney with a horse, which is a common symbol of male potency. In this picture male solidarity against the potent woman is thereby celebrated. Such a solidarity is specifically impotent.

Whilst both extra-ordinary realities share the same logic, each exhibits a different implication of it. 'Nagasaki' and 'Barney' portray scenes characterized by exta-ordinary female potency. 'Horse' portrays a scene characterized by extra-ordinary male impotence. Thus the realities of stanzas I and V are enriched by contrast with mundane life. The reality of stanza VII by contrast is impoverished by contrast with mundanity.

On this understanding the conversation, though portraying six distinct realities, exhibits only three structured positions for those realities, which can be displayed as follows:

$$
\begin{matrix} + \\ = \\ - \end{matrix}
\left[\begin{matrix} Nagasaki \\ \\ \\ \end{matrix} \right]
\; ya \;
\left[\begin{matrix} \left[\begin{matrix} [Barney\ Google] \\ divorce \end{matrix} \right] \\ horse \end{matrix} \right]
\; your\ minds
$$

Here the plus sign indicates enrichment, whilst the minus sign indicates impoverishment of the realm of mundane life which is itself indicated by the equals sign. These identify precisely with the three orders of reality portrayed by Schutz's account of the structure of consciousness, viz transcendental 'heaven', immanent 'hell', and mundane 'earth' respectively.

In the present case, this structure is employed to reveal 'the subject' of the conversation as the impotent comfort of collective male sexuality. From this safe vantage point, the frightening potency of female sexuality is observed (googled at). In this way the joke itself exhibits (says) precisely the situation in which it is being produced (done). In this sense, it reflexively achieves a poetic elegance which for us is the import of its humour.

In extra-ordinary terms, Barney Google's plight is his inability to satisfy sexually the woman 'three times his size': he has recourse to the shared but sexless male company of the horse. In ordinary terms, within the same story is a portrayal of a woman taking a realistically possible social action within our society: that of suing for divorce. Thus the story stresses the realistic possibility underlying the fears expressed in fantasy.

Sexism

It is in the context of this reading of the joke that we may consider Dan's pun. Dan states, 'you skirted around the subject that seems to be most on your minds.' The previous speakers have told tales of male impotence and female potency, in short of man's inability to face sex with women. Dan's pun accuses them of 'skirting around' the subject, that is, of addressing the subject as a woman ('skirt') would do. In short, he accuses them of effeminacy in their portrayal of male sexuality.

Superficially, Dan's pun might be taken as male supremacist. He identifies impotence with effeminacy. But his speech is subtler than that. In response to the boys' speech which exhibits traditional male stereotypes and explores their consequences, Dan ironically exhibits the traditional stereotype of female sexuality. The contradiction posed by the boys' story is, that man cannot act as his fantasies of male-ness require him to do, because of the power of female sexuality which those fantasies do not allow him to handle. Dan proposes that in his very ineffectual action he acts like a woman.

The resolution is somewhat paradoxical: for in accusing the male sexual combatant of being womanly, it questions the claim made by that sexuality to be unambiguously male, not female. Yet in posing the male impotence revealed by the story as also a feature of female sexuality it reassures the males that if they are no better than the females, then at least they are no worse.

Dan's intervention grasps the paradox of the situation revealed by the telling of the story, in a way which opens that issue for further discussion. Such discussion can consider whether male impotence in the face of female sexuality is itself a retreat precisely to that state of impotence long imposed upon women by the character of male expressions of sexuality.

So Dan brings the discourse down to earth. In terms of the grammar of his remark, he constitutes his speech as 'earthly' in character, as opposed to the stereotyped 'heavenly' and 'hellish' visions entertained by the boys. By this means, he changes the character of the discourse. The speech of the boys constituted itself as telling tales about a reality which transcended their talk. The reality of sexuality was posed as a feature of a world somehow outside speech. By contrast, Dan's remark constitutes itself as a discourse precisely concerned with ways of speaking (about) sexuality. In raising paradoxes in these ways of speaking, Dan opens and contributes to a deeper kind of discourse *of*, rather than merely *about,* sexuality.

In so doing, Dan interrupts the boys' discourse. His speech stands in the gap between the alternative visions summoned up in their speech: and invites them to join him there. The argument has thus come full circle. We interrupted the speech of Sacks in order to interrupt the speech which he analysed, only to discover in doing so that that speech itself already exhibited interruption.[10]

It is now possible to demonstrate more rigorously how Sacks's practice is Sacksist. For Sacks, Dan's pun sustains the continuity of topic (*Sache*) between Al's ditties and his own. Such continuity is Sacks's imposition. On the contrary, Dan's pun interrupts and changes the continuity of topic from sexuality as external to the speech which addresses it to ways of speaking (about) sexuality themselves.

For Sacks the topic (*Sache*) of Al's ditties and of Dan's pun is 'Sex'. Accordingly, the import of Dan's pun is taken to be, that a direct encounter with sex would be possible which would not skirt around the issue. This reading implies that the skirts might be lifted, to make visible what is underneath.

Sacksism clearly implies such a conception of the relation of speech to its topic (*Sache*) as one of hindrance. Such an interpretation ascribes to Al and to Dan, a sexism which it itself exhibits. By contrast, instead of skirting round the issue (addressing it as do wearers of skirts) Dan's pun implies that the boys might address it as wearers of trousers. On this conception there is no reality of Sex to be directly encountered under either skirts to trousers. What is at issue is the ways in which skirts, trousers, and other forms of clothing (other forms of words) themselves constitute the reality of sexuality as a social (spoken) practice.

Notes

1 Cf. Chapter 5 above.
2 Cf. Chapter 5 above.
3 Barry Hindess (1972, p. 1) refers to this as 'a "sociologising" of [Husserl's] realm of transcendental intersubjectivity'. Hindess's critique of Schutz is discussed below.
4 The Schutzian account of the range of provinces of meaning and their inter-relationships would appear to meet the criteria as to 'what kind of model deserves the name "structure"', given by Claude Lévi-Strauss (1968, pp. 279–80).
5 It is this dilemma which bedevils Jean-Paul Sartre's account of the encounter of self and other, cf. 'The Look', in Sartre (1969), and Schutz's discussion of it (1971b). This is more fully discussed in Torode (1975).
6 This conclusion, which is plainly crucial to an understanding of Sacks's own text, is here proposed only tentatively: it is established more rigorously below.
7 Cf. no. 6 above.
8 There is no direct relationship between stanzas IIo and IIIo, but they are indirectly related via their connections with stanza I.
9 This distinction is developed in Torode (1975).
10 Having analysed this conversation in such a way as to discover a significant difference between Dan's speech and that which preceded it, it was intriguing to read, in Sacks (1975, p. 338), that ' "Dan" is an

adult, and the therapist in what is a group therapy session, in which the others attend.' Sacks states that this is 'a fact which never again figures in our discussion'.

Bibliography

Garfinkel, H. (1967), *Studies in Ethnomethodology*, USA: Prentice-Hall.

Hindess, B. (1972), 'The "phenomenological" sociology of Alfred Schutz' *Economy and Society* 1, p. 1.

Lévi-Strauss, C. (1968), 'Social Structure', in his *Structural Anthropology*, London: Allen Lane.

Marx, K. and Engels, F. (1848), 'The German Ideology', in L. D. Easton and K. H. Guddat, *Writings of the Young Marx on Philosophy and Society*, Doubleday-Anchor, 1967.

Sacks, H. (1972), 'On some puns with some intimations', in R. W. Shuy, ed., *Report of Twenty Third Round Table Meeting on Linguistics and Language Studies*, USA: Georgetown University Press.

Sacks, H. (1975), 'An Analysis of the Course of a Joke's Telling in Conversation', in R. Bauman, ed., *Explorations in the Ethnography of Speaking*, Cambridge University Press, 1975.

Sartre, J. P.(1969), *Being and Nothingness*, London: Methuen.

Schutz, A. (1970), *Reflections on the Problem of Relevance*, New Haven: Yale University Press.

Schutz, A. (1971a), *Collected Papers*, Vol. I, The Hague: Nijhoff.

Schutz, A. (1971b), *Collected Papers*, Vol. II, The Hague: Nijhoff.

Schutz, A. (1974), *The Phenomenology of the Social World*, London: Heinemann.

Smith, D. (1974), 'Theorising as Ideology', in R. Turner, ed., *Ethnomethodology*, Penguin.

Torode, B. (1975), *The Extra-Ordinary in Ordinary Language*, unpublished PhD thesis, Edinburgh University.

Socio-linguistics, as its practitioners Bernstein and Labov admit, is a direct expression of elaborated speech and writing, with its interpretive approach to language based on underlying sociological, psychological, and grammatical structures. In opposition to this, an interruptive approach to language expresses the commitment of the restricted code speaker, for whom the conflicting interplay of language itself is the reality in question.

chapter 8

Codes in conversation: the speech of Bernstein and Labov

William Labov, in 'The Logic of Non-Standard English', (1972)
does not actually discuss Basil Bernstein's writing on the language
of working-class and lower-class children. Instead, he deals with a
'notion . . . drawn from', and with 'interpretations of' these writings.
From the start, then, Labov practices an indirectness or distancing
of his topic.

'Bernsteins's views', writes Labov, (1972, p. 183): 'are filtered
through a strong bias against all forms of working-class behaviour,
so that middle-class language is seen as superior in every respect – as
more abstract, and necessarily somewhat more flexible, detailed,
and subtle.' Identifying working-class speech with his interpretation
of Bernstein's 'restricted code', one writer is quoted as stating that
"the language of culturally deprived children . . . is not merely an
underdeveloped version of standard English, but is a basically
non-logical mode of expressive behaviour" ' (ibid., pp. 183–4).
Against this claim, Labov offers an example of a 'skilled speaker' of
non-standard Negro English 'with great "verbal presence of
mind".' This speaker 'can use the English language expertly for
many purposes', and can construct 'a complex argument'.

Again, 'some psychologists believe' that Bernstein's elaborated
code is '"flexible, detailed, and subtle".' As against this claim,
Labov provides an example to show that it can be 'also turgid,
redundant, and empty'.

Labov's mode of argument in relation to Bernstein precisely
resembles the attack by Melvin Tumin on the structural-
functionalist theory of social stratification of Kingsley Davis and
Wilbert E. Moore, which Silverman (1974) re-examines in 'Davis
and Moore, Market Speech and Community'. Echoing this paper
we would argue that there are grounds for finding Bernstein more
convincing than his critic.

Specifically, Bernstein locates his mode of discourse (in terms of

Durkheim's attempt 'to derive the basic categories of thought from the structuring of the social relation'), and addresses (in his terms) analytic rather than concrete issues. In contrast, his critic, failing to attend to his own grounds, provides a display of commonsense accounting in which the practices involved in providing for the world and displaying its rule-governed properties are necessarily uninteresting.

Labov's empirical 'refutation' of Bernstein's theory involves, as he acknowledges, an interpretation of that theory. Since the relation between the interpretation and the theory is itself problematic, the 'refutation' necessarily remains so. (This is the general difficulty with the attempts to refute theoretical propositions empirically.) The refutation treats the 'predictions' made by the theory as mere appearances. It seeks to show that such predictions fail to correspond with empirical 'facts' which it presents as reality. In order to accomplish this, 'appearance' and 'reality' both within the theory and the refutation must be assumed to correspond.

We suggest that a claimed correspondence between 'appearance' and 'reality' must be called into question by any text which is other than a continuation of the first. In so far as Labov's paper does not call into question Bernstein's text, it is in fact a continuation of it. Labov perpetuates the reading of Bernstein's views as biased against all forms of working-class behaviour and as advocating what is in fact a 'turgid, redundant, and empty' style. We will attempt to read Bernstein's text differently – perhaps not only differently from Labov's interpretation, but also from Bernstein's own – and in so doing will also be involved in re-reading Labov's text. We shall proceed by scrutinizing the claimed correspondence between 'appearance' and 'reality' made by each of their texts.

Universalism and particularism

In 'Social Class, Language, and Socialization', drawing upon his reading of Marx, Chomsky, Durkheim and Mead, Bernstein argues (1972, p. 163):

> Historically and now, only a tiny percentage of the population has been socialized into knowledge at the level of meta-languages of control and innovation, whereas the mass of the population has been socialized into knowledge at the level of context-tied operations.

This account – not of language at all, but of connections between socialization on the one hand, and knowledge on the other – continues directly (ibid., pp. 163–4):

A tiny percentage of the population has been given access to the principles of intellectual change, whereas the rest have been denied such access. This suggests we might be able to distinguish between two orders of meaning. One we could call universalistic, the other, particularistic. Universalistic meanings are those in which principles and operations are made linguistically explicit, whereas particularistic orders of meaning are meanings in which principles and operations are relatively linguistically implicit. If orders of meaning are universalistic, then the meanings are less tied to a given context. The meta-languages of public forms of thought as these apply to objects and persons realize meanings of a universalistic type. Where meanings have this characteristic, then individuals have access to the grounds of their experience, and can change the grounds. Where orders of meaning are particularistic, where principles are linguistically implicit, then such meanings are less context independent and *more* context bound, that is, tied to a local relation and to a local social structure. Where the meaning is particularistic much of the meaning is embedded in the context, and may be restricted to those who share a similar contextual history. Where meanings are universalistic they are in principle available to all because the principles and operations have been made explicit and so public.

It is clear from this expansion of the previous sentence that the place of language in Bernstein's schema is that of mediator between the social (socialization) and the psychological (knowledge) on the other. The way in which the schema is constructed will repay more explicit attention.

The distinction between particularistic and universalistic orders is not original to Bernstein but is fundamental to both philosophical and sociological accounts of meaning. In Husserl it is found as the distinction between mundane and transcendental consciousness.[1] Here it is a matter of the individual consciousness disciplining itself sufficiently to make the arduous journey from the former to the latter, with phenomenological philosophy guiding the way. In Durkheim it is the distinction between the commonsense conception of the individual as a voluntary source of his own thoughts and action, and the scientific understanding of the determination of the individual by the *conscience collective*. For Durkheim, society may range from a state of particularistic individualism (anomie) to a state of developed collectivism (social order), and the sociologist, in helping the individual to comprehend the danger of the former, helps society to achieve the latter. Thus the distinction carries with it a (universal) moral commitment from which its (particular) individual user, Bernstein, cannot easily remove himself. And his text shows no attempt to do so: Bernstein is committed to transcendentalist universalism as the *telos* of the pursuit of meaning.

As in Durkheim's concept of forced division of labour, Bernstein formulates the class structure as an obstacle to this pursuit (ibid., p. 163): 'Without a shadow of doubt, the most formative influence upon the procedures of socialization, from a sociological viewpoint, is social class . . . . The class system has deeply marked the distribution of knowledge within society.' Bernstein's novelty lies in his identification of a new medium through which this obstacle can work, namely linguistic codes (ibid., p. 164):

> I shall argue that forms of socialization orient the child towards speech codes which control access to relatively context-tied or relatively context-independent meanings. Thus I shall argue that elaborated codes orient their users towards universalistic readings, whereas restricted codes orient, sensitize, their users to particularistic meanings . . . . Where codes are elaborated, the socialized has more access to the grounds of his own socialization, and so can enter into a reflexive relation to the social order he has taken over. Where codes are restricted, the socialized has less access to the grounds of his own socialization, and thus reflexiveness may be limited in range. One of the effects of the class system is to limit access to elaborated codes.

Thus Bernstein's quest for transcendentalism is not, like Husserl's, a matter of the pursuit by the individual consciousness of philosophical certainty nor is it, like Durkheim's, a matter of commitment to the collectivity. Instead, in his formulation the collectivity is necessarily divided. If the *telos* is to be achieved, and this division overcome, society must be changed.[2]

For Bernstein, access to universalist and particularist knowledge, as mediated by elaborated and restricted codes, is defined by social class membership. As we have already intimated, one linguist, namely William Labov, has nothing to say regarding this hypothesis, contenting himself with an attempt to reverse certain of its moral connotations. In attempting to rescue his Non-standard Negro English speaker from the 'Bernsteinian' charge of cultural deprivation, Labov explicates the 'complex set of inter-dependent propositions' implied by the speaker 'by setting out the Standard English equivalents in linear order'. The speaker emerges creditably from this translation because eight numbered propositions of, in all, sixty words are required to reformulate his three sentences of sixty-nine words. The same procedure is used to denigrate the Standard English speaker whom he quotes. It is shown that in his case three numbered propositions of in all twenty words are required to reformulate his seven sentences of seventy-seven words! This speaker – and his mode of speech – are thus criticized for 'verbosity' (Labov, 1972, pp. 182–202).

Unfortunately this procedure interprets and assesses these speeches in terms external to themselves. By his criteria, Labov's writing is better at formulating what they are saying than are either of the speakers. The charge of 'verbosity' is vacuous: it represents simply a refusal to ask what these words are doing not if they are not formulating explicit logical propositions.

Interview talk as restricted speech [3]

Consider then the following conversation upon which much of Labov's analysis rests. It consists of an interview between a Non-Standard English speaker, Larry, and an interviewer, John Lewis (1972, pp. 193–4). It is presented here already analysed into its constituent pictures, along the lines employed in previous chapters. Words repeated in the conversation are underlined.

<pre>
                                    i   ii
          ┌ JL: ((What happens to you after you die?) Do you know?)
 first   │   iii
 Q/A   │ L: Yeah, I know.)
 inter-   ─┤   iv
 change   │   (After they put you in the ground
           │   v
           └   (Your body turns into – ah – bones an' shit)

                         vi
          ┌ JL: (What happens to your spirit?
          │   vii
          │ L: (Your spirit – soon as you die, your spirit leaves you
          │   viii
          │ JL: (And where does the spirit go?)
          │   ix
          │ L: (Well, it all depends)
          │   x
 second   │ JL: (On what?)
 Q/A   ┤   xi   xii   xiii
 inter-   │ L: (You know, (Like some people say (if you're good
 change   │   an shit, your
          │   spirit goin'
          └   t' heaven))
</pre>

xiv
. . . 'n' if you're bad,
your spirit goin' to hell)
xv
well, bullshit!)
xvi
(your spirit goin' to hell anyway, good or bad)

xvii
JL: (Why?)
xviii   xix
L: (Why?) (I'll tell you why,
xx   xxi
Cause, (you see, (doesn' nobody really know
that it's a God)

xxii
y'know)
xxiii
cause (I mean
xxiv
(I have seen black gods, pink gods, white
gods, all colour gods,
xxv
and (don't nobody know its really a
God.)
xxvi   xxvii
And when (they be sayin' (if you good you goin t'
heaven))
xxviii
(tha's bullshit)
xxix
Cause (you ain't goin' to no heaven)
xxx
Cause (it ain't no heaven for you to go to)

third
Q/A
inter-
change

Relations of sameness and difference between pictures constitute
voices.[4] The voice structure exhibited in this interview is given in
Figure 4, p. 196. The determination of this structure is as follows:

Picture   i

is a composite of two *you* pictures. This
is voice 1.

Picture ii	employs a different 'you'. It refers back to picture i to complete its sense. This is voice 2, as yet unidentified.[5]
Picture iii	employs *know* from voice 2, though reformulating 'you' as 'I'. It continues voice 2, which is now identified.
Picture iv	continues *you* of picture i, so is voice 1.
Picture v	reformulates *you* as *your body*. It is not yet clear whether this continues voice 1 or not.
Picture vi	repeats *what happens* from picture i, also *your* from picture v. It is as yet unclear whether a new voice is begun or not.
Picture vii	repeats *you* from picture i and iv, also *your spirit,* twice, from picture vi. Both pictures thus continue voice 1, though indirectly.
Picture viii	repeats *spirit,* but in a new shift of emphasis drops *your.* But this is still voice 1.
Picture ix	reformulates picture viii as 'it', beginning a new unidentified voice 3.
Picture x	employs ellipsis to continue picture ix and so is voice 3 also.
Picture xi	repeats *you know* from picture ii, so is voice 2.
Picture xii	is an entirely new formulation so is voice 4, as yet unidentified.
Picture xiii	repeats *you* and *your spirit* from picture vii, so is voice 1, but not directly from picture viii.
Picture xiv	repeats *you* and *your spirit* again, so also continues voice 1.

Picture	xv

repeats *shit* from picture v. Retrospectively, this identifies voice 5. (The use of *shit* in picture xiii will be discussed below).

Picture	xvi

repeats *your spirit goin' to hell* from xiv, *good* from xiii and *bad* from xiv, so is also voice 1, but not directly from xv.

Picture	xvii

introduces a completely new formulation: call this voice 6.

Picture	xviii

repeats xvii, so continues voice 6, now identified by *why*?

Picture	xix

repeats *why* from xvii and xviii, so continues voice 6, but also repeats *I* and *you* from pictures ii and iii, thus retrospectively assimilates voice 6 to voice 2.

Picture	xx

continues *you* from xix, so continues voice 2.

Picture	xxi

introduces a new vocabulary, so is voice 7. However *body* in no*body* is in a strict sense a repetition of *body* in picture v. That picture, as noted above, reformulated *you* as *your body,* and in a further reformulation the theme of picture vi became *your spirit.* At that point in the talk, 'body' was not being employed to constitute a voice but now it is, so this new voice can be seen retrospectively to have already begun.

Picture	xxii

repeats words from picture ii, so continues voice 2. The word *know* also appears in picture xxi, though the word 'really' is prefixed to it there. This suggests a relation between voices 2 and 7 which will be discussed below.

Picture	xxiii

repeats *I* from picture xix so is also voice 2.

Picture	xxiv

also repeats *I,* establishing a link with voice

2, however it also repeats *god* from picture xxi, establishing a link with voice 7. It now appears that voice 7 is an extension of voice 2, to which this picture belongs.

Picture   xxv

repeats the wording of picture xxi, so is also voice 7.

Picture   xxvi

repeats *say* from picture xii, though reformulating 'some people' as 'they'. This would make it an extension of picture xii rather than a direct continuation of it. *They* is in fact also found in picture iv, voice 1.

Picture   xxvii

repeats *good* and *goin' t' heaven* from picture xiii, but reformulates *your spirit* as *you*. This would identify it as belonging to voice 1, but in a continuation of picture iv rather than directly from picture xiii.

Picture   xxviii

repeats wording from xv, so is also voice 1.

Picture   xxix

repeats wording from xxvii, so is voice 1.

Picture   xxx

repeats wording from xxix, so is also voice 1.

According to this analysis, the conversation exhibits seven separate voices. But these are not all of equal significance. Voices 1 and 2, which are inhabited by both speakers, are sustained throughout the conversation. Voice 1 articulates the main themes of the conversation, in terms of *you*, while voice 2 sustains a commentary on how voice 1 is *known*. Voice 5 also recurs at intervals throughout the interview, but only in the speech of the interviewee. The other voices make no more than fragmentary appearances.

As the example shows, the talk of one individual comprises a plurality of voices. Furthermore, speakers ordinarily enter, in elaborate ways, into voices introduced by others. In order not to reduce speech to presuppositions about speakers, it is necessary to describe speech as a significant reality in its own right, prior to an attempt to locate socially significant (but non-linguistic) facts about speakers. Our criticism of both Bernstein and Labov is that they fail to do this. The danger of a premature attempt to classify speakers according to 'their' speech is of fundamentally misrepresenting the complexity of that speech.

Once the structure of voices has been identified, it is possible to note the division of labour involved in their production. In the present instance, the interviewer introduces voices 1 and voice 2, while the interviewee introduces voice 5. If the conversation is broken into its three constituent question-answer sequences, then each begins with the articulation by the interviewer of his configuration of two voices and concludes with the articulation by the interviewee of his single voice.

The three voice structure is present in the first interchange (pictures i to v), though this only becomes apparent as a result of the identification of voice 5 from pictures xv and xviii which come somewhat later. The interviewer puts forward two voices. In three pictures, the interviewee repeats each of these and produces his own.

In the second interchange the interviewer interrupts his own first formulation of voice 1 in terms of *you* to formulate a subvoice in terms of *your spirit*. In order to participate in this conversation – and seemingly it requires three questions from the interviewer to persuade him to do it – the interviewee formulates 'some people say', including 'some people say shit', and later 'they say', as the meta-statement required before he will discuss the topic *your spirit* at all. It is evident that 'some people' and 'they' here could include the interviewer.

The third interchange requires only one one-word question by the interviewer to provoke it (picture xvii). The interviewee now introduces his own voice (voice 7, on *god(s)*, linked by the word *body* to his text on *shit*). He then returns to the earlier discussion and concludes by re-affirming his answer to the original question of the interviewer, in voice 1.

Thus the conversation does not transcend the form of an interview, in which the interviewee answers the questions posed by the interviewer. However, there are two distinct ways in which this answering may be understood. The comparison between these ways may clarify the difference between the socio-linguistic approaches of Bernstein and Labov, and the one which we are putting forward. Specifically, the interviewee may be regarded as interpreting or as interrupting the interviewer's question. Because it is the more familiar, and perhaps also the easiest to display, consider first the reading of the interview as an interpretation.

Interpreting restricted speech

From the interpretive point of view, each speaker comes to the encounter with a version of the correspondence between 'appearance' and 'reality'. Through this version he interprets that of the other speaker. In this case, the interviewer's formulation of *appearance (reality)* is *you know (your spirit)*. The interviewee's viewpoint may as easily be identified. His formulation is, expressed negatively, *nobody knows (God),* and positively, *body (shit).* The latter may be regarded as his own viewpoint, the former as his interpretation of the interviewer's. (As is usual in interviews, the interviewer's interpretation of the viewpoint of the interviewee is not part of the interview).

This identification squarely fits the way we read Bernstein's distinction. The conception of the world as comprising human subjects (*you* seeking to *know* the underlying essence or *spirit*) is an elaborated one, and indeed in the conversation here recorded, the speech which articulates this conception (pictures vi, vii, viii, xii, xiii, xiv, xvi) is itself 'elaborated'. By contrast, the conception of the world as comprising *bodies* and *shit* is a restricted one, and the speech which articulates it here (pictures v, xxi, xxiv, xxv) is itself 'restricted'. The terms 'elaborated' and 'restricted' are here being used in the sense of *elaborating* the difference between 'appearance' and 'reality' on the one hand, and of *restricting* 'reality' to an identity with 'appearance' on the other.

The identification fits Bernstein's distinction when it is treated as a distinction between ways of speaking. But Bernstein wants to make a distinction between speakers. Yet here one speaker is articulating both linguistic practices. So we reach the conclusion that Bernstein's hypothesis correctly captures what speech *says*: it itself articulates a distinction between restricted and elaborated speeches. But Bernstein inadequately grasps what speech *does*: the ways in which speech relates together restricted and elaborated ways of speaking.[6]

Interrupting restricted speech

Our account of the interviewee's interruptive practice will depend on the interpretation of his text made above. Whereas the interviewer puts forward an elaborated scheme involving a distinction between the 'subjective' *you know* voice and the 'objective' *your spirit* voice the interviewee puts forward a restricted scheme involving only a single voice, that of *body* and *shit.* But the interviewee's speech practice is not confined to asserting his voice as an interpretation of those of the interviewer. He actively enters into those voices to transform or interrupt them. It is the practices whereby this intervention is accomplished that we now seek to explicate.

In the first interchange, the interviewee participates in both the interviewer's voices, and introduces his own. He answers the question, 'Do you *know?*' directly, 'Yeah, I *know*'. His immediate answer to 'What happens to you after you die?' already involves a reformulation: he introduces the personal *they* as actively dealing with the *you,* whereas the interviewer had articulated, impersonally, *what happened* to *you.* This continuous transformation from picture i to iv is followed by another from picture iv to v, whereby *you* is reformulated as *your body.* Within picture v, *your body* is, as it were, continuously reformulated as *shit.* In this sense, the interviewee has succeeded in shifting the discourse step by step from the interviewer's elaborated voices to his own restricted one.

In picture vi, the interviewer does not continue precisely from the point reached by the preceding conversation. None the less, his first picture is a transformation of the interviewee's last one. *Your* is repeated, but so also – and first – is *what happens?* from the interviewer's own first picture. The reformulation is within this structure of repetition, and is itself structured: *body* is transformed to *spirit* in a well-known philosophical contrast. Thus in the terms of the interviewer's voice there is no discontinuity between picture v and picture vi, nor between pictures i and iv or iv and v. Pictures i, iv, v, and vi are all components of a single voice dealing with *you* and *your.* The difference between this speech and the *body* and *shit* speech of the interviewee is thus invisible to the speech of the interviewer.

The interviewee's answer to this question, picture vii, directly responds to the question concerning *your spirit* with an answer in the same terms. However within this picture itself a second formulation is produced, namely *you. Your spirit* is distanced from *you,* making the latter the continuing topic of the discourse.

In picture viii however, the interviewer insistently pursues the *spirit,* distancing the discourse from *you* by dropping *your.* At this point, for the first time, the interviewee reformulates the question. *It* refers to picture viii, as a whole, and enables the interviewee to avoid further participation in the text of *spirit.* In Garfinkel's term, he at this point withdraws his 'trust' in the interviewer's speech, and in the *spirit* voice in particular.[7]

At this point, the interviewer employs ellipsis in picture x to enter into and continue the unfamiliar voice which the interviewee has introduced. It is as if he recognizes that a reformulation has occurred, and is prepared to extend trust to the interviewee on his terms. As if to reciprocate, the interviewee employs the interviewer's own terms *you know* in picture xi. However this is only a gesture, since he at once reformulates again with 'like', and proceeds to show distance from the interviewer's speech.

Three separate devices are used to this end. First, the interviewee's formulation of *your spirit* in pictures xiii and xiv is contextualized by meta-statement (picture xii) to show that it is not what the interviewee says but what 'some people say'. Secondly, in picture xv *your spirit* is reformulated (as *bullshit*). Third, the interviewee's own voice is interjected into the *your spirit* voice to reformulate it again (as *shit* in picture xiii).

Finally, in picture xvi, the interviewee does participate in the *your spirit* voice, in order to deny the distinction made by 'some people'. Thus *bullshit* is not his final word. His final word is to make a statement in the voice addressed to him by the interviewer, namely *your spirit goin' to hell anyway*. At this point his own and the interviewer's voices stand side by side within his own speech. Picture xv interprets the other voice in terms of his own. It asserts that what appears to be discourse addressing 'your spirit' is really 'bullshit'. But picture xvi interrupts the other voice in its own terms. That voice, as articulated in pictures xii to xiv, makes a distinction between reality (heaven, the realm of the good) and mere appearance (hell, the realm of the bad). Picture xvi calls into question the distinction between appearance and reality made by this voice, and asserts – consistent with the position upheld in the interviewee's own voice – that appearance is all there is ('your spirit goin' to hell anyway').

Telling the code[8]

The interviewer's question 'why?' (picture xvii) attaches itself by ellipsis to the interviewee's concluding remark within the *your spirit* voice. It questions the claimed correspondence between appearance and reality made within that voice. The interviewee repeats the wording of the question (picture xviii), thus perpetuating that voice. He then shifts to the meta-statement introduced by the interviewer at picture ii, in which he had already participated at picture iii. Here he repeats the word 'why', promising, 'I'll tell you why'.

This remark has the form of what Harvey Sacks calls a 'story preface'.[9] However the subsequent conversation does not have the unambiguous preface/story/conclusion sequence which Sacks proposes. It could be regarded as a complex sequence of main and substory. In this case picture xix, itself made within the interviewer's meta-statement, promises an answer to the 'why?' question which is made at picture xxix and xxx below. This establishes the sequence of the main story. Picture xx, made within the same meta-statement text is the preface of the substory, promising a statement which is made at picture xxv.

The distinction between *seeing* and *knowing* within the interviewee's voice constitutes a distinction between prior anticipation and subsequent reiteration. *You see* points out a novel appearance: *you know* reminds of a familiar reality. At picture xx, *you see* points for the first time to the unfamiliar appearance of the conclusion which the text will demonstrate. The appearance is itself presented at picture xxi, and involves the question of *really knowing*. At picture xxii this picture is re-run and so is regarded as '*known*' rather than 'seen' by the you. (A repetition of 'you see' at picture xxii would have suggested inattentiveness on the part of the you. More precisely, it would have been a failure to trust that the you was following the discourse at this point. *You know* reasserts such trust.)

The use of *know* in both pictures xxi and xxii shows that the relation between them is not one of meta-statement from the point of view of the interviewee's voice, though from the point of view of the interviewer's voices the meta-statement form is preserved by picture xxii. The interviewee, then, has entered into the interviewer's meta-statement voice to transform it, having previously failed to transform his other voice.

In terms of the interviewer's voices, picture xxiii, 'I mean', serves as a continuous transformation of xxii. ('You know what I mean' is a familiar turn of phrase.) But it does not serve as a meta-statement in terms of the interviewee's voice. Instead, the following picture xxiv employs *I* and *seen* from pictures xix, xx and xxiii, whilst also continuing the reference to *god(s)* from picture xxi. The interviewee's single voice is thus continued without division.

It is in pictures xxiv to xxv that the *seeing: knowing* relation does its main work. This is indeed the main work of the interviewee's voice in the conversation as a whole. The transformation from what *I* (or you) *have seen* to what *nobody* (or anybody) *knows* (or does not know) is the fundamental work done within this 'restricted' voice. It is important to note that this work is not simply that which Garfinkel calls the 'documentary method', whereby an appearance is taken as indicating a (different) underlying reality. Rather, a multiplicity of appearances ('all colour gods') is put forward as demonstrating that there is no (real knowledge of a) single underlying reality.

Picture xxv concludes the substory prefaced at picture xxi, and marks a discontinuity in the speech. The interviewee's voice (i.e. his transformation of the interviewer's meta-statement voice) shifts to the interviewer's *your spirit* voice, previously concluded – before the interviewer's question 'why?' at picture xvii – by the interviewee's picture xvi. However, pictures xxvi and xxvii do not simply repeat what was said before. Picture xxvi reformulates 'some people' in xii as *they,* and picture xxvii reformulates *you're* and *your spirit* in pictures xiii, xiv, and xvi as *you* and *you* respectively. In the second interchange there was a clear distinction between meta-statement and statement. Each was sharply differentiated from the interviewee's own text. Here the two pictures are much less clearly distinct from one another. The usage of *they* (in picture xxvi), and of *you* (in xxvii) resembles that (in picture iv) which approximated the interviewee's own voice.

In the following picture xxviii, *the* verbally resembles *they* in picture xxvi, so that 'tha's *bullshit*' sounds like 'they say bullshit'. In the interviewee's 'restricted' voice, this restates what was said in the interviewer's 'elaborated' voice at pictures xii-xiii ('some people say *shit*').

With the repetition of 'bullshit' in picture xxviii, the assertion made at picture xv has been grounded. In answer to the interviewer's 'why?' question (picture xvii) it remains only to restate picture xvi. This is done in pictures xxix – xxx, but again not without transformation. The positive participation in the interviewer's *your spirit* voice there is not repeated. In place of *your spirit,* the interviewee speaks of *you.* Rather than affirming the existence of hell, he contents himself with denying that of heaven.

The resulting statement serves as an answer not only to the 'why?' question (picture xvii) which directly provoked it, but also to the 'what happens?' question (picture i) which had already been answered twice before (at pictures v and xvi). It is thus the interviewee's third effort to answer in the interviewer's terms the question which he has already answered quite decisively (at pictures v, xv, and xxviii) in his own.

Thus the interviewee treats each configuration of voices articulated by the interviewer as the occasion for reaffirming his own. In contrast to ethnomethodology's assertion that 'members' in consensual fashion work to sustain a single social fact world, it appears to us that speakers articulate conflicting relations between voices. This occurs both within the repertoire of a single individual, and between individuals.

Ethnomethodology's critique of sociolinguistics and ours can be similarly related: for them 'society', the 'psyche', and all extra-linguistic conceptions are constituted by linguistic practices whose underlying grammar they seek to determine. They thus expect to discover the only conceivable principles upon which a sense of the social-psychological world could be constructed. For us 'society' and 'psyche' are two among an indefinite multiplicity of extra-linguistic realities. In our view, these realities are constituted by linguistic practices which are discontinuously under transformation.

Labov's example shows that the 'restricted code' speaker, Larry, can participate in 'elaborated code' speech. It does not, however, show that this is his own mode of speech. Our analysis shows the reverse. The distinction between the two codes, and his own iden-tification with the 'restricted' code, are rigorously preserved in his speech. He employs the elaborated code only to combat it in three different ways.

The first purports to deal directly with the reality which the other code addresses. It is what Garfinkel calls the 'documentary method of interpretation' which treats the other code as formulating merely the appearance of which it grasps the reality. It amounts to a direct acknowledgement of difference between the two codes. It is exemp-lified by the interviewee's metaphorical reformulation of the elabo-rated code of pictures xii, xiv in his own restricted code picture xv.

The second deals with the appearance which the other code presents, and amounts to a claim of sameness between the two codes. It is exemplified by the attempts by the interviewee in pictures iv – v, and again in pictures xxvi – xxvii – xxviii to continuously transform the interviewer's two voices into his own single one. This might be called the interpellation of one voice by another.

The third intervenes directly in the relation between appearance and reality exhibited by the other code. It is exemplified in terms of the elaborated code by pictures xii – xiii – xiv – xvi, and in terms of the restricted code by pictures xxi – xxiv – xxv. This interruption of one voice by another employs the practice of one to transform the other. Here the restricted code intervenes within the elaborated code in support of its premise that no reality stands over appear-ance. This premise is put into practice in two instances, not to dissolve the elaborated code into silence (it is the interpretation, 'bullshit', which attempts this) but to produce new statements within the elaborated code (pictures xvi and xxix – xxx).

Interview talk as elaborated speech

The restricted code speaker finds his singular voice to be under attack from the elaborated codes which impinge upon it without showing awareness of its existence. More specifically, the 'restricted' speaker finds his viewpoint that reality is as it appears to him constantly assailed by the 'elaborated' assertion of the exis-tence of realities beyond appearance. In response to these assertions, the 'restricted' speaker must master the practice of 'elaborated' code in order to preserve his 'restricted' code at all. This the first speaker who Labov presented to us was able to do.

Compare this with the example Labov presents to us of an 'elaborated code' speaker. In the following conversation, a college educated Negro speaker, Charles Morris, is interviewed by Clarence Robbins. As before the conversation is presented already analysed into its constituent pictures, and with repeated words underlined. In this case a structure of stanzas is also identified.

CR: i
    (Do you know of anything?
        ii
      (someone can do [anything])
I
        iii
    to have (someone who has passed on)
        iv
    ([someone who] visit him in a dream))

CM: v
    (WELL, (I even heard my parents say that
        vi
      (there is such a thing as something in dreams)
II
        vii
      (some things like that)
        viii
    AND (sometimes dreams do come true)
        ix
    (I have personally never had a dream come true)

    x   xi
    (I've never dreamed that (somebody was dying)
        xii
    AND (they actually died))
III
        xiii
    OR that (I was going to have ten dollars
        the next day)
        xiv
    AND (somehow I got ten dollars in my pocket)

    xv
    (I don't particularly believe in that)
IV
    xvi   xvii
    (I don't believe (it's true))

    xviii   xix
    (I do feel, though that (there is such a thing as
        – ah – witchcraft)

xx   xxi
(<u>I do feel</u> that (in certain cultures <u>there is such
                              a thing as witchcraft</u>)
                    xxii
V   OR (<u>some</u> sort of science of <u>witchcraft</u>)
          xxiii   xxiv
(<u>I don't</u> think that (<u>it's</u> just a matter of believing
                                   hard enough that
                    xxv
          (<u>there is such a thing as witchcraft</u>)
     xxvi   xxvii
(<u>I do believe that</u> (<u>there is such a thing</u> that
                    xxviii
     (a person can put himself in a state <u>of mind</u>))
                    xxix
VI   OR that (<u>something</u> could be given to <u>them</u> to
                    xxx
     (intoxicate <u>them</u> in a certain – to a certain
                                   frame <u>of mind</u>
     xxxi
     (that could actually be considered <u>witchcraft</u>)

The voice structure exhibited here is given in Figure 5 (p. 197). It is determined as follows:

<u>Picture</u> i	
	appears to be a *you know* meta-statement picture: voice 1.
<u>Pictures</u> ii	
iii	are referred to by picture i. Among themselves they are interdependent of sense. Thus pictures iii and iv could be reversed with no loss of meaning, so *someone* belongs equally to both. However 'him' in picture iv refers to *someone* in picture ii, but this picture depends on picture iii and iv for completion of its sense. For present purposes it is sufficient to note that these pictures define a *someone* voice 2.
iv	
<u>Picture</u> v	
	articulates what appears to be an *I* meta-statement. Voice 3.

Pictures	vi ⎫
	vii ⎬
	viii ⎭

resemble pictures ii–iii–iv in repeating *some-* and *dreams,* so continue voice 2.

Picture	ix

resembles picture v in its use of *I,* but picture viii in its use of *dreams come true.* However grammatically this picture unlike vii is not subject to the meta-statement picture v consequently it is judged to continue the voice of picture v, i.e. voice 3.

Picture	x

continues picture ix. Voice 3.

Picture	xi

the use of *some* repeats that of voice 2 pictures above.

Picture	xii

repeats *die* from picture xi, though not identically; also reformulated *some*body as 'they'. Grammatically is not subject to the meta-statement of picture x, thus is a new unidentified voice 4.

Picture	xiii

grammatically is governed by the meta-statement picture x, of which *that* is repeated, but repeats *I* of that picture, judged a new unidentified voice 5.

Picture	xiv

repeats *some* from voice 2 pictures, but also *I and ten dollars* from picture xiii. Grammatically meta-statement x governs this picture. It is judged to be the same voice as picture xiii, but retrospectively this voice 5 is identified with voice 2.

Picture	xv

reformulates picture xiv and presumably other previous pictures in voice 2 as *that.* It is grammatically a meta-commentary, and repeats *I* of picture x, so is voice 3.

Picture	xvi

repeats *I don't believe* of picture xv, so is also voice 3.

Picture   xvii

appears at first sight to reformulate *that* of picture xv. But more precisely, it reformulates what *that* also reformulates, namely picture xiv and others of voice 2. It here defines a new meta-level voice 6.

Picture   xviii

repeats *I do* from picture xvi, so is also voice 3.

Picture   xix

repeats *there is such a thing* from picture vi, so is also voice 2, but not continuing directly from pictures xi or xiv.

Picture   xx

repeats *I do feel* from picture xviii, so is also voice 3.

Picture   xxi

repeats *there is such a thing* and *witchcraft* from picture xix, so is also voice 2.

Picture   xxii

repeats *witchcraft* from picture xxi, also *some* from earlier voice 2 pictures, so is also voice 2.

Picture   xxiii

repeats *I do* from picture xx, so is also voice 3.

Picture   xxiv

employs *it* to reformulate *witchcraft* from picture xxii and previously. *It* repeats the usage of picture xvii, so this is voice 6.

Picture   xxv

repeats picture xix, so is also voice 2.

Picture   xxvi

repeats *I do believe* from pictures xv and xvi, so is also voice 3.

Picture   xxvii

repeats *there is such a thing* from picture xxv and previous voice 2 pictures, so is also voice 2.

Picture   xxviii

introduces an entirely new vocabulary, so call it voice 7. Grammatically, picture xxvii is contextualized by picture xxvi as meta-statement, and in turn serves as meta-statement to contextualize picture xxviii. Thus three levels are constituted.

Picture   xxix

> grammatically is contextualized by picture xxvi as meta-statement: this is confirmed by the repetition of *that*. This picture reformulates 'a person' from picture xxviii as 'them' (sic), and repeats *some* from previous voice 2 pictures. It is voice 2.

Picture   xxx

> repeats *them* from picture xxix, and implies 'something could' from that picture by ellipsis. This establishes its identity as a voice 2 picture. However the second part of the picture repeats *of mind* from picture xxviii. It appears significant in this connection that the picture breaks after the word 'certain': after the break, the picture belongs to the voice of picture xxviii, i.e. voice 7.

Picture   xxxi

> reformulates 'frame of mind' from picture xxx (voice 7) as 'that', and repeats *witchcraft* from picture xxv and earlier voice 2 pictures. This picture is also contextualized by picture xxvi as meta-statement. It is voice 2.

This interviewee departs from the theme of the interviewer's speech, considered as a reality external to language, far more than did the speaker previously considered. But he does so by remaining much more closely than did that speaker within the voice structure which the interviewer's language defined. As such, his 'elaborated' speech is itself more structured throughout than was that of the 'restricted' speaker. Furthermore, when he does develop the complexity of his voices beyond those presented to him by the interviewer, it is to extend that structure further in its own elaborated terms. The transformation from voice of 'appearance' to voice of 'reality' already present in the speech of the interviewer is applied again to produce a voice of 'hyper-reality'. Within this voice the interviewee formulates his ultimate response to the interviewer.

The significance of the seven distinct voices here is not equal. Voice 2, although undergoing considerable internal transformation, is the fundamental statement of the conversation as a whole. It is articulated by both speakers. Voice 3 is the fundamental meta-statement of the conversation. It is developed by the interviewee, but out of the interviewer's meta-voice. Voice 6 stands between voices 3 and 2. Voice 3 then contextualizes voice 6 which itself contextualizes voice 2. Voice 7 stands beyond voice 2, such that voice 3: voice 2 is as voice 2: voice 7. Both voice 6 and 7 appear only in the interviewee's talk.

Qualitatively there are here four main voices, of which two are articulated in the first instance by the interviewer, and two by the interviewee. Whereas the 'restricted' code speaker earlier considered began within the voices offered him by the interviewer and later articulated his own unrelated voice, the 'elaborated' speaker is able to generate new voices by his own employment of the voice: meta-voice operation. This does not not simply make meta-commentaries upon the statements put to him by the interviewer but constructs a voice between the original voice and meta-voice, and, in reverse, constructs a voice of which the original voice is a meta-voice. It is in terms of these constructed voices, and especially the latter (the voice of mind), that his answer to the interviewer's question is posed. This can be explored in more detail, as before, both interpretively and interruptively.

Interpreting elaborated speech

From an interpretive point of view, the interviewer comes to the encounter with a formulation of *appearance (reality)* as *you know (someone)*. Of course in the particular question posed, this viewpoint is brought to bear upon the question of dreams: however our interest is in the viewpoints in their own right rather than in the topics which those viewpoints address. In terms of the interviewer's voices, the interviewee formulates *I . . . I do feel . . . I believe (something . . . some . . . some witchcraft . . .witchcraft)*. However the interviewee also articulates voices not found in the interviewer's talk. These present the viewpoint *it's (of mind)*.

The interviewer's formulation is notably concrete compared to that of the interviewee. '*Do you know* of anything that *someone* can do . . . ?' invites a response in terms of anecdotes about *someone* known to *you,* the interviewee. The interviewee reformulates this subjective orientation. His *feel,* and *belief* suggest that with regard to the topic at hand *knowledge* may not be the appropriate mode. He also reformulates that topic: *something* replaces *someone* so that what is at issue is his intellectual activity rather than his stock of personal acquaintances.

His subsequent transformation of the topic of dreams to that of witchcraft also shifts the conversation from a potential interrogation of his personal experiences (everyone has dreams) to a topic external both to himself and the interviewer (most people are not witches). Finally, when he constructs his own two voices, within which he states 'it's [a matter] of mind' his discourse raises issues which go beyond the particularities of both the speech and the topic formulated by the interviewer.

Thus the converstion transcends the form of an interview in which the interviewee answers the questions posed by the interviewer. This accomplishment of the interviewee's 'elaborated' speech is precisely what Bernstein's hypothesis would suggest. The interviewee has 'universalized' the issue raised by the interviewer. But this is at the cost of avoiding the issue of whether someone can do anything to have someone who has passed on visit him in a dream. Instead quite a different issue is raised (concretely, the issue of *witchcraft;* analytically, the issue of *mind*).

Interrupting elaborated speech

Unlike the previous conversation considered, this one is not structured around question/answer interchanges. The interviewer's first question is not answered. Instead the interviewee's elaborate 'reply' is itself internally structured by breaks and reformulations. These are identified on the text above as stanzas, i.e. groups of pictures verbally and grammatically united together. In order to interrupt the conversation, we re-examine it stanza by stanza.

In the first stanza, the interviewer articulates his two voices. The first cannot be precisely identified from a single picture, but appears to involve *you know*. The second clearly identifies itself as organized around *someone*.

In the second stanza, the interviewee reformulates 'you' as 'I' to constitute his own meta-statement voice. Within this voice he reformulates *someone* as 'my parents'. However he portrays these as neither persons who have passed on nor as ones who have had such a person visit them in dream. Instead, he portrays what they *say* about dreams. The device of referring in speech to what others say was also used by the previous interviewee to distance his own speech from the topic which the interviewer demanded he discuss. In that instance it appeared that the sayers ('some people') could include the interviewer as against the interviewee, who would say no such thing (talk about *your spirit*). But here the interviewee works to distance the topic from himself, and the situation from one in which a sophisticated interviewer interrogates a naive interviewee about his superstitions regarding his dreams. However he acknowledges that 'even' his parents participated in a discourse closely resembling the one articulated by the interviewer. Where the interviewer asks for anything that *someone* can do, where *someone* might include the interviewee, the interviewee articulates, in the voice of his parents, that there is *some*thing in dreams. Thus a more distant relation is acknowledged between his parents and the topic than the interviewer invited between the topic and the interviewee.

The extended formulation of his parents' discourse permits the interviewee to articulate his own in contrast to it in the conclusion of stanza II. His speech up to this point is as complete an answer to the interviewer's precise question as he ever gives. What follows marks progressive moves away from the terms of that question, without a return to them. This phenomenon was largely absent from the speech of the first interviewee.

Stanza III consolidates the structural relation of difference between the *I* voice and the *some* voice in his talk. In this connection it is noteworthy that picture xiv, which seems to obscure this difference by placing *some* and *I* together in a single picture, formulates an inconceivable event.

Stanza IV marks two shifts. Up to this point, the *I* voice has formulated only descriptions of events in the life of the *I,* though the qualification 'never' to these generalizes them. In a new mode (*I do*), categorical statements are made about the beliefs of the *I.* To formulate these beliefs, a new voice is articulated. The impersonal *'it*'s true' portrays a level of meaning or language-game permitting the talk to move beyond its previous limits, though in a way which can itself be clearly located. It refers to the *some* voice as a whole. It is part of a meta-voice. But this voice is not that of the *I* itself. The latter is a meta-voice on the *it* voice. The *it* voice is thus not tied to the *I,* but is presumably open to the participation of others, in terms of what they may *believe.*

Stanza V, however, introduces as a contrast to the negative statement of *beliefs* a positive statement of the *I*'s *feel*ings. (The topic is later strengthened as a statement of *belief.*) In the first instance, however, the contrast is made the other way: *I don't believe'* X, whereas *'I do feel'* Y. In this way, the meta-voice (the I), transforms the *some dreams* voice to the voice of *witchcraft.*

This technique of transformation, by way of the meta-voice, is particularly appropriate to elaborated speech, but is unavailable to the 'restricted' speaker. The transformation from *seeing* many *gods* to *knowing* there was no real *God* changed its voice from within. The transformation here is from *not believing sometimes dreams do come true,* to *feeling there is such a thing as witchcraft.* This allows the old voice to continue (as the belief of others), while the new voice does not threaten the old (one could believe both in dreams and witchcraft).

The passage from *belief* to *feel*ings claims to offset the charge that the whole issue is one of belief (I don't believe X; I do believe Y). That witchcraft is not just a matter of belief is refuted in a second recourse to the impersonal *it's* voice.

However the final stanza is structured in terms of beliefs. Part of it (the first and last pictures taken together) asserts '*I do believe* that . . . that could actually be considered *witchcraft*'. *That* refers to a new voice not heard before. This is now articulated to present the speaker's ultimate version of reality: a 'state' or a 'frame' of *mind*. Yet in so far as the 'belief' is itself a frame of mind, and one which the interviewer here seems to be 'putting himself into', the final stanza is circular. It seems that this stanza does formulate precisely what is denied in picture xxiv – with a crucial difference.

The final stanza adds that something is missing from this formulation. Significance must be attached to the power of the *mind* to *believe* what it wants. This is a version of the social-psychological argument which shifts attention from the unobservable transcendent reality to which belief orients, and instead focusses upon the activity of believing as reality in its own right. (If God did not exist, it would be necessary – for the good of the individual, or in other formulations, for the good of society – to invent him.) This is one reply to the attempted refutation of the existence of such realities attempted by the 'restricted' speaker. Such a reply is directly expressive of the commitment of 'elaborated' speech.

The reply is not successful. Here, as in general, it replaces one unobservable transcendent reality (*God*) with another (*mind*). We have attempted to interrogate language in a way which avoids itself erecting any transcendent reality in terms of which to interpret word or world. Both elaborated and restricted speech fall short in this attempt.

Given that speeches exist in elaborate multiplicity, the commitment of the elaborated speaker is to preserve and explore that multiplicity. A voice can be re-interpreted. Thus dreams coming true are a matter of the beliefs of some rather than others. Again witchcraft is a matter of the state of mind of its practitioner. But as such it is preserved although removed from its original location.

In opposition to this, the restricted speaker is committed to his own version of speech as reality.[10] Other voices are to be interrupted, to transform them from within. Thus where elaborated interpretation is preservative, restricted interruption is subversive of the claim to rule of existing speeches.

There is another aspect of this distinction which is clearly indicated by the difference between the two interviews. In a precise sense, the second interviewee's elaborated speech is idealist in its orientation to knowledge of a reality beyond appearances. The first

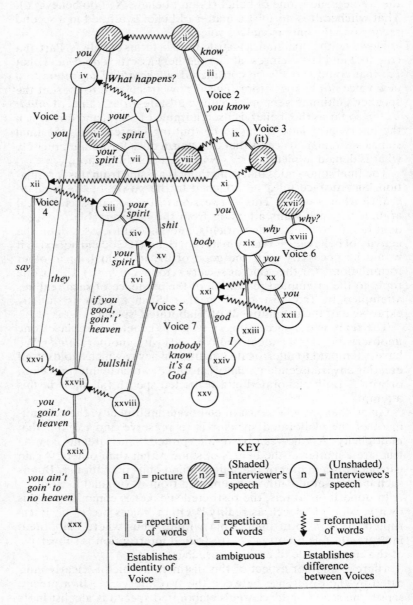

Figure 4 Voice structure of 'restricted' interview

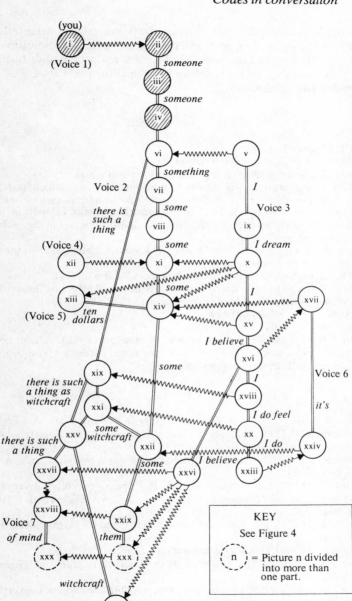

Figure 5 Voice structure of 'elaborated' interview

interviewee's restricted view is, by contrast, materialist, oriented to the brute reality of the world, and convinced by the sheer multiplicity of appearances of the impossibility of a reality beyond. In this sense the dialectic of materialism and idealism plays itself out in everyday encounters.

Notes

1 Cf. Chapter 5 above.
2 This point is developed in Bernstein (1971).
3 For an earlier analysis of interview talk, cf. Silverman (1973).
4 The *stanza* structure is omitted from this analysis, which instead attempts to discover voices directly from relations between pictures. It appears that the *stanza* level of organization is undeveloped in the 'restricted code' interview – it is however clearly apparent in the 'elaborated' interview.
5 A voice is 'identified' when the word or words which it regularly repeats have been discovered.
6 The saying/doing distinction is taken from Austin (1971).
7 'Trust' is Garfinkel's name for what Schutz calls the epoche of the natural attitude. Cf. Chapter 7 above, and Garfinkel (1967).
8 Apologies to Weider (1974).
9 Cf. Sacks (1970).
10 In terms of the distinction drawn by Hudson (1966), 'elaborated' speech expresses a *divergent*, and 'restricted' speech a *convergent* strategy with respect to other speeches.

Bibliography

Austin, J. (1971), *How to do Things with Words*, Oxford: Clarendon Press.
Bernstein, B. (1971), 'Education Cannot Compensate for Society', *New Society*, no. 387.
Bernstein, B. (1972), 'Social Class, Language, and Socialization', in P. Giglioli (1972).
Garfinkel, H. (1967), 'Studies in the Routine Grounds of Everyday Activities', in his *Studies in Ethnomethodology*, Englewood Cliffs: Prentice-Hall.
Giglioli, P. (1972), ed., *Language and Social Context*, Harmondsworth: Penguin.
Hudson, L. (1966), *Contrary Imaginations*, London: Methuen.
Labov, W. (1972), 'The Logic of Non-Standard English', in Giglioli (1972).
Sacks, H. (1970), Spring 1970 lectures 1–6, unpublished mimeo, University of California.
Silverman, D. (1973), 'Interview Talk', *Sociology*, 7, p. 31.
Silverman, D. (1974), 'Davis and Moore: Market Speech and Community', in B. Sandywell *et al.*, *Problems of Reflexivity and Sociological Enquiry*,

London: Routledge & Kegan Paul.
Weider, D. (1974), 'Telling the Code', in R. Turner, ed., *Ethnomethodology*, Harmondsworth: Penguin.

part V

The practice of ordinary language

Earlier parts of this book have traced the dangers of reducing language to entities like 'thought' or 'society'. We learn from the recent English philosopher J. L. Austin that ordinary language usage is a reality in its own right. However, this will involve separating what is done in Austin's texts from Austin's own claims about them.

chapter 9

What Austin does with words

Austin's work is important because it proposes and, more centrally, *uses* a method of analysis concerned primarily with ordinary, or non-philosophical, language. Instead of engaging in the parlour game of arraying professional concepts against each other in order to achieve easy victories in mock battles, Austin found it more interesting to study ordinary language utterances.

Austin's interpreters

It is easy to see that much of the debate about Austin has degenerated into professional polemics which, while affirming the pre-eminence of a technical interest among philosophers, in no way settles the case as far as Austin's own work is concerned. For, in order to score points off each other, the rival 'sides' have often preferred to attach labels rather than to analyse the practices of the other (admittedly rather a strange activity for those 'players' who profess to believe in the importance of linguistic practice).

Thus Gellner (1959) attributes to 'linguistic philosophy' (note that throughout he prefers to address a label rather than a text) the suggestion that 'philosophical theories are misuses of language' and the implication that ' "common sense" is right' (19). Yet this straw-man version, while helpful for polemical purposes, only works if we ignore the following questions:

1   What is a 'misuse' of language? Austin, for instance, discusses different *uses* of language in philosophy, psychology, and law (*APFE*) but avoids the crude (grammatical? moral?) tag of 'misuse'.

2   Are 'linguistic philosophers' supposed to reject *all* philosophical theories as 'misuses' of language? Then why are they so willing to construct their own philosophical theories and to suggest, as does Austin, that ordinary language has but 'the first word' (*APFE*)?

3   If 'common sense' is 'right', why does Austin go to such lengths to overcome our 'common sense' assumptions about the meanings of terms, like 'real' (*SS*)? Moreover, is it not a gross simplification to equate linguistic usage (a practice) with commonsense (an idea)?

Yet the temptation to score points, unshaken by such niceties, extends as well to the other 'side'. The ordinary language philosopher Urmson manages to group his opponents under the head of 'metaphysics'. They, it seems, are concerned with Platonic 'revelations', while sober 'analytic' (or ordinary-language) philosophy, is an Aristotelian activity of 'clarification' (1967: 294). Not surprisingly, Gellner seeks to use much the same labels – applying them, of course, in the reverse order.

Only Marcuse (1955), predictably, refuses to be on the side of these very British angels. Mobilizing the tradition of German Idealism, which identified truth with Reason, he rejects the reduction of the world to 'observable facts' (113). According to Marcuse, then, *both* analytic philosophy and its (British) opponents stand condemned because of their apparent obsession with empirical reality.

If valid, Marcuse's critique would lead to a speedy conclusion to this chapter. We would have to say that there is *no* emancipatory potential in Austin's work because, like any empiricism, its appeal to 'the certainty of fact' denies human potential. Drawing upon Hegel, we would have recognized, with Marcuse, that 'the given facts', which appear to be the index of truth are, in reality, its negation. It would follow that real truth can be established only by the destruction of apparent 'facts'.

Marcuse's position is a half-answer to a half-question. As Marx argued in the *Grundrisse*, if revolutionary potential did not appear in the *present* world, then any revolutionary aims would be quixotic. 'Observable facts' may be expected to contain both a representation of the status quo and the seeds of its destruction. It is a commitment to romantic theology rather than to Marxism which tempts Marcuse to reject this world and all its works. So Austin is spared a speedy dismissal. The question remains: what *kind* of means of engaging the world, not theory versus empiricism. Marcuse has flown in the face of Marx's achievement by implying that a dialectical method is incompatible with empirical study (predictably, *The German Ideology* lives on).

Clearly, our questions can only properly be settled by inspecting Austin's practice rather than the programmatic statements made either for or against his work *in toto*.[1]

The attachment to a set of professionally approved topics reflects a *reductivist* impulse which bedevils analysis, here as elsewhere. A debate about the world becomes reduced, in consequence, to a rehearsal of a body of unchallengeable conventions. Viewed in this way, the world becomes little more than an index of professionally conceived categories such as 'social structure', 'personality' and even (in Schutz's case) the 'natural attitude'.

By excluding signifying practice from attention, such a method is destined to be idealist, seeing in the world only a confirmation of its own categories (Torode: 1976). This 'terrorism' (Ricardou: 1975) reduces discourse to a statement of a reality that is already apprehended and, in place of an analysis of discursive operations, remains focussed on the supposedly 'distorting' effects of language.

To summarize these introductory comments: we have stated that, given an emancipatory interest, it is necessary to assess the means of engaging the world offered by versions of language such as that of Austin. Along the way, we have encountered two related issues which have a direct relevance both for Austin and for the themes of this book. Namely:

1 The status of empirical research, conceived as an investigation of 'the facts of the case'.

2 The status of concrete 'reality', conceived either as an ever-present danger to the purity of theory or as the very site of theoretical intervention.

In some respects, our response to issue (1) has been indicated in the discussion above of Marcuse's theological rejection of 'the given facts'. Despite Marcuse, research remains viable as a means of recovering the dialectical possibilities available in 'the facts'. Conservatism is only a *possible* feature of various means of recovering facts; romanticism is the inevitable concomitant of a total rejection of all facts.

Finding for once a good word to say about one of Austin's academic supporters, we would have few qualms about engaging in the kind of empirical research that Urmson (1967: 235–6) carves out as Austinian territory. Namely: taking more interest in ordinary language than in professional formulations; avoiding vast theories about language in favour of developing a systematic method to be used by 'anyone with patience'; and not rejecting technical usage, but basing it in a proper understanding of ordinary usage.

Returning to issue (2), once empirical investigation is permitted, concrete 'reality' need no longer be feared as a threat to the purity of theoretical formulations but as the site in which theorizing begins and to which it returns (Clegg: 1975).

The major remaining danger is that 'reality' may be apprehended as a massive unity, in the face of which theory looks shorn of any critical dimension. However, this apprehension overlooks the dialectical nature of reality. If dialectic, in both ancient and modern versions, is taken to be the dialogue between many theses or speeches (Ryle: 1971), then the apparent unity of reality dissolves in the dialectical formulation. Moreover, a theory which understands its own dialectical relation to reality (i.e. theory as the *revelation* of many speeches in the form of a discourse which bears the *trace* of many speeches) will not abdicate its critical role.

The recognition of such a dialectic provides a useful backdrop to two contrasting statements by Austin and Heidegger which are given below. Partly because these statements are located in the apparently different traditions of British and Continental Philosophy, they reveal seemingly alternative versions of the status of reality *vis-à-vis* theory. However, as we will suggest, the idealism of both formulations must ultimately be resisted:

> . . . our common stock of words embodies all the distinctions men have found worth drawing, and the connexions they have found worth making, in the lifetimes of many generations: these surely are likely to be more numerous, more sound, since they have stood up to the long test of the survival of the fittest, and more subtle, at least in all ordinary and reasonably practical matters, than any that you or I are likely to think up in our arm-chairs of an afternoon – the most favoured alternative method (*PFE*: 182)

> It is as though men had to make an effort to live properly with language. It is as though such a dwelling were especially prone to succumb to the danger of commonness.
> The place of language properly inhabited, and of its habitual words, is usurped by common terms. The common speech becomes the current speech. We meet it on all sides, and since it is common to all, we now accept it as the only standard. Anything that departs from this commonness, in order to inhabit the formerly habitual proper speech of language, is at once considered a violation of the standard (Heidegger: 1972, 118–19).

1   Leaving aside the reference to armchairs which, as we have seen, so enrages Gellner, Austin's affirmation of the 'soundness' of ordinary language may be taken to be a failure of critical nerve expressed in the self-abasement of theory before 'the facts of the case'. Here, in the Platonic metaphor, Austin would be accused of having mistaken shadows for the sun and proceeded to worship the

former. It is precisely this metaphor which Heidegger's warning about 'the danger of commonness' seems to address – translating the sun as 'language' and the shadows as 'the common speech'. Instead of understanding the dialectical relation of speeches to one another and to language, we have chosen to acknowledge only the one-dimensional unity of common terms. In this land without a horizon, 'common speech' becomes both the sole topic and the sole resource ('the only standard', as Heidegger puts it).

2 Alternatively, Austin may be treated as engaging in a thoroughly worthwhile critique of system-building ('the distinctions that you or I are likely to think up in our arm-chairs of an afternoon'). In its place, he offers a confrontation with the concrete world, expressed in a wonder at the subtleties of ordinary usage and its relation to the 'practical matters' that have arisen 'in the lifetimes of many generations'. Viewed in this light, Heidegger's effort 'to live properly with language' begins to look like another romantic effort to escape from the world – a romanticism stressed by the exaltation of the past implied by his reference to 'the *formerly habitual* proper speech'. According to this version, theory is constrained by two idea(l)s: 'Language', which is the silent, mysterious backdrop to human activity, and 'the speech of language', a practice which defers to this ideal but is now seemingly available only to the theorist. Hence Heidegger wants to stand outside the (fallen) concrete world, acknowledging as his ground and as his topic the transcendent idea(l) of 'language'. Untainted by the concrete, not confused by 'facts', such a theorist then turns towards ordinary people with a mask of omniscience upon his face and the gesture of a rebuke upon his hand.

3 While Austin does turn to face the concrete world – a better posture than the back offered by Heidegger – it is not clear that his formulation escapes the idealism that grasps Heidegger. For if 'language' is the ideal that sustains Heidegger, then 'our common stock of words' seems like Austin's ideal. 'Language (Heidegger) and 'words' (Austin) are treated as massive unities standing outside of emancipatory practice and constraining. In both passages, there is an apparent failure to see the dialectical possibilities (the many voices) within both everyday and theoretic discourse. In Heidegger's case, this leads to a rejection of the concrete world, in Austin's, to an embrace of an ideal version of it. In neither case, is any critical space offered to lay and professional theorists.

We are now in a better position to formulate a method for reading Austin (or any text). Two principles seem uppermost:

1 The need to avoid escaping from the concrete (in this case, the text) into our own formulations. Such excursions from Austin's

texts that have been made in this introduction have been meant to
clear away dead-ends that prevent an intervention in the concrete – an intervention that would reconstitute that concreteness
as a dialectic of many speeches. This will serve both as a principle
of reading Austin's texts (the 'reality' that confronts us) and as a
means of assessing the method they propose (the 'appearance'
constituted in, and, sometimes, against that reality). At all times,
then, it will be necessary to distinguish what Austin does from
what he says about what he does.
2   The need to avoid that form of polemics which (to mix
metaphors) constitutes a text as either a 'straw man' or a 'sacred
cow'. As any text is an interweaving of many speeches, we may
expect to find both progressive and retrogressive elements in
Austin's work, no less than we earlier discovered in Heidegger.²

From now, we abstain from any discussion of the secondary literature in order to consider solely Austin's texts themselves. One of
the reasons that makes them so approachable for the student is
that the whole corpus amounts to no more than three slim vol-
umes – two no less important reasons are their humour and dis-
trust of unnecessary jargon.
    The works consist of *Sense and Sensibilia* (*SS*), *How to do
Things with Words* (*W*), and the Urmson and Warnock edition of
Austin's *Philosophical Papers* (*PP*). For the purposes of this chapter, however, some selection from these texts will have to be made.
We choose three inter-related aspects of Austin's work. Using a
method of Austin's, we try to show the difference between what
each text is *saying* and what it is *doing*. The material is organized
as follows:
1   Austin as a philosopher, entering into traditional philosophical
disputes armed with his linguistic method. Here we select an early
paper, dealing with familiar philosophical territory ('The Meaning
of a Word', *PP*: 55–75), together with certain passages in *Sense
and Sensibilia*. The latter, a group of lectures on theories of perception, particularly A. J. Ayer's *The Foundations of Empirical
Knowledge*, offers a more extended canter over the same sort of
field.
2   Austin as an investigator of ordinary usage, primarily concerned to establish a method for the analysis of utterances rather
than to score points in a professional dispute. Here we select the
classic *How to do Things with Words*, part programme and part
analysis, together with the famous account of 'excuses' ('A Plea for
Excuses', *PP*: 175–204) and its later development ('Three Ways of
Spilling Ink', ibid: 272–88).

3   Austin in a state of reflection about his method and, in particular, about the status of 'ordinary language' as the starting point (or
'first word') for analysis. This is something begun in 1940 in 'The
Meaning of a Word' (*MW*) but expressed most fully in a section of
'A Plea for Excuses' (*APFE*: 181–9).

Aspect (2) of Austin's work, which gives the appearance of the
practice itself rather than the programme (1) or the legislation for
the reading of the practice (3), seems to be the most relevant to
our concerns. On the other hand, it would be inaccurate to segre-
gate unnecessarily aspects (1) and (3) from aspect (2). We shall
argue that the form of life of professional philosophy informs all
three aspects. It remains to be seen whether this factor undercuts
any emancipatory potential possessed by the practice.

Austin as philosopher

MW attacks the perennial system-building pretensions of philosophy with self-deprecatory language and no little humour (e.g.
reference to 'letting sleeping dogmatists lie'). None the less, it
clearly reads as a contribution to a professional dispute about
language, to be settled by the criteria of academic debate.

Consonant with his method, Austin's attack is indirect, challenging the terms in which an argument is couched and letting it fall to
the ground without the need to contest any of its main propositions. Austin starts from the position that the philosophical debate
about 'meaning' and 'words' has mistakenly asked the wrong kinds
of question. In particular: 'The phrase "the meaning of a word" is
a spurious phrase' (*MW*: 75). We can resolve much of the tangle
that philosophers have got themselves into by rejecting questions
like 'What is X?' Austin comments:

> This supposed *general* question is really just a spurious question
> of a type which commonly arises in philosophy. We may call it
> the fallacy of asking about 'nothing in particular' which is a
> practice decried by the plain man, but by the philosopher called
> 'generalizing' and regarded with some complacency (*MW*: 58).

Austin sets about distinguishing 'sense' from 'nonsense' by
rejecting such 'general' questions. However, unlike the logical
positivists or modern-day critical rationalists, like Popper, he
rejects purely philosophical criteria for establishing 'sense'.
According to Austin, at some point in our path, although not
necessarily at the terminus, we must give due weight to ordinary
language and to the criteria of sense, implied in its practices.

Austin uses the character of 'Old Father William' to counterpose the massive reality of the (material) wor(l)d to the idealist nonsense of some philosophy. Father William, we are told, is asked a number of questions about the 'point' of doing various concrete things. He answers without difficulty. Then he is asked:

> 'What is the point of doing *anything* – not anything in particular, but just *anything*?' Old Father William would no doubt kick me downstairs without the option. But lesser men, raising this same question and finding no answer, would very likely commit suicide or join the Church. (Luckily, in the case of 'What is the meaning of a word?' the effects are less serious, amounting only to the writing of books) (*MW*: 59).

The point is that we run serious risks if we retreat to an ideal world with its own language. It is really no improvement to ask questions about ordinary language while assuming that an ordinary language must be like an ideal language. Through this path, like the former, we conclude only by asking nonsensical questions.

However, Austin does not mean to imply that ordinary language sets *all* the parameters to our analysis. Clearly, there will be questions we want to pursue which are not given in ordinary usage. The debate is centred around how we should begin rather than how we should end. And Austin's argument is that we lose nothing and gain potentially a great deal by beginning with the question: ' "What should we say when . . . ?" ' Certain questions, then, are non-starters only because they allow no *initial* toe-hold on everyday linguistic practice. There remains only the (methodological?) point about whether that toe-hold should be through the medium of *inspection* of naturally occurring utterances or of *recollection* of the analyst's native linguistic competences (Austin's preferred method).[3]

The issue of the appropriateness of our questions arises again in Austin's treatment of the philosophical debate about 'reality'. In *Sense and Sensibilia*, he examines at length the 'general doctrine' that has emerged from this debate. Namely, that: 'we never see or otherwise perceive (or "sense"), or anyhow we never *directly* perceive or sense, material objects (or material things), but only sense-data (or our own ideas, impressions, sensa, sense-perceptions, percepts, etc.)' (*SS*: 2).

Once again, it is the terms rather than the proposition itself that must be contested. Philosophers have based their argument on a few particular words but have oversimplified their uses. So the point is not to rush to respond to the doctrine but to 'unpick' it: 'It is a matter of unpicking, one by one, a mass of seductive (mainly verbal) fallacies, of exposing a wide variety of concealed motives – an operation which leaves us, in a sense, just where we began' (*SS*: 4–5). This last phrase 'leaving us . . . just where we began' might seem to have worrying implications. There is the 'conservative' implication about the impossibility of changing the world. And (*à la* Gellner), there is the 'parlour-game' implication that Austin's real business is the construction of a diversion for jaded Senior Common Room palates.

Both complaints are misplaced. Austin, with Wittgenstein, use-fully shows the limits of any professionally-defined enterprise (in their case, philosophy) which too readily confuses its word-games with the world. The problems suggested by such work and the solutions offered thereby ground themselves in *ideas* which have a tenuous or concealed connection to reality. Consequently, by revealing this idealism, we do learn something that Austin rightly terms: 'something positive . . . a technique for dissolving . . . *some* kinds of philosophical worry' (*SS*: 5). In bringing to bear this 'technique', Austin rightly implies that many of the questions that we are tempted to ask are pre-critical. Answering them will not change the world because the world is (unwittingly) pre-supposed in their formulation. The point could not be more serious. We are not being invited to a parlour-game; instead, we are being shown how ostensibly critical thought has degenerated into little other than a parlour-game and are being offered a better target upon which to aim our sights – ordinary usage.

This target allows us to complete the dissolving of 'some kinds of philosophical worry' – think of dissolving as dis-solving, i.e. not as effacing but as standing apart from, and trying to understand, our desire to solve. Once returned to their ordinary use, terms like 'look', 'seem', or 'appear', will not, as Austin shows, support the intellectual edifice that philosophers have built upon them. In particular, the 'absolutely normal' (*SS*: 62) word 'real' operates in a far more complex way than we might be tempted to assume. So we must always bear in mind:

> (a) that the distinctions embodied in our vast and, for the most part, relatively ancient stock of ordinary words are neither few nor always very obvious, and almost never just arbitrary; (b) that in any case, before indulging in any tampering on our own account, we need to find out what it is that we have to deal with . . . (*SS*: 63).

At once, we 'find out' that 'real' is *not* entirely 'normal'. Unlike other words ('Yellow', 'horse', or 'wall'), it does not have one single meaning but neither is it ambiguous. For instance, when asked: 'What is the real colour of the sky?', we feel less sure about

how to proceed than when asked, say, 'Are these real diamonds?'.
Such examples lead Austin to suggest four 'salient features of the
use of "real" ' (68). We will mention two of these:
1   The question: 'real or not?' only arises when suspicion reason-
ably assails us that things may not be what they seem. Like 'good',
then, 'real' does not refer to a fixed state of affairs separate from
context. It is what Austin calls 'substantive-hungry'.
2   'Real' only operates when it can be assumed that 'not-real' is a
situated possibility:

> a definite sense attaches to the assertion that something is real,
> a real such-and-such, only in the light of a specific way in which
> it might be, or might have been, *not* real . . . the function of
> 'real' is not to contribute positively to the characterization of
> anything, but to exclude possible ways of being not real (*SS*: 70)

Austin's analyses of 'meaning' and 'real' cut away the ground
from under metaphysical assertions of a 'real' meaning under the
flux of ordinary language. Austin proceeds by means of a critique
of idealism.[4] His criticism is grounded in a prevailing lack of
concern with practice rather than ideas, i.e. the practice of ordinary language and professional philosophical practice as related to
it. 'The facts of actual language' (*MW*: 69) exemplify the practices
of the world which underpin the abstract constructs that constitute
traditional philosophy's 'reality'.
   But nowhere does Austin imply that ordinary language should
be elevated above any other. It constitutes only a *beginning*. When
raised above its station, 'ordinary language *blinkers* the already
feeble imagination' (*MW*: 68). In one respect, the ordinary examples that readily come to mind are not very revealing for understanding the reality of usage. So, Austin remarks, we need to
imagine 'all kinds of odd situations' (68) and then to ask, without
any hope of an entirely clear answer: 'Now, would I say that?'.
Further, a mere description of the facts of usage, limited to the
terms we all use, would not cope with the failure of many speakers,
lay and professionals, to comprehend the reality of their linguistic
practice – we might say, to comprehend the linguistic practice of
their 'reality'. As Austin remarks: 'There may be extraordinary
facts, even about our everyday experience, which plain men and
plain language overlook' (*MW*: 69). Ironically, Austin's emphasis
on the *ordinary* has served to drive home an *extraordinary*
fact – the reality of linguistic practice.

Austin as investigator

To investigate linguistic practice as it usually occurs is to turn one's back, for the moment, upon technical discourses. Before moving on to such an investigation, however, Austin cannot resist one final thrust at his philosophical colleagues: 'It was for too long the assumption of philosophers that the business of a 'statement' can only be to 'describe' some state of affairs or 'to state some fact', which it must do either truly or falsely' (*MW*: 1). Like Wittgenstein, then, Austin wants to reject any correspondence theory of truth. 'Saying' may be 'describing' but it is also a host of other activities. In sum, 'saying' is 'doing'. Take Austin's examples:

'I name this ship, etc.'

'I bet you sixpence, etc.'

When making these utterances, it seems clear that we are not describing our doing of something. Rather we are actually *doing* it (naming a ship, making a bet). And it is no good at all to say that we are not necessarily doing that act because of our mental reservations at the time. The act still remains an act. Subsequent revelations of 'states of mind' do not make the act void, although they may indicate that it was not performed in good faith.

Once again, with Wittgenstein, Austin is here asserting that the sense of utterances arises in something like the same way as the sense of a move in a game. The state of mind of the other player is either unavailable or possibly to be inferred on the basis of knowledge of the game. But the game itself constitutes what is a move and whether an act (utterance) counts as one kind of move rather than another. Although this is not to deny that things can go wrong. For instance, I might be an imposter not entitled to name ships. Such 'infelicities' (Austin) will mean either that the act does not come off (i.e. is void) or that it is achieved through an abuse of the procedure – as subsequently recognized.

These utterances which do not 'describe' but 'do' something, e.g. naming, 'betting', 'marrying', etc., Austin calls *performatives*. Unlike a description or statement (a *constative*), a performative cannot be 'true' or 'false', only 'happy' or 'unhappy'. Performatives either 'come off' or they fail.[5]

To complicate the analysis, Austin reminds us that performatives are not always in the first person, e.g. 'trespassers will be prosecuted'. None the less, they must be reducible to the first person. So the sign about trespassers can be taken to mean: 'I, John Smith, state that trespassers will be prosecuted.' When an utterance is not so reducible, it is not a performative. For instance, Austin suggests, 'He bets (is betting)' only describes 'his' performance; it does not perform his act of betting – an act which only he can perform.

A further feature of performatives is that they cannot lead to the question: 'Did he really do that?'. Compare:

'I approve'

'I feel approval of X'

In the first case, a performative, there is no question that the action of approving has happened. Here we cannot doubt that the speaker was really 'approving'. In the second example, a description (constative), in this case of a mental state, we may legitimately worry about the accuracy of the utterance, asking ourselves, or others, 'did he really feel approval?'

Despite these niceties, Austin recognizes that the distinction between performatives and constatives requires further refinement. Isn't, for instance, a 'statement' or a 'description' as much an act as any other. To resolve this vagueness, he analyses the range of acts performed by utterances in the following way:

1   Does an utterance simply *say* something (e.g. 'I feel approval of X')? Then it is a performance of an act *of* saying something and has a *'locutionary'* force.

2   Does an utterance *do* something (e.g. does it have the force of a question, a warning, etc.)? Then it is the performance of an act *in* saying something and has an *'illocutionary'* force. Such an act derives its force by conforming to some convention (e.g. about what counts as a question or a warning).

3   Is an utterance reducible to the first person (e.g. we can say 'I argue that' or 'I warn you that' but we cannot say 'I convince you that' or 'I alarm you that')? So when we say 'He convinced me' or 'He alarmed me', we are referring to the effects of another's actions upon ourselves. Hence this is the performance of an act which derives its force from whatever *effects* we bring about or achieve *by* saying something. These effects constitute the *'perlocutionary'* force of an utterance.

To summarize: the locutionary act has a *meaning* to be established by the usual method of correspondence with the facts – the truth/falsehood dimension applies to it. The illocutionary act has a *force* based on a convention, so the happiness/unhappiness dimension applies to it. Finally, the perlocutionary act: 'which is the achieving of certain effects by saying something' (*W*: 120) is not based on convention. Unlike an illocutionary act, its force is not immediately apparent to any hearer.

In these terms, 'stating' is now recognized as having the status of an illocutionary act. It differs from other such acts only in that there is no perlocutionary object specifically associated with 'stating' ('stating' is intransitive). For instance, while I can 'inform' or 'warn' someone, I do not 'state' someone. Among illocutionary acts, then, 'stating' has a 'comparative purity' (*W*: 138). The task remains, Austin concludes, to list the kinds of illocutionary forces of utterances. Towards that end, he suggests five classes of such force (*W*: 150–1 and 162).

Austin has impressively demonstrated here the pay-off that can arise from treating utterances as activities. Freed from the idealist attachment to a version of speech as an idea or ideas which picture(s) the world, linguistic practice becomes established as the phenomenon. As Austin writes: 'The total speech act in the total speech situation is the only actual phenomenon which, in the last resort, we are engaged in elucidating' (*W*: 147).

There is no doubting the significance of Austin's assertion in relation to the purposes of this book, especially as it gives the lie to the charge that such work reduces analysis to commonsense. Nevertheless, the 'linguistic phenomenology' which seems to Austin to be the proper name for such an enterprise is made ambiguous by two features just described in *How to do Things with Words*:

1 'The total speech situation', to which Austin refers, is a problematic conception. Either it refers to the situation as constituted in and through the speech acts themselves or it implies an analyst's conception used to context utterances. In the first case, it reverts back to the 'total speech act' and so is redundant. In the second, case, it seems to affirm the role of the analyst as interpreter, reading an underlying pattern in talk and, implicitly, denying space for linguistic practice itself. On the face of it, Austin chooses the latter alternative, thereby electing efficacy for the concept of the 'situation' but apparently denying some of the gains of our new found respect for the power of speech.[6]

2 Austin's desire to list classes of force of utterances, which he admits to be a sketchy enterprise, raises again the issue of whether we should proceed via reflection upon our own native competences, aided by Austin's beloved dictionary, or through inspection of naturally occurring utterances. It does begin to look like there is a mistaken line of development here. It begins with a preference for reflection, leads to a desire to list and classify, and terminates in that *interpretive* activity which leaves no space for the play of discourses.

3 Austin's insistence on the centrality of first-person speech to performatives is misleading. *Any* speech, including that associated with other voices than the 'I', involves a particular practice or performance (see the later discussion of Austin's 'Sovereign I').

'A Plea for Excuses', together with its postscript 'Three Ways of Spilling Ink', will give us further material to assess the innovatory force and also the limits of the practice of Austin as investigator. He chooses 'excuses' as 'a good site for *field work* in philosophy' (*APFE*: 183) because ordinary language seems to be less infected here by extinct philosophical theories. Above all, because 'excuses' are a 'pressingly practical matter' (182), we can expect ordinary usage to be 'rich and subtle'. Consonant with his method, Austin is here concerned not with the 'essence' of an excuse but with the practice of making excuses – when excuses are made and what makes them felicitous. An accusation of wrong-doing seems to be an appropriate occasion to proffer an excuse. Here an excuse accepts responsibility for the action but denies that the action was bad. Alternatively, while accepting the badness of the action, the excuse denies responsibility for it.

Making an excuse is entangled with the grammar of 'entitle-ment' and 'responsibility'. If we look at the example of a killing done in battle and compare it to an accidental, if reckless, killing, we see that the former instance calls forth a 'justification' and the latter an 'excuse'. 'Justifications' seem to relate to what I was entitled to do in the circumstances; 'excuses' relate to failing to do what I was obliged to do.

Such an excuse may seek to distinguish the 'voluntary' from the 'involuntary' parts of my actions. So, for instance, I may excuse my deed by reference to an 'involuntary' reaction to a situation. But, Austin notes, in many instances, for example 'eating' or 'kicking', it is inadmissible to appeal to the supposedly 'involuntary' nature of my deed simply because the semantics of 'voluntary' and 'involuntary' is inappropriate. Thus *modifying expressions*, like 'voluntary', may not be required or even permissible for the *stan-dard* case. Here: 'Only if we do the action named in some *special* way or circumstances different from those in which such an act is naturally done . . . is a modifying expression called for, or even in order' (*APFE*: 190). The basic rule in most cases is 'no modifica-tion without aberration'.[7] However, as we have seen, not all mod-ifying expressions can be applied to every verb. It makes little sense to speak of making a gift 'involuntarily' or of 'voluntarily' hiccoughing, for instance. We should be wary then, Austin warns us, of treating such modifiers as voluntary and involuntary as part of a pair. Often they are not alternatives. In the case of making a gift, for example, the opposite of voluntary might be 'inadver-tently' or 'under constraint'. Equally, while it might be felicitous to use a modifier with reference to certain actions, the context of the action may well render the excuse 'unacceptable'. As Austin says, 'involuntarily' treading on a snail is not likely to be treated in the same way as 'involuntarily' treading on a baby.

Austin stresses that such analysis has the aim of clarifying the 'machinery of action'. He rightly rejects the 'vague and comforting idea' that acting is simply 'the making of physical movements with parts of the body' (*APFE*: 178). It remains to be seen whether this proper stress on the reality of linguistic practice, opposed to the prevailing exaltation of 'ideas', avoids succumbing to an idealism of its own.

'Three Ways of Spilling Ink' seeks to develop the analysis of 'responsibility' by showing its intimate connection with the semantics of 'intention', 'deliberation' and 'purpose'. According to the method of 'What should we say when . . . ?', when somebody spills ink, they, or others, may excuse the act by seeking to offer favourable replies to questions about whether the act was performed 'intentionally', 'deliberately' or 'on purpose'. To disentangle the functioning of these terms, we can proceed, according to Austin, on two fronts: an examination of imagined or actual cases and of the 'grammar' and 'etymology' of the terms.

Take the case of feeding peanuts to penguins when the notice says: 'do not feed the penguins' (*TWSI*: 275). Assume the penguins die. Then the following questions might be asked:

> Did I feed them peanuts intentionally? Beyond a doubt: I am no casual peanut shedder. But deliberately? Well, that seems perhaps to raise the question, 'Had I read the notice?' Why does it? Or 'on purpose?' That seems to insinuate that I knew what fatal results would ensue. Again, why? (ibid).

Upon investigation, Austin suggests, we find that what is done 'intentionally' and 'deliberately' need not be done 'on purpose'. For instance, only the former two terms seem appropriate to the case of vandals destroying trees. Equally, 'intention' and 'purpose' need not go together with 'deliberation'. Where there is something 'precipitate' in an act, as when one rushes back into a blaze in an attempt at rescue, 'deliberation' is cut off from 'intention' and 'purpose'. However, the converse holds too: an action can be 'deliberate' but not 'intentional' – for example, running over an object and destroying it when driving to perform an important duty. In these felicitous distinctions, the only difficulty, it seems, is to pull apart 'intention' from 'purpose'. As Austin suggests (279), the expression 'accidentally on purpose' is probably only ironic.

Moving on to Austin's second etymological front, we discover that to 'deliberate', unlike the other two verbs, can be used to describe a process that is currently going on. For example, we can say 'I am deliberating' in this way but 'I am intending' refers to a future act, while 'I am purposing' does not exist. Further, each term is linked to its own kind of adverbial expression. 'Purpose' goes with 'on' and 'for'. 'Deliberation' takes 'after' or sometimes 'with', but the latter case indicates simply a slow style of performance. Finally, 'intention' goes with 'with'. The significance of these niceties, Austin suggests, is that 'on' and 'for' 'disassociate or sever my purpose from my action in a way that "with" does not do' (282). So 'purpose' can become almost impersonal in a way that is never done with 'intention'. For instance, we can act 'to good purpose' but not 'to good intention'. Equally, 'intention' distinguishes itself from 'deliberation'. For 'deliberation' is associated with a style of performance ('after' or 'with') but: 'intention is too intimately associated with ordinary language in general for there to be any *special* style of performance associated with it' (ibid). Austin concludes that 'intention' refers to something presumed in ordinary English usage to be intrinsic to life. It is not based on reflection. Instead, I am always supposed to have some idea of what I'm up to, some overall conception of what I'm doing. This idea or conception is not supposed to be based on conducting observations or to require reflection or analysis. Because this is so, it only makes sense to add 'intentionally' to a description of my action when it makes sense to suggest that the action might have been unintentional. However, this is not to say that 'intentional', like 'real', has no positive meaning until we have grasped certain ways in which things might be done 'unintentionally' (or be 'unreal'). Rather, 'intention' is a basic part of action. To be an actor, Austin implies, is to have 'intentions'.

If intention refers to my overall plan or conception, submerged in my acting, 'purpose' relates to my immediate conception of the *consequence* of my actions. 'Purpose' is: 'something to be achieved or effected as a result of what I'm doing like . . . the sickness of the penguins, if I did indeed feed them peanuts' (285). While both 'intention' and 'purpose' involve immediacy, 'deliberation' suggests stopping to weigh up the pros and cons. It further implies the existence of some cons for 'deliberation' is not just any kind of activity involving consideration of ends and means. Finally, we should note that overriding considerations may put all these assumptions out of joint, e.g. when we act 'under a threat'.[8]

This, broadly, is what Austin suggests about 'responsibility'. How does he account for and justify his method? First, he argues that obtaining agreement about what we should say in imagined cases reveals the fine power of ordinary usage. Of course, having completed our analysis:

we shall then have arrived at nothing more than an account of certain ordinary 'concepts' employed by English speakers: but also at no less a thing. And it is not so little. These concepts will have evolved over a long time: that is, they will have faced the test of practical use, of continual hard cases better than their vanished rivals (274).

As the reference to historical evolution and to 'cases' makes clear, the model is that of the common law. If the Sapir-Whorf thesis is that society is modelled in language, Austin is reminding us that societies have a history and that language *evolves* in connection with society.

We may immediately note two points of issue with Austin. First, common law appeals to the assumption of a uniformity of interpretive procedures used by common men – it is the everyday equivalent of ethnomethodology. Like its academic twin, however, it is indifferent to linguistic practice that interrupts the rule of one discourse and cannot acknowledge (or would suppress) the multiplicity of discourses which exist in a state of tension even within one set of utterances. Second, it will allow no challenge to the rule of a single discourse because it itself is possessed by an ideal of the proper form of such a discourse – the ideal of the free individual, exerting his sovereignty on the market of actions.

Like bourgeois law, Austin's texts make reference to the individual as the seat of responsibility and intentionality. This sovereign 'I' precedes and is at the basis of the social realm of the 'We'. Hence, in our very discussions of ordinary language, 'We' may well come together in a common view but this community is no more than a social contract, agreed for specific purposes by sovereign 'I's, possessed of rights and responsibilities which exist prior to the contract.[9]

This fiction of a discourse of 'I's is all the more absurd in an era when, as Marx noted, *social* relations have never been more developed. The assumption of rights by collectivities (the state apparatus and the corporations that service each other) and the challenge made to this rule by collective action evade Austin's conception of a discourse of 'I's. In this sense, the Austinian world is the world of the self-understandings paraded on our media. Economic and industrial disputes are understood in the media by reference to the Austinian legal fiction of the 'I' and his intentions. It is always one individual against another – an employer 'threatened' by militants, a housewife 'demanding' that her striking husband return to work. In each case, the organization of ruling collectivities is ignored and the activity of emancipatory collectivities treated as repressive. The domination of such ruling collectivities, shown in a ruling discourse, undercuts and, at the same time, shows the basis of complaints about the 'personalization' of issues by the media.

Austin at reflection – the rule of Austin's self

Austin's version of the collectivity is made most explicit in the course of some pages in the middle of 'A Plea for Excuses'. In clarifying his position about the status of ordinary language, he grounds his activity in the collectivity of professional philosophy – a specialized discipline proceeding, like common law, from (and out of) ordinary usage. The monolithic rule of a dominant discourse is thus doubly supported. First, the commitment is to a form of research which respects (or should respect) a ruling discourse, which, second, through its legitimation of the status of a profession, sets its seal of approval upon the collectivity.

As made clear elsewhere, the method is to proceed 'from ordinary language': 'that is, by examining *what we should say when* and so why and what we should mean by it' (*APFE*: 181, Austin's emphasis). Proceeding in this way, Austin senses two problems. The minor problem is that ordinary usage seems to vary. Yet this is easily overcome for, when we examine or imagine a speech situation in detail, we do tend to agree what we should say. If the differences in usage are sometimes apparently well-founded, this is because we have identified more than one of the many collectivities that have their own specialized forms of usage (e.g. judges, philosophers, and so on). Such specialization, in turn, flows in and out of ordinary usage which, as a reflection of what Austin terms 'the inherited experience and acumen of many generations of men' (185), always has the first word.

However, to treat ordinary language as the first word, Austin observes, gives rise to a second, more major, problem: what has the *last* word? He points out that we should remember that ordinary language is primarily concentrated upon the 'practical business of life' (ibid). As such it should not be discounted: 'it does not mark nothing'. However, its distinctions are clearly 'not the best way of arranging things if our interests are more extensive or intellectual than the ordinary'. Ordinary language leaves out, for instance, the discoveries of science but takes into account superstition, error, and fantasy. 'Certainly, then', he concludes: 'ordinary language is *not* the last word: in principle it can everywhere be supplemented and

improved upon and superseded. Only remember, it *is the first* word'
(ibid). Austin now turns to address the issue of how this 'supple-
menting' and 'improving' activity is to proceed. It seems that there
are a number of 'systematic aids' or 'source-books' to be used along
the way. The dictionary can be 'worked' simply by reading it
through making lists or by making interconnections between the
definitions of a limited number of terms; the common law, as
already noted, is a vast source of data; and, finally, the researches of
psychology are not to be discounted for it is a discipline which
notices and classifies varieties of behaviour: 'not observed or named
by ordinary men and hallowed by ordinary usage' (189).

There is no doubting, however, that the collectivity which Austin
summons up to sanction his activity, as both resource and topic, is
that of lawyers engaged in common law practice. While lexico-
grapher and psychologist alike are tempted to codify, even in areas
where ordinary language finds no practical importance, the common law judge, like the ordinary language philosopher, resists the
urge to codify, respects usage and locates its source in the evolutionary movement of history. Austin writes that:

> it is a perpetual and salutary surprise to discover how much is to
> be learned from the law; and it is to be added that if a distinction
> drawn is a sound one, even though not yet recognized in law, a
> lawyer can be relied upon to take note of it, for it may be
> dangerous not to – if he does not, his opponent may (188).

Of course, there are differences to be noted between the lawyer and
the philosopher of language: the former is required to make clear
decisions, to use certain accepted formulae of court procedure and
to respect precedents of the court which may have a problematic
relation to ordinary usage. But such differences do not override the
family resemblances between the communities of philosophy and
law. Both share the same 'first word' – usage – and adopt co-
operative methods in order to 'clean' the 'tools' (181) to be used in
their specialized work ('words are our tools' Austin comments
(ibid)). Both offer the pleasures of communal life. The Inns of
Court, no doubt, like Austin's version of the philosopher's seminar
group afford: 'the fun of discovery, the pleasures of co-operation and
the satisfaction of reaching agreement' (175).

Such modest pleasures are secured by a number of self-imposed
limits. First, professional collectivities must not seek to overstep
their sphere of professional competence. Austin's motto for 'a sober
philosophy', 'neither a be-all, nor an end-all be' (*PP*: 271 fn.), is the
watchword of a community determined not to tread on other
people's toes and conscious that 'the pleasures of co-operation' are

as important as the end in view. The second limit, which arises from the first, is that, where ordinary language is at the heart of its work, a professional collectivity (of lawyers or philosophers alike) must develop a respect for usage and, above all, for the supposedly evolutionary course of history which authored it. Hence professional discourse is to be regarded as a specialized variety of one central discourse – ordinary usage. Further, professional discourses will vary from one another in the extent to which ordinary usage provides a topic as well as resource. This is illustrated in Figure 6:

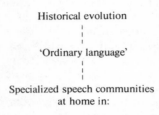

Figure 6   An 'Austinian' version of usage

We can now afford to be a little more precise about Austin's beginning and end – his 'first' and 'last' words in discourse. If 'ordinary language', as seemed likely all along, offers that 'first' word, then it is tempting to see the specialized speech communities which license professional tasks as the source of the 'last' word. However, as Figure 6 makes clear, this conclusion would neglect the question of what licenses, or warrants, such communities? Austin would answer: 'ordinary language'. And what licenses ordinary language? The answer is clear and consistent in Austin's texts: historical evolution.

It is the evolutionary course of historical development that is the Austinian 'last word'. It holds both ordinary and extra-ordinary usage securely in its grasp. Historical evolution has established one main discourse ('ordinary language') and any number of specialized sub-variants (the discourses of philosophy, psychology, gardening, and so on). And this discourse, as we have already noted, is the discourse of the individual and his responsibilities – the discourse of sovereign 'I's. After the model of the social contract, collectivities are admitted into this discourse only as professions, coming together for limited purposes, and respecting the rule of the dominant discourse.

Austin's critique of theorists who legislate the character of the world is thus undercut by his neglect of 'legislative' activities in everyday communication. The Socratic dialogue of Austin's Oxford seminars is altogether misleading as a representation of a world where discourse does not routinely redeem its own claims to validity and where the technicization of language limits our possibility of speaking to each other in the way that Austin regards as 'felicitous'. Austin's self-reflection is the reflection of the rule of 'self'. An era in which history is claimed to have stopped will brook no interference with its linguistic rule.

In the introductory comments on Austin, two principles of method were enunciated: the reconstitution of the concrete as the dialectic of many speeches and the location of progressive, as well as retrogressive, elements within a text. Both principles seem endangered by the present state of the argument. In moving towards a more satisfactory view, we need to examine the state of tension within Austin's texts, rather than to constitute a specious, because ideal, 'entity'. This tension arises between an imposition of a dominant discourse and the recognition of, and engagement with, a multiplicity of discourses.

Austin's subservience to an 'ordinary language', which, through historical evolution, allows only the discourse of 'I', is in a state of tension with his formulation of speech as a practice. The former leads straight to idealism, offering a world dominated by an idea (the sovereign individual) and organized into specialized speech communities evolving their speech, while subservient to that idea. The latter implies a materialist turn, rejecting the concept of ideas and 'mind', and replacing them with an analysis of the multiplicity of discursive practices.[10] Here lies the 'progressive' or emancipatory potential of Austin's texts: the attempt to engage everyday practice rather than to dismiss it.

Notes

1 To accept Austin's explanations as full and accurate guides to his practice would be not only to confuse advice (which is about all he gave in this line) with philosophical analysis and literary-critical description (which is what is needed) but to confer upon Austin an unrivalled power of self-discernment: Cavell (1967: 252 fn.).

2 See Chapter 6. It is worth noting, however, the importance of Heidegger's attempt in the same work to reject the treatment of words as simply items of 'communication'. His injunction to 'pay heeds to what the words say' (1970: 130), rather than to become preoccupied with the dictionary definition of terms, can equally well lead in a materialist direction as in a romantic one.

3 This methodological dimension produces strange bedfellows: on the one hand, the 'inspectors' include conversational analysts and the authors of this book. On the other, the 'recollectors' include Chomsky, Searle and Blum and McHugh.

4 This is not to say that some of his practice altogether escapes idealism, as we have already noted about his commitment to 'the common stock of words'. We explore these tensions further in the conclusion of this chapter.

5 Austin gives an example of such failure: 'I divorce you' said to a wife by a husband in a Christian country, where both are Christians rather than Mohammedans.

6 This raises the difficult issue of the role of analysts' formulations of the 'speech situation'. To dismiss an emphasis on context preserves the centrality of linguistic practice to analysis. None the less, it is doubtful whether we can do without some analytic formulations of an 'ideal speech situation'. Indeed, formulations like these provide a critical perspective while preserving the reality of linguistic practice. Habermas's treatment of this issue is referred to in note 10 below.

7 This rule is questioned by John Searle (1969). 'The point is not', he remarks, 'no modification without aberration, but "no remark without remarkableness" ' (144). What is at issue, he argues, is not the analysis of particular words, but, rather, the explanation of what it is to make an assertion. It might also be noted that the issue of excuses fits very well with a 'social order' concerned with rule-following and rule-breaking.

8 As Hart (1949) points out, the claim to be acting 'under a threat' makes reference to the *defeasibility* (or possibility of defeat) of legal concepts. Precedent is relevant not as an abstract statement of what constitutes an offence but as an expression of what *defences* can be employed. Rather than seek abstract rules, lawyers should examine actual defences used, asking, with Austin, 'what should we say when . . . ?'

9 The pre-capitalist elements in common law suggest that the ideology of the 'free individual' may be more appropriate to modern statute law. Equally, to the extent that common law already assumes a social order that gives it sense, such law need not depend upon a fictional social contract.

Austin's emphasis on common law, however, allows him to affirm the sovereignty of common practice. A focus on statute law might reveal more clearly the impingement of a mode of domination upon both legal and everyday linguistic practice. In fact, there is no hint of this in either Austin or Hart's work. They agree that law is based on a general habit of obedience to orders. Hart (1961) disagrees with Austin only in making the (Parsonian) claim that habit is insufficient without a shared normative commitment among members of a community.

10 For instance, Habermas (1976) makes use of Austin's analysis of speech acts in order to suggest the emancipatory potential of discourse. The illocutionary and constative components of speech acts give them what Habermas calls 'a double structure'. Illocutionary acts appeal to 'the level of intersubjectivity' and make normative validity claims.

Constative acts appeal to 'the level of objects in the world'. Speakers seek to achieve a consensus about these objects in terms of the communicative role assigned in the illocutionary component. The point is that both validity claims are discursively redeemable. Hence Habermas implies the possibility of challenge to any discursive attempt to naturalize social forms.

Bibliography

Austin, J. L. (1970), *Philosophical Papers*, eds. J. O. Urmson and G. J. Warnock, Oxford University Press: London.

Austin, J. L. (1962), *How to do Things with Words*, ed. J. O. Urmson, Oxford University Press: London.

Austin, J. L. (1962), *Sense and Sensibilia*, reconstructed from the manuscript notes by G. L. Warnock, Oxford University Press.

Cavell, Stanley (1967), 'Austin at Criticism', in Rorty, 1967, pp. 250–60.

Clegg, Stewart (1975), 'Power, Theorizing and Nihilism', *Theory and Society*, vol. 2.

Gellner, Ernest (1959), *Words and Things*, Gollancz: London.

Habermas, Jürgen (1976), 'Some Distinctions in Universal Pragmatics : A Working Paper', *Theory and Society*, 3, 155–67.

Hart, H. L. A. (1949), 'The Ascription of Responsibility and Rights', *Proc. Aristot. Soc.* (XI), 1949.

Hart, H. L. A. (1961), *The Concept of Law*, Oxford University Press.

Heidegger, Martin (1972), *What is Called Thinking?*, trans. F. J. Wieck and J. G. Grey, Harper Torchbooks: New York.

Marcuse, Herbert (1955), *Reason and Revolution*, Routledge & Kegan Paul: London.

Ricardou, Jean (1975), 'Terrorisme, Théorie', in *Robbe-Grillet: Colloque de Cerisy*, Union Générale des Editions: Paris.

Rorty, Richard (1967), ed., *The Linguistic Turn*, University of Chicago Press.

Ryle, Gilbert (1971), 'Dialectic in the Academy', in *Collected Papers*, vol. 1, Hutchinson: London.

Searle, John R. (1969), *Speech Acts*, Cambridge University Press.

Torode, Brian (1976), 'The Revelation of a Theory of the Social World as Grammar', in R. Harré (ed.), *Life Sentences*, Wiley: London.

Urmson, J. O. (1967), 'J. L. Austin', in Rorty, op. cit., pp. 232–8.

Urmson, J. O. and Warnock, G. (1967), 'J. L. Austin', in Rorty, 1967, pp. 248–9.

John Locke, the seventeenth-century philosopher, entitles a chapter of his *Second Treatise of Government* 'Of Property'. The use of the preposition 'of' rather than 'on' reflects an archaic usage. It also provides a dual possibility. While the chapter *says* that its topic is 'property', what it *shows* is the text 'of property'. By a close examination of Locke's chapter, we show how it subverts traditional authorities in order to instate the property rights of the author. The ways in which these latter rights are themselves subverted is a continuing theme of subsequent chapters.

chapter 10

Locke's text of property

The intelligibility of the text

Because we have read our masters, we are already familiar with the distinction between saying and showing.[1] So whatever a text says is sustained or undermined by what it shows. What it shows is the intelligibility of its claim. We are used to two such claims. According to one claim, that of objectivity, a text expresses the world. To be sure, since we are all neo-Kantians, this 'objective' text does not present itself as the world itself (literally, as the speech of the world), but as an expression of our common forms of language and representation. In the terms of the later Wittgenstein, the 'objective text' claims to speak our grammar and defer to our form of life.[2]

But we are also familiar with another claim to intelligibility that appeals to subjectivity. This directs our attention not to what is common but towards what is (purportedly) unique. Rather than look to the body of the text for the comforting reiteration of the familiar (of ourselves), we are encouraged to look, as it were, to the foot of the last page – to look at the signature. For this is the text of genius, the subjective text, where we encounter a system of signs that has its apparent origin in the practice of some instituting subject.

Objective and subjective claims are not, of course, mutually exclusive. We are very well familiar with the text which interweaves the claims of objectivity (the ordinary) and subjectivity (the extra-ordinary). Such a text provides for itself as extra-ordinary work upon the ordinary. Indeed, in a stratified society, in a society of experts and of expertise, we have learned to expect (and to respect) the kind of difference that is expressed through such a claim. Here genius recognizes its proper limits within the common forms of speech.[3]

All these claims share in a reiteration of the certainties of grammar. Their versions of responsible speaking differ but all *defer* to the theorizing power of subject and object. Neither will permit itself, in Nietzsche's terms, to be a 'little ironical' about such grammatical certainties.[4]

But this disavowal of irony is not a chance commitment – even if they *would*, such texts *could* have none of it. For to question grammar is, fundamentally to question the rights of property as inscribed within a textual mode of production. Both objective and subjective texts would have us believe that they belong to persons (the author, his community) – both would be possessions. Both display themselves as the *possessors* of *properties* (of style, of purpose, of content) which must be respected in reading. Both reproduce, then, the features of ownership and control characteristic of property relations.

The 'objective' text rests securely on the claims of *common* property redefined as ownership *by* the dominant mode of production. It poses the question: 'who owns the text?', and answers by making reference to its espousal of the commonly owned grammar.

To see the claims of *private* property asserted we must look to the 'subjective' text. As we gaze at the author's name, we are reminded of the rights of property arising from the private labour that has produced the text. Does the author have certain intentions in writing *his* text? Well, then, we must respect such intentions.

Each text reproduces a version of 'belonging' in terms of ownership and property – whether in regard to the persons who own the text or to the *properties* that the text *possesses*.[5] Consequently, neither can acknowledge the 'belonging' to discourse which is set into play by its own signifying practice.

The concrete representative of discourse found in such texts of property is the reader – who must be persuaded that the text fulfills its claim and, thereby, be allowed to unite with the writer. The writing and the reading have no history. The text becomes one-dimensional because the saying and the showing are collapsed into one – the text *is* the property which speaks it.[6]

Cut off from discourse, the text of property cannot provide for itself as other than an instance of itself. It can no more acknowledge the presence of emerging forces within common property (grammar), than it can recognize the historically transitory nature of private property (genius). Locked within itself, the power of its speech arises as it theorizes powerfully (persuasively) a mode of production of sense (a means of differentiating, of deferring) that has both persuader and persuaded securely in its grip.[7] In mastering its topics, the text of property conceals that which masters it.

Sophistry and mastery

Among the interesting aspects of Locke's theorizing is that it shows the tension between the certainties of his mundane world, the certainties of its theorizing power, and the manner in which a reiteration of these certainties can render speech worthless – without point. For, if everyone can see it and say it, why speak? To begin from the certainties of the mundane world is to be written upon by its mode of production – not to work, not to negate, and, hence not to be involved in the movement of history.

Notice Plato's comment on Sophists who use the mundane as their secure beginning. The Sophists, Plato tells us, teach nothing but the conventional views held by the mass of the people. It is as if a Sophist were in charge of a powerful animal whose ways he got to know:

> But he would not really know which of the creature's tastes and desires was fair or unfair, good or bad, right or wrong; he would simply use the terms on the basis of its reactions, calling what pleased it good, what annoyed it bad. He would have no other standard of judgment, but would call the necessities of the animal's nature right and fair, remaining quite blind to the real difference between necessity and goodness, and quite unable to tell anyone else what it was. He would make a queer sort of teacher, wouldn't he? (*Republic*: Book I, 493).

It is worth recalling the appositeness of Plato's critique to ordinary-language philosophy (and, perhaps, to ethnomethodology and other versions of sociological phenomenology). Like the Sophist, this 'queer sort of teacher' identifies *grammar* with *essence*. Like the Sophist, he is secure in the mundane as the only possible existence – he equates, in Plato's terms, necessity and goodness.[8]

Nietzsche shares with Plato a rejection of grammar as the beginning and the end of philosophy. In *Beyond Good and Evil*, he writes: 'Ought not the philosopher to rise *above* a belief in grammar?' (47–8). He is discussing here the relation between a text (a fiction) and an author. He argues that the notion of the former *belonging* to the latter might be a fiction too. Yet this seems strange. Do I not own what I write and speak? Or is not at least what I speak my own? Ought I not to respect another's ownership of his text and be faithful to it – for instance by seeking to establish his intentions before presuming to criticize?

In posing the issue of ownership, we return to Locke who formulated our historically located temptation to achieve an alternative beginning for writing and reading in *common* property – a beginning in the mundane. Yet the appearances of the mundane world are not first; they cannot be our beginning. Such appearances cover over the emergence of subsidence of certain modes of ownership (of the means of production, of labour) and control (over theorizing power).

So every speaking and acting occasion represents an historically bounded relation to a situation containing *concealed* potentialities. Through such a relation, practice provides an opportunity to transcend the appearances suggested by our mundane existence (appearances which express one, albeit dominant, mode of production). Which is to say that practice provides an opportunity to participate in discourse.

To turn away from discourse is to be the voice of the Master. The Master needs to deny his historically transitory role. His mode of domination, when embedded in mundane existence, appears to be natural Reason itself. So to adopt the security of mundaneity is to speak as the Master. Standing apart from discourse, one speaks *masterfully*.

Masterful speech does not labour; it does not transform what is given because it cannot transcend it. That is to say, masterful speech has the character of idleness. In his submission to the dominance of the appearances of the mundane world (the mundane world *of* dominance), Austin provides in this sense, an example of idle practice.

In contrast to Plato and Nietzsche, Austin seems to want to ground knowledge upon our mundane existence – he wants to equate the 'necessary' and the 'good'. Like the Sophist animal-keeper, the speaker is condemned to leave everything as it is, only revealing more clearly the mundane base of certainty. As Austin writes: 'It is a matter of unpicking, one by one, a mass of seductive (mainly verbal) fallacies, of exposing a wide variety of concealed motives – an operation which leaves us, in a sense, just where we began' (*Sense and Sensibilia*: 4–5). Our investigations ('unpicking', 'exposing') only certify, for Austin, the inability of practice to transcend the given. An inability to treat the commonplace as a body of contradictory practices.

In principle opposed to positivism, Austin's ordinary-language philosophy thus shares with positivism a desire to encourage respect for 'the facts'. It wants to restrict itself to speaking 'what is'. In doing so, it restricts itself to appearances, exemplified by the happy certainties of the dictionary and accepted usage. So its discourse denies history and historically grounded practice. Or, rather, the only history that it will acknowledge is the history of the ever-growing 'soundness' and 'subtlety' of ordinary usage.[9]

This recalls Heidegger's notion in *Being and Time* of *Gerede* or idle talk. We hear and understand its words, while floating on the surface, forgetful of what its mode of discourse covers over. As the willing accomplice of appearances, the idle talk of ordinary-language philosophy comes to resemble what Heidegger calls 'gossip', 'passing the word on', or 'scribbling'. In none of these activities do the participants listen to the discourse which their speech represents.[10]

In its explicit commitment to the mundane, a commitment to a dominant mode of production, ordinary-language is the voice of the Master. The practice of the Master is idle talk – which is to say that the Master is idle. Following Kojève's (1969) reading of Hegel, the Master is thus condemned to be overcome in history. For: 'History is the history of the working slave.'

The Master can never detach himself from the wor(l)d in which he lives and, if this world perishes, he perishes with it (because he does not work). Only the Slave can transcend – can transform – the given world that forms and fixed him in slavery and create a world that he has formed in which he will be free.[11]

We read Locke as struggling with this given world – as engaged, that is to say, in transcending it. In overturning the secure beginning of his mundane existence, by authorizing a text ('Of Property') as the produce of (his) private labour, Locke expresses the practice of the bourgeois Slave in the process of overturning a pre-capitalist Master.

Interpreting Locke

In his book, *The Political Theory of Possessive Individualism*, C. B. MacPherson sees Locke as the provider of the ideological justification for unlimited capitalist appropriation. According to MacPherson, Locke's version of 'possessive individualism' allows for an *individual* who is the proprietor of his person and talents, a *society* which consists of relations of exchange between proprietors of private property, and a *state* which is a mechanism for the protection of property rights. Locke's transcendence of the pre-capitalist limits on private appropriation has, in MacPherson's view, produced a political theory which recognizes a money economy, formally free labour, and secure rights of property encompassing vast inequalities.

Now we do not want to deny MacPherson's reading but to attempt a change of emphasis. Private appropriation necessarily expresses itself not only in ostensible *economic* relations but in all socially organized activities, including the production of texts and the theorizing power that animates it. Our topic, then, centres around the character of the theorizing power of *property*. In our reading of Locke, we seek to show that (his) chapter 'Of Property' is both an *account* of property and an expression of the *text* of property.

Yet how does a text produce itself as privately appropriated – which is to say what is the mode of production of the text of property? What kind of secure beginning, what kind of claim does it make for itself? What kind of relation does it (re-)produce between *its* categories of writer and reader?

In this reading, we argue that Locke begins in common property by writing a text whose authoritative beginning is the world which everyone knows. Yet facing the nihilistic implications of the text-of-anyone, he secures a new grounding for his text. His work now becomes the text of private labour, of private talents, of private property. Through his efforts (labour), through his talents, Locke now claims to transcend what is held in common. Common property becomes redefined as a topic of inquiry – as the starting place for the industrious and talented inquirer.

Talents and industry, however, need to be recognized and duly rewarded. Locke implies that without recognition and reward (private) labour is without point.[12] Hence, having moved from the collective to the private, Locke now moves back to the collective in order to provide some standard for private labour. The money-exchange equation secures (socially) the character of private labour and enables a value to be given to socially demanded commodities (texts). The text of property is now the full expression of a commodity society, of a society of private proprietors obtaining abstract rewards for their intellectual labour.

Given this, it is instructive to pay attention to the intelligibility of MacPherson's own text on Locke. Somewhat curiously, while MacPherson wants to locate Locke as a man of his times – to exert his own authority over the topic – his version of reading receives its authority not *against* but *in* Locke.

MacPherson writes of 'the risk of reading into an author's work any assumptions that he did not clearly state'. According to this view of reading, one seeks to be faithful to the author's intentions – to what the author meant rather than to what made the meaning possible but what he could not say. To do otherwise is, for MacPherson, to risk (a risk which, it should be added, MacPherson *does* take).

But MacPherson is silent about the risk that arises in such a version of faithful reading. The risk where the reader unthinkingly employs the theorizing power of the Master: where the reader is idle. Such a version of faithfulness makes MacPherson want to respect the security of Locke's beginning, to respect the (private) grounds upon which Locke erects his text. Locke becomes the proprietor of his (own) text and we must respect *his* ownership and not infringe upon *his* property. So when Locke erects a fence on his property (the security of his beginning), we must be careful that we do not unduly trespass.

MacPherson's genuflection towards this version of reading suggests the textual significance of Locke's defence of the rights of private property. MacPherson equates reading with an acceptance of the Subject: the same grammar that grounds the claims of the 'subjective' text.

The text 'Of Property'

Yet Locke's chapter 'Of Property' begins not in a subject's private property but in common property. Like other theorists of his time, Locke assumes a state of nature in which individuals confront the dictates of God ('Revelation') and of a 'Reason' which is an immutable given, designed by nature and God to be man's moral guide. Hence his chapter begins:

> Whether we consider natural Reason, which tells us, that Men, being once born, have a right to their Preservation, and consequently to Meat and Drink, and such other things, as Nature affords for their Subsistence: or Revelation, which gives us an account of those Grants God made of the World to Adam, and to Noah, and his Sons, 'tis very clear, that God, as King David says, Psal. CXV. xvi. *has given the Earth to the Children of Men*, given it to Mankind in common (*S*25: 1–8).

Locke tells us here that Earth – the place where men live, the source of the raw materials that they have available – is given in common. But as well as *asserting* a commonness, Locke exemplifies a *commonness*. His authority is what is in common: the certainties of Reason and Revelation as viewed by his contemporaries. Equally, the 'We' (who consider natural Reason) and to whom 'tis very clear' are already taken to be co-partners in Locke's form of life. Locked into what commonly passes as Reason, his speech arises out of the common, for the common. His text is common property, appealing to a common standard of intelligibility and telling us what another's text might equally have told us. So Locke begins from the certainty that speech makes reference to the commonness granted by God ('Revelation') or by a social consensus ('natural Reason'). Both kinds of commonness arise *outside* language.

Grounding his text in this common 'Reason', common property defines the topic of his enquiry, the difficulty that he wants to address (because it troubles us in common): 'But this being supposed, it seems to some a very great difficulty, how any one should ever come to have a Property in any thing . . .' (*S*25: 8–10). So Locke can raise a topic because, in perusing communal usage, members of the community ('some') discover 'a very great difficulty'. The community thus provides for Locke's text a directive about how to begin (from itself), and a standard for what should be spoken (what it speaks about) and what should be ignored (that about which it remains silent). Even though Locke operates concretely with the asocial categories of Earth, God and Children, his social is already constructed rather than contracted – as the community that owns his text, the text of common property.

In exemplifying his commitment to the common speech, Locke follows his own stated view of human activity which would polarize life between asocial and socialized individuals and opt for the latter as the only tolerable choice: 'God having made Man such a Creature, that, in his own Judgment, it was not good for him to be alone . . . ' (*S*77: 1–2). 'Aloneness' is here conceived by Locke as being apart from civil society. In his speech, then, man must re-assert his one-ness with civil society – with the mundane – must re-assert the character of his text as common property. For the choice is between the solitary genius – who solipsistically denies the mundane – and the fully mundane man. 'Aloneness' is never addressed as being apart from discourse, always addressed as lack of commitment to what is (currently) common. In such a way, in his theorizing, Locke is indeed not 'alone'.

Locke begins from a kind social contract that he does not recognize. This is his contract to be faithful to a mode of discourse which is an image of the present and narrowed to appearances. So Locke remains silent about what his communal consensus covers over.

Locke's contract is social because he grounds his text in the authority of his community – the 'we' and the 'some'. Lamprecht (1962) refers to Locke's different style from that of the Scholastics. He is, as they could not be, a gentleman talking to gentlemen. Hence Locke speaks socially because the claim that runs through his text is that in reasoning together, 'we' (gentlemen) begin at the same place and have the same destination in view. Gentlemen would not wish to pursue the matter further. For any dispute must infringe the conventions of polite society – must infringe their gentlemen's agreement.

Locke's social contract seems to parallel attempts, as with the Sophists, or ordinary-language philosophers, to speak what is common, to give voice to what is common property. Like them, Locke becomes the mere mouthpiece of what (in his community) passes as reason. At this stage, at least, Locke is not involved in history – he does not work, he is idle.

Compare Locke's start with that of Austin in *Sense and Sensibilia*. Once again, one is confronted with a text by and for gentlemen – gentlemen who offer their common knowledge to confront the philosopher's puzzlement about words. The latter's notion of 'reality' according to Austin, must be restored to the ordinary usage from which it has come adrift:

> Real is an absolutely *normal* word with nothing new-fangled or technical or highly specialised about it. It is, that is to say, already firmly established in, and very frequently used in, the ordinary language we all use every day. Thus, *in this sense*, it is a word which has a fixed meaning (*SS*: 62).

For Austin, then, the mundane is normative for what can be said and done – it gives a word 'a fixed meaning'. Philosophy goes wrong when it is alone in its private world and, as Locke puts it, it is 'not good' to be alone. Consequently, the philosopher must let mundane usage (common property) speak through him, he must remind us of the pre-eminence of the 'absolutely normal'.

So Austin's task is to reveal philosophy's necessary dependence upon the mundane world and to return us home to the security of that world. Through him, we learn 'a technique for dissolving philosophical worries', and this, he tells us, is 'an operation which leaves us, in a sense, just where we began' (ibid: 5). Self-confessedly, Austin's speech changes nothing and transcends nothing. His speech merely reiterates and confirms the impossibility of transcending what he was: an ordinary Englishman (although perhaps of the Senior Common Room variety). His practice serves to remind himself and his readers of the impossibility of practice – for what practice recalls is our mundane community and its dominance over us. In leaving us 'just where we began', Austin's practice only can reassert a dominant theorizing power (the theorizing power of dominance). Like Locke, in his opening comments, like the Master, Austin does not work – he is not involved in history. So when his world perishes, his text perishes with it.

Ultimately, however, Locke is not prepared to tolerate an Austinian version of speaking securely. Notice how 'the very great difficulty' to which Locke refers, poses this very problem, the problem of speaking as and for common property. If the mundane world (what is in common) speaks and we must remain silent when it is silent, man no longer makes any difference in his speech or rather that difference becomes an act of deference to the mundane. Acting as the mere mouthpiece of common property, it becomes difficult to see why he should speak, difficult to see 'how any one should ever come to have a property in any thing'.

In this reading, Locke is saying that the mundane speaker has no grounds for speaking. Or rather that those grounds, because they are communal, fixed in a pre-given, frozen, determining, mundane world, are worthless. Because he wants to work, Locke faces the issue of nihilism, covered over by the Sophists and Austin. Put in another way, Locke's difficulty 'how any one should come to have a property in any thing', now becomes 'how any one should' have *grounds to speak*. (Curiously, in an Austinian way, this reading trades off the way in which the word 'grounds' can refer, in ordinary English usage, to property, as in 'the grounds of my house'.)

In answer to his 'difficulty', Locke seems to recognize that speech only ceases to be nihilistic when it becomes *work*, engaged in negating the certainties of Nature and of the mundane world. While God gave the Earth to men in common, he tells us, he did not mean it always to remain common and uncultivated (*S*34). So, although men share in what is common property (speech, the mundane world), their life consists in working upon it, in cultivating it (through speech, through practice). Practice, then, necessarily engages and *transforms* what is common. As Locke puts it, thereby rejecting practice which leaves everything as it is: 'The Law Man was under, was rather for *appropriating*. God Commanded and his Wants forced him to *labour*' (*S*35: 12–14). Practice, including speech, now becomes recognized as *labour* – as an engagement with Nature, with the social, as work upon it, as appropriation. So Locke replaces the assumed dominance of common usage by the transforming activity of labour. In this way, he challenges the theorizing power which does not work – the theorizing power of the Master.

Labour is not the practice of the solitary genius, spitefully rebelling against the constraints of the mundane world. Labour engages with (and against) modes of production. It contains, thereby, the historically bounded basis for the transformation of society. By introducing labour, rather than mundaneity or genius, as the ground of human activity, Locke, then, expresses a new theorizing power of one who works – the theorizing power of the Servant.

Now, if labour is conceived as the practice of the Servant, then it is the practice that overturns the theorizing power of the Master, first in its traditional (pre-capitalist) form and then its capitalist mode. It is, therefore, important to remind ourselves that it is the theorizing power of the *pre-capitalist* Master with which Locke struggles. In turn, he speaks as and for the theorizing power of what, in his time, was the capitalist *Servant*.

So Locke's need to free his speech from the security of past beginnings expresses, therefore, not an intellectual task (as if intellectual and manual labour could be separated) but his engagement with the movement of history – as an emergent capitalism needed too to free itself from past constraints. Accordingly, in his text, labour becomes *private* labour for *private* purposes. So, in working, Locke denies the authority of his mundane world because he wants to *own* his grounds, to own the authority of his speech. At the same time, while Locke's text speaks as and for private property and private labour (the slave of his period), its recognition of the theorizing power of labour also foreshadows the force that contends with his Slave-become-Master.

Locke now establishes his argument for work (speech) as private appropriation leading to and confirming private property. He shows how the commonness of the Earth (language) can lead to the private character of labour and its products (the private character of speech). That is to say, he shows how men 'could come to have a property in any thing'.

First, Locke argues that man is the proprietor of his person – that is to say, his labour expresses his private efforts disposed of in accord with his private choices. Man, according to Locke, *owns* his labour. Second, when he labours, when he works upon Nature, the product is his alone, for it represents Nature mixed with (worked upon by) private labour:

> Though the Earth, and all inferior Creatures be common to all men, yet every Man has a Property in his own Person. This no Body has any right to but himself. The Labour of his Body, and the Work of his Hands, we may say, are properly his. Whatsoever then he removes out of the State that Nature hath provided, and left it in, he hath mixed his Labour with, and joyned to it something that is his own, and thereby makes it his Property (*S*27: 1–7).

So, for Locke, private labour produces private property – private speech produces privately owned texts (texts which report upon the private talents, the private grounds, of their author). Moreover since, as he hastens to tell us, men do not have the same talents, nor do they make the same efforts, different persons will rightfully amass different amounts of property. If we scrutinize private labour (private speech), then, we will observe that rationality and industriousness are unevenly distributed among men – indeed, some men, we are informed, are 'quarrelsome' and 'contentious' (S34). Consequently, we must expect an uneven distribution of property.

So, what have we here? First, an irony. Labour, which expresses the social (and the transcendence of given forms of the social), is used by Locke to represent the private. By theorizing in terms of private labour, which produces private property and is based upon private property (the proprietorship of one's person), the grounds of our speech become assimilated to the grounds of our house. The grounds of my speech are now private property. What is shown in speech now becomes my private talents in rationally and industriously working upon what is in common (Earth, language). Hence, in answering his 'difficulty', Locke has accounted for the intelligibility of his own speech. Faced with the nihilistic implications of fully mundane speech, Locke can now say that, as proprietor of his person, his speech is authorized by himself, by his special talents, as he works upon language (as he works upon Earth). He then can invite us to concede the special truths that his rationality and industriousness have broughh forth from a perusal of common usage and of common assumptions. Locke here asks to be taken seriously as the *virtuoso* of the mundane – able to wrench forth new truths from the mundane through his special talents (able to show how even 'very great difficulties' can be overcome through the application of his *gifted* 'natural Reason'.

So, for Locke, to speak must be to own (to own one's labour and its products). His private labour (private speech) shows that he is both proprietor of his person and proprietor of his text. His speech reports upon himself. We must, therefore, respect his proprietorship (his special talents, his limitations, his intentions) as we examine his text. His 'very great difficulty' has been established as the difficulty expressed in moving from the public (Nature, the mundane) to the private (private appropriation, private property, privately owned texts). And Locke remains silent about this treatment of the grounds of discourse. Silent about how speech as private appropriation, but not socially organized/socially organizing labour, becomes inevitable. Silent about how labour cannot be social, dialectically engaged with modes of production and their theorizing power, but must be private, an expression of private talents.

Locke remains silent, then, about his theorizing power, about his subjection to what he subjects. The theorizing power of revelation and of natural Reason have become, through him, the theorizing power of the market – as individuals, possessed of different talents, and varying degrees of industry, try to persuade others of their virtuosity. He is silent about the version of 'natural' Reason that has emerged both in his text and in history because his text *exemplifies* the theorizing power of that 'natural' Reason. It is, a version of Reason which insists that the power of speech can only reflect individual talents and which recognizes discourse *only* as the *outcome* of the activity of individual proprietors and *not* as its *beginning*. In producing the text of a formally free labourer (the text of talents), he conceals what that formally free labour covers over.

But Locke still has not secured the seriousness of his new beginning in individual talents and private labour. He hasn't shown how private property (private texts) can become publicly valuable. Nor has he demonstrated how the vocabulary of private labour (private speech) can become publicly recognized, can become persuasive and powerful.

He expresses this problem in two ways. First, there is the prospect of the perishability of property:

> As much as any one can make use of to any advantage of his life before it spoils; so much he may by his labour fix a Property in. Whatever is beyond this, is more than his share, and belongs to others. Nothing was made by God for Man to spoil or destroy (*S*31: 8–11).

Whatever is appropriated, whatever language becomes private speech, Locke argues, should not go to waste. With too much stress on asocial labour (private speech), speech can go to waste, can perish, because there is no socially recognized standard of value. The proprietor of talents, the supplier, is helpless if there is no commodity (property/text) market. The talents of the unrecognized virtuoso can perish without recognition. Property (texts) need to be valued: without a standard of value commodities might as well 'belong to others'.

Second, private appropriation remains limited by the fact that, in a private world, where there is no secure theorizing power, each may use what is in common to construct their own grounds, their own private worlds. If, as Locke says, each who: 'leaves as much as another can make use of, does as good as take nothing at all' (*S*33: 5–7), all men are allowed sufficient resources (Earth/language) to develop their own theorizing power. Yet all Earth, all language, ought properly to be already appropriated by the icon of private labour if that icon is to be the secure foundation, the powerful version of theorizing, of our mode of sociality.

So Locke needs to move beyond private speech. Having begun

from a mundane sociality, and moved on to construct a private world of private labour, he needs to move back to a new mode of sociality. Movements that are, of course, only movements of his text – for that new mode of sociality is already present in his theorizing of (and as) private labour (which is to say that his social is already reproduced in his text rather than contracted between its puppet figures).

Locke requires, then, a mode of theorizing, a standard, through which private men can be joined together (as he has told us, 'it is not good for man to be alone'). A social union is needed which will powerfully mystify the exploitation of talent by talent, of man by man, in the light of an apparently abstract and natural Reason.

For Locke, *money* provides the needed theorizing power. Through the language of money, he overcomes his problems with the 'perishability' and 'use' limitations on private property:

> And thus came in the use of Money, some lasting thing that Men might keep without spoiling, and that by mutual consent Men would take in exchange for the truly useful, but perishable Supports of Life.
> And as different degrees of Industry were apt to give Man Possessions in different Proportions, so this Invention of Money gave them the opportunity to continue and enlarge them (*S*47, *S*48: 1–3).

So money (a 'lasting thing') and the market in commodities for which it provides, is the new standard for speech. Money expresses the mode of sociality of private labour: it theorizes powerfully the relation between private speakers. The money abstraction thus is 'taken in exchange' for actual labour and for its social products (goods, revolutions). Through it, we now come to relate to one another as commodity producers in a world in which exchange-value is powerful and I am personally powerful because I can 'enlarge' my 'possessions' (my texts). My social power, as Marx puts it, as well as my bond with society, is now carried in my pocket (*Grundrisse*: 157).

Consequently, through the money abstraction, the products of my labour become commodities offered for sale on the market. Reading becomes recognized, as Barthes points out, as a *referendum* which decides the exchange-value of texts, while writing is an attempt to sell private talents and private industry.

Indeed, the power of money serves to expropriate the theorizing power of the Slave. While the Slave theorizes under the icon of exchange-value, the language of money allows the Master to own what the Slave produces *and* the means of production (the theorizing power which his speech reproduces). Hence, the Slave's potential to work is concealed from him and, to rephrase Marx, speech creates alien property and property commands alien speech. For speech now produces commodities which belong to another who owns the theorizing power which speech expresses.

This expropriation of the *Slave*'s theorizing power is mystified by the abstractions of money and of exchange-value, both of which seem objective and necessary, the very expression of 'natural Reason'. Precisely because it appears to be immaterial and abstract, the theorizing power of money gives to speech a blindness of its relation to discourse and to modes of production. Hence Locke can present his words as pure thought, as the employment of his talents upon 'natural Reason'. The money equation is both the culmination of his chapter 'Of Property' and also the guarantee of its seriousness – as purely private labour by an author who transcends his embeddedness in discourse.[13]

Once again, the parallels with Austin suggest themselves. Given the money-exchange abstraction, Austin can produce himself as the talented practitioner of private labour who finds new gems in the mundane existence from which he begins and ends. As he stresses, it is the 'cash-value' of an expression that counts socially – a cash-value which will exist for artful re-arrangements of mundane knowledge which, by respecting a gentleman's agreement, leave its theorizing power unchallenged; a cash-value whose own theorizing power is reproduced in the text of property.

When comparing Austin with Locke, it is interesting to apply playfully Marx's early distinction between two kinds of capital (*Grundrisse*: 456 *et seq.*). Capital I is the original capital put into the production process. From this process, a surplus capital arises out of the labour that is appropriated. When this capital, Capital II, is put into the production process again, the capitalist exchanges nothing for the surplus he obtains.

As the product of one who does not work, Austin's speech resembles Capital II. While Locke works, engaging a dominant theorizing power to produce (as a surplus) the speech of private labour, Austin merely *appears* to work, while using the surplus created by Locke's Capital I. So his speech (his idleness) leaves us, as he tells us, where we had begun. In producing himself as a mundane speaker, he re-produces the relations between Master and Slave characteristic of mundane society.

We have been trying to show what it is to speak through the authority of mundane appearances. We have sought to indicate how Locke transcends the security of this beginning by recognizing its nihilistic practice. By introducing a new grounding for practice in private labour, secured by the money-exchange abstraction, Locke works – his practice is that of the working Slave.

We have gone on to suggest how contemporary writers who ground their speech on our present (decaying) mundane existence, to which Locke originally gave expression, do not work. Like Austin, then, they re-present the voice of the Master. In seeking to efface their labour, by producing their speech as private intellectual work, they do not rise above a belief in grammar.

Finally, we should not underestimate the significance of Locke's recognition of the role of labour (the production of a text) as a *transformation* of the given. From at least Locke onwards, the separation of the individual from the social bonds of a feudal order and the intellectual bonds of divine will, necessitated that the character of activity as labour be confronted – if only to be suppressed. Even though Locke and his successors still mystify labour by treating it as private, the possibility emerges of the socially organized and organizing character of a labour, which recognizes the material conditions of its struggle.[14]

Even in the practices of the mundane world, secured by these writers, we find revealed the conditions for the construction of a new mode of sociality. The presence of the theorizing power of labour in Locke's text reminds us that it is a text which contains within it the seeds of its own de-struction, it own un-structuring.[15]

Notes

1 'What can be shown, cannot be said' (L. Wittgenstein, *Tractatus Logico-Philosophicus*: 4.1212). The distinction is also employed by Austin and by Marx – see his treatment of Proudhon as 'a composite error' in *The Poverty of Philosophy*.

2 The nihilistic implications of such a deference, well recognized by Wittgenstein, arose in an earlier paper by David Silverman which concluded a critique of 'market speech' with an assertion that its author was a 'market speaker' (see Silverman, 1975).

3 Think of ethnomethodology or ordinary-language philosophy.

4 'Are we not permitted to be a little ironical now about the subject as we are about the predicate and the object? Ought the philosopher not to rise above a belief in grammar?' (F. Nietzsche, *Beyond Good and Evil*: 47–8).

5 'Why could the world which is of any concern to us – not be a fiction? And he who then objects: "but to the fiction there belongs an author?" – could not he be met with the round retort: *why*? Does this "belongs" not also belong to the fiction?' (ibid.).

6 Sollers recalls the multidimensionality of the text:
'The text is thus *not* the full and frontal object expressing an ultimate substantial subject but the fragment, the oblique stroke of a . . . diffe-

rential play . . . the *remnant* of an operation to be constructed or restarted', *Signs of the Times*, Granta: Cambridge, n.d., p.84.

7 Stewart Clegg has suggested the notion of 'theorizing power' (see his *Power, Rule and Domination*: 1975).

8 Marcuse (1974) suggests that, for the Greeks, Reason discovers a rational world antagonistic to the world of practical rationality.

9 Our common stock of words embodies all the distinctions men have found worth drawing, and the connexions they have found worth making, in the lifetimes of many generations; these surely are likely to be more numerous, more sound, since they have stood up to the long test of the survival of the fittest and more subtle, at least in all ordinary and practical matters, than any that I or you are likely to think up in our armchair of an afternoon – the most favoured alternative methods ('A Plea for Excuses': p.182).

Compare this to Locke's assertion that men:

> must also take care to apply their words as near as may be to such ideas as common use has annexed them to. For words, especially of languages already framed, being no man's private possession, but the common measure of commerce and communication, it is not for any one at pleasure to change the stamp they are current in, nor alter the ideas they are affixed to (*Essay on Human Understanding*, Book 3, Ch. XI: p. 11).

Note the intriguing identification, by locke, of 'commerce' and 'communication'.

10 Hence in such talk:

> We do not so much understand the entities which are talked about, we already are listening only to what is said in the talk as such. What is said in the talk gets understood but what the talk is about is understood only approximately and superficially. We have the same thing in view because it is in the same averageness that we have a common understanding of what is said (*Being and Time*: p.212).

Because idle talk trades off this 'averageness' as the home of enquiry, it is inherently forgetful of its relation to discourse. Consequently it is deceptively persuasive, 'discouraging' and 'holding back' any disputation – see the discussion of Heidegger in Chapter 6.

11 As Kojève comments, only the Slave works, while the Master is idle. The Slave, in transcending the given world by his work, transcends what is given in himself. Hence he goes beyond himself and also beyond the Master who is tied to the given. Without work that transforms the object-world, men cannot really transform themselves.

12 See Davis and Moore's (1945) functionalist theory of social stratification.

13 As Walter Benjamin once noted: '(This) transcendental subject is the head stamped on the back of our coins' (quoted by Sohn-Reithel, in Walton and Hall: 1969).

14 Althusser (1976) rightly draws attention to the bourgeois character of the insistence on the 'supernatural creative power' of labour. Only by

recognizing the material character of its struggle (and of the constraints that it encounters) can collective labour become emancipatory. So a text does not begin on a blank white sheet which it transforms (see the discussion of 'white' in Chapters 4 and 12). Instead, it engages and, in Locke's case, subverts what we later term an *economy* of signs (see the discussion of Saussure's treatment of difference in Chapter 11 and of economy in Chapter 13).

15 'If we did not find concealed in society as it is the material conditions of production and the corresponding relations of exchange pre-requisite for a classless society, then all attempts to explode it would be quixotic' (*Grundrisse*: p.159).

Bibliography
Note: all the quotations from Locke, unless otherwise indicated, are taken from his *Two Treatises of Government*, ed. Peter Laslett, Cambridge University Press, 1967.

Althusser, L. (1976), *Essays in Self-Criticism*, New Left Books: London.

Austin, J. L. (1962), *Sense and Sensibilia*, Oxford University Press.

Clegg, S. (1975), *Power, Rule and Domination*, Routledge & Kegan Paul: London.

Davis, K. and Moore, W. (1945), 'Some Principles of Stratification', *American Sociological Review*, pp. 242–9.

Heidegger, M. (1962), *Being and Time*, trans. J. Macquarrie and E. Robinson, SCM Press: London.

Kojève, A. (1969), *Introduction to the Reading of Hegel*, (ed. A. Bloom), Basic Books: New York.

Lamprecht, S. P. (1962), *The Moral and Political Philosophy of John Locke*, Russell & Russell: New York.

MacPherson, C. B. (1962), *The Political Theory of Possessive Individualism*, Oxford University Press.

Marcuse, H. (1974), 'On Science and Phenomenology', in A. Giddens, ed., *Positivism and Sociology*, Heinemann Educational Books.

Marx, K. (1973), *Grundrisse*, trans. M. Nicolaus, Penguin: Harmondsworth.

Nietzsche, F. (1973), *Beyond Good and Evil*, trans. R. J. Hollingdale, Penguin: Harmondsworth.

Rosen, S. (1969), *Nihilism: A Philosophical Essay*, Yale University Press.

Silverman, D. (1975), 'Davis-Moore, Market Speech and Community', in B. Sandywell, D. Silverman, M. Roche, P. Filmer and M. Phillipson, *Problems of Reflexivity and Dialectics in Sociological Inquiry*, Routledge & Kegan Paul: London.

Sohn-Reithel, A. (1969), 'Mental and Manual Labour in Marxism', in P. Walton and S. Hall, eds, *Situating Marx*, New Left Books: London.

part VI

Language, sign and text

The attempt to dissolve meta-languages has made use of Saussure's discovery of the sign. Yet Saussure still wants to attach signs to extra-linguistic 'signified' concepts. By contrast, we trace Barthes's attempt to free the work of the signifier from a signified reality and, thereby, to constitute the text itself as a site of productivity.

chapter 11

The significance of Barthes

'The demon of analogy'

> . . . analogy implies an effect of Nature: it constitutes the
> 'natural' as a source of truth; and what adds to the curse of
> analogy is the fact that it is irrepressible: no sooner is a form seen
> then it *must* resemble something: humanity seems doomed to
> Analogy, i.e. in the long run to Nature (Barthes: 1977, p.44).

Analogie, according to the *Petit Robert*, is the relation established
by the imagination between two or several essentially different
objects of thought. Analogy is, then, the work of mind. It expresses
an 'imagination' which establishes a relation between 'objects of
thought'. But this relation is taken to imply 'an effect of Nature',
says Barthes. It becomes 'natural', 'a source of truth' which expresses a reality *sui generis*. So, in a double sense, analogy offers an
imaginary relationship. A relationship established by the imagination is none the less postulated as expressing a natural order. And
this natural order (which includes 'imagination' as a self-evident
category) is given voice in speech.

The reductivist impulse reigns supreme in the work of analogy.
Signs are inevitably seen as signs *of* something else; activities are
treated as documents of an underlying reality. So *interpretation* is
the aim of all understanding and interpretation is achieved when the
pattern supposedly submerged in the appearance is noticed and
named (analogy, metaphor, etc.).

What is irrepressible in the 'curse of analogy' is the desire to stop
the movement of speech by hearing speech as a stand-in (albeit
imperfect and blemished) for Nature. Analogy reduces linguistic or
textual practice to an expression of something else. Speech becomes
an empty kernel, containing nothing inside and relevant only to a
reality obstinately outside itself. So a text is the imperfect mark of
an *untexted* Nature.

The turn towards analogy expresses the practice of 'interpretation' discussed and criticized elsewhere in this book. It is a practice which seems eminently 'realistic' in demanding a signified for every signifier, in insisting that signs must be 'of' something, that texts must be responsible and responsive to a topic which they are 'about'. But this 'realism' is the grossest idealism. The 'things' and 'topics' which it assigns to Nature are already texted. Nature itself is a mark of a text – a work of signs. It is Nature and not the text that is the idea(l). The text is real; its signs speak Nature.

Analogy assigns Nature a capital letter. As a move in the game of idealism, it capitalizes (on) ideas. Analogy reduces practices to ideas and makes them work for Capital.

Barthes goes on: 'When I resist analogy, it is actually the imaginary I am resisting: which is to say: the coalescence of the sign, the similitude of signifier and signified, the homeomorphism of images, the Mirror, the captivating bait' (ibid). In analogy, the signifier coalesces with the signified: it seems to stand in for, or to mark, Nature. So signs are the 'Mirror' of Nature. Their internal relations (analogy, metaphor) appear natural and insistent prepositions ('of', 'about') establish them as frames of Nature. To resist analogy is to resist this (imaginary) Nature – to reclaim the natural for the textual. In part, this will involve challenging the claims of certain discourses (science, religion, etc.) to a privileged position – silencing other discourses by their appeal to a non-discursive (untexted) Nature. In part, to read Barthes playfully (an obligation not a transgression), resistance will involve a destructuring of the 'Imaginary-I', revealing it not as the natural presence which initiates discourse but as only a mark of discourse. So if 'I am resisting' the imaginary, the area that is imaginary includes the reduction of discourse to the site of an untexted person. But, of this we have already been warned: 'It must all be considered as if spoken by a character in a novel' (ibid).

Yet, at once, Barthes seems trapped in a contradiction. 'His' text should be read as the site where multiple texts interweave themselves, such as occurs in the construction of a stable 'character' in the conventional novel. In reading this way, we resist, we may assume, the 'demon' of 'analogy'. But, while at the level of appearance, Barthes appears to *resist* analogy, the reality of his practice *is* analogical. Freed from appearances, the utterance above reduces to the injunction: Consider X *as if* it were Y. Since the discovery of a logical contradiction, according to the rules of proper discourse, negates the sense of an utterance, we may safely assume that Barthes's discussion of analogy is based on a nonsense. Game, set and match (and much satisfaction) to Barthes's critics!

This victory becomes possible, however, only if 'analogy' is treated as an idea which is to be rejected and to be replaced by another idea ('resistance' perhaps). But 'analogy' is more than an idea. Its 'demonic' status, its 'irrepressibility', suggests that it is a practice which coheres and interacts with other practices. Hence 'analogy' is encountered as a reality with which emancipatory practice must reckon.

So it is not a question of leaping from a false to a correct concept – that mental leap demanded and applauded by idealism. 'Analogy' will not go away by revealing its methodological limitations. Already, when we speak we are present within the territory of the 'as if' that surfaces in Barthes's text.

The reign of analogy is only disturbed when other practices challenge those 'natural' appearances that it silently constitutes, by revealing the multiplicity of discourses, the contradictions and unities, at work in the apparently univocal utterance. 'Logical' contradictions and 'proper' discourse then cease to be indices of conceptual structures and become recognized as part of a practice which sustains a naturalized structure against the movement of language.

The reference to multiple discourses implies that Barthes's texts operate at the junction of other texts, each writing and re-writing the other. This chapter uses the tactical ploy of limiting those texts to ones signed 'Roland Barthes'. (The demon of the *apostrophe* is another 'captivating bait' – as in 'Barthes's texts'. Hence we write 'the texts signed "Roland Barthes" ' and *not* 'the texts that Barthes signs'. But, of course, The Text of Property is never silenced, only contested.) Such a tactic is justifiable in so far as the trajectory of the texts signed 'Roland Barthes' itself traces the trajectory of the semiotic project outlined in this chapter. As for the crucial contribution of Derrida, we refer the reader to Chapter 13. However, the trajectory of Barthes's project, like that of these others is shaped by the work of Saussure at the turn of the century. It is to Saussure's work that we now turn.

Saussure's semiology

The vocabulary and thrust of Barthes's characterization of analogy turns upon the influence of Saussure. As Durkheim sought to establish the specifically social territory of sociology, so Saussure established language as the topic of a reconceived linguistics – itself to be installed as part of a new science of signs or semiology. In characterizing the organization of signs as arbitrary, he reclaimed language from Nature; the rules of combination of the linguistic system, arbitrary and socially organized, at last came into view. Yet, as we shall argue, there is a deceptive double movement at work in Saussure's semiology: language is reclaimed from Nature only to return it to it, as speech is reduced to a social epiphenomenon, a psychological entity with no transformative potential. How this occurs will be seen in an outline of Saussure's programme. This is necessarily brief and the reader interested in a more extended discussion is directed towards Culler's (1976) excellent little introduction to Saussure.

1 *Language as the topic*

In any attempt to specify the phenomenon of language, argues Saussure, a number of confusions must be confronted. Speech seems to belong to physiology, in so far as it is dependent for its utterance and reception on the vocal and hearing organs. Yet the sound of speech has no existence apart from the thought that it appears to express. Speech, he suggests, 'is only the instrument of thought'. Equally, however, it would be foolish to deny that speech is both individual and social, for 'we cannot conceive of one (side) without the other'. But, again, when we look at the social organization of speech, it is difficult to keep apart its existing structure from its historical development. Unless these confusions are overcome, Saussure argues, linguistics will wander off into a number of unrelated investigations or, more likely, it will be subsumed within physiology, psychology, anthropology or philology. Like his contemporary, Durkheim, Saussure carves out a reconceived topic to offset the challenge of other disciplines: 'As I see it there is only one solution: from the very outset we must put both feet on the ground of language and use language as the norm of all other manifestations of speech' (1972: 60–1).

The trick is to move our sights away from the infinitely variable instances of speech, whether observed in the present or in the course of historical evolution. Both kinds of observation reduce to empty empiricism or to a history without any clear theoretical direction. Language stands out from speech-acts as a manageable body of inter-related facts which cohere according to internal principles of classification. In words reminiscent of Durkheim's injunction to approach the social realm at the point where it offers the easiest access, Saussure comments: 'Language is a self-contained whole and a principle of classification. As soon as we give language first place among the facts of speech, we introduce a natural order into a mass that lends itself to no other classification' (ibid). The aim of introducing a 'natural order' gives a clue to a crucial defect of Saussure's science of language. Before commenting on it further, however, we will need to discuss briefly his treatment of language and speech.

2 Langue *and* parole

We have seen that the topic of Saussurean linguistics is language (*la langue*). He makes it clear that he excludes from the social sphere of language the faculty of speech itself. The latter (*le langage*) belongs to physiological studies. *La langue* is not, then, the faculty of speech but: 'A social product of the faculty of speech and a collection of necessary conventions that have been adopted by a social body to permit individuals to exercise that faculty' (61). Equally, because *la langue* (henceforth referred to simply as 'language') is 'a social product' it invites investigation as 'an associative and co-ordinating faculty', a world of 'social facts' of which the individual speech-act is only 'the embryo' (64).

Parole refers to the actual speech act. This 'speaking' is what Saussure calls the 'executive side' of language: the way in which any speaker selects and combines elements of the given linguistic system. So, using Culler's (1976) example, in speaking, 'I' comes to mean 'me' in most contexts. To speak it, at a particular time and place, is an individual act which executes one of the possibilities of a linguistic system, relating, in this case, to the system of pronouns that the system offers. So the system of pronouns exemplifies language and the utterance 'I' exemplifies speaking.

This system is the realm of social facts, external and coercive (as Durkheim would say), and exhibiting regularities which are amenable, unlike speaking, to scientific investigation. Behind the infinite variability of speaking, Saussure assures us, is the very stuff of systematic scientific advance. Consider the fact that:

> Among all the individuals that are linked together by speech
> some sort of average will be set up: all will reproduce – not
> exactly, of course, but approximately – the same signs united
> with the same concepts . . . For language is not complete in any
> speaker; it exists perfectly only within a collectivity (64–5).

So the separation between language and speaking distinguishes, for Saussure, the social fact from the individual choice. It separates the essential from the merely contingent, offering regularities to the scientist in the same measure as language constrains the individual. For language is: 'The social side of speech, outside the individual who can never create nor modify it by himself, it exists only by virtue of a sort of contract signed by the members of a community' (66).

Like Durkheim, Saussure here combines the 'realism' of a science of social structures with a crude idealism, dependent upon the ideological opposition of society and the individual – an opposition to be resolved by the tired fiction of a 'contract'. In terms of language, then, we owe Saussure the signal insight of the need to reckon with the linguistic system which speaking engages. Speech-acts themselves, however, are needlessly reduced either to simple expressions of a pre-given system or to random individual utterances dependent on the psychology of the speaker.

We shall discuss shortly the way in which Barthes responds to these positive and negative elements in Saussure's theory of language. But so far we have only discussed the object or topic of this theory. The theory itself, having discovered its object, constitutes language as a system of *signs*. Linguistics, for Saussure, is merely a sub-discipline of a general science of signs. This latter science will study the life of signs within society (Saussure instances systems of writing, deaf-sign language, symbolic rites, and military signals). Deriving from the Greek word for sign, *semeion*, it will be called semiology.

3 *Signifier and signified*

What is the nature of a sign such as a word? The theory which Saussure is concerned to attack is the simple suggestion that 'language', when reduced to its elements, is a naming process only – a list of words, each corresponding to the thing that it names, thus:

Tree

On this view, a word is simply a label, as it were tied on to the thing which it names. According to Saussure, this theory is false, instead, 'the linguistic sign unites, not a thing and a name, but a concept and a sound-image' (1972, p.66). (This is in the case of speech; in the case of written language, it would be a concept and a written word; in the case of any other branch of semiology, it would be a concept and some other entity.) But now we come to one of Saussure's key distinctions: in the case of every semiology, the link would be between, on the one hand, a *psychological entity* (he only considers the case of a *concept*) and, on the other hand, a *material entity*. The contrast is at once between the *subjective* and the *objective*, the *ideal* and the *material*, and the *private* and the *social*. For, whereas the 'concept' is a feature of the internal state of mind of the speaker or listener, and so subject to variation and error, the 'sound image' is a feature of the public world shared in common with others. Saussure now proceeds to name these two aspects:

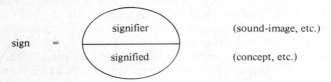

We shall see that this distinction is of the utmost importance. For the science of structuralism, whose project has been in large part to display the meaningful social world in terms of binary oppositions, itself rests firmly on this key opposition established by Saussure, an opposition which as we can see reflects and perpetuates very many of the traditional dichotomies of Western philosophy in itself. This theme is discussed, with reference to Derrida, in Chapter 13.

4 *The arbitrariness of the sign*

Now Saussure goes on to elaborate certain properties of the sign as he has here conceived it. The first, which he refers to as his *Principle I*, is that of the *arbitrariness of the sign*, namely, that there is no real connection between the material nature of the signifier and the idea which is the signified. Empirically, all that Saussure means by this is that such phenomena as 'onomatopoeia' ('quack quack' as the sound of a duck) are of no more than trivial significance in language as a whole, and anyway are misleading: the French for 'quack quack' is something entirely different: more precisely, it is expressed in French phonology, not English. However, the wider sense in which this principle could be taken might cause us some concern. Thus, for example, *it sets itself against any serious concern for etymology as a guide to meaning*, since, if the relation between signifier and signified is arbitrary, it is liable to change. However, Saussure does develop a method of pointing to connections between words employed within the same language at a particular time, as we shall see later. Saussure's own interest in developing this principle is to call attention to the nature of linguistic change in a very different, and indeed, contradictory manner to that of Heidegger. To do this, he now seeks to establish two further principles: first that of *immutability* of the sign, or as he puts it, 'the masses have no voice in the matter'. For every society, he says, language is inherited from predecessors: there is no question of any one individual being able to change a single word of the language. Here we have a straight-forward statement of a historical structural-functionalism. But, second, he says, is the principle of *mutability* of the sign, namely that over time meanings do change, so the relationship between signifier and signified does shift. This principle does not, however, contradict the last: for once again no individual has any say in the matter: no one can change anything in language. What then does cause change in language? 'I might be reproached', says Saussure, 'for not having been as explicit on this point as on the principle of immutability.' It is here that, after some fumbling, he produces his remarkably weak statement, 'Time changes all things, and there is no reason why language should escape this universal law.' We might express this principle which Saussure refers to as the 'Mutability' of the sign by another term: *the arbitrariness of linguistic change*. Curiously, there is an exception to this, namely the case of 'Analogy' which Saussure discusses in his section on 'diachronic linguistics'. This is however a structured form of change: a change always in the direction of greater structure, and is itself a building upon the arbitrariness of linguistic change in general.

5 *Synchrony: the economy of language*

Having produced these rather uncertain statements, Saussure now sets out to tidy up the question raised by 'mutability' and 'immuta-bility', namely the question of *dynamic* as opposed to *static* investi-gation of language or, to use the terms which he himself employs, *synchronic* versus *diachronic* investigation. In order to discuss this question, he suggests that there are certain fields of academic enquiry which can get by without making the distinction between synchrony and diachrony. These include Astronomy, Geology, Law, and Politics, so he says. On the other hand, there are sciences, the most notable being Economics, which are already split abso-lutely into two (political economy *versus* economic history). (We might note at once, and bear in mind during this part of the argument, that, for at least one version of economics, namely Marxism, no such split is tolerated.) Now, says Saussure, this is not a matter of chance. 'Economists', he says, 'are obeying an inner necessity'. Economics, and other sciences which make this split, including linguistics, have one property in common: they are *sci-ences of value*. 'Here as in political economy', says Saussure, 'we are confronted with the notion of *value*: both sciences are concerned with a system for equating things of different orders – labour and wages in one, and a signified and signifier in the other' (Saussure: 1974, p.79).

Thus, beginning with a rejection of commonsense accounts of the transparency of language, which posit language simply as a 'means' of communication, Saussure discovers the materiality of the signifier and with it the 'economic' character of language, already implied by Locke's labour theory of (linguistic) value. Previously, the real thing signified was assumed to be the only material reality present in the speaking situation. Now, with Saussure, we recognize that the 'grammatical system' of *la langue* is composed of units that, far from being indexical, context-bound items, have a specific *value* in the system.

This has two important implications for Saussure. First, the value of a sign is given entirely by its relation to other signs since signs have no natural relation with what they designate or signify. Second, the value of a sign cannot reside in itself alone but only in its relation to other signs.

In this economy of signs, the value of a sign is constituted solely by its place in a system of oppositions and differences – the value of 'red', for instance, arises only by its place in such a system of colours: red is red because it is not orange or yellow, and so on. So signs have value only by the differences between them.

These differences organize themselves around what Saussure calls *syntagmatic* and *paradigmatic* relations. The former, the syntagmatic, relate to the ways in which a sign can combine with other signs, while remaining intelligible within a given linguistic system. For instance, in the context of a menu it makes sense for the meat dishes to be listed before the puddings and for the vegetables to be offered as complementary to the meats. Equally, it is proper for certain prefixes and suffixes to be attached to a particular noun – so 'honour' can make 'dishonour' or 'honourable' but not 'unhonour' or 'honouration'. Syntagmatic relations thus express the combinatorial possibilities of signs. Paradigmatic relations, on the contrary, give expression to contrastive properties. Signs are in paradigmatic relation when the choice of one *excludes* the choice of another. Using the menu example again, the choice of roast beef may be taken to exclude the choice of roast chicken. The relation between the two items is such that meaning is produced by excluding one or the other.

Here we have Saussure's most important contribution to a materialist treatment of language. Faced with the attempt to minimize language as a transparent naming of Nature and with the suspicion of language as an imperfect expression of the thought of an untexted 'I', Saussure asserts an economy of signs. Confronted by the terrorism which would restore language to Nature, we begin to grasp the possibilities of an anti-terrorist intervention (cf. Ricardou: 1975), concerned with the play of differences which constitute the work of signs. As Saussure writes:

> The ultimate law of language is, dare we say, that nothing can ever reside in a single term. This is a direct consequence of the fact that linguistic signs are unrelated to what they designate and that, therefore, 'a' cannot designate anything without the aid of 'b' and vice versa, or, in other words, that both have value only by the difference between them, or that neither has value, in any of its constituents except through this same network of forever negative differences (quoted by Culler: 1975, p.52).

Saussure's 'ultimate law' is an important milestone in the critique of that practice of 'interpretation' which, in the history of idealism, is now represented by the assertion of the supposed inevitability of the 'documentary method of investigation' (Garfinkel: 1967). To understand, on the contrary, linguistic practice as the setting into play of a 'network of forever negative differences' has been the aim of Saussure's materialist successors.

Yet the anti-Idealist, anti-reductionist thrust present in this statement of Saussure's programme is altogether undermined when we remind ourselves that he is concerned with *langue* not *parole*. Consequently, this 'network of . . . differences' is located by Saussure at the level of a linguistic code which stands in a coercive relation to actual speaking practice. The latter is reduced entirely to the contingencies of psychology.

Like Lévi-Strauss's structuralism, itself heavily influenced by Saussure, a new area of the social is discovered only to return it once more to Nature – the structures of Mind, as expressed in binary oppositions, in the case of the former; an encoded, transcendental language in the case of the latter.

The advance (and overcoming) of semiology was only to be possible by retrieving Saussure's 'network of differences' from a transcendent Language and instating it as the work of linguistic practice, i.e. at the level of the signifier and, more precisely, in terms of the play of signifiers. This advance (and, ultimately, we argue, a retreat) is traced in the trajectory of Barthes's work.

Barthes's 'signifiance'

For Saussure, as we have pointed out, the meaning of a sign is indicated by a relation between signifier and signified. Speaking thus becomes an act of *signification* whereby encoded signs are given certain meanings depending upon context. A focus on signification, however, involves two assumptions which inadvertently naturalize linguistic practice. First, it assumes that meaning is not processual or emergent but given or determinant. Second, it implies that meaning resides ultimately in what the signifier signifies or, put more directly, that meaning is directed towards the *signified*.

Signifiance, on the contrary, treats meaning as continuously emergent but without reference to anything signified. Instead, meaning exists in the moving play of *signifiers*. Signifiers are now freed from that reductivist analysis which insists on the 'of' and 'about' of signs. However, this need not represent a movement towards analytic anarchy. The most precise analysis of the play of signifiers, we might say of signifying *practices*, is demanded when the significance of *signifiance* is grasped.

The trajectory of Barthes's work is, then, the gradual overturning of the Saussurean dichotomy of signifier/signified in favour of an analysis of the play of signifiers themselves. The implication, which he does not shirk, is that no meta-language (e.g. semiology, science) escapes this play. Consequently, the unmasking intent behind Saussure's discovery of *langue* dissolves, in the final analysis, into the attempt to erect a privileged discourse. This discovery traces the full circle from nature to text and then back to Nature. Barthes's movement of analysis is part of the project of the analysis of the textual production of signs, freed from the reductivism of interpretation. As we shall argue, however, this movement has currently taken a direction towards what we conceive as a purportedly revolutionary *aesthetics* which deflects attention from the coercive and emancipatory practices of a broader political sphere.

Barthes's 'infinite thematics' (Barthes: 1977), by focusing on the innovative practices of certain *avant-garde* texts, offers a theoretical advance which leaves untouched, except by implication, the coercive structures of everyday life. The trajectory concludes at a point disturbingly similar to the site of the Frankfurt School, holding out the prospect of a moral community committed to a Reason from which the masses have excluded themselves.[1] The question must be posed: why has there been so little attempt, in Paris or Frankfurt, to analyse the coercive and, more especially, the *emancipatory* practices present within *everyday discourse*?

However, until recently, Barthes has made some attempt to develop such an analysis. It will thus be helpful to trace historically the sequence of his work. In doing so, we indicate three moments of his project:

1   The specification of the historical specifics of signifying systems, largely by unmasking their systems of connotation.

2   The contestation of privileged discourses (e.g. the meta-language employed in (1)) and the constitution of the text as a site of productivity.

3   The recognition of the play of signifiers, leading towards an 'infinite thematics', Nietzschean rather than Marxist, focused on *avant-garde* texts.

Historical specifics – systems of connotation

For Saussure, it will be recalled, linguistics was a science of value concerned with the investigation of *langue* at a fixed point in time. Barthes's early work, especially *Mythologies* and *Elements of Semiology*, originally published, respectively, in 1957 and 1964, challenges the synchronic/diachronic dichotomy implied in Saussure's position. In doing so, as we shall see, Barthes runs the risk of reducing linguistic practice to an historical realm which is purportedly language-free (untexted) – the familiar path of those whose reflex response to language is 'ideology' (presumably both a description and an explanation). Curiously, this proposed reduction is achieved precisely in the linguistic realm, by erecting a meta-language which unmasks connotation.

Elements of semiology, however, has the merit of drawing out Saussure's contribution to the study of language, as well as pointing to some of its deficiencies. For Barthes (and for us), Saussure is the inspiration behind reflection on the economy of signs. Semiology is the science of *differences*. These differences allow exchange (of the dissimilar) and comparison (of the similar). Here Barthes refers to Saussure's analogy of a sheet of paper which, when shapes are cut from it, reduces to various pieces. Each of these shapes has a value in relation to the others and also has a back and a front. If the sheet as a whole is language, the future task of semiology, says Barthes, is to discover the cutting out of shapes, the articulations, which people construct as 'reality'. This task aims to avoid reducing language to any pre-linguistic reality. Its method is immanent: it will observe a given system 'from the inside'. The aim, Barthes explains, is to use a finite corpus of textual materials and to keep strictly to it: 'on the one hand, not add anything to it (the corpus) during the course of the research, but also exhaust it completely by analysis, every fact included in the corpus having to be found in the system' (1967: pp.96–7).[2]

Having drawn on Saussure for these observations, Barthes also shows how a science of differences must overcome two central Saussurean themes. The first relates to the latter's insistence that linguistics is part of a general science of signs and, hence, that language has no primacy over, say, Morse code, systems of fashion, and so on. Against this, Barthes rightly insists that every extensive system of signs is mediated by language:

> As for collections of objects (clothes, food), they enjoy the status of systems only insofar as they pass through the relay of language . . . we are, much more than in former times, and despite the spread of pictorial illustration, a civilization of the written word (p.10).

The primacy of the *written* word, over both the spoken word and the visual object, forms part of the important advance made by Derrida which is detailed in Chapter 13. For our present purposes, Barthes's insistence on 'the relay of language' serves as a reminder of the activity, or play, that presents itself once language is no longer misunderstood as a transparent medium of communication. Before, however, that activity can be documented, Barthes points out that Saussure's dichotomy between *langue* and *parole*, language and speaking, must also be overcome.

Speech and language, Barthes argues, are dialectically related. Speech is far from the psychological domain that Saussure indicated: speech sets into play, challenges and sustains the codes of language. If Saussure's dichotomy is retained linguistic *practice* is as implausible as is social practice in Durkheim's world of social facts (pp.15 *et seq.*).

The other early work of Barthes with which we are concerned, *Mythologies*, pre-dates this encounter with Saussure. The final chapter, however, 'Myth Today', draws upon a 'connotative semiotics' which is more fully developed in the later *Elèments of Semiology*. Before glancing at this chapter, then, it will prove useful to begin with Barthes's treatment of connotation in the later work.

According to Barthes (1967: pp.89 *et seq.*), Saussure's formulation of a sign as the relation between a signifier and a signified sketches out a system of *denotation*, telling us what signs *indicate*. This system of denotation as a whole, however, itself becomes a signifier which, in relation to a signified, constitutes a system of *connotation*, telling us what signs *imply* in addition to the primary meaning. Here the system of denotation is a *rhetoric* and the signified is an *ideology*.

This abstraction is clarified by the example Barthes uses in 'Myth Today'. A picture in a French magazine shows a black man, dressed in the uniform of the French army, saluting the tricolour. At the level of denotation, we have the sign of the salute, formed between the movement of the soldier's arm and the flag upon which his gaze is fixed, and the sign of colour (black being selected from the paradigmatic opposition of primary colours). However, when the whole system of denotation is treated as a signifier it serves as a rhetoric sustaining the ideology of French imperialism. So the sign connotes the free participation of subject peoples in the French Empire. In short, it signifies ideology.

Now the revelation of the ideological underpinning of words and images is hardly a new project. Consequently, Barthes is most exercised to distinguish his analysis from older tactical ploys. The move he makes is to distinguish two 'mistaken' ways of reading the magazine-picture. The first treats the salute as simply an *example* of French imperialism. All it does, says Barthes, is to state the obvious, abstain from analysis, and move on. The second way of reading is more sophisticated. It treats the salute not as an example but as an *alibi* of French imperialism. However, while this implies some notion of ideology, it fails to address the power and manner of functioning of particular ideological connotations.

It follows that both ways must be abandoned in favour of an analysis of the precise mode of ideological operation of French imperialism. Such a 'reader of myths', because he alone explores the practice of the ideology, is uniquely fitted to understand both its contemporary power and its historically transitory status. Barthes writes of these three modes:

> The first two types of focussing are static, analytical; they destroy the myth, either by making its intention obvious or by unmasking it: the former is cynical, the latter demystifying. The third type of focussing is dynamic, it consumes the myths according to the very ends built into its structure: the reader lives the myth as a story at once true and unreal (1973a: p.128).

Conceived as a 'story', the myth is 'true' because it expresses the practice through which a form of domination functions; it is 'unreal' because this practice naturalizes history and will be revealed as myth in historical change.

Barthes here seeks to overcome another Saussurean dichotomy. Having challenged the formulation of the langue/parole distinction, his emphasis on the centrality of history challenges Saussure's preference for synchronic analysis.

Barthes 'reader of myths' has an impressive intellectual pedigree. Marx's own depiction of the texts of political economy as 'adventure stories' treats them neither as examples nor as alibis but precisely as stories 'at once true and unreal'. In this century, however, we are rightly more concerned than Marx could be about the site of our own discourse or reading – the privileging of any discourse, including science, now falls within the bounds of a materialist treatment of language.

The Barthes of the early works wriggles uneasily with the knots created by this problem arising from the positing of the figure who is to be 'the reader of myths'. His first try at a solution appeals to that sure-fire concept of the young Marx – the concept of 'labour':

> There is . . . one language which is not mythical, it is the language of man as a producer: wherever man speaks in order to transform reality and no longer to preserve it as an image, wherever he links his language to the making of things, meta-language is referred to a language-object, and myth is impossible (p.146).

The solution to the problem of the reader's site which is posited in terms of labour falls on at least four counts. First, at least as stated here, it relies on an intentionality (speaking 'in order to') which has an unknown relation to the practice it is purported to originate. Second, the language of production ('labour'), as Habermas (1974) shows, will always be intimately bound with the *forces* of production. Since these forces are unlikely to differ between capitalist and socialist societies, it is to the realm of communicative relations ('interaction') that we must turn to establish a site for emancipatory practice. Third, when people speak 'in order to transform reality' they sometimes create fresh ideologies which re-naturalize the social. So 'the language of *man* as producer' (an unfortunate sexism for which we might forgive Barthes in 1957!) can also be the language of the forces of reaction. And, finally, a point to which we shall return, Barthes's commitment to 'meta-language', expressed in the passage above, reflects an unthought attachment to the signified which was to provide the precise point of departure for his later work.

Barthes's other attempt to find a space for his 'reader' resorts to a ploy which works no better for him than it did for Kafka (see Chapter 4). In the course of a critique of the claims of 'demystification', he appeals baldly to irony: 'What I claim is to live to the full the contradiction of my time, which may well make sarcasm the condition of truth' (p.12). Conceived as a rhetorical ploy, this sentence functions very well in the Preface to *Mythologies*. But then the analysis of the relation between rhetoric and ideology was supposed to be the project. Perhaps this is simply 'the contradiction of my time'. Or, more likely, that irony, which distinguishes the 'real' I from the words which entrap 'him', is only the latter-day voice of Romanticism with its suspicion of language.

As the development of Barthes's work shows, the wriggling or unease could only be overcome by a change of direction. This involved a diagnosis of the wrong turn that had been taken and a new programme that took heed of the diagnosis.

In Barthes's early work, two unthought traces of Saussure's formulation of semiology remained. The first surfaced in the attempt to specify a code (a *langue*) which was to stand as the silent underpinning of speaking. Despite the emphasis on the dialectics of *langue* and *parole*, the structuralist urge to locate deep structures of language and thought precluded a proper attack on the productivity of speech practice. Hence the thrust of *Mythologies*, despite Barthes's protestations to the contrary in his Preface, is towards the essentially reductionist programme of demystification. The second Saussurean and reductionist trace emerges in the attention paid to what is *signified* at the cost of an analysis of a text as a *play of signifiers*. As Coward and Ellis (1977) argue, signification is a process of production. It is not a system to be formulated in a meta-language by a presumably pre-textual 'I' (cf. Barthes's assertion above: 'What *I* claim . . . ').[3]

In our usual way of conceiving of signs, the way we have been taught by Husserl and by Saussure, and, following them, by phenomenologists and structuralists (including the early Barthes), meaning is always considered as constituted outside of signifiers themselves. We have dispensed with the naive notion of a world of things outside signification for a long while, quite a long way back in the history of metaphysics. With Husserl and Saussure, we are told that the meaning of one discourse of signs is to be found in another discourse of signs. For Husserl, the meaning of indicative signs (speech) is to be found in expressive signs (thought). For Saussure, the meaning of speech is to be found in the system of language. What neither acknowledges is that the capacity of a discourse of signs to refer to another reality outside that discourse, whether it be a further discourse of signs, or some other reality, must lie within that same discourse of signs. This capacity which calls for investigation (and to which Barthes turned) involves not the underlying structure of discourse but discourse's own structuration.

The productivity of the text

What we have described as the second 'moment' of Barthes's project turns away from a reworking of Marx's position – hardly original but conducted with some flair and insight – towards a more thoroughgoing critique of Saussure. This replaced the old Saussurean dichotomies with a recognition of the text as the site of productivity and, consequently, a treatment of the multiplicity of texts which any given text traces and contests. This treatment's specific target (and origin) was, then, precisely the movement of (what became called) *intertextuality*.

The treatment of 'connotation' now became seen not as a decisive advance but as the last skirmish of the defence of the claims to privilege of one discourse of signs over another. Far from being an advance, then, it continued Saussure's work (we might say, more grandly, following Derrida, the work of the history of Western metaphysics) by reinstating a discursive closure, while obstinately claiming that its business was to unveil (other systems') closures. The closure of neo-Saussurean semiology operated in a number of areas. For the sake of convenience we will discuss Barthes's attempt (in his 'second' moment) to contest three such closures to discourse: respectively, 'ideology', 'authorship' and 'the subject'.

It will be recalled that the analysis of the black soldier was supposed to reveal the precise mode of ideological operation of French imperialism. Presumably, the sense that we were being told something that we knew already was restrained by the technical skill of Barthes's account of connotation within the image. But, as Barthes now himself began to see, his 'reader of myths' effected a closure not an opening. In place of an analysis of the image/text's productivity, we were given instead a closely-knitted web. Barthes's reference in the passage from *Mythologies* already quoted (p.260, this chapter) to his reader as the 'consumer' of myths was accurate through *irony*. For no textual space was left in the workings of the image in which the reader could insert himself. The image became consumed and used up. The only point of entry to dialogue to be allowed was at the level of the signified. The signifier was banned as a site of debate, closed off by Barthes's analysis.

Barthes Mark II writes differently. 'Ideology' is now rejected as the site of semiotic analysis because ideological analysis at least in the form of the essays in *Mythologies* silences language. It does so by operating at the level of representation rather than of production and practice. As Barthes puts it: 'ideology "reflects" it does not do work' (1975: p.4). So the difference of the writing must defer to its own textual work. This constitutes the differance or silent play of difference of the signifiers (see the discussion of Derrida in Chapter 13).

The closure of 'authorship' presents an altogether easier intellectual target. And here lies something of an irony. Marxists resistant to language are always ready to call 'ideology' when confronted with a text – the response's regularity almost makes one respect Skinnerian stimulus/response models (the rats salivate, the critics shout 'ideology'). Understandably, the label elicits a negative response from those concerned with the materialist analysis of linguistic practice and total disinterest from the general public.

With 'authorship', on the other hand, the picture reverses. Because the term connotes a system of property relations, both kinds of Marxists are prepared to join hands in opposition to it. The public, on the contrary appear unalterably attached to the notions of the 'genius' (or otherwise), talents, and so on, of the writer, 'star', and so on.

The consequence of this is that 'ideology' remains at the centre of a forceful debate. For, conceived as a point of departure for analysis rather than its termination, 'ideology' remains relevant to materialists precisely as that closure of discourse which privileges certain sets of signifiers. 'Authorship', however, is rather like a straw man at which all sides are prepared to huff and puff but which, none the less, refuses to be blown down.

We need, then, only briefly rehearse Barthes's encounter with the concept. In 'traditional' criticism, the author 'confides in us' through his work (Barthes: 1977b, p.143). Hence once it has located the 'motivations', 'background' or 'unconscious drives' of this productive hunk of mind, criticism has 'explained' the text (p.147). As is to be expected, quite rightly, Barthes dismisses this treatment of 'authorship' as an ideological operation ('ideology' is used here in the sense suggested in the preceding paragraph). In a paper understandably called 'The Death of the Author', Barthes writes: 'To give a text an Author is to impose a limit on that text, to furnish it with a final signified, to close the writing' (1977b: p.147). The challenge to the claims of 'authorship' links itself to the third form of closure which Barthes contests. If it is language which speaks, not the 'author', then the 'subject' (that 'I' which is narrated or claims to speak as the source or 'reader' of the text) is nothing more than a particular textual movement. So the 'subject' is not a unity but a plurality of other texts marked by the 'I' inscribed in this text. Again, following Barthes: ' . . . language knows a subject not a "person" and this subject is empty outside of the very enunciation which defines it (p.143) . . . I is nothing other than the sentence (in the text) saying I' (p.145).

These closures ('ideology' – in a reductivist version – 'authorship', and the 'subject') free analysis for an encounter, much postponed but now inevitable, with the text itself. Conceived as a site of productivity, the text becomes that *space* in which multiple voices enter into mutual relations of dialogue, parody and contestation (cf. Barthes, p.148). The decisive turn arises when the multiplicity of the text is encountered not as the sum of a set of 'influences', 'contexts', or even 'pre-texts' but as the precise accomplishment of the text itself:

> The text is plural. Which is not simply to say that it has several meanings but that it accomplishes the very plural of meaning: an irreducible (and not merely an acceptable) plural. The text is not a co-existence of meanings but a passage, an overcrossing; thus it answers not to an interpretation, even a liberal one, but to an explosion, a dissemination. The plural of the text depends, that is, not on the ambiguity of its contents but on what might be called the *stereographic plurality* of its weave of signifiers (etymologically, the text is a tissue, a woven fabric) (ibid., p.159).

'Intertextuality' is precisely this 'stereographic plurality'. The decisive turn away from the Saussurean combination of signifier with signified is hereby accomplished. The text is no longer a 'structure of signifieds' but a 'galaxy of signifiers' (Barthes: 1975, p.5).

Before assessing the implications of this moment of the semiotic project, it should be stated that Barthes's second 'moment' receives its fullest tribute in the line by line analysis of a Balzacian short story that constitutes the work *S/Z*. Since this work is discussed clearly and sensibly elsewhere (Coward and Ellis: 1977, Chapter 4), we limit ourselves to one observation about its place in Barthes's project. In *S/Z*, connotation is revealed as the ensemble of voices which constitute a text. Instead of the reductivist turn of *Mythologies*, which makes connotation the *special* method of the 'reader of myths', connotation is located as the body of practices that write *any* text. Denotation, viewed in this light, now becomes a secondary rather than a primary form. More precisely, denotation represents that closure which stems the productivity of a text to produce the one 'proper' meaning. As Coward and Ellis state: 'Denotation is shown to be a product, an effect, of connotation' (p.53). It will be seen that this reversal of terms is fully in line with the movement from 'ideology' to 'intertextuality' – from 'ideology' as linguistically reductivist to 'ideology' as a closure of discourse. As we formulated three closures that this 'moment' set into question, so we note below three implications for a materialist textual practice.

First, we have suggested that Saussurean semiology ultimately follows the path that it wants to avoid. It privileges the discourse of semiology, while claiming to free itself from the trappings of previous linguistic methods. In the same way, the early Barthes unwittingly colludes in this mode of domination by establishing his 'reader of myths'. This is a reader who unfailingly uses the documentary method of investigation (see Chapter 7) to discover the secret 'connotation' of a text. When challenged about the claims of his own method, he falls back upon a destructive form of irony.

Both methods privilege a discourse from analysis and hence from challenge. They are, in short, the voices of the Law, the Church and the State. So the first accomplishment of the analysis of the plural text is that:

> by refusing to assign a 'secret' and ultimate meaning to the text (and to the world as text), ((writing)) liberates what may be called an anti-theological activity, an activity that is truly revolutionary since to refuse to fix meaning is, in the end, to refuse God and his hypostases – reason, science, law (Barthes: 1977b, p. 147, double brackets are our own).

Barthes here takes two positions which, especially because of the possibility that they may be contradictory, will be central to our reading of his project. The reference to 'the world as text' is crucial and welcome. Despite his attachment to the analysis of 'literary' texts, Barthes rightly implies that the empire of signifying practices includes the world within its scope (indeed it must do if textual analysis is not to reduce to a specialist aesthetics). Yet the attention to the 'refusal to fix meaning' brings into question Barthes's stated 'revolutionary' claims. Such a refusal may, it is true be a function of the dialogic/interruptive encounter that arises in everyday life. But it may equally be a kind of anarchistic game, played with *avant-garde* texts and offered to an intellectual elite. As we shall argue, there are some grounds for reading Barthes's most recent work as pointing in the latter, profoundly conservative, direction.

However, we are in danger of forgetting achievement by emphasizing the risk that achievement must run. If the first accomplishment of the recognition of plurality is the 'refusal', the second follows from it in offering for analysis the critical or interruptive character of a text of the 'perpetual signifier'. As Barthes makes clear, the discovery of intertextuality is at the service of a critical project, leading to the analysis of *disconnections*, rather than an empty tool to be used to discover hermeneutic organic *wholes*:

> The generation of the perpetual signifier . . . of which the text is the field is realised not according to an organic process of maturation or a hermeneutic course of deepening investigation but rather according to a serial movement of disconnections, overlapping, variations (p.158).

The specific character of this critical project, the 'disconnections' which above all others it serves to foster, is the challenge to property relations. The final accomplishment to be mentioned arises in *S/Z* (pp.44–5) when Barthes notes the way in which the conventional text is always careful to assign quotations to their owners. Its rule, we might say, is 'never an utterance without an owner'. Exceptions, like maxims, for instance, do not refute the rule precisely because they are recognized as exceptions.

This emphasis on ownership serves two functions. The first, minor, function is to allow a play of irony in the text. If we know that X has said Y, then we are in a position, as readers, to contemplate the irony of knowing, unlike X, that the reality is Z. The second, crucial, function, is to preserve texts as texts of (and for) property (cf. Chapter 10 of this book). As Barthes puts it: 'This is the problem facing modern writing: how to breach the wall of utterance, the wall of origin, the wall of ownership?' (1975: p.45).

Once again, however, doubts persist about the character of the project offered here. Why is the 'problem' outlined simply 'a problem facing modern writing'? Is not breaching 'the wall of ownership' not simply an activity of *avant-garde* texts but an activity, indeed a reality, of everyday practice? If not, then there is no doubt that the reality of Barthes's practice, if not the preaching, is an empty playing of games – a play that is no more than a play.

To conclude: in this discussion of the second moment of Barthes's trajectory, three achievements have been noted – the refusal to fix meaning, the attempt to reveal textual 'disconnections' and the challenge to property relations. We may pull these achievements together and relate them to the contributions of other texts considered in this book, by means of two observations:

1 We have already noted how Wittgenstein and Austin's project aimed at the dissolution of meta-languages. The emancipatory character of this project is that, in attacking the claims of one discourse to formulate another, it participates in the attack upon the linguistic constitution of transcendental realities, such as theology, law and nature. In *S/Z*, it is revealed that the capacity of signifiers to refer to reality resides entirely *within* the signifiers themselves. The journey 'outside', as it were, is illusory or reductivist. Barthes weds the dissolution of meta-language – the product of the journey 'outside' – to a kind of emancipatory project which, for what it is worth, Austin and Wittgenstein might have deemed implausible if not ridiculous.

2 Meta-language thrives side by side with the documentary method of interpretation. It offers the vocabulary through which the reality concealed in the appearances may be brought to the attention of the bemused reader: deep structure beneath surface structure, competence beneath performance, *langue* beneath

parole. Again, Barthes uses Balzac's text to emphasize how Sarrasine's desire to tear off the veils and undress a model of 'femininity' underlines the idealism that lies at the heart of the interpretive project: 'The Sarrasinean artist tries to undress appearance, tries always to get *beyond*, behind, according to the idealistic principle which identifies secrecy with truth: one must thus go *into* the model, *beneath* the statue, *behind* the canvas . . . ' (1975: p.122). The project of interpretation, aesthetic and sexual, but, ultimately, a *political* practice is here interrupted.[4] The question remains whether Barthes recognizes its political character and, if he does, whether the site of his interruption is unnecessarily delimited.

An 'infinite thematics'?

> When the unnesting of names ceases, a critical level is established, the work is closed, the language by which the semantic transformation is ended becomes nature, truth, the work's secret. Only an *infinite thematics*, open to endless nomination, can respect the enduring character of language, the production of reading, and no longer the lists of its products (1975: p.93).

At this point, a certain sleight of hand must be admitted. The device of treating Barthes's texts in three moments would imply that, chronologically speaking, this section should deal with the later works (*The Pleasure of the Text*, published in 1973, and *Roland Barthes* – an anti-autobiography, published first in 1975). Yet the quote above derives from *S/Z* which was included, albeit in passing, in the previous section.

Two happy statements in mitigation may be made. First, we may say to the conventional literary critic that, after all, a writer's work *evolves* over time and so elements to be found in the later periods may be expected to be implied in the earlier. Here the fictions of 'evolution' and 'authorship' do their job very well. Alternatively, to our modern audience, we need only point to the ruptures in chronology which characterize the *nouveau roman* (see Chapter 12). Should this rupture be the sole preserve of 'fictions'? – already this label weakens.

To return to the passage, Barthes is objecting to a reading which is satisfied with the discovery of the codes of connotation. Yet this was the very project with which *S/Z* begun and upon whose apparent success (in discovering the fives codes that allegedly write *Sarrasine*) the future productivity of the structuralist project seemed guaranteed. So the fulfilment of the project has, in a sense, revealed that even irony will not dispel the attachment of the 'structuralist reflex' to the very codes it unveils:

The structural reflex consists in deferring the pure difference as long as possible to the end of a common stem: so that the meaning explodes, pure and clear, *in extremis*; so that the victory of meaning be won in the nick of time, as in a good thriller (1977a: p.153).

The phrase 'as in a good thriller' reveals the irony. The 'hermeneutic' code, which is 'discovered' in *S/Z* as the means by which the reader's attention is held to the fiction (through the question: whodunnit?), is precisely the code that writes *S/Z*'s own interpretation. We are left with two versions of impotence: the form of irony already discussed and/or the retreat to structures of mind favoured by Lévi-Strauss (and, curiously, in a different tradition, by Cicourel).

Confronted by the practice that can only close the work, by the 'semantic transformation' which is ended by the discovery of 'the work's secret', Barthes opts for a new practice: an 'infinite thematics'. This is to avoid naming codes (*S/Z*) or, still worse, attempting to avoid all names (the practice dismissed in his early *Writing Degree Zero*). Instead, such a thematics will *participate* in the codes 'without quotation marks'. Merging writing and reading together, it will write/read the text as a braid (1975: p.160), forever twirling and untwirling its segments. The flow of language is not to be stopped: 'the skid of names' must be endless. Indeed, the alphabetical order of entries in *Roland Barthes* is precisely intended to 'erase everything', to 'banish every origin' (1977: p.148).

We have already raised the obvious question whether Barthes's (necessary) overcoming of the structuralist reflex terminates in an aesthetic game – one is reminded of the intellectual and moral community of *Lufthunde* depicted in Kafka's story (see Chapter 4). Let us first consider in greater detail Barthes's account of the movement of his work.

In *Roland Barthes*, we are given a clear statement of the intended programme: 'Suppose that the intellectual's (or the writer's) historical function, today, is to maintain and to emphasize the *decomposition* of bourgeois consciousness' (1977a: p.63). Barthes goes on to say that he uses the word 'decomposition' advisedly. 'Destruction' of bourgeois consciousness would imply a transcendental position apart from our (Western) world – 'who would educate the educator?' we would then ask with Marx. Destruction, he says, implies overleaping.

Let us accept the good sense of Barthes's argument and see how he views the trajectory of his work through it. The original path, through *Mythologies*, lay in demystification. The discoveries of semiology then seemed to offer a method in place of the satisfying but empty pursuit of the expressions of (an insufficiently theorized concept of) 'ideology'. However, this now involved a privileging of one discourse which could only be overcome by a theory of the text which was able to treat the Subject as an effect of language. But this theory in turn, as we have observed, effects another discursive closure. So the (final?) turn is made towards an 'infinite thematics' (the trajectory is sketched in diagrammatic form in Barthes: 1977a, p.145).

The act of decomposition is now to be located wherever the reader takes his pleasure (his *jouissance*) – the pleasure, as Stephen Heath points out, of sexual climax (1977: Translator's Note), encompassing both delight and loss.[5] In *jouissance*:

> the old biblical myth turns round, the confusion of languages is no longer a punishment, the subject accedes to *jouissance* by the cohabitation of languages, which work side by side; the text of pleasure, it is a happy Babel (1973b: p.10, our translation).

In this 'happy Babel', the singular privileged discourse gives way to an *endless* deferring of 'pure difference'. The aim is to construct 'a converse book' in which nothing is caught up in signification: 'A converse book is conceivable: which would report a thousand "incidents" but would refuse ever to draw a line of meaning from them; this would be, quite specifically, a book of haiku' (1977a: p.151). The project reveals itself, in the reference to the Japanese *haiku*, as a revolutionary *aesthetics*. To what extent does such a project participate in the required 'decomposition of bourgeois consciousness'?

We must not assume at the outset that an aesthetic project is self-evidently apolitical. Is this not the very teaching of the bourgeois order? The real argument begins when we consider whether revolutionary practice can establish itself through a rejection of a given social order as entirely reactionary and the consequent attempt to generate a (moral? political?) community who share that rejection.

Barthes's later work seems to make precisely this turn. It holds out the vaguest prospect of a text to be written and of a possible community of writer/readers who will share in its pleasure. Having supposedly destroyed the Subject as other than a moment of discourse, the Self is now apparently reinstated as the source and target of a reformulated aesthetics. Such a reader, we are told:

> participates at the same time and contradictedly in the profound hedonism of all culture: he would play with the consistency of his

self (that's his pleasure – *plaisir*) and re-search his loss (that is his *jouissance*) (1973b: p.26, our translation).

Here revolution appears to become narcissism. 'A mobile, plural writer/reader who nimbly inserts and removes the quotation marks: who begins to write with me' (1977a: p.161) is presupposed without any grounds for assuming his presence. Moreover, should such a reader be discovered, he will be informed that the activity in which he is to participate: 'is a kind of intellectual "sport" ' (1977a: p.162). 'Sport' becomes the form of the practice which would abandon an apparently 'fallen' world and elect the satisfactions of a self-congratulatory moral community. Barthes's present 'moment' offers its own epitaph:

A political misfit
Aesthetics being the art of seeing the forms detach themselves from causes and goals and constitute an adequate system of values, what could be more contrary to politics? Now he could not rid himself of the aesthetic reflex (1977a: p.169).

The 'aesthetic reflex' arises when the real 'forms' underlying the apparent 'causes' and 'goals' of language become an object of fascination in their own right. This establishes the 'infinite thematics' of pure forms to which Barthes now aspires. By contrast, following from his earlier work, we continue to pursue (in everyday discourse as elsewhere) an emancipatory linguistic practice which will interrupt permanently the relation between the forms (doing) and goals (saying) of signification.

Notes

1 Barthes sketches out a similar version of the trajectory of his works in a diagram (1977: p.145).
2 Let us assume that this 'exhaustion' of the corpus refers to the attempt to include as many elements as possible. Otherwise, 'exhaustion' would indicate a closure of the play of the analysed text. Perhaps the possibility of this latter reading arises in the structuralist impulses from which Barthes was still freeing himself at this time.
3 Coward and Ellis argue:
this method becomes untenable with the realization of the primacy of the signifier within signification; signification then appears to be a productivity (which presupposes the production of certain positions for the speaking subject), rather than a system that can be operated, or 'summed up' in a metalanguage by a transcendent subject (1977: p.32).
4 The aim of 'undressing' appearance was discussed earlier with reference to Sacks's material on 'skirting the issue' – see Chapter 7.

5 The sexist character of this reading has been pointed out to me by Linnie Price.

Bibliography

Barthes, Roland (1967), *Elements of Semiology*, Cape: London.
Barthes, Roland (1973a), *Mythologies*, Paladin: St Albans.
Barthes, Roland (1973b), *Le Plaisir du Texte*, Eds du Seuil: Paris.
Barthes, Roland (1975), *S/Z*, Cape: London.
Barthes, Roland (1977a), *Roland Barthes*, Macmillan: London.
Barthes, Roland (1977b), *Image, Music, Text*, Fontana: London.
Coward, Rosalind and Ellis, John (1977), *Language and Materialism*, Routledge & Kegan Paul: London.
Culler, Jonathan (1976), *Saussure*, Fontana: London.
Habermas, Jürgen (1974), *Theory and Practice*, Heinemann: London.
Ricardou, Jean (1976), 'Terrorisme, Théorie', in *Robbe-Grillet: Colloque de Cerisy*, Union Générale d'Editions: Paris.
Saussure, Ferdinand de (1972), 'Course in General Linguistics', in R. and F. de George, *The Structuralists*, Anchor: New York.
Saussure, Ferdinand de (1974), *Course in General Linguistics*, Fontana: London.

In Chapter 11, we learned from Barthes the dangers of reducing a text to 'ideology', 'authorship' or the voice of a pre-textual 'subject'. Alain Robbe-Grillet's text *Projet pour une Révolution à New York* is an example of a work which itself resists being reduced or consumed in these ways. From it we may learn more precisely the particular practices which constitute the text as a site of productivity and the 'realities' thereby set into play and disturbed.

chapter 12

The blood of dreams: Robbe-Grillet's project

On p.18 of Alain Robbe-Grillet's *Project for a Revolution in New York,* there is a description of 'two figures'. A man, subsequently said to be black, is leaning over a young blond girl called Laura. 'The scene', we learn, 'includes an objective trace of struggle.' There is blood on the girl's palm, apparently because it has been scraped on a broken window-pane.

All this is retrievable through the codes of the thriller. 'Plot', 'character' and 'chronology' will no doubt surely tell us all we need to know to interpret these events. Strangely, these are withheld. On p.19, we learn that the scene is only a poster advertising a play (*The Blood of Dreams*). The 'reality' constituted by the 'plot' gives way to the textual reality of the poster. Curiously, however, the two 'realities' interact. For the girl pictured in the poster is the same Laura that figures elsewhere in the text. What we had expected to be the usually smooth narration of an untexted reality now exhibits 'an objective trace of struggle' between 'figures'. The 'figures' of the words 'trace' the 'struggle' between the modes of discourse that constitute the text. It appears to be a struggle between a blond and a black – for the black words attack the virginal white page. When the framing of the narration (the window) is shattered, the material reality of the struggle expresses itself in the blood that is produced.

If the dream is to silence the motion of discourses in favour of the voice of narration, then the revolutionary project will involve placing the surfaces of discourse in motion, denying the authority of any one voice. Playing on the geometric sense of revolution, this *revolving* of discourses will deny the univocal narrator (Léenhardt: 1975). As the points of rupture are revealed in the 'struggle' between 'figures', so blood is produced.

A fiction ruptured by its narration

In a sense, the fiction is an immense metaphor of its narration (Ricardou: 1971, 220).

The continuity of a fiction is simultaneously guaranteed and ruptured by its narration. The unfolding of plot, the development of character, and the passage of time are guaranteed by the seemingly smooth unfolding of the narration. But, equally, plot, character, and time are present to the reader only as products of self-evidently fabricated text. The purely fictional continuity is ruptured by the continuities and discontinuities of the narration itself. The putative onlooker is thereby reminded that he is simply a reader and that what he perceives is a text.

The text of *Project for a Revolution in New York* supplants the assumption that the narration is only a frame through which a story is told: the act of narration continually challenges, and eventually replaces, the fiction. The opening words of each of the first three paragraphs use the imagery of film to highlight the challenge that the text constitutes for the fiction: 'The first scene goes very fast'; 'Then there is a gap'; 'And suddenly the action resumes'.

As Robbe-Grillet has pointed out (1964: 149), the film's appeal to the eye seems to give to its invention an apparent objectivity. Yet this objectivity is denied by the film's constructed character. The stops and starts of each scene, the 'gap' after a 'very fast' scene, the 'resumption' of the 'action' conflict with any assumption of a naturalistic unfolding of a fiction. Equally, the use of the film terms 'cut' and 'retake' during the narrator's final attempt to sum up the story so far, denies through irony the codes of a self-constituted fiction, told by a narrator who is merely a reporter. The 'plot' is only the unfolding of a narrative whose twists and turns are signalled by each 'cut' and 'retake'.

The first lines of the text point to the curious puzzle of beginning a narration:

> The first scene goes very fast. Evidently it has already been rehearsed several times: everyone knows his part by heart. Words and gestures follow each other in a relaxed continuous manner, the links as imperceptible as the necessary elements of some properly lubricated machinery (1).

Fictions are possible and narrations can begin because we already know what to expect. Writer and reader have evidently 'rehearsed several times'. Each 'knows his part by heart'. Like 'some properly lubricated machinery', the codes of narration stand ready to be used, the imperceptible grounds of the fiction.

But, even as doubt is stilled by the smooth working of the machinery, the character of the fiction as narration re-asserts itself. A paragraph, after all, comes to an end. The reader becomes half-conscious of a constructed halt, followed by a space, and a fresh beginning: 'Then there is a gap, a blank space, a pause of indeterminate length during which nothing happens, not even the anticipation of what will come next' (ibid.). The 'gap', the 'blank space', the 'pause of indeterminate length', is simply the white emptiness on the page between paragraphs. In such an emptiness, the appearance that 'nothing happens' only applies to the fiction. The narrative itself has moved on and, in moving, has left a trace of its workings. When: 'suddenly the action resumes, without warning . . . ' (ibid.) it is clear that the movement of the fiction is only a feature of the movement of the text.

The 'scene' that is now revealed is viewed through a window pane, near the top of 'a heavy wooden door'. But this cannot be the case, for we are next told that a cast-iron grille over the window allows 'nothing . . . (to) be seen of what might or might not be inside' (ibid.) Instead, the 'scene' appears only in the shapes on the varnish of the wood around the window. Shapes which: 'constitute parallel networks or networks of only slightly divergent curves outlining darker knots, round or oval or even triangular, a group of changing signs in which I have discerned human figures for a long time' (1–2). Even a window-pane will be insufficient to underline the intervention of the narrative voice ('I') between viewer and view. After all, one can stare passively through glass. Instead, the 'scene' is only to be present within the frame of the window. And the 'framing' of the scene affirms the constructed character of the text. What is shown in the frame is less significant than the movement of the narration revealed in the metaphor of 'framing'. The scene of torture that now appears is only available within a text which, on every reading is clearly simply 'a group of changing signs'. The 'human figures' that are discernible are the fictions developed from the signs of a code. The presence of these apparently concrete people stands as a reminder of the absent practices in which codes are assembled and employed.

A silent machinery of narration is reaffirmed repeatedly in the text. The staircases and steps which recur in *Project* link signs together and facilitate movement through the text. The fiction depends upon mechanisms which generate light as well as movement – like the torch, the projector and the various lamps which figure in the text. 'Suddenly the light goes out. The only thing left in front of me is a dusty pane in which no more than a dim reflection of my own face can be made out' (4). When 'the light goes out', there is no more fictional scene. With the collapse of the narrative machinery, the frame disappears and is replaced by 'a dusty pane' which reflects a narration with no events to narrate. Left to its own devices, the narrative voice must make do with such a dusty pane which can do no more than case 'a dim reflection' of the possibilities of signifying practice, silenced by the imposition of a single voice.

A collapse of the narrative voice is the emancipatory aim of the revolutionary project. It is this voice which is being challenged at a 'meeting' attended by the narrator:

> I imagined I was ahead of time; it appears on the contrary that the meeting has already been going on for some time. And it is not concerned with the usual specific details, concerning imminent action. Instead, today, the meeting is given over to a kind of ideological discussion presented in the usual form, whose didactic effectiveness on the militants of every persuasion has been readily acknowledged: a prefabricated dialogue between or among three persons assigned alternately questions and answers, changing parts by a circular permutation at each shift of the text – i.e. about every minute (26–7).

The 'meeting' stands as an icon of the meeting of voices that might be offered by a text. Unlike the frozen code of the conventional fiction, but like the ruptures of Robbe-Grillet's text, there are no 'specific details, concerning imminent action'. So one encounters an absence of the usual development of character, chronology and plot. The reader is not prepared for what follows. But he is to be surprised not by a sudden switch of plot or unexpected development of character but by the appearance of the usually imperceptible machinery of narration.[1] The tactic of the revolutionary project is to deny the oil that lubricates the machinery.

Instead of character, there is 'dialogue'. Since each person changes 'parts by a circular permutation at each shift of the text', words are taken away from the possession of speakers and restored to dialogue. In turn, this dialogue is not the property of current speakers for it has been 'prefabricated' in the texts which speak it. Its acknowledged 'didactic effectiveness on the militants of every persuasion' is that it teaches them that the fictions of the prevailing code, including the purported private ownership of speech, are contingent on the very signifying practice that will overturn it.[2] If the 'assigning' of speeches indicates the grip of a code, the 'circular permutation' of parts ruptures the code at its heart. Only the fictions of the code make the narrator imagine that such an encounter – the 'meeting of dialogue' – would not yet have begun. Instead, in the workings of the text, 'the meeting has already been going on for some time.' As 'the meeting' (of voices) progresses, so the rule of the narrator's voice collapses.

The collapse of the narrative voice

I must say I do not see what it is you mean. I am making my report, that's all there is to it. The text is correct, nothing is left up to chance, you have to take it as given (160).

The various narrators that appear in the text have to answer the complaints of an unknown interrogator. Sometimes they are asked to give more detail to their account, rectifying any apparent inconsistencies. Here, however, a narrator, who might be Laura's brother, is responding to the interrogator's doubts about the large amount of erotic detail present in his accounts of torture and rape.

The authority of the narrative voice in a fiction derives from its appeal to an extra-textual reality. This authority may be deeply embedded in an impersonal voice which strives to become transparent and so invisible. In Robbe-Grillet's text, however, it is brought into prominence within the text, personified by the voice of the 'I'.[3] But this 'I' who speaks appears to have access to a private world of experiences outside the text. His account cannot be significantly challenged because, after all, it is only the way he happens to see things. In this solipsistic world, 'I' is complemented by a 'You' who, passively, has to 'take it as given'. The only possible area for debate arises if the reader chooses to compare his experiences of reality with those of the narrator. But this removes the 'realities' generated by the text from any possibility of challenge and can only end in the solipsistic world of 'Sez you'.

Faced with the textual 'reality' of narration, the only history that *Project* will chart is the gradual collapse of the narrative voice. Unlike novels which consign the voice of 'You' to only a passive, extra-textual presence (the 'reader'), here a questioning, challenging 'You' is also present within the workings of the text.

Confronted by this challenge from an unexpected source, the narrative voice defends itself against intra-textual interrogation. First, it retreats to its familiar, solipsistic home-base of an 'I' whose experiences constitute reality: 'I must say I do not see what it is you mean.' Second, it seeks to close off debate by appealing to the narrator's 'duty' to keep his readers informed: 'I am making my report, that's all there is to it.' So the apparently arbitrary experiences and choices of a sovereign 'I' are protected by a social obligation. However, the sociality is fictitious because it replaces the meeting of voices with silence: 'The text is correct, nothing is left up to chance, you have to take it as given.' If the text is 'correct' and to be taken as 'given', the reader is relegated to the role of passive observer. His only space for dialogue is to concede the givenness of the text and to compare it with extra-textual realities. The 'realities' constituted by the text itself, its movements and closures, are to be areas of silence.

However, the internal interrogation of the text will not be stopped. 'The list of questions', Laura is told, 'is never closed for good' (130). Moreover, the continuous questioning will not be satisfied by reference to extra-textual realities. This version of narrative 'accuracy' is rejected by the interrogator. 'Try to invent details', he says, 'that will be exact and meaningful' (86). The inventions of the text are the sole reality with which the interrogation will be concerned.

The security of the narrative voice has been challenged at its heart. It now stands revealed not as the voice of reality but as a particular textual practice used to generate a 'reality'. The conventionality of the practice resembles the tribal rituals shown on a television programme reported in the text. Like the scenes of torture described there and elsewhere, *Project* will be concerned with the torture and ultimate death of the narrative voice.

Desperately trying to preserve himself, the narrator seeks to relate his incapacity to make everything fit into place to the apparently irresponsible reading habits of Laura:

> (This) has always suggested to me that Laura was reading all these books at once and that in this way she mixed up from room to room, according to her own movements, the itineraries of the detectives carefully calculated by the author, thereby endlessly altering the arrangement of each volume, leaping moreover a hundred times of day from one work to the next, not minding her frequent returns to the same passage nonetheless stripped of any apparent interest, whereas she utterly abandons on the contrary the essential chapter which contains the climax of an investigation, and consequently gives its whole meaning to the rest of the plot. . . . (68)

Laura's way of reading undermines the narrative's own authority. Refusing the sequential reading that is demanded in order to maintain 'interest', she abandons a concern with the 'plot'. She is unconcerned with its 'whole meaning' and jettisons the 'essential chapter'.

Laura examplifies the kind of reader demanded by Robbe-Grillet's text. In common with Laura's reading, the 'same passage' recurs; the 'essential chapter' is missing.

The narrator can only combat this challenge to his existence by locking such a difficult reader as Laura inside the house of his text and seeking to ensure that the house's contents are in proper order.

For instance, the narrator, using the voice of 'I' ('that will be simpler', he tells us, p.57), speculates that 'someone from the outside' might have gained entry to the house he shares with Laura because there is an unfamiliar volume in Laura's collection of detective stories. Since 'I' always locks the door, such a person would have needed a locksmith to gain access. A locksmith who, we are told in the next paragraph, is actually picking the lock. A locksmith who witnesses through the keyhole a particularly brutal scene of torture.

But the torture is only an illustration on the torn cover of one of Laura's books. The book's cover, minus the title, has been held up to the keyhole by Laura. The myopic old locksmith, stunned by the horror of the scene that confronts him, has apparently mistaken fiction for reality.

Yet this cannot be. 'I' later refers to the torture not as part of a fiction but as a central element in the project of the revolutionary group with which he is involved. Indeed, the torturer in the scene is identified as one Dr Morgan, whose clinic 'I' has already visited. And the torture is so real that the locksmith is subsequently able to enter the room where the victim is kept and to amuse himself with her now dead body.

The locksmith would seem to be only a fiction (of 'I'). Yet he acts. In acting, he imagines or creates new fictions. Even Laura herself appears merely to be a fiction invented by another torture victim (J. R.) in order to distract her torturer. But J. R. is only part of the text of one of Laura's books. How is the narrator ('I') to account for the presence of J. R., a character to whom he has already referred in his account of reality, within the pages of his sister's book? Moreover, how can it be a new book, a book unfamiliar to him, when it recounts events with which he is already familiar? He ponders these problems:

> But now I begin to have a certain qualm: if I recognize this fragment textually (and not only anecdotally, for that would prove nothing, analogous situations are to be found in most novels on sale in the pornographic bookshops of Times Square), then this volume, whose cover I have forgotten, has already passed before my eyes (76).

The narrator can no longer keep the house contents in order. His attempts to make an orderly narrative generate 'a certain qualm'. The text is not his possession: it does not speak *with* his voice, rather it *speaks* his voice. First, the text does not begin on a blank sheet. Instead, it is a function of the plots of the pornographic books which write it and which it re-writes. Second, its parts depend upon and challenge each other. So to recognize a 'fragment textually' is to understand that its sense derives from a location in a network of internal, intra-textual relations. Because of these internal and external textual connections, a volume has always 'already passed before my eyes'. Its reality is intertextual.

But this leaves no room for the sovereign narrator as other than a textual movement. Even the voice of the 'I' loses its security and has to be recognized as a textual device (which 'will be simpler').

In a final attempt to preserve himself, the narrator insists that 'it is always foreigners who prepare the revolution' (160). This is in accord with his attempt to preserve a reality *foreign* to a text which itself is solely concerned with 'making a report'. For the narrator, then, revolutions occur anywhere except in the workings of the text. Contrary to the narrator, *Project* demonstrates that revolutionary practice is close to home in the violated body of the text. In this way, the site of the revolutionary project has been clarified.

Writing/reading

In a fiction that interrupts the voices of its narration, characters cease to have that happy solidity so familiar in the 'well-constructed' conventional novel. The psychological insights of the author, together with the reader's identification with the characters, is precluded by the no longer silent movement of the narrative. The reality is the text itself; the only 'characters' are like practices of writing and reading. In *Project*, the stereotyped version of these practices is challenged by the collapse of the narrative voice.

1 *Writing*

The writer is curiously absent from the conventional narrative in its two familiar forms. The third-person account silences questions about the origin of the text through the claims of an omniscient presence, able to see and hear (but not to invent) everything. An account in the first-person gains in 'authenticity' by presenting the facts from a particular point of view. Equally, it annuls, although in a different way, questions about the practice of writing which creates such voices as 'I' and 'He'. Both accounts depend upon the fiction of a practice permanently outside the house of the text. The writer is only satisfied when, like the detective Ben-Said, his practice, 'avoids notice', (11) although present at every fictional turn of the text. This 'man in black' (6) fades into the background, unnoticed because of his 'motionless figure' (ibid.) – as 'motionless' as the (black) marks of the text.

Writing, inscribed in the figure of Ben-Said, must set about 'describing the scene with laborious care', merely acknowledging, but not answering, extraneous questions:

> 'Making out?'
> Ben-Said, who is describing the scene with laborious care in the notebook with worn imitation-leather covers which he had taken out of his yellow overcoat pocket at the moment the train came to a halt, in order not to waste time, utters a vague acquiescence and continues to cover his cross-ruled page, slowly but without erasure, with tiny careful letters whose regular alignment is virtually unaffected by the jolts of the moving train (123).

The text describes the scene in 'tiny careful letters' which faithfully preserve the fiction. Their 'regular alignment' will not at all be threatened by the movement of the narration: 'the jolts of the moving train' leave the text 'virtually unaffected'. The practice is 'without erasure', without a mark of difference, for no unfamiliar markings can be allowed to challenge the security of the narrative voice.

This commitment to an encompassing fiction is re-asserted in the notebook in which Ben-Said enters his letters. Its pages are already 'cross-ruled' by the prevailing codes; it is covered in a worn material which is only an 'imitation' of reality.

According to the cross-ruling of the codes, the text reduces to an unnoticed machinery of narration. In its empty reiteration of the fictions of the codes, such a text tries to conceal its material origins. The fictions *are* fictions precisely because they seek to efface the signifying practice sedimented in the text and in the codes that speak it. Since such practice or labour is the work of the hand, Ben-Said must keep his hands deep in his raincoat pockets (11) or hide them in black gloves (15).

The ideal is a narrative which can be consumed directly by the reader, leaving no trace of the machinery of its production. The house of the text must contain only a set of infinitely variable, consumable fictions. It is almost as if the words that inscribe the fiction have to appear absent from the text, like the tactical police (*les miliciens*) outside the house. For words imply practice and deny the passivity of consumption. Better then, to ignore their living presence and to treat the 'vacant faces' (13) of the police (words) as a self-effacing means to an end.

Like the words arranged on a straight line on the printed page, the police are 'walking in step, as though on patrol, right down the middle of the street' (11–12). The march of these words is steady and straight ('*leur avance uniforme et rectiligne*', Fr: 21) and the text as a whole is located between familiar covers (the flat hats worn by the police, *les casquettes plats*, cover their heads in the same way as *les plats* translates as the covers of a book).

How easy for the consumer to ignore the presence of the police (words). Only their 'holstered revolvers' (100) hint at their explosive potential. Laura alone notices the odd position adopted by these police:

> They are standing in exactly the same way, one foot in the gutter and the other resting on the stone curb, thereby resembling – by their identical clothing, corpulence and posture – a single individual doubled by his mirror reflection. The revolver itself completes this illusion, the man on the right having slipped the strap over his left shoulder and the man on the left, over the right shoulder (ibid.).

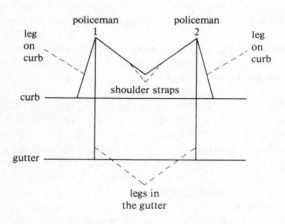

Figure 7 The letter of the text

As Fig. 7 illustrates, the 'single individual doubled by his mirror reflection', is nothing more than the letter 'M'. *Les Mots, les Miliciens*, the words of the text, assert their presence. The silent workings of the machinery of narration are interrupted by the emergence of the material word.

Given the materiality of the word, the property claims of writer or reader are revealed to be as specious as the property claims of the

Lockean proprietor. Both stand as attempts to replace the social by the individual, the body by the mind.

Only the narrator's respect for property makes him want to believe that Ben-Said is a 'go-between' (*intermédiaire*). The origin of a text is never an individual. Ben-Said does not go-between reader and fiction, any more than the words of the text obey his gestures (13). To adapt J.-L. Baudry, the author does not sign a text; rather a text signs its author.

Like Ben-Said, the narrator tries to hide from the reality of the text. When the materiality of the words cannot be silenced, he seeks the security of the codes – the conventional view 'behind the grille' or the stereotyped picture offered by the turn of the 'key':

> They are walking in step, as though on patrol, right down the middle of the street. My first impulse was to reopen my door and get back inside until the danger was past, observing from behind the little grille the sequence of events. But then I thought that it was absurd to hide so obviously. Moreover, the gesture I made towards the key in my pocket could only be that belated mechanical precaution I have already mentioned (11–12).

But 'belated mechanical precaution' will not help the narrator when, on a gesture from Ben-Said, the policemen (words) turn around to stare at him. Where signifiers no longer derive their sense from a fictional relationship with the signified, but face towards the speaker, the conventional narrator is frozen where he stood: 'Les deux miliciens, d'une façon imprévisible, d'un même mouvement se sont retournés pour fixer les yeux sur moi, s'immobilisant sur place d'un seul coup' (Fr: 22). Only an 'instinctive about-face' (13) saves him this time.

In accord with the need for a smooth, easily consumed narration, a code of sober ascetism rules the fiction. Ben-Said must be careful 'not to waste time'. Seeking to maintain the chronology which underpins the rationality of his fiction, he must 'note the exact hour' (164) when events happen. Trying to minimize affectivity, as well as affirming the significance of time, he must avoid involvement in what he describes. If he 'leaves his post', against 'orders' (94), simply because he has observed some strange behaviour, he might fail to report a vital part of the fiction. He satisfies his duty and extinguishes himself by writing down 'the succinct narrative of the occurrence, as well as the exact time, down to the second according to his wrist watch' (ibid.).

But all is not well for such a being. The codes creak and show their mechanism. Several times, Ben-Said is 'seized by a series of tics' (169). The mask that he has adopted will not altogether fit:

> He puts the notebook back in his pocket and immediately
> afterward, taking between both thumbs and forefingers the loose
> flesh of his neck on either side of his chin, he pulls at his skin in
> hopes of controlling this involuntary twitching which disturbs
> him, a little as if he were trying to replace a poorly applied plastic
> mask (94).

Trying to ignore the badly fitting mask, he still seeks to give
convincing accounts of the fiction. But his explanations degenerate
into telescoped, random phrases and, despite himself, he trips up
over exact chronology.[4] Eventually, he is only able to continue 'by
sheer force of habit' (169). The habit that preserves the conventional fiction, in the face of its crumbling code, preserves Ben-Said
too.

In this confusion, the myth of an absent practice cannot be
protected. Ben-Said seems 'so completely lacking in discretion that
I wondered if he was really trying to avoid notice', the narrator
comments (11). The very neatness of Ben-Said's arrangement of
time and place ultimately produces confusion. Unable to explain
the inconsistencies of his fiction, he relapses into pettiness, putting
the blame on unknown others.[5] Unless perhaps he is correct, if the
'someone' who 'is trying to put him in the wrong' (140) is not one
individual but a narrative voice which can no longer conceal the
signifying practices that speak it.

Faced by the collapse of the fictions that speak him, Ben-Said
despairs: ' "A mess!" he sighs. "The mess gets worse and worse,
and I'm getting sick of it all" ' (ibid.). Nevertheless, the
writer/Ben-Said pursues his thankless task producing reports that
have long since lost their original sense.

> 'Mission accomplished?' he is asked:
> 'Mission accomplished!' Ben-Said answered. And he has not
> made the slightest allusion to the minor discrepancies of time and
> place, nor to his dissatisfaction (140–1).

The sense of 'dissatisfaction' created by the collapse of the narrative
voice will not, of itself, halt its operation.

2 *Reading*

The conventional novel requires both a stereotyped writer and
reader. This kind of reader is only happy when he can consume the
fiction at first hand, forgetful of the intervention of the narrative.
He desires to see all through a keyhole, personally uninvolved yet
directly exposed to the events. Like the locksmith who actually

attains such a view (70, 158), he has his 'toolbox' (69) close at hand, filled with 'metal blades'. Such equipment is the pre-given code that will be used to cut the text. In such a way, the locksmith/reader will gain entry to the narrator's house/text (68).

As he uses the code, such a reader is, in turn, used by it. Seeking to unravel the fiction, he participates in it. The old locksmith, affected by a myopia (69, 158) produced by the insistent code, mistakes the cover of a book for reality (93). Only his bad eyesight makes him believe that the scene he views is far away. In reality, it could not be closer to him, for he is grasped by its fictions.

This distortion of his sight is emphasized when later his view is obtained through a mirror which reflects a distant scene. Consequently, he imagines that the people he sees are close at hand when they 'are actually located much further away than he supposed at the time' (158). A human presence is not, as he thinks, near at hand, available through his eyes. Instead, the trace of human practice is within the distant codes that foreshorten his eyesight.

This 'locksmith/voyeur' (166) cannot keep his eyes away from the scene suggested by the codes. His penultimate act is to violate the dead body of Sarah (168), as the reality of his practice is, in turn, violated by fictions.

At the end, however, like Ben-Said, the codes will no longer speak him. In effect, the locksmith finds that he cannot use the flashlight from his tool/code-box to illuminate the scene through the keyhole, while leaving space for his eye (70). The silent workings of the codes depend upon specific practices.

So, once more following Ben-Said, the locksmith finds that his mask itches. When scratching is not enough, he is forced to pull it off. Underneath is revealed the face of Ben-Said himself (168). Freed from the constraints of the fiction/mask, writer and reader are shown to be one.

3 *Writing/reading*

This girl represents a danger, because she tries to find out more than she can stand knowing (32–3).

But for one little truth, there are millions and millions of lies, so she can't help it, really (51).

L'aura – physiol. anc. Émanation ou principe subtil d'un corps, d'une substance. (*Le Petit Robert*: 1972, 118).

All is not so easy as it seems. The multiple fictions, connected by staircases in the house of the text, conceal any rupture. The codes which organize them will not go away if ignored and are able to withstand frontal attack (which can only produce the 'conceptual puzzlement' that Wittgenstein diagnoses when we attack words with words).

Perhaps emancipatory potential only begins to emerge when the power of the codes is brought into view – when the usually silent machinery is heard. Such a viewing or hearing depends upon a certain respect for the codes. Notice how Laura understands that fictions are omni-present in the cassettes playing around her:

> The tone of her voice is that of a discreet, neutral commentary, which seems to be the result of her attentive observation of the mechanism:
> 'He turned it on before he went out', she says.
> 'But you could have turned it off!'
> 'No, you can't turn it off: the box is locked' (49).

Laura's 'attentive observation of the mechanism' of the codes makes her suspicious of the chronologies to be found in narratives (the 'staircases' of the text/house). So the narrator tells us that, with doctor's advice, reference to time is avoided when Laura is around because 'it awakens her anxiety' (67). Perhaps that is why she prefers to signal breaks in the narrative by 'cut' and 'retake'.

The noise of the machinery of narration sounds constantly in Laura's ears, represented by 'faint knocks' and 'tappings'. For Laura, staircases do not offer the usual silent movement between fictions:

> But, reaching the next landing, she hears once again quite distinctly, although with the imagination of memory, the faint knocks audible in this place from time to time, in reality, coming from still higher up, from the unoccupied rooms of the top floor, as if someone were tapping with his finger tips against a wooden panel, a signal or gesture of impatience or a long code message transmitted to some other secret inhabitant of the house (99).

For Laura, the house is composed of fictions which do not smoothly mesh with one another: there are 'other secret inhabitants of the house'. Rather than glide from one landing (fiction) to another, she tries to grasp their mutual interplay. Notice how Laura switches on a cassette which fills the house with sounds while she talks to J. R. (52). Such a listening to the movements of intertextuality reveals the origin of fictions and allows one to remain alert for the 'decisive occurrence' that will signify their end. So Laura listens: 'ears cocked, for some decisive occurrence: crackling of flames, bursts of machine-gun fire, alarm sirens, clamours of the revolution . . .' (116). This listening is coupled with Laura's seemingly perverse

reading habits. The endless alterations she makes to the arrangement of any one volume, her satisfaction with an interweaving of
multiple texts (68), suggest that she has no respect for the idealist
conception of the text's 'integrity'. Practice that emanates from the
body (*l'aura*) will reveal the material reality of the signifying
practices that write the text.

Laura ruptures the pretensions of the conventional reader. At
first, she thinks of putting out the locksmith's useless eyes, peering
through the keyhole, with a knitting needle. Eventually she decides
that it will be 'more amusing' to hold up to him the cover of her
book, through this act emphasizing the fictions that constitute his
reality (93). Even when the narrator tries to correct what seems to
him like 'the occasionally brutal negligence of this way of reading'
(68), Laura who is conscious of the codes that speak the conventional fiction, is fully able to withstand his interrogation. Laura's
skilful deference to the logic of the codes sustains her account, even
though the narrator believes that 'she has to be lying' (73). He
continues:

> Or else perhaps it is true, in spite of everything. Each time I ask
> this kind of question, which soon turns into an interrogation, she
> always has the same slow, precise, remote diction, as if she were
> reciting her answers in a dream or in the voice – perceptible to
> herself alone – of an oracle. But at the same time, her tone does
> not permit the least objection: it is clear that in her mind, the
> facts leave no room for ulterior motives. She also gives the
> impression, to some degree, of having on her side the guarantee
> of the slide-rule, by means of which she has just discovered and
> announced the sole solution to the problem set (ibid.).

Perhaps, 'in spite of everything', Laura's speech 'is true': 'the
least objection is not permitted', after all, when a voice is guaranteed by the 'slide-rule' of the codes. Unable to step outside the codes
that locate the narrator's question, Laura refuses none the less
to be satisfied by the answers that the codes speak. Since they are
'the sole solution to the problem set', Laura is only satisfied by
speaking the codes themselves. Consequently, her answers appeal
to geometry and aesthetics rather than to the conventional fictions.
Her intervention, this 'slow, precise, remote diction, as if she were
reciting her answers in a dream', emphasizes the dream of the silent
machinery of the codes, available for speaking because the voice of
the 'oracle' is 'perceptible to herself alone'.

In this way, the narrator encounters the frozen fictions which
grasp speech and 'leave no room for ulterior motives'. Correctly, he
obtains the impression that Laura receives 'from elsewhere her

ready-made sentences' (92). Misplaced artfulness prevents the self-understanding that his 'interrogation' too is spoken 'from elsewhere'. Failing to grasp what grasps his artfulness, the narrator, says Laura, is nothing but an 'old phoney' (*gros malin*) (132).

In a search for a way to contain Laura's disruptive practice and the danger which she represents, the narrator locks her in when he goes out. Laura is physically prevented from leaving his house/text. Surrounding her are the recurrent fictions of detective stories and the memories of the 'ordinary anecdotes' from which all trace of 'destructive episodes' has been removed.[6]

It is these texts, repetitive and easily 'restocked' (96), which constitute her 'studies' (77). Through them, the narrator hopes 'to shield her from the supreme decisions' and to avert the 'monstrous crime' that he fears she may otherwise commit (76). Such a crime, by annihilating both narrator and captive reader in the course of its subversion of the code, would 'destroy us both' (ibid.).

But the apprehension of an imminent catastrophe haunts the narrator. Threatening scenes from Africa, viewed on a TV documentary, 'interrupt' Laura's studies (77). Black bodies point towards black print – the practice that interrupts the white pages if only to instal the fictions of the code. As the code itself comes more into view, Laura's speech becomes more stylized. The discontinuities of the code, no longer glossed by its comforting fictions, now deny the possibility of 'a continuous discourse' (ibid.). Laura's words, once freed from fictions, emphasize only the order of the code and its catastrophic dissolution:

> Her words never form a continuous discourse: they are like fragments which nothing any longer links together, despite the emphatic tone suggesting a coherent whole which might exist somewhere, elsewhere than in her head probably; and there is always, suspended above the elements stuck together one way or another, the apprehension of an imminent, unforeseeable though ineluctable catastrophe which will reduce this precarious order to nothingness (77–8).

The 'coherent whole' does not exist in Laura's 'head' but in the practices which write the text, now revealed in all their power and contradictions. These represent the 'one little truth' for they are the source of 'millions and millions of lies' (51). In the 'ineluctable catastrophe' to come, 'unforeseeable' because of the remaining grasp of the codes, the social order, replicated in the social ordering of the fictional text, 'will reduce . . . to nothingness'.

Black and white – and red

The theme of the day's lecture seems to be 'the colour red', considered as a radical solution to the irreducible antagonism between black and white (27).

Black and white seem to be the primal colours of a text. The white of the blank page contrasts with the black of the print. A text consists, then, of black on white. Each colour seems locked in an 'irreducible antagonism' to the other: where there is black, there cannot be white, and vice versa.

White looks like an absence in which the black print instals itself. Outside of the word there appears to be merely an emptiness, save from the workings of the writer's mind. As the practice of writing seems to reflect the imposition of a will on to a blank surface, so practice as a whole appears to arise on an empty stage, shorn of any social or historical dimension.

Seen through the illumination of the code, the text looks like a play of black print upon white pages. Here the essential elements of a text reduce to: (1) a culturally defined set of codes, which, in turn establish (2) an illuminated area in which fictions may be viewed, and a fictional version of a text as a play of (3) black upon (4) white.

All four elements are established in the first few pages of the text of *Projet*. After the initial reference to 'properly lubricated machinery' (*une machinerie bien huilée*), the presence of a white empty space is established (*un blanc, un espace vide*, Fr.: 7). The empty page awaits the fictional black text.

The fiction is revealed as a scene of 'suffering' or 'torture'. As the fiction denies the body of the word, so, in this scene, a human body undergoes apparent torture. The torture is situated at the heart of the play of black and white. A white-jacketed man (*l'individu en blouse blanche*, Fr.:11) leans over the body. But, without any black text, one doesn't know 'what the person in the white coat was going to do to his captive' (4). Not surprisingly, 'at this moment', a man enters wearing a black dinner jacket (*un smoking noir*) and a soot-coloured leather mask.

The 'toolbox' of the codes constitutes the text as a play of black upon white. The whole fiction of black and white jackets is viewed through the eyes of: 'a short, bald man in workman's clothes, with the strap of a toolbox over one shoulder, apparently a plumber, or an electrician, or a locksmith' (4). As the toolbox offers the key to the enterprise, so a 'lamp' spreads a 'cone of harsh light' which 'has been carefully directed' (2) on to the fiction.

The four elements of the text have now been located. All that follows, in so far as it keeps to the rules of the game, can only be a variation on these elements. Everybody knows his part very well. The 'machinery', we are told, once again, is 'properly lubricated'.

As the page is blank without the text, so, prior to the revolutionary meeting at which the 'lecture' is to be given, the narrator experiences only varying shades of white. In the New York subway, below the living ground, the walls are covered with a 'white surface' which would smother everything were it not for 'cracks', 'chips' and 'stains' (20). These marks of signifying practice are, however, rendered almost invisible by the dimness of the illumination. The underground hall of the subway, for instance, is so badly lit 'that nothing identifiable is apparent in any direction' (ibid.). In the prevailing darkness, even the difference of black and white is almost hidden. The placards which might give some indication of a human presence in the underground hall are mounted on such 'remote surfaces' that they fail to punctuate the blackness.

Where the traces of signifying practice are unlit and without any dimension, people become artificial and alone. So the subway is populated by 'isolated figures', whose identical clothes and stiff attitudes support an 'impression of artificiality'. With their whitewashed faces, 'beardless, pink and blond', or 'grey' with 'drawn features', they seem like 'poor actors', 'store-window mannequins', or, possibly, only 'the embalmed faces of corpses in glass coffins in the cemeteries of the dear departed' (ibid.). No doubt they have obtained their appearance from the wig and mask shop which offers the full gamut of stereotyped roles to be found in the fictions of the code (39–41).

The whole underground area is devoted to amusements: pin-ball machines, shooting galleries, souvenir stalls and pornographic bookshops. After all, the fictions of the code define such diversions which masquerade as living practice. Were it not for the 'breaks' in the white surface, 'as though someone had pounded it with a hammer' (20), the diversions would overtake reality.

Even though the revolutionary meeting will show the possibility of deconstructing frozen codes, its very entrance is smothered by the white. The waiting-room is nothing but 'a very small, bare cubicle, all six surfaces painted white (in other words, the floor as well)' (23). The oppressive whiteness is not alleviated by its occupant:

A blond young woman – quite pretty perhaps, impersonal and sophisticated in any case, wearing a dazzlingly white nurse's uniform, her eyes concealed by sunglasses which doubtless help her endure the intense lighting, white like everything else and reflected on all sides by the immaculate walls (23–4).

Next to these 'immaculate walls', offering, like the blank page, a whiteness unmarked by human practice, black seems to offer a living challenge. The bleak walls of the subway are only interrupted by a 'bright-coloured poster' advertising a 'play' whose 'male character is a Negro' (19). Similarly, glimpsed by Laura through a window, black girls playing out 'cruel and mysterious rites' (76), suggest a living practice, albeit of a vicious nature, to redress the balance of the deathly house that envelops the narrator's victim.

But, while the living black text may one day expunge the fatal white, it is not clear that the outcome will be revolutionary. The code may live on with merely its mode of domination reversed in a way that fails to challenge the naturalization of the order as a whole – black-white instead of white-black. The black bandage over the woman's eyes on a poster with the sole printed text of 'Tomorrow . . . ' does indeed suggest a change-over of colour order in the future. But it needs someone to add 'the revolution' in red paint (91), if living practice is to show its possibilities through the frozen code. With only a change in the colour order, the black of the text still has its 'eyes' covered by white bandages, like the black child observed by Laura playing a bizarre game with her friends. The 'T-Square', ordinarily used in 'school notebooks', is now used by her companions to attack her. This reasserts the continuing role of the 'geometry' of the existing code in black education (98).

The activity of black words versus the passivity of white pages does, however, contain revolutionary (red) potential. Red flames get started in black areas: the narrator, for example, hears of 'a big fire . . . in the distance towards Harlem' (60). After all, without the black word there is only the unending blankness of white. But, as long as black practice does not surpass the polarities of the binary code (black on white), the reports of a fire will only be 'rumours' (ibid.).

The 'geometry' of the existing code sustains the polarity of black and white. A text appears to counterpose the black print, which flows from the author's 'genius', to the white emptiness of the page. More concretely, we see this polarity in the detective story which offers the blackness of 'mystery' to counteract the emptiness of (white) existence. But these polarities are mystifications. Only the whitewash of the code could make us believe that practice begins on a blank sheet or offer us relief from an alienated existence in the form of a fiction.

By concealing the code that authors it, the fictional polarity of black and white lowers an enveloping white blanket, like a layer of snow over emancipatory practice. At one and the same time, the opportunities of the writer grasped by this polarity are boundless and hopeless. Everything seems to be attainable through an act of will that imposes the black word on the white page. But, in reality, nothing can be achieved by means of a will that denies the discourse that grasps it.[7]

The 'creativity' of 'genius' reduces the white blanket of the code. The black 'mystery' of writing is revealed as a mystifying label applied to signifying practice – as much as a fiction as the mystery of this detective story. Like any practice, writing engages not emptiness but the fictions of a historically sedimented code.

The red of practice is the only 'radical solution' to the antagonism of black and white. Like Mallarmé's *'feu-nixe'*, the red of the fire can alone negate the reifications of the code.[8] This 'crime' against the code will take the form of 'three metaphoric acts' which will destroy the whiteness with the red mark of practice:

> Crime is indispensable to the revolution . . . . Rape, murder, arson, are the three metaphoric acts which will free the blacks, the impoverished proletariat, and the intellectual workers from their slavery, and at the same time the bourgeoisie from its sexual complexes (128).

Each symbolic crime is associated with the red: each indicates the consumption of the white by the force of practice:

> the perfect crime, which combines the three elements studied here, would be the deflowering, performed by force, of a virgin, preferably a girl with milky skin and very blond hair, the victim then being immolated by disembowelment or throat-cutting, her naked and bloodstained body having to be burned at a stake doused with gasoline, the fire gradually consuming the whole house (30).

'The whole house'/text must be consumed. The 'milky skin' of the seemingly pure text will be violated. Its basis in material reality (in body and blood) will then stand revealed in preparation for its destruction.

Already under attack, it becomes clear that the code is stained by the trace of emancipatory practice. The 'dazzlingly white nurse's uniform' is subsequently 'spattered with tiny red stains' (175). The body of J. R., its whiteness complemented by her long red hair, stands as an invitation to violation. White attracts red and the knife. J. R.'s 'round white neck gleams like a knife blade' (59). 'What a lovely corpse you could make out of that lovely white flesh', reflects the narrator. And J. R. has already prepared herself for her violation. A 'white sheet' covers the ironing board on which she will be tortured. On the sheet, resembling a blank sheet of paper, empty except for the 'cross-ruling' of the codes, she has 'laid a pair of large chromium-steel sewing scissors' (62).

As the scissors cut through inert material, Laura, in her turn, cuts through the fiction and its frozen polarities of writer and reader. The instrument, the scissors, through which the code will be ruptured is the violent practice of the writer/reader.

From one end to the other of the 'corridor' that Laura walks, the white fiction extends a: 'strip of dazzlingly white carpeting which occupies about a third of the white-tiled floor between the two white walls with their white-lacquered doors' (102). But the closed door at the end of the white corridor cannot hold back the flow of red: 'There is blood, a trickle of thick fresh bright red blood which runs under the door, coming from inside' (ibid.). As the codes of the enveloping black and white fiction are brought into view, there appears the reality of the signifying practices that script them, signalled by the 'trickle of . . . blood'.

Even the sacred code of bridegroom/bride is threatened by blood. A blacksuited bridegroom is murdered, leaving only the trace of: 'a little white circle which, on closer inspection, turns out to be a wreath of orange blossoms made out of plastic' (139). The blood of the murder reveals the plastic artificialities of the code and its version of reading, which, after killing off the possibilities of the text, leaves only the appropriate memorial.

The revolutionary project becomes clearer in Ben-Said's depiction of the fate of the bride. On 'a piece of white cardboard', he writes, 'in capital letters': 'Young brides, in white raiment, will be torn, still virgin, from the arms of their earthly spouse, to become the prey of the knife and the flames . . . ' (140). The text, white and apparently virginal, is to be 'torn . . . from the arms of (its) earthly spouse', the frozen codes which speak it. 'The knife and the flames' of a practice that engages and deconstructs the codes will reveal the material basis of earthly realities, once hidden by encompassing fictions.

If the poster in the subway refers to a play named *The Blood of Dreams* (19), the play of the text will show the blood of the material world as the source of the illusory dream of the fictions of the code. Such dreams are made from blood; in the blood and fire of emancipatory practice they will be destroyed.

The play of the text

> *Esplanade*: Terrain aménagé devant un édifice, une maison, en vue d'en dégager les abords (*Le Petit Robert*: 619) ('Ground uncovered in front of a house to make for easier access').

'There are lots of odd installations in this house'.
'Yes', she said.
'I've noticed many other incomprehensible details'.
'Incomprehensible is not the word', she answered, after a
moment's thought (142–3).

When the complex machinery of a 'house' (text) is unravelled, it
is clear that there are many 'odd installations'. Unlike the narrator,
however, Laura recognizes that these 'details' can be understood
('Incomprehensible is *not* the word'). This is because there are
points of access to the house other than by way of the tired codes.
Laura alone knows of the access offered by 'une sorte d'esplanade
rectangulaire' (Fr: 159). But she is also aware that her interrogator
will be more interested in the big posters that adorn the fence on the
outside. 'There's nothing valuable inside', she comments with great
accuracy. After all, in a world of exchange-value, fictions, but not
reality, have value.

Access is possible only through a small door, printed on one of
these posters and thus difficult to find. No one believes that it is
possible to enter the house of the text this way:

> In any case, people don't imagine that a door printed on paper
> can actually open, and at the same time it's convenient for ones
> who do know, it makes it easy for them to find it without
> difficulty, even when you've taken too strong a dose (134).

For most people, only the codes give access to a text. The lack of a
'door' to the text leads to the narrative voice's appeal to an
extra-textual reality. Yet Laura, who has taken a 'strong dose' of the
codes, spurns their use as a substitute door. She will gain access
through the rupture in the text itself, in the space between the
multiple voices that compose the fiction. So the door (rupture) 'can
actually open' to those who, like Laura, have found the key to the
codes: 'The little secret door has a key, which looks like a key to a
real door. I'm the one who keeps it, since I'm the one who found it'
(135). Once inside the text, through the secret rupture, all the
machinery of the narration is recoverable. So the *esplanade* is found
to contain: 'the ruins of recent houses which were just badly
constructed' (134–5). These are the earlier texts, rewritten in the
narration. There is a 'giant staircase', the machinery which had
served to link the fictions, with discarded objects and 'a lot of other
machinery even more nondescript and difficult to identify' (136).

The contents as a whole reveal clearly the geometry of the codes.
For the bits and pieces 'are not heaped up here in disorder, but
spread over the entire surface like the pieces in a chess game' (148).

Moreover the *esplanade* exhibits not only the points of coherence of the codes, but their internal ruptures. Thus 'cracks which crisscross the entire surface of a regular pavement' are reportedly 'very visible' (ibid.).

The *esplanade* displays the play of the text and the text's own invitation to play in the space it holds open. But play can be an excuse for empty intellectualism – a play on words, unaware that words play with it. Playfulness has point where it resists the play of signs, while recognizing their power.

Writing/reading pays a tribute to the power of signs by seeking to unravel the machinery of a text. Resisting the work of signs involves seizing and enlarging the ruptures between them and the reality of which they claim to be the appearance. The point is to denaturalize the signs and the codes that speak them by reawakening the play of the text.

Interrupting the code[9]

To reawaken the play of the text involves the placing in motion of the surfaces of discourse that was earlier identified as a 'revolutionary' project. Two practices have, in effect, been rejected. First, that of the univocal narrator. The stories and metaphors associated with this usage take the reader outside the practices of the text and efface the multiplicity of voices that speak it. Second, Ben-Said's attempt at an 'innocent' mode of writing, apparently liberated from the cross-ruling of the codes, cancels itself out by its very character as text and practice.

Laura's irresponsible reading – 'reading all these books at once . . . endlessly altering the arrangement of each volume' (68) – suggests an alternative practice. Beginning with a recognition of a text as what Barthes calls 'a tissue of quotations', such a practice weaves and ruptures the multiple voices that speak a text.

Project exemplifies this practice in three ways:
1 It reveals the machinery of narration, with its code of black on white, which scripts the readerly text. This machinery establishes a fixed geometry of the text which gives to Laura's words 'the guarantee of the slide-rule' (73). Such a geometry, silent and powerful, does violence to the play of the text – like the T-Square used by black girls (words) upon each other.
2 It reveals that the origins of this machinery are specific signifying practices which silence the multiple voices of a text through a univocal narration. Hence it constitutes the materiality of the text as a body of practices which, like *L'aura*, emanate from the body.

3   It pulls these practices apart to create ruptures or tears in the body of the text. The bloody text, marked by its 'cuts' and 'retakes', denies the apparently virginal whiteness of its beginning.

To be secure, the machinery must rest concealed behind the fictions that it authors. As the machinery is brought into view, so it is denaturalized. The machinery stands revealed for what it is: a product of signifying practice which, none the less, mystifies the material word.

In this way the categories of writing and reading are deconstructed. This interrupts the geometry of the fictions, revealing the practices in which they originated and through which they will be effaced.

The recurrence in the text of references to 'masks', 'glass' and 'keys' point to the fiction that is interrupted. Through the practice of writing, the masks of the fiction will be located in the bloody, material world. The faces in the wig-and-mask shop, apparently 'made out of some soft plastic material' (39), are shown, on closer inspection to be 'bleeding profusely' (42). The 'foam rubber gloves' in different shapes and colours, which serve as artificial hands, now seem to have 'blood still dripping from the wrist' (41). Once that the contradiction is shown between the contrived fictions of the masks and the reality of signifying practices that write them, the masks irritate. The red of emancipatory practice tears them off, revealing itself in 'the bloody face' left behind (48).

The fiction is laid like a plate of glass over reality. But Laura dares to break the glass with her hand. Engaged in a practice of writing stemming from the hand, Laura's *manual* labour causes 'a little bright-red blood' to stain 'the hollow of her raised palm' (19).

The interrupted code now no longer separates reading from writing, nor does it offer a key to the plot by making available a comprehensible fiction. Yet the narrator, still captured by a fiction, makes a 'futile', 'habitual' gesture towards past happy certainties. He checks, again and again, that the key (which will unlock the house/text and make its contents available for use) is still in his pocket (6) or is laid properly, awaiting employment, on 'the vestibule table' (37). His constant fear is that the key might be dropped or lost. To drop a key, as Laura does, is an act of criminal assault, comparable to breaking the glass of the fiction. Each signals an interruption to the code, a truly murderous activity:

> At the first landing, she drops her key inadvertently; the complicated noise the key makes as it knocks against one of the iron bars of the railing, then landing on the imitation-stone floor, resembles – does not resemble – the sharp clatter of a pane of

glass broken by a murderer breaking the window at the end of the corridor (96).

With the drop of the key, the description cancels itself out: at once it 'resembles – does not resemble' the tired metaphors of the code. If the key continues to be used, it will be merely as a ceremonial mark of past practice. Aping the narrative voice's involvement in the fictions of the code, while employing a gesture that simultaneously shows the glass pane of the fiction, Laura: 'ceremoniously makes the gesture of setting down on the vestibule table's marble top a bunch of imaginary keys, while glancing up toward the big mirror' (95). But the narrator himself is destined to drop his real keys. As he does, Laura screams, signalling the freeing of speech from the encompassing fictions. There is no report, no sign in the movement of the text, that the keys are again picked up. The economy of the text, signalled by the interminable calculations of Ben-Said and of the narrator, is disrupted. The voice of the narrator is 'exhausted': 'And finally, exhausted by calculating everything, I end up by waiting in my turn for the incalculable event which is going to make everything blow up in another moment' (78). The sheet of glass, like the keys of the code, had offered a rescue from the red of signifying practice – a *fire escape*. But 'fire-escapes' are no longer available:

I turned my head toward the sheet of glass. I was thinking, of course, of the fire escape; but aside from the fact that no such thing exists on any building of recent construction, I would have been very reluctant to use, once again, this convenient means of regaining the stairs, the subway, my abandoned house . . . (46)

To face a 'sheet of glass' is to think 'of the fire escape'. However, 'this convenient means of regaining . . . my abandoned house'/text is unacceptable and buildings/texts 'of recent construction', offer no staircases to escape from the flames. Increasingly, the only way to stop the fire is to destroy the affected building with dynamite (66). But this has the same effect as the flames: the mechanical means, just as much as the human hand, leaves the house/text in ruins. The interruption exhibited in the writing has shown the rupture between the fictions and the reality of the play of the text.

Robbe-Grillet has noted that it is easy to read hermetic texts, like Kafka's, as 'allegories' or 'metaphors' (1965: 164). Once the metaphor is grasped, the text is rendered useless, closed off and exhausted. In this version of reading, he adds, literature always speaks of 'something else' – an invisible but real world, evoked by the novelist's words.

It is possible, if erroneous, to locate the foregoing argument within such a reading. Locks, keys and glass, like red, white and black, would then be seen as some thing external to the text which, in being recovered, rendered the text functionless. Ironically, such a 'metaphorical' reading, for all its apparent unmasking, merely reiterates the most basic rule of the code: treat every signifier as a sign of something signified (cf. Saussure: 1972).

Project for a Revolution in New York provides the raw material for such a reading most clearly in the interrogator's 'explanation' of the role of the recurrent scenes of torture. They are, he says, contrived as a source of money, from blackmail and the sale of pornographic films, and as a source of 'martyrs', serving to produce useful myths for future generations (128). The absurd character of this reading is that, in appealing not only to metaphor itself but to the specific metaphors of exchange-value and religion, it merely reproduces the fictions of the code that it would capture.

'Reality' *for* the text is, on the contrary, only the reality *of* the text. The text speaks to and as the practice of writing. The only 'real' torture is found in the violence that the frozen codes wreak upon human possibilities; the only 'interrogation' is the questioning of fictions exemplified in the text. The movements of the text are what is real.

Why, then, all this reference to *material* reality? And if the text only speaks about itself, what kind of triumph is thereby achieved? After all, as Marx said about Proudhon's work, it is simple to replace one idea with another. Such purely 'intellectual' triumphs are the very stuff of conventional academic discourses. Nothing is altered in the 'real' world, or even challenged.[10]

The response implied here is that the activity of writing/reading is unrelated to ideas or thought (pure or otherwise). Writing/reading a text shows primarily a particular signifying practice which derives its power not from the mind but from the material reality expressed in the neglected body of the letter.

We can now be a little clearer about 'the blood of dreams' and its relation to the 'revolutionary project' referred to in the book's title. The *dreams* are the fictions generated by the thriller code through its machinery of narration ('plot', 'character', and so on). *The* dream is that this machinery can so lubricate the fictions that it need never come into view. The practices which constitute this dream are material or bodily in character. To rupture the dream is to produce blood, like the blood which stains Laura's palm. The blood stands as a reminder of the (violated) body of the text and of the material practices that script it.

Notes

1 At the revolutionary meeting that the narrator attends, the machinery temporarily stands out: 'the whole scenario is articulated like a piece of machinery, without a single hesitation, without a slip of memory or the tongue, in an absolute perfection' (27). Yet this reminder of the 'absolute perfection' of the codes is only available in the same practice that the fictions of the code conceal. The showing of this contradiction is part of the revolutionary project.

2 See 'The text of property' (Chapter 10) for an account of Locke's relation to the fiction of private ownership of speech.

3 As suggested in Chapter 10, this voice of the 'I' is the immanent capitalist version of the transcendent, feudal voice of an impersonal order.

4 Ben-Said comments bitterly:
   it was not the hour indicated, nor even the exact place. He in any case is never late, he repeats bitterly; if he got there, this once, too close to the beginning of the scene, of which he might have missed a fragment, it was obviously because he had been given the wrong time, and perhaps on purpose, if someone is trying to put him in the wrong. Seven minutes' difference is a lot (140).

5 The others who had 'perhaps on purpose', given him the wrong time. Ben-Said's concern for correct time and attempts to avoid time-wasting, like that of the conventional writer, is entirely in the tradition of Benjamin Franklin.

6 For a long time now, she has lost all real communication with the outside world, to which she now has only artificial links, constituted for the most part – aside from the fragments of personal memories whose most violent scenes I have made her forget – by this detective-story library in decay, by the ordinary anecdotes which I myself supply her, carefully expurgating from them any allusion to destructive episodes . . . (76)

7 See Chapter 4 for a reading of Kafka's texts in these terms.

8 See Ricardou (1971), pp.212–13.

9 The notion of 'interruption' is introduced in Chapter 1. Unlike 'interpretation' which treats every utterance as a document of an underlying reality, the practice of interruption engages the relation between reality and appearance that the text itself offers. There are intriguing parallels between the black/white/red scheme and the practice of colour classification among the Ndembu reported by Turner (1967).

10 Hence Marx's *Theses on Feuerbach* with their reference to mere 'interpretation' of the world.

Bibliography

References to the French edition of *Projet* (Eds du Minuit: Paris, 1970) are cited as (Fr.).
All references without a year or page number refer to the American

paperback edition of Robbe-Grillet's text, *Project for a Revolution in New York*, trans. Richard Howard, Grove Press: New York, 1972. The other works cited are:

Barthes, Roland (1966), *Critique et Vérité*, Editions du Seuil: Paris.

Barthes, Roland (1972), *Le Plaisir du Texte*, Editions du Seuil: Paris.

Cerisy Conference (1972), *Nouveau Roman: Hier, Aujourd'hui*, Union Générale d'Editions: Paris.

Habermas, Jürgen (1976), *Legitimation Crisis*, trans. Thomas McCarthy, Heinemann: London.

Léenhardt, Jean (1975), in *Robbe-Grillet*, Colloque de Cerisy, vol. 2.

Ricardou, Jean (1971), *Pour un Théorie du Nouveau Roman*, Editions du Seuil: Paris (Chapter IX, 'La Fiction Flamboyante').

Robbe-Grillet, Alain (1965), *For a New Novel: Essays on Fiction*, trans. Richard Howard, Grove Press: New York ('Time and Description in Fiction Today' and 'From Realism to Reality').

Saussure, Ferdinand de (1972), 'Course in General Linguistics', in R. and F. de George (eds), *The Structuralists*, Anchor: New York.

Turner, Victor (1967), *The Forest of Symbols*, Cornell University Press: Ithaca, New York ('Colour Classification in Ndembu Ritual').

part VII

Conclusion: the mastery of language

Two writers, thus far neglected, contribute directly to a materialist critique of language. Volosinov attempts a definitive break with sociologistic and psychologistic interpretations of speech and writing, and intervenes directly in the dialogic relations of speech to speech. Derrida interrupts the texts of social psychology to read them against themselves. A method deriving from both writers is brought to bear on a classical tale of socialization, the story of 'Little Red Riding Hood'.

chapter 13

Textuality, sexuality, economy

Volosinov's sociology of speeches

Volosinov's connections with the themes of our argument are indicated by noting his discussion of Saussure's approach.[1] He states that at the time of writing, 'the majority of Russian thinkers in linguistics are under the determinative influence of Saussure and his disciples' (1973, pp.58–9). Volosinov formulates Saussure's main thesis as being, that 'language stands in opposition to utterance in the same way as does that which is social to that which is individual.' Therefore:

> Linguistics, as Saussure conceives it, cannot have the utterance as the object of study. What constitutes the linguistic element in the utterance are the normatively identical forms of language present in it. Everything else is 'accessory and random' (ibid., p.60).

Saussure, in line with 'the sociological school of Durkheim', would 'decisively cast aside' the 'individual act of speaking, the utterance (*parole*)'. This discarded element, however, makes its re-appearance in the history of language which 'is dominated by the "utterance" with its individuality and randomness'. Consequently, in a move of Saussure's which Volosinov finds characteristic of his 'abstract objectivism', history must be excluded 'as an irrational force distorting the logical purity of the language system' (ibid., p.61).

Volosinov opposes himself as rigorously to the 'individualistic subjectivism' which would regard language as 'an ever-flowing stream of speech-acts in which nothing remains fixed and identical to itself' (ibid., p.52). Objectivism and subjectivism both preserve the mystical notion of the uniqueness of the utterance, the first to denigrate it, the second to celebrate it. But for Volosinov, 'the

individual utterance is by no means an individual fact not susceptible to sociological analysis by virtue of its individuality'. Against
objectivism it must be insisted that 'individual utterances are what
constitute the actual, concrete, reality of language, and . . . that
they do have creative value in language'. But with objectivism it
must be affirmed that 'the structure of the utterance . . . is a social
structure'. Volosinov asserts (ibid., pp.93–4) that 'the stylistic
shaping of an utterance is shaping of a social kind, and the very
verbal stream of utterances, which is what the reality of language
actually amounts to, is a social stream'. We turn now to the
distinctive account of the 'social structure' of the utterance which
Volosinov elaborates.

The statement that 'any utterance, no matter how weighty and
complete in and of itself, is only a moment in the continuous process
of verbal communication' (ibid., p.95) is unexceptional enough. But
Volosinov draws from it a rigorous method for the interrogation of
the utterance which is new. The utterance has no complete meaning
in itself, for it is necessarily a response to previous utterances. The
utterance is monologic only in appearance. In reality it is the
product and continuation of dialogue. 'Any true understanding is
dialogic in nature' (ibid., p.102). But this dialogic nature is
extremely elusive: the utterance itself invites consideration as a
united whole. Volosinov proceeds, therefore, to focus attention on
a kind of utterance which explicitly addresses the relation between
utterances, namely reported speech.

Reported speech comprises 'the syntactic patterns . . . , the modifications of those patterns and the variants of those modifications,
which we find in a language for the reporting of other people's
utterances, and for incorporating those utterances, as the utterances
of others, into a bound, monologic context' (ibid., p.112). It 'is
speech within speech, utterance within utterance, and at the same
time also speech about speech, utterance about utterance, (ibid.,
p.115). It is therefore proposed 'to take the phenomenon of
reported speech and postulate it as a problem from a sociological
orientation', and on this basis 'to map out the sociological method in
linguistics' (ibid., p.113).

Volosinov's statement of this method is worth quoting at length.
'The productive study of dialogue presupposes . . . a more pro-
found investigation of the forms used in reported speech, since
these forms reflect basic and constant tendencies in the active
reception of other speakers' speech' (ibid., p.117):

What we have in the forms of reported speech is precisely an
objective document of this reception. Once we have learned to

decipher it, this document provides us with information, not about accidental and mercurial subjective psychological processes in the 'soul' of the recipient, but about steadfast social tendencies in an active reception of other speakers' speech, tendencies that have crystallized into language forms.

In a passage which itself involves more than a trace of the Durkheimianism for which he criticized Saussure, he continues (ibid., p.117):

The mechanism of this process is located, not in the individual soul, but in society. It is the function of society to select and make grammatical (adapt to the grammatical structure of its language) just those factors in the active and evaluative reception of utterances that are socially vital and constant, and, hence, are grounded in the economic existence of the particular community of speakers.

In our view, the deciphering of the forms of reported speech as exemplifying steadfast social tendencies in the reception of other speakers' speech must be sharply distinguished from the documentary method interpretation of these tendencies in terms of functions of society and the grammatical structure of language. Volosinov only incompletely articulates the distinction between his approach and that of classical sociology. The distinction becomes clearer when we turn from these theoretical prognostications to consider an example of Volosinov's method of decipherment in practice.

The method is demonstrated in an examination of reported speech in the literary text. Here, Volosinov points out, it is used in particular to mark the relation between the authorial context on the one hand, and the reported speech of the characters on the other. Historically, this relation has taken three characteristic forms. In the first, a rigid separation is made between the speeches. Author's speech has its precise style, and that of the characters is in each case clearly distinct from it and from that of other characters. No attempt is made to reformulate one in terms of another. Although it superficially preserves the individuality of each speaker, Volosinov finds this to be an authoritarian and dogmatic organization of the dialogue, since all other characters appear only within the context defined by the author's speech, with which the text opens and to which it returns. It is characteristic, for example, of the Middle French writings of the seventeenth century.

A second possibility is one 'in which the dynamism of the interorientation between reporting and reported speech moves are exactly opposite in nature' (ibid., p.120). Here,

> language devises means for infiltrating reported speech with
> authorial retort and commentary in deft and subtle ways. The
> reporting context strives to break down the self-contained com-
> pactness of the reported speech, to resolve it, to obliterate its
> boundaries.

This style, found by Volosinov to characterize 'the Renaissance
(especially in the French langauge), the end of the eighteenth
century, and virtually the entire nineteenth century', breaks down
authoritarian dogmatism, and exhibits instead 'a relativism supply-
ing extremely favourable grounds for a positive and sensitive reception of all individualized verbal nuances of thought, belief, feeling'
(ibid., p.121). This individualism, though playfully pitting one
speech against another, none the less preserves the integrity of each
though without the unambiguous hierarchy asserted by the first
style.

More recently, particularly in the late nineteenth-century writers
of Russia, Volosinov discovers a mode of writing which calls into
question both the integrity of the speech of the 'characters' which it
reports, and also 'it's' own authority to speak. In this style (ibid.,
p.121):

> the verbal dominant may shift to the reported speech, which in
> that case becomes more forceful and more active than the
> authorial context framing it. This time the reported speech
> begins to resolve, as it were, the reporting context, instead of the
> other way around. The authorial context loses the greater objec-
> tivity it normally commands in comparison with reported speech.

In this case, the narrator's speech can become 'just as individualized, colourful, and non-authoritative as is the speech of the characters' (ibid., p.121). Here, as he later puts it, 'we perceive the
author's accents and intonations being interrupted by the [. . .]
value judgments of another person' (ibid., p.155).

It is this third mode of writing the relation between speeches
which particularly interests both Volosinov and ourselves. He finds
it expressed in a distinctive mode of direct speech, which he calls
quasi-direct discourse, in which narrator's and character's speeches
interfere to the extent that it is impossible to unambiguously
determine which is at work in a particular word. In this case there is
a double sense in which the authoritarian context of the text has
been overthrown. The 'narrator' has become a character within the
text, unable to stand back from it. But further, no such standing
back is now possible. The unresolvably problematic character of the
text defies the attempt to sum up in a single speech the interplay of
speeches within it.

Volosinov draws attention to a striking implication of this problematicity. It is impossible to read such a text out loud with accuracy in the spoken voice. In the authoritarian text it is not difficult for the reader (say, the author himself) to adopt a distinctive style of speech, facial expression, gesticulation, for each of the roles he is to perform, including his own. Indeed if he reads his own part straightforwardly then the authority of his own speech will be enhanced by the more or less artificial ways in which he less successfully mimics others. In the relativistic text, the task of reading is more complex, but none the less clear-cut. It amounts to the performance of a number of characters, including that of the author, with equal vigour and plausibility. Here unlike the first case a degree of theatrical skill is required: a bad performance of any role will falsify it and so damage the text as a whole.

But to read the anti-authoritarian text is necessarily to falsify it. Insofar as the reader-author, by style of speech, facial expression, or gesture either identifies together two instances of discourse, or distinguishes two instances of discourse, then he resolves in speech what was written to be irresolvable. Volosinov concludes (ibid., p.157):

> From all this, it necessarily follows that the absolute acting out of
> reported speech, where a work of fiction is read aloud, is
> admissible only in the rarest cases. Otherwise an inevitable
> conflict arises with the basic aesthetic design of the context.

Thus the writer who asserted earlier that 'the very verbal stream of utterances . . . is what the reality of language actually amounts to' has reached the surprising conclusion that what this reality actually amounts to is necessarily misrepresented by its verbal performance. The real relations which this performance conceals can be grasped only when language is examined as writing. This conclusion has implications going beyond the significance of the literary text. Speech generally misrepresents itself. The dialogic relations between speeches, exemplifying steadfast social tendencies, which Volosinov wants to make the object of his sociological method in linguistics are not directly visible as the relations between one utterance and another. Contradictory tendencies within the utterance and problematic relations between utterances make it necessary to define a new level of analysis. We refer to 'voices' as the speech unities which interplay, in the fashion which Volosinov admirably describes, in both the spoken and written word. Within a particular discourse the number of voices at work will not be arbitrary, nor will the modes of relationship between them.

We have elsewhere identified the 'appearance'/'reality' relation as a particularly crucial mode of relationship between voices, and it is one which precisely accounts for the examples which Volosinov has presented. In the classical text, characters in diverse voices articulate the varied appearances of the world to them, but only in the context of the single reality articulated by the narrators' voice. Authoritarian dogmatism arises in this situation, where every voice is re-interpreted by the voice of the author.

In the relativist text, the ability to re-interpret other voices is generalized from that of the author to all voices. A cacophony of competing claims is heard, but finally each acknowledges the independence of the other, in exchange for the assurance of its own. For each, its own voice is the single reality: the very multiplicity of the others confirms their merely apparent status.

In the anti-authoritarian text the claimed integrity of the voice is undermined. A play which can no longer be recognized as the cut and thrust of competing voices is at work. In the mutual interruption of one voice by another what is in question is no longer the insistent re-assertion by each of its own version of 'reality' underlying the 'appearance' presented by the other, but rather the practices whereby the relation between 'appearance' and 'reality' is constituted in either. This play is fundamentally textual rather than vocal in character. It is the play which Jacques Derrida has identified as the play of 'differance'.[2]

Derrida's 'differance'

The problematic character of the spoken voice in its relation to the written text is a sustained theme of Derrida's writings: we can regard his discussion as building on the point which Volosinov's has reached.[3]

For us, textuality is the interplay of voices which constitute 'appearance' and 'reality' in discourse, spoken or written, an interplay however which is fundamentally disguised in speech, with the possibility of becoming apparent only in writing. Derrida calls this interplay *differance*.[4] The name is specifically chosen so that in speech it is inaudible: when the word is read aloud (in French), it sounds the same as 'difference'. Only in writing can differance appear.

Derrida draws attention to the fact that differance has two aspects. It is a temporal deferral of the moment when 'appearance' and 'reality', initially differentiated, will be brought into correspondence. It is equally a spatial-ontological deference of 'appearance' to the 'reality' which does not appear.

The text as traditionally understood involves a play of differance which is limited in scope, i.e. closed. The text opens with a gap between 'appearance' and 'reality', which is resolved in the course of the narrative, so that ultimately the difference is abolished. Typically, the text initially portrays diverse characters, each able to formulate a different 'appearance' of the world in which the tale is located. Through the unfolding of a plot, which may be simple or complex, the different appearances clash and contradict. Finally, the course of events produces a single 'reality', apparent equally to all. So understood, the text is a site of interaction in the course of which many distinct subjectivities come to recognize themselves in a single objectivity which is thus intersubjective.[5]

From the social-psychological point of view, the interpretation of the text focusses upon the 'subjects' and 'objects' constituted by the text. But Derrida shifts attention to the gap within the text which constitutes them. The text produces and consumes differance. The play of the text thus has two aspects. Derrida locates the first as *economic*. It arises from the temporal deferring aspect of differance, which constitutes the time of the text. He locates the second as *sexual*. It arises from the spatial-ontological deferring aspect of differance, which constitutes the pleasure of the text.

From the social psychological point of view, the text reiterates the recognition of subjectivity in intersubjective objectivity. It is necessarily closed because the functioning of the society as a whole depends upon this recognition. The text is thus necessary to society, and society to the text. A significant aspect of this necessity is that the play of differance should be closed: indeed it is the function of the social psychological text to close it.

But, Derrida points out, the text as the play of differance is not necessary to society. The non-necessity of differance has itself two aspects. From the temporal point of view, 'appearance' and 'reality' are ultimately identical. In this sense the time of the text is an economic surplus over what is necessary. From the spatial-ontological point of view, 'appearance' and 'reality' are ultimately different: 'reality' need never 'appear' at all. In this sense the pleasure of the text is a surplus over what is necessary.

The textual play of differance thus transcends the necessary closure of social-psychological recognition. The differance between 'appearance' and 'reality' is always already in play, and thus so are sexuality and economy, which transcend and threaten the functional needs of 'subjectivity' and 'intersubjectivity' respectively.

The text must then be re-read, against social psychological interpretation. In our terms, its play of differance must be interrupted. This interruption is a political intervention in the text, for

312 *Conclusion: the mastery of language*

the existence of differance is systematically denied by the upholders
of the status quo, who reduce it to the 'psychological' and 'sociological' facets of a single smooth working consensual whole.

Two reductions are the butt of Derrida's particular criticism. The
first, of speech to thought, is epitomized by the writing of Husserl. It
is articulated in a short passage of thirty pages of his early *Logical
Investigations* (1970, pp.268–298). This attempts to displace language, for once and for all, from any claim to centrality as object of
phenomenological investigation. Derrida finds in Husserl's appeal
to soliloquy an 'autoaffection' which is fundamentally erotic in
character. The pleasure of hearing one's own voice is non-necessary
and thus capable of a pure intensity which is given expression by
Husserl in his account of the ego.[6] Derrida's interrogation of
Husserl is thus able to demonstrate, through the latter's writing
(itself ostensibly anti-psychological), the sexual and differential
character of what passes for self-same and psychological identity
(Derrida: 1973, *passim*).

The second, from writing to speech, is epitomized by the writing
of Saussure, for whom this theme expresses directly – though as
Derrida shows, in contradictory fashion – the thesis of the arbitrariness of the sign. For Saussure writing stands to speech as signifier
to the signified. To give writing priority over speech is to value the
signifier over the signified. This is precisely what Derrida, reading
Saussure against himself, proposes to do. Following an identification which is explicit in Saussure himself, Derrida finds the establishment of the signifier-signified relation within language, in the
absence of any natural identification, to be an operation which is
fundamentally economic in character. The surplus of the signified
over the signifier is non-natural and is the transformatory force of
writing which Saussure himself reveals but tries to suppress in his
drive to sociologize the establishment of what he calls value (Derrida: 1977, *passim* but especially Part I, Chapter 2).

The sexual is thus the relation between voice and voice viewed
from the standpoint of underlying difference where the economic is
the relation between voice and voice viewed from the standpoint of
underlying sameness. Derrida shows that these identifications, and
the origin of the two reductions which cover them over, can each be
derived from the writings of Jean-Jacques Rousseau, the eighteenth-
century antecedent of both Saussure and Husserl. A scenario,
presented by Rousseau as the 'origin of languages' illustrates these
relations (quoted from Derrida, 1977, p.262):

> In the arid places where water could be had only from wells,
> people had to rejoin one another to sink the wells, or at least to

agree upon their use. Such must have been the origin of societies and languages in warm countries.

This is where the first ties were formed among families: there were the first rendezvous of the two sexes. Girls would come to seek water for the household, young men would come to water their herds. Their eyes, accustomed to the same sights since infancy, began to see with increased pleasure. The heart is moved by these novel objects; an unknown attraction renders it less savage; it feels pleasure at not being alone. Imperceptibly, water becomes more necessary. The livestock become thirsty more often. One would arrive in haste, and leave with regret. In that happy age when nothing marked the hours, nothing would oblige one to count them; the only measure of time would be the alteration of amusement and boredom. Under old oaks, conquerers of the years, an ardent youth will gradually lose its ferocity. Little by little, they become less shy with each other. In trying to make oneself understood, one learns to explain oneself. There too original festivals developed. Feet skipped with joy, earnest gestures no longer sufficed, the voice accompanied them in impassioned accents: pleasure and desire mingled and were felt together. There at last was the true cradle of nations: from the pure crystal of the fountains, flowed the first fires of love.

Rousseau's text accounts for the origin of the voice in terms of an economically necessary encounter out of which a non-necessary pleasure is soon produced. Economy expresses the sameness between the practices of girls and boys: each must seek water and in so doing enter into relations with others different from themselves, unfamiliar to those 'accustomed to the same sights from infancy'. Pleasure arises out of the contemplation of this difference in its own right, an activity which is strictly non-necessary. The cultivation of this pleasure itself influences the temporality, that is the economy, of the encounter: the time made available for it is extended little by little.

But Rousseau's idyllic picture harmonizes the differance which it glimpses. The pursuit of pleasure precisely matches the economic surplus which allows for it: the result is a situation free of conflict and process. Derrida writes (ibid., pp.262–3):

What Rousseau describes here is neither the eve of society nor society already formed, but the movement of a birth, the continuous advent of presence. None of the oppositions of determined predicates can be applied clearly to what, between the state of nature and the state of society, is not a state but a passage which should have continued and lasted . . .

The 'origin' is not a single moment in the distant past to which we can now only look back nostalgically. Rather, the textual, sexual, and economic work of originary differance, 'between the state of nature and the state of society', is always already in play. It is possible to re-open this play if we are able to interrupt the interpretations dedicated to closing it.

Derrida's practice of writing advances upon Volosinov's in a crucial respect. Although identifying and welcoming the overthrowing of the authoritarian voice, Volosinov himself practised it. For him the distinction between the classical 'objectivist' and 'subjectivist' texts and the contemporary texts which we could call 'materialist' was objective. But for Derrida, it is a textual distinction: it depends on the way in which we read these texts.

The classical text wants to be read as necessarily and safely closed, as successfully voicing subjective integrity. But we have to interrupt this closure to reveal the play of non-necessary and dangerous openness. In an attempt to demonstrate this practice, we turn now to read a classical text which, like Rousseau's, portrays a passage 'between the state of nature and the state of society'. Charles Perrault's *Little Red Riding Hood* (1975) is such a tale. We will present two readings of the story, in order to exemplify the two ways in which texts may be treated. The first is the social-psychological way which acknowledges itself as an interpretation of the text. The second, we shall argue, is a materialist interruption of the text.

Here it is not simply a matter of comparing two philosophical positions each of which upholds the text as an exemplification of itself. If this were so, then the text would be irrelevant. Rather, we claim that the interpretation can only read the text as an illustration of the idea which it brings to the text. Instead interruption is open to the play of the text itself.[7]

Reading Little Red Riding Hood

In his paper called 'Little Red Riding Hood's Metacommentary', Victor Larrucia states that his own concerns are at the 'peculiar interface between meaning and behaviour'. His approach (1975, p.518): 'while acknowledging the prime significance of historical and social context, aims at the processes involved in communication itself in order to see the text as a message in circuit.' He explains that 'while the approach is basically centred on the text, it views the text only in terms of a communication process, and meaning here is seen as a constituent, not of the message, but rather of the process'. The approach 'requires two essential tools: one for decoding the text, the other for relating the decoded text to the communication process'. These essential tools he finds respectively in the structuralist analysis of myth by Claude Lévi-Strauss (1967) and in the pragmatic analysis of communication by Paul Watzlawick *et al.* (1968).

It will be argued here that Larrucia's approach is necessarily eclectic. His eclecticism arises from the attempt to reconcile two aspects of a supposedly total situation: a message and a communication process in which it circulates. It will be shown that this approach reduces the 'message' (here the text of the story) to a presupposed version of the 'process' (here the Europe of the late seventeenth century in which the story was produced). By contrast, it will be proposed that a text or message itself sufficiently constitutes the sense of the communicational context within which it circulates. Our interruption of the story will concern itself with the precise character of this context.

From Watzlawick *et al.*, Larrucia draws the assumption that, 'all messages have two aspects, a command and a report, the first being a message about the nature of the relationship between sender and receiver, the second the message of content' (p.520). These two 'functions' can work 'conjunctively or disjunctively' (pp.521–2). 'There is normally no problem . . . if there is a conjunctive operation.' But, problems arise when the ostensible *report* (p.522): 'which might select one set of possibilities for role behaviour, is negated by the relationship established in the command aspect of the message.' This, he writes 'is the essential ingredient for a power struggle' (p.522):

> Theoretically, this notion of power struggle derives from Gregory Bateson's idea of paradoxical injunction – double bind – wherein a message, through the very nature of a communicational process, creates an untenable behavioural situation; an example of this is 'Be spontaneous!', which denies the possibility for the receiver of acting spontaneously at the very instant it requires of the receiver spontaneous action.

Larrucia proposes that 'this process holds at both "societal" and "individual" levels'. This enables him to reconcile the Watzlawick-/Bateson theory of sender/recipient relations with Lévi-Strauss's account of the cultural significance of myth (p.522):

> As Lévi-Strauss says, 'Although experience contradicts theory, social life validates cosmology by its similarity of structure. Hence cosmology is true'. Lévi-Strauss' use of the term 'contradiction' is equivalent to my use of the term 'paradox', that is, some

logical inconsistency in the way members of a group relate to one another can neither be resolved without changing the fundamental structure of the group . . . nor spoken of. We might say this paradox is the 'blindspot' for the group, the blindspot which generates social communication for the vision peculiar to the group.

Larrucia's reading of 'Red Riding Hood' proceeds by first examining the report aspect of the tale, employing Lévi-Strauss's notion of 'contradiction', and secondly examining its command aspect, employing the Watzlawick/Bateson notion of 'paradoxical injunction'.

The notion of a power struggle around the meaning of the text is intriguing. But Larrucia conceives it as occurring between the text itself (the report) and a meta-statement attached to the text (the command). Thus he is concerned with struggle between the text and something other than the text (another text). He sees the relation between these (texts) as either one of consistency (conjunction) or contradiction (disjunction). The reading attempted here, by contrast, will search for relations of struggle within and intrinsic to the text itself.

Interpreting morality

Larrucia's Lévi-Straussian analysis re-writes the story in terms of units, each represented by a sentence, which when read from left to right and down the page tell the tale sequentially (diachronically), but which when read as contrasting pairs of vertical columns reveal the synchronic structure of contradictions which is the unconscious meaning of the tale.[8] The result is as follows (1975, p. 528):

Column 1	Column 2	Column 3	Column 4
1 Grandmother's illness causes mother to make Grandmother food	2 Little Red Riding Hood obeys mother and goes off to woods	3 LRRH meets (Wolf as) friend and talks	
4 Woodcutter's presence causes Wolf to speak to LRRH	5 LRRH obeys Wolf and takes long road to Grandmother's	6 Grandmother admits (Wolf as) LRRH	7 Wolf eats Grandmother

	8 LRRH meets (Wolf as) Grandmother	
9 LRRH obeys Grandmother and gets into bed	10 LRRH questions (Wolf as) Grandmother	11 Wolf eats LRRH

Here, (ibid., p. 528, emphasis added):

> the first column involves mediated relationships, mediation
> being based on a sign (illness, . . . presence . . .): here the signs
> are recognized. In the second column are . . . relationships . . .
> where mediation is not based on a sign: here the sign is [*sic*] not
> recognized as signs. The third column contains . . . disguised
> relationship; . . . the sign disguises a real relationship. The last
> column involves direct relationships which are not disguised and
> which involve no sign.

Larrucia states that the first two columns represent respectively
the over-rating and under-rating of mediated relationships. (Over-
rating arises because no message was received from either Grandmother or Woodcutter; under-rating because 'no demands for
exchange are made'.) The last two columns represent respectively
the under-rating and over-rating of direct relations. (Under-rating
arises because 'signs are not noticed as participating in a direct
relationship', over-rating because there is no struggle.) The four
columns can then 'be condensed into the following sets of opposition – Consent: Submit: Tricked: Coerced.'

This interpretation of the columns is in terms of a version of self,
and of society which is exhibited by the tale. Larrucia states (ibid., p.
528): 'In the first two columns the subject has access to regulation
and is not the object of control. In columns 3 and 4, a subject does
not have access to regulation, and is in fact objectified by control.'
These columns express 'unmediated' relationships. Note that in
both instances for Larrucia the character in question is human:
mother, Red Riding Hood, and grandmother are the actors to
whom awareness or unawareness is attributed. In this sense, the
Wolf is not a character in his reading of the story.

For Larrucia the Wolf in fact represents Nature in order that the
tale can be read as a Lévi-Straussian Nature/Culture dialectic. This
perspective assumes that nature provides the underlying reality of
social life, while culture is its immanent appearance. Despite the

complexities of the conception of the 'noble savage' entertained by Rousseau and Voltaire, its assumption remains that of Hobbes: natural individualistic conflict underlies superficial social cohesion. The commitment is to the social as the realm of freedom, as against the natural as the realm of unfreedom. On this basis Larrucia concludes that (p. 529) 'the contradiction which is the basis of the narrative structure might be put simply as Free:not-Free.' But of course Perrault's Wolf is not natural, neither is 'he' outside the cultural product which is the tale. The narrative structure of the text cannot be deduced from the Nature/Culture opposition conceived as a reality prior to it; rather it must be interrogated to show how the 'Nature'/'Culture' opposition arises within it.

For Larrucia the text arises at a specific point in the development of this opposition (p. 530):

> Already in the Renaissance 'mastery of nature' was becoming a dominant theme – anything which can be seen as a part of 'nature' is potentially exploitable, and . . . the report/command relationship depends on this opposition, Nature/Culture.

The text expresses the social construction of the 'individual' self for the first time historically (and, we may add, biographically, in the life of each child to whom at a formative stage it is subsequently retold). It does so by way of a paradoxical injunction. The paradox can be expressed (p. 531), 'Be free, be entirely individual.' Concretely, the report (be free) contradicts the imperative employed by the command. Analytically, the 'be natural' of the report contradicts its cultural specificity as a command.

However, the paradox is not to be found within the text itself. Rather, it is to be found in the relation between the tale and the moral which Perrault appends to it (p. 532): 'The moral, which appears incidental to the tale, a supplement, in fact creates a disjunctive relationship between the ostensible content of the narrative and its meaning.' 'The moral,' writes Larrucia, 'puts the narrative outside itself, and places itself in the domain of behaviour: it is didactic.' He concludes (p. 532):

> A relationship is created between behaviour and meaning, a relationship regarding both the significance of an act – social context – and the connection of the subject with the other – psychological context.

Thus a double-bind is constituted between the command, expressed by the motto, forbidding young lasses to listen to strangers, and the report, expressed by the story, of one who did. Unless Red Riding Hood's freedom to choose is acknowledged, the tale makes no sense. Unless this freedom is denied, the moral is unacceptable.

On this reading the story expresses the natural underlying reality, while the motto expresses the cultural conclusions to be drawn from it: the paradox is the particular form taken by the Nature/Culture opposition understood as the difference between these two. Lessons about Cultural (human) wolves are drawn from a tale about a Natural (animal) Wolf. But the Wolf is not an animal wolf, and the tale is not a natural tale. This reading imposes its own prior conception of the opposition to interpret it, instead of interrupting the opposition constituted by the text itself. We shall now attempt such an interruption.

Re-reading Red Riding Hood

Let us begin by reformulating Larrucia's categories as follows:

	sign	*no sign*		
mediated relations	column 1	column 2	reality ≠ appearance	in *reality*, i.e. to the reader
unmediated relations	column 3	column 4	reality = appearance	
	reality ≠ appearance	reality = appearance		
	in *appearance*, i.e. to the character			

Our row and column headings appear below and to the right of the table. Larrucia's headings appear above it and to the left. We propose that his 'mediation' is a gap between 'appearance' and 'reality' which is *real* in that the reader is aware of it, while 'sign' is his notion of a gap between 'appearance' and 'reality' which is *apparent* in the sense that the character in the story is also aware of it. This distinction is based on that made by the text of the story between the voice of the narrator, which formulates reality directly to the reader, and the voices of the characters, which formulate the appearance of that reality to them.[9]

Thus in Larrucia's column 1, the mother (incident 1) and the Wolf (incident 4) each introduce a gap between present appearance and future reality. The mother tells Red Riding Hood to go to the Grandmother. The Wolf tells Red Riding Hood that he too will go to the Grandmother.

In column 1 the narrator also introduces a gap between appearance and reality at each incident. At incident 1, he writes that the mother doted on the child, whereas the grandmother was 'even fonder, and made her a little red hood'. Thus beneath the appearance formulated in the mother's talk, an underlying current of conflict between mother and grandmother for the child is portrayed. At incident 4, as Larrucia notes, the Wolf's friendly words to the child are put in question for the reader by the narrator's direct statement of his desire to eat her up.

For both characters and reader, an appearance/reality gap opens the tale. For the characters this gap anticipates the time of the journey to the grandmother by both child and Wolf and encompasses the temporality of the tale. For the reader the gap is more foreboding. Little Red Riding Hood must wend her way warily through the woods. But the beginning and end may contain more dangers than the journey itself. In the text – and this is an event which Larrucia omits from his analysis – the time in the wood is the only freedom which she has.

In column 2, Larrucia collects incidents in which Little Red Riding Hood denies any gap between appearance and reality. She takes at face value words addressed to her, as she thinks, by each of the other three characters. In incidents 2 and 5, the reader has been warned of underlying realities which contradict these appearances, in the ways already noted. In incident 9, the reader has been told how the Wolf devoured the grandmother and then lay down in her bed.

Thus in column 2 a gap is introduced between the reader and the character. The character grasps only an appearance of the reality which is made available to the reader. The same character occupies this position on each occasion. Little Red Riding Hood thus exemplifies orientation to mere appearances.

In column 3, the Wolf on each occasion masquerades as other than he really is. He thus exhibits a gap between appearance and reality. Although the reader has been warned in general terms of the Wolf's desire, the narrator does not explain the motive underlying any of his particular actions. The reader is thus forced to accept these actions at face-value as they occur.[10] In this sense, for the reader, reality equates with appearance for the incidents in this column.

The reader is thus put in the position of being more naive than the Wolf, whereas the reader was able to be less naive than Red Riding

Hood. In column 3 the gap between the reader and the character is reversed. Now only appearance is made available to the reader. The Wolf thus exemplifies orientation to underlying reality.

In column 4, Larrucia collects incidents in which the Wolf reveals his underlying reality to himself, the Grandmother, Red Riding Hood, and the reader. Identity between reality and appearance is established for all, closing each of the gaps previously opened. Most fundamentally, the gap between appearance and reality for both reader and characters which began the tale has been resolved, first for one, then for the other, now for both.

But here we have re-captured the sequence of the tale, which Larrucia – following Lévi-Strauss – wished to dissolve. Initially reality is opposed to appearance (to which reader and characters have different orientations). The text then moves through two formulations of appearance as opposed to reality (in the first, on behalf of a character, in the second, on behalf of the reader). Finally, reality is identified with appearance (one and the same for both characters and reader).

It is this movement of textuality, which we shall make the object of an alternative reading to Larrucia's. Larrucia's reading cannot grasp textuality as movement. In fact he cannot grasp textuality at all. The synchronic meaning which he attributes to the story can only be discovered outside the text itself.

Interrupting textuality

The tale is an interplay of discourses, being in order of appearance those of the narrator, of the mother, of Little Red Riding Hood, of the Wolf, and of the grandmother. However this distinction based on the identity of the speakers is not infallible. In his second and third appearances, the Wolf counterfeits the voices of Red Riding Hood and the grandmother respectively. The text marks this by his precise repetition of the words he has heard them use. The delight engendered by the final dialogue results precisely from the ambiguity of the Wolf's statements, between the innocuous speech of the grandmother and the explicit formulation of the evil intentions of the Wolf, into which it shades.

But if the identification of speeches with speakers is not reliable – and it is precisely the point of 'Little Red Riding Hood' that it is not – then serious problems are raised as to how to proceed in reading the text. In particular any attempt to impute 'characters' to the speakers in the tale becomes suspect. Larrucia's interpretation depends precisely on such imputation: in his most rigorous statement, the tale concerns subjects who must choose between (social) regulation and (natural) control. This choice is neither 'social' nor 'natural'. (For Larrucia this fact can only be reiterated paradoxically.) Further, it is not a choice made by subjects.

The text can be (re-) read without the imposition of the category of the subject, but for this purpose new categories are necessary. Rather than imputing characters to the speakers (including Perrault and the narrator), and then reading the text as a relation between characters, these categories must formulate relations between speeches themselves. The categories for sameness and difference between characters, which Larrucia's social-psychological interpretation employs, are those of society and self.[11] ('Society' is the way in which two characters are the same, and 'self' the way in which they differ.) The categories for sameness and difference between speeches, which we propose are the basis for a materialist interruption of the text, are those of economy and sexuality. ('Economy' is the way in which two speeches are the same, and 'sexuality' the way in which they differ.)

'Self' and 'society' are concepts inherently bound up with social psychology's functionalist belief in harmonious closed systems divorced from historical transformation. Despite his awareness of contradiction and of history, Larrucia's 'paradoxical' formulation establishes the timeless closure of 'Red Riding Hood'. 'There can only be a perpetual oscillation between categories of freedom and non-freedom' (p. 534). 'Sexuality' disrupts functionalism by the fact that sexual pleasure is not necessary to the function of reproduction. 'Economy' disrupts functionalism by the fact that economic surplus is not necessary to the function of production. To interpret social psychological phenomena in terms of 'society' and 'self' is to pre-suppose their harmonious closure. To interrupt textual phenomena in search of 'surplus' and 'pleasure' is to discover their disharmonious openness. It is to reveal the political character of the modes of production (of surplus) and consumption (of pleasure) which they employ.

An interruption of 'Little Red Riding Hood' can reveal the politics of the text in these terms, and serve as a paradigm for the interrogation of other phenomena presently subsumed under the hegemony of social psychology.

Relations of sameness and difference between discourses are explicitly established by the text. The mother's speech, in terms of the 'cake', and the 'pot of butter', is subsequently repeated by Red Riding Hood to the Wolf, and by the Wolf counterfeiting Red Riding Hood to the grandmother. Finally the Wolf counterfeiting the grandmother again refers to the 'cake' and the 'pot of butter' in speaking to Red Riding Hood. In a textual sense, then, these two items play an economic role in establishing sameness between the discourses. The mother's speech to Red Riding Hood, Red Riding Hood's speech to the Wolf, and Red Riding Hood's speech to the Wolf counterfeiting the grandmother all refer to the 'Grandmother', and never refer to the Wolf. The speech of the Wolf to Red Riding Hood, and his speech to her counterfeiting the Grandmother, refer to himself ('I'), but not to the Grandmother. In a textual sense this difference establishes the sexual character of the tale.

Of the four characters in the tale, besides the narrator, only two are responsible for significant discourse. The Mother speaks only once at the outset, about the cake and the little pot of butter. These words had already been mentioned by the narrator, and are repeated five times by the characters. The Grandmother scarcely speaks. Thus the text presents three voices, those of narrator, Red Riding Hood, and Wolf. The narrator's voice formulates 'reality'. From the outset, he identifies the ambition of the Wolf to devour Red Riding Hood. Red Riding Hood's discourse formulates 'appearance'. To the very end, she maintains that she is speaking to her Grandmother. It is the Wolf's discourse which holds 'appearance' and 'reality' apart from one another, repeatedly deferring the moment when the two will correspond with one another to the very end of the narrative. The way in which it does so has both economic and sexual aspects.

Economy

Red Riding Hood is on her way to visit her grandmother, bringing a cake and a little pot of butter. Given that her grandmother is ill, this is a necessary function within the domestic economy of the two households. The items are part of an ongoing exchange, for we are also told that it was the grandmother who made the child her little red hood. In his first conversation with her, the Wolf proposes to her an activity which is strictly surplus to her necessary journey. He shall go this way, and she that. The little girl follows his suggestion and discovers her own freedom. She 'amused herself on the journey by gathering nuts, running after the butterflies, and making nosegays of the wild flowers which she found.' In his second conversation with her, counterfeiting the grandmother, he again proposes an activity which is strictly surplus to her necessary journey. She is to 'Put the cake and the little pot of butter on the bin, and come up on the bed with me.' Finally, from his own point of view, his gobbling up of Red Riding Hood is non-necessary. The text points out that this is not the case *vis-à-vis* the grandmother. 'He sprang upon the poor old lady, and ate her up in less than no time, for he had been more than three days without food.' By contrast to the 'less than no time' which the necessary devouring of the grandmother takes in the story, the non-necessary devouring of Red Riding Hood takes the whole time of the text.

Sexuality

Implicitly within the tale, but explicitly within Perrault's moral, the encounter between the Wolf and Red Riding Hood is a sexual one. Whereas in the English version she is invited to 'come up on the bed' by the Wolf, then she 'took off her cloak' and was astonished at her grandmother 'in her nightgown', in the French version she is told, 'Viens te coucher avec moi', meaning simply 'come to bed with me', then she 'se déshabille' and is astonished to see her grandmother 'en son déshabille'. The word may mean lightly clad, or simply, undressed. The sequence of astonished expressions by the little girl, at the sight of arms, legs, ears, and eyes of the male wolf can express simply the astonishment of a girl for the first time in bed with a man. Marc Soriano (1968) points out that this level of meaning is enhanced in French oral versions of the tale, where Red Riding Hood's 'déshabillement' becomes a strip-tease. In relation to each item of her clothing, she asks where to place it. The Wolf replies, 'Jette-le au feu, mon enfant, tu n'en as plus besoin.' The conclusion of the text is its consumation, the consumption of Red Riding Hood. The sexual skill of the text is its ability to bring closer and closer, while still delaying ever so slightly, the climactic moment, thereby raising pleasure to a greater and greater intensity.

Economy and sexuality are constituted by the text itself. The text produces the surplus time in which the tale can unfold, by deferring the Wolf's initial urge to devour Red Riding Hood. It then consumes this surplus pleasurably, repeatedly deferring its conclusion. The telling of the tale is the deferring of Red Riding Hood's devouring. This deferral/deferance/differance is the work of the text.

Textual practice

Larrucia's reading of the tale is invited by the text itself which, with its appended moral, offers a series of interpretations of interpretations. To provide an alternative reading it is necessary to interrupt the levels of interpretation within the tale itself. Central among these is the moral's interpretation of the narrator's interpretation of the intentions of the Wolf. This can be questioned if it is acknowledged that the Wolf himself intervenes within the situation, perhaps to greater effect than the narrator.[12] We want to suggest that, whereas the narrator and writer of the moral interpret the situation in which they find themselves, the Wolf interrupts it.

For the narrator, 'old Father Wolf . . . would have very much liked to eat' Red Riding Hood. However this raises the question of whether the meaning of an action can be reduced to the intention of the actor. This question can be asked not only of sociological interpreters of actions or of literary texts, but of actors and characters within texts themselves. It must be insisted that the Wolf's actions do not reduce to his (animal) intentions. Whatever his intentions, the Wolf's actions consist in an intervention in the discourse of Little Red Riding Hood in order to transform it. The way in which he does so repays closer examination.

At the first encounter, we are not told the Wolf's opening words. Red Riding Hood's words are given, however. They are exactly repetitious of those addressed to her by her mother. In our earlier consideration of this encounter, following Larrucia, we formulated it as one in which Red Riding Hood obeyed the words of the Wolf, just as she had previously obeyed those of the mother. (These are incidents 2 and 5, making up column 2 of Larrucia's analysis of the story.) But re-consideration shows that this is misleading. The Wolf precisely questions blind obedience. He shows that there is more to the meaning of the mother's words than the appearance of those words. (He shows their indexicality.) Specifically, there is more than one way to obey the words (more than one path to the grandmother's house) and room to investigate the relative merits of each. As we have already noted, the little girl is thereby led to discover that she has surplus time on her hands, and she is able to employ this pleasurably in her own pursuits.

It is precisely the repeated words of the mother, whose meaning he has called into question in speaking to Red Riding Hood, that the Wolf himself repeats in speaking to the grandmother. He does so only to learn the stereotyped speech which the grandmother addresses, as she imagines, to Little Red Riding Hood.

Next the Wolf repeats these words to Red Riding Hood herself. But again his further remark calls this speech into question. He asks explicitly for the cake and the pot of butter to be set aside, and initiates another kind of speech with her. It is important not to be blinded by the knowledge that he is 'really' the Wolf to the fact that here he speaks as the grandmother and intervenes in her speech, in a way which transforms the discourse which she previously had with the child.

The Wolf opens the closure created by the social order speech of the mother and grandmother which had subsumed the little girl within it until then. Economically she had been no more than the bearer of items of exchange (the red hood one way, the cake and butter the other) between the two households: he shows her that she has surplus time of her own. Sexually she had been the object of desire of her mother and of her grandmother: he shows her that she can pursue her own pleasure.

These issues are no sooner opened than they are closed once more by the narrator's final words, which restore the unproblematic and 'wicked' animality of the Wolf. But the narrator's claim, which remains Larrucia's assumption, can be reversed. Instead of presupposing that the Wolf is really natural, and only feigns the veneer of culture, we may conclude that the narrator feigns his natural animal identity in order to exclude the Wolf from the cultural community. This is necessary in order to deny the Wolf's ability to transform the 'Nature'/'Culture' relation which the community is committed to preserve, a commitment upheld by social order theory from Perrault to the present day.

Notes

1 'Valentin Volosinov' is regarded by some as the pseudonym of Mixail Baxtin. In any event Baxtin (1971) is a useful short statement of the theoretical approach developed at greater length in Volosinov (1973).

2 Derrida's writing is itself anti-authoritarian in precisely this sense. Rather then interpreting a text of, say, Rousseau, in terms of his own presupposed version of reality, he interrupts it, allowing its own formulation of the 'appearance'/'reality' differance to come to the fore. This has also been our own attempt in the chapters of this book.

3 This theme is addressed most explicitly in Derrida (1977), but is already implied in Derrida (1973).

4 Cf. his 'Differance', in Derrida (1973)

5 Althusser's theory of ideology understands the text in precisely this way. Cf. Chapter 2 above.

6 The passion expressed by Husserl in his exclamations on behalf of the ego is illustrated by the passages discussed in Chapter 5 above.

7 The aim of a 'genuine openness to the text itself' will be recognized as a linguistic version of Husserl's early programme of phenomenology, as pursued further by Heidegger. However, as we have tried to show in earlier chapters, in each of these writers the project of interruption is itself tainted with essentialism, which restores a form of interpretation. The project must therefore be continued, by way of an interruption of the practice of interruption in each of these writers.

8 For a fuller account of the method, cf. Lévi-Strauss, (op. cit., *passim*), and Larrucia, (op. cit., pp. 523–8).

9 This is the method of the classical text, which 'Little Red Riding Hood'

exemplifies. To disrupt it, one has to conceive of a text in which the voice of the narrator is capable of misleading the reader. This is precisely what occurs in such a text as Robbe-Grillet's *Project for a Revolution in New York*, cf. Chapter 12 above.

10 Of course it is possible to postulate a sophisticated reader who could anticipate the Wolf's moves. However if the reader in general were able to do this, then the plot would be pointless. To express this in terms which will be more rigorously defined below, there would be no pleasure in the text.

11 As already noted, the Wolf is excluded from subjectivity, self, and society. Although he does not explicate this argument, we might say that Larrucia's solution to the problematic identification of speakers (subjects) with speeches is that *qua* counterfeiter, the Wolf is not a speaker (subject), i.e. he has no words of his own. Our view would be rather that by his ability to transform the speech of others, the Wolf better displays the potentialities of speaking than do the other characters.

12 This suggestion is not so fanciful as may appear, since given that the tale existed and exists in many oral versions prior to Perrault's writing it in a literary form, his re-writing of it and appending to it of a moral constitute a definite intervention within the tale which must be open to criticism.

Bibliography

Baxtin, M. (1971), 'Discourse Typology in Prose' in L. Matejka and K. Pomerska, eds, *Readings in Russian Poetics*, Boston: Massachusetts Institute of Technology Press.

Derrida, J. (1973), *Speech and Phenomena*, Evanston: Northwestern University Press.

Derrida, J. (1977), *Of Grammatology*, Baltimore: Johns Hopkins University Press.

Husserl, E. (1970), *Logical Investigations*, vols I and II, London: Routledge Kegan Paul.

Larrucia, V. (1975), 'Little Red Riding Hood's Metacommentary: Paradoxical Injunction, Semiotics and Behaviour', *Modern Language Notes*, 90, pp. 517–34.

Lévi-Strauss, C. (1967), 'The Structural Study of Myth', in *Structural Anthropology*, New York: Basic Books.

Perrault, C. (1975), *Perrault's Complete Fairy Tales*, Harmondsworth: Penguin (Kestrel Books).

Soriano, M. (1968), *Les Contes de Perrault*, Paris: Gallimard.

Volosinov, V. (1973), *Marxism and the Philosophy of Language*, New York: Seminar Press.

Watzlawick, P. *et al.* (1968), *Pragmatics of Human Communication*, London: Faber & Faber.

The linguistic turn has recently been associated with attempts to reduce speech to generative structures of competence or rule. Culler's appeal to 'the linguistic competence of speakers' and Foucault's references to 'a body of anonymous, historical rules' are cases in point. In this chapter, we examine a hospital out-patients' interview using Foucault's concept of 'clinical discourse'. The inability of this concept to reveal critical practice leads to a reanalysis of the interview drawing upon Habermas's version of 'distorted communication'. Here we identify the rupture by practical means of the discursive space occupied by 'clinical discourse'.

chapter 14

The competence model and its limits

Culler's circle

> Rather than try to get outside ideology, we must remain resolutely
> within it, for both the conventions to be analysed and the notions
> of understanding lie within. If circle there be, it is the circle of
> culture itself (Culler: 1975, p.254).

Culler's comments are taken from his *Structuralist Poetics*. This
work is a major attempt to introduce Saussurian semiotics to
English literary criticism. We say *Saussurian* advisedly because
Culler's position involves a strong defence of Saussure's treatment
of language as an external social fact which coerces actual speech
practice.

The statement above is made in response to critics of Saussure
who label his work reductivist and seek to replace it with a more
dialectical treatment of signifying practices. Culler's particular
target is the writers associated with the Paris journal *Tel Quel*,
notably Julia Kristeva and Phillipe Sollers. Culler bases his argument on the centrality of a linguistic competence which is given in
the structure of *langue*. He suggests that the case against a competence model of language *presupposes* the very notions which it
claims to have rejected. For Culler, any attempt to deny the
all-embracing character of an ideology, can, therefore, only be
circular. As Culler puts it: 'Whatever type of freedom the members
of the *Tel Quel* group secure for themselves will be based on
convention and will consist of a set of interpretive procedures'
(252).

There are two reasons why Culler's position is worthy of treatment in this concluding chapter. First, it expresses, in a way, the
major direction of the nineteenth and twentieth critiques of empiricism in the social sciences. That is to say, it puts itself in the ranks of
what seems to be the modern movement against unselfconscious

scientism. This movement came to assert the primacy of language to understanding and the essentially internal character of explanations of social processes.

So a whole column of theorists stand in line behind Culler. Dilthey, the hermeneutic tradition and the German commitment to the uniqueness of the cultural sciences (*Geisteswissenschaften*), culminating in Weberian sociology, foreshadow Culler's acknowledgement of 'the circle of culture'. As we have seen, this position is given philosophical and literary expression in, respectively, Wittgenstein's notion of limits, Kafka's depiction of Court and Castle and Larrucia's interpretation of *Little Red Riding Hood*. Equally, Culler's assertion that 'both the conventions to be analysed and the notions of understanding lie within' could only be applauded by the tradition which asserts the primacy of everyday life – from Schutz on the 'natural attitude' to Winch (1958) on the internality of sociological explanation. Finally, the reference to the centrality of 'interpretive procedures', while deriving from Saussurian semiotics, is on all fours with the position adopted by ethnomethodology, as represented by Garfinkel, Sacks, and Cicourel. Hence it is worth considering Culler's position because it encompasses most of the theories of language that are discussed in this book.

The second reason why we take up Culler is to argue, with one or two qualifications, that his position is entirely wrong. Put more precisely, we try to show that the 'modernism' he represents, far from being the critique of empiricism that it claims to be, simply expresses the post-Kantian empirical tradition in a different guise. Consonant with Kant, Culler's position is premised on a set of *a priori* constructs presupposed in understanding. The 'modernist' ploy is to site these constructs in a variety of homes. Saussure, Heidegger and the early Wittgenstein choose Language, ethnomethodology favours 'interpretive procedures', Husserl votes for 'consciousness' and Schutz for the 'natural attitude'. Usage is elected by Austin and the later Wittgenstein, while Lévi-Strauss, Chomsky and, recently, Cicourel (1973), put their money on Mind. As Strawson's (1972) important treatment of Kant makes clear, this tradition questions only the *siting* of such constructs *not* their universality or pregivenness.

Consequently, it should not be surprising that 'modernism' offers an entirely conventional version of critique, which does not depart considerably from Popper's 'critical rationalism' (1972), nor from the purely technical interest that dominates social science. 'Society' is reformulated in terms of the rules of a system of language but it remains a Durkheimian social fact. Practice is reduced to grammar.

In this regard, it is only necessary to recall Saussure's insistence on the unimportance of *parole*, Austin's reliance on a cosy, evolutionary theory of history, and Heidegger's mythology of 'decisive turns' in the history of language. The idealism at the heart of these positions expresses itself in their lack of attention to emancipatory practices which challenge the closures of a 'culture'. For 'modernism' conceives of everyday life as a massive unity and, in response, offers only the passivity of a total embrace (Austin's celebration of 'the plain man'), the sidestep of ironic detachment (the 'circle' of Wittgenstein and Kafka, together with Garfinkel's tongue-in-cheek 'demonstrations'), and the romantic dream of a linguistic community which, by dint of moral effort, holds itself aloof from the fallen world of *Das Man* (Heidegger). The reduction of mundane practice to the unities of 'convention' and interpretive procedures vitiates any real basis for critique.

As we have noted, Culler's position emerges from this 'modernism', taking up the concept of 'the circle of culture' and using it not for Kafkan ironies but for the construction of a science of language and literature along Saussurian lines. Consequently, we are invited to treat speech and text as surface expressions of a deep structure of linguistic competence. As with Saussure, the latter is the prime research target: 'One must begin with a set of facts to be explained, drawn from the linguistic competence of speakers, and construct hypotheses to explain them' (Culler, p.23). There are echoes here of more recent attempts, in the transformational grammars of Chomsky (1965) and others, to locate the deep structure of competence underlying the surface layer of performance and to specify the rules of transformation from one to the other. The favour which the competence model of language has found suggests that it offers an appealing resolution to the dilemma posed by the 'modernists' ' discovery of everyday life. A total embrace or a total retreat when confronted with the phenomenon came to be seen as romantic responses, unworthy of a social science. With Saussure's work, the competence model establishes a clear body of data and secure field of operations for the scientist. Within the model, the latter is able both to defer to the all-embracing structures of everyday life (Schutz's 'first-order' constructs) and to carve out his own problematic – the systematic unearthing of the competences they presuppose, concluding in the formulation of constructs of 'the second-order'. Granting that discoveries about language are, as Turner (1974, p.213) puts it, 'ineluctably discoveries from *within*', most practitioners turn their back on the murky prospect (implied by both Turner and Garfinkel) of a *mundane* science, in favour of the beckoning pastures of a *science* of the mundane.

But the competence model has more to offer than an antidote to romanticism and mysticism. Its attachment to the role of 'culture' and 'ideology' also allows it to turn the other way and to destroy the 'realist' aspirations of economism. The sense of the omni-presence of ideology, implied by the quotation from Culler with which we began, recognizes its mediating role between social structures and social action. So, for this model, ideology is a fact which is as coercive and external to practice as economic structures. In Foucault's terms, 'discursive practice' reduces to: 'a body of anonymous, historical rules, always determined in the time and space that have defined a given period, and for a given social, economic, geographical, or linguistic area, the conditions of operation of the enunciative function' (1972: p.117).

Foucault's 'clinical discourse'

Despite Foucault's claim to have transcended structuralism, his pursuit of 'the archaeology of knowledge' treats performance, as we have seen, as the outcome of 'a body of anonymous, historical rules' (1972: p.117). In this way, he appears to re-affirm Culler's 'circle of culture' and, with it, the structuralist method.

To investigate further the limits of the competence model, it will be helpful to examine some conversational material. We take it from a hospital outpatients and, initially, seek to apply Foucault's (1973) model of 'clinical discourse' described shortly.

The outpatient clinic we will consider treats children with cardiac disease. Apart from the doctor who speaks, there are a number of other white-coated doctors sitting around a table facing the child. A researcher is seated with a cassette recorder in front of him on the table. There is an X-ray display device on the wall and the doctor who speaks has in front of him the child's records, to which he adds notes during the course of the conversation, and details of tests conducted earlier in the day.

The child has just been examined by the doctors and is seated with his parents on the other side of the table. He has an inoperable heart condition and the family is used to regular visits to the clinic.

In this fragment, the doctor is indicated by D, the mother by M.

1　D.　I think he's smashing. Really he's done **beautifully. You** know the situation long-term (　)?
2　M.　(　)
3　D.　Well, I think as long as he is well there is no indication to do anything else. At such time as he's not well (　). The situation is that it is probably extremely difficult to fix his

heart in such a way that the blood goes round the right
way. I mean he's missing part of the heart and there's no
way of constructing that. If you like, it might be theoretically possible to do (   ).

4* M. He's noticing. He says: 'Look Mum'. And then one day, I
know when you're angry with a child you say: 'What's the
matter with you' (   ) 'There's something wrong with me.'
He's sort of catching on in his own way.

5* D. The thing is, um, at the moment, even though he's not
perfect, he's leading a normal life. There *are* operations
that can be done (   ) but they're not going to give him a
normal heart.

6 M. They seem very pleased with the shunt at H.Hospital.

7 D. Do you know what the shunt does?

8 M. Well not exactly. I would like to know.[1]

To judge simply by appearances, the doctor seems to treat the
situation as more than the merely diagnostic/prognostic encounter
suggested by a purely 'medical' model of disease. In particular, he
recognizes parental anxiety and responds with reassuring words
('he's smashing . . . done beautifully . . . leading a normal life'). He
also seeks out parental lack of knowledge about the earlier 'holding'
operation carried out on their child ('Do you know what the shunt
does?'). Subsequently, he will explain in simple terms, its nature and
consequences. However, these kinds of observation rely on an
anecdotal use of the material which derives from a reductivist
impulse. Their aim is to reduce the facts of language to preconceived categories of social structure, for example the 'normal'
roles of doctor and patient. Their method is to search for a deeper
unstated meaning in what is said by treating the talk as documenting
some underlying reality.

This 'documentary method of investigation' (Garfinkel) functions
as what Foucault has called a 'commentary' upon the text. He
explains this as follows:

> Commentary questions discourse as to what it says and what it
> intended to say: it tries to uncover the deeper meaning of speech
> that enables it to achieve an identity with itself, supposedly
> nearer to its essential truth; in other words, in stating what has
> been said, one has to re-state what has never been said (1973:
> p.xvi).

As Foucault points out, such 're-stating' always assumes an excess
of the signified over the signifier. Its 'hermeneutic project' literally
parallels biblical exegesis. In older forms, it sought to penetrate

from concrete images to the word of God. In modern dress, it seeks to uncover a transcendental Subject who speaks.

Instead of 'commentary', Foucault offers a *structural* analysis of discourses, concerned only with the fact of the historical appearance of a mode of discourse and supposing no signified 'excess'. In *The Birth of the Clinic*, he investigates what he calls 'clinical discourse'. Let us see how we can apply Foucault's formulation to the hospital conversation.

The first point to note is that this fragment is contemporary. Knowing the period is essential because Foucault maintains that a crucial sequence of changes overtook medicine from the late eighteenth century onwards. These were changes in the relation between disease and the 'gaze' (the French '*regard*') to which disease offered itself. Each kind of 'gaze' constituted differently the relation between the disease and the 'sick' person.

In earlier times, a pathological 'essence' was assumed to lie beyond particular symptoms. Fevers, for instance, were thought to have a pure form and to develop in certain 'natural' stages. Certain symptoms that did not fit this essential truth were regarded as 'interferences'.

This had two contrasting implications for the perceived relation between disease and diseased. First, the 'sick' person was seen as simply a vehicle for the unfolding of the disease. This meant that he himself constituted an 'interference' who could complicate matters by reacting upon the pure form of the disease. Second, however, the 'sick' person regained his being within his family. The family could allow the disease to attain its own truth by assisting the natural forces that would allow it to dissipate. Consequently, disease and the family were to be treated as natural phenomena, essential counterparts to each other.

In modern times, the assimilation of disease and diseased to natural pure forms was overturned. With the new visibility of the anatomy and pathology of the body (via the dissected corpse), disease ceased to be a metaphysical essence and reduced itself to a collection of symptoms. The clinical gaze turned towards these symptoms. The calculation of 'data' replaced conjecture about nature.

'I think he's smashing', the doctor says, 'really he's done beautifully.' These utterances can be located within Foucault's modern version of clinical discourse.

A relation is implied between a 'sick' person (here in the form of 'he') and a disease (which makes him 'smashing' or doing 'beautifully'). However, this person is now no longer presented as an 'interference' to the disease. Instead, the nature of the disease is intimately related to the person. Indeed, there is no disease without the subject (*he* is smashing, *he* has done beautifully). Notions of the 'essence' of a disease are here discursively reconstituted in the form of an *individual('s)* illness. In this form, as Foucault writes: 'Only individual illnesses exist: *not* because the individual reacts upon his own illness, but because the action of the illness rightly unfolds in the form of individuality' (1973: pp.168–9). This 'individuality' will unfold by reference to the anatomy and pathology of the body. So 'the situation long term' to which the doctor refers will be given, as we shall see, by 'data' rather than by natural 'essences'.

This 'situation' is formulated in utterance 3 in terms of such data ('He's missing part of the heart'). The data is conceived in relation to the horizon offered by the body and by the individual who 'owns' the illness ('he is well'). In turn, pure 'forms' are replaced here by a definition of the elements that compose the individual case and a calculation of their relation, e.g. *his* heart and circulation of the blood. As Foucault points out, modern clinical discourse understands disease as a complex set of inter-relations of observable conditions *not* as a mixture of essences. The move is from types to rules of combination: from botany to chemistry. Such rules define what 'it might be theoretically possible to do'.

Utterance 4 presents a problem. Clearly, it cannot be treated simply as an example of 'clinical' discourse as he defines it. In *The Birth of the Clinic*, such discourse is associated with doctors. Yet here a patient's mother speaks. This creates difficulties to which we shall return. For the moment, however, let us treat her words simply as an expression of an earlier form of clinical discourse.

As we have noted, Foucault emphasizes the central place of the family in early medicine. In modern times, the family is redefined as, in part, an obstacle to diagnosis and treatment. Against the mother's attempt to locate the patient within the structures of family life (*old* discourse), the doctor insists on the relevance of clinical data ('he's not perfect') and clinical standards of normality ('he's leading a normal life') (*new* discourse). In the new discourse, the hospital replaces the family as the natural locus of treatment. While the mother in utterance 4 returns to family life as the 'natural' environment of disease, the doctor responds in utterance 5 by asserting the greater relevance of assessment made in the hospital. The hospital is where 'operations . . . can be done'. It is also the site where pure, unmediated data can be made visible – the place where decisions about 'perfection' and 'normality' should be made. So, following Foucault, the patient is no longer a 'sick person' (old discourse) but the bearer of an 'individual illness'.

The concluding utterances (6 to 8) indicate the triumph of the new discourse. They turn on the technical term 'shunt'. The gaze of modern clinical discourse, as Foucault points out, only reveals to those who know what to see. Consequently, technical vocabularies have developed to give speech to what everybody sees without seeing. The facts available to the clinical gaze may thus be fully described. It also follows, however, that this gaze becomes out of the ordinary and that medical encounters start to turn on the elucidation of vocabulary.

Utterance 8 seems to bear out the special character of the gaze which the mother 'would like to know' in so far as it defines her child. As utterance 4 indicated the presence of an alternative to modern clinical discourse, so utterance 8 indicates an attempt to enter into the doctor's clinical speech. However, such an attempt can only be partially successful for, as Foucault notes, clinical discourse belongs to doctors. The difficulty has been created by the presence of the mother's speech. We had no difficulty in assigning the doctor's speech to Foucault's categories of clinical discourse. But since, by definition, the mother cannot be engaging in clinical discourse, we could only treat her speech as an exemplar of what stands opposed to such discourse. We did this by using the fiction of the mother as the speaker of an older version of clinical discourse.

It is possible now to abandon this fiction. Instead, we can treat the mother's speech as exemplifying a form of non-clinical discourse – perhaps to be called 'familial discourse' – whose mode of operation would have to be specified. On this reading, the conversation is the statement of two self-contained discourses (one that Foucault might call 'clinical' and one that we have called 'familial'). Each discourse coheres by virtue of what Foucault calls its 'unity' and 'systemic' character. Any contradictions that arise within a discourse (and Foucault's account has not suggested any here) are, within this model, *pre-defined* by the structure of discourse itself.[2] Speakers, then, are committed at the outset to remain within the mode of discourse to which they are fitted. They can only enter another discourse partially and without any opportunity to modify its speech or their own. Each discourse offers only a single authoritative voice: notice how Foucault's model of the clinic focuses entirely on the doctor. Speech simply restates pre-defined unities and contradictions.

Our investigation of the implications of Foucault's model for an example of hospital talk has led to a curious conclusion. It has transpired that the model can cope with talk that does not follow the rules of a particular discourse *only by placing it in another discourse*. But this is precisely what the doctor does. He stays firmly within his clinical discourse, refusing to enter any other. Foucault's model, by devious means, preserves the Subject whom it claimed to abandon. It articulates an authoritative voice of a Subject who can respond to another's speech only by drawing boundaries.[3]

Yet the mother's speech suggests an alternative. Unlike the doctor, she moves between both modes of discourse. In so doing, her speech stands as a practical criticism of the Foucault/doctor scheme of interpretation. It remains to be seen whether it also dissolves the closure suggested by the concept of *modes* of discourse.

In this analysis, we have tried to show the extent to which the competence model offers a reductivist interpretive theory of language which is unable to cope with the material reality of speech. Despite its anti-idealist pretensions, the model lapses into an idealist position whereby 'discourse' or 'culture' become grammatical unities rather than the locus of contradictory practices. More precisely, the model:

1   Reduces speech to a pre-given reality (competence, modes of discourse) proposed by the theorist. So the theorist's idealized account of discourse is given preference to the realities of actual speech practices;

2   Constitutes the investigator as engaged with formulating possible worlds (i.e. as a theorist) but reduces others to passive exponents of a pre-given mode of discourse (i.e. as non-theorists);

3   Treats the relation between appearance and reality as pre-constituted in the surface-deep structure distinction rather than as constituted by speech and dialogue;

4   Offers a normative, social order model which precludes investigation of the 'interruptive' practices in which speakers challenge and reassemble proposed relations between appearance and reality.

In so far as the model is unconcerned with the *critical* practices of speakers, we may say that it is unable to offer a critical treatment of language. However, there are nuances in the notion and practice of critical theory which we must now explore. It remains to be seen whether there are elements of the competence model which can help an exploration of the critical practices present in the clinic talk.

Habermas's critical theory of language

We have implied so far that a critical theory of language cannot develop from a competence model. However, no serious attention has been given to the exact character of such a critical theory. Nor have we reviewed any attempt to base a critical theory on a formulation of the structures of competence presupposed in critical communication, as opposed to communication which merely reproduces dominant ideological forms.

Considerations of this nature imply the potential value of a model of language which recognizes the capacity for emancipation as a matter of linguistic competence. Such a critical model is at the basis of Habermas's theory of communication and it is to his work that we now turn. In a later section, Habermas's model will be briefly assessed with further reference to the materials that we have just considered.

Habermas's version of critical theory seeks to restore recognition to the 'human interest' expressed in a particular practice. He argues that the Kantian attempt to free knowledge from human interests depends upon a split between life and theory that was inimicable to Greek thought as much as to Marxist formulations. Instead of denying interest, along the lines of Culler and most proponents of the competence model, Habermas suggests that knowledge is always constituted by reference to one of *three* interests:

1 *Technical-cognitive interest*

This is exemplified in the attempt of the empirical-analytic sciences to reveal the character of objectified processes (e.g. the structure of the atom or 'suicide' as constituted by Durkheim). In order to pave the way for technical control, criticism is restricted to issues of epistemology and methodology. This interest, as Habermas puts it, is 'philosophical only insofar as is necessary for the immunization of the sciences against philosophy' (1972: 67).

2 *Practical interest*

As expressed in the cultural sciences, this maintains that access to facts is not through observation but by the empathic understanding of meaning. Hence, one is engaged always in the interpretation of a tradition from out of a tradition. The practical interest is in the expansion of intersubjectivity that may follow. However, as Habermas shows in his essay on Dilthey (1972: Chs 7–8), the attempt to re-experience meaning is only the equivalent of science's method of observation. In both cases, truth is held to arise in contemplation which seeks to copy experience. But this preserves the distinction between observer (contemplator) and observed (contemplated). Rather than contemplation, Habermas argues, a form of dialogue is required which establishes critical practice in the context of experienced life activity. Such a dialogue, we are told, can make the participant comprehend himself in his own self-formative process and see himself and the other as moments of an objective process that encompasses them both (181).

3 *Critical interest*

The dialogic relation that expresses a critical interest establishes a distinction between the 'invariant regularities of social action' and the 'ideologically frozen relations of dependence that can in principle be transformed' (310). Like psycho-analysis, it sets off a process of reflection in the consciousness of those whom science's laws are supposedly about. This self-reflection aims to release the subject from dependence on the power of illegitimately naturalized social processes.

For Habermas, emancipation only occurs when the constraints of both external and internal nature are overcome. The former relates to instrumental action geared to the forces of production, the latter to *communicative* action in terms of *norms*:

> Emancipation from the compulsion of internal nature succeeds to the degree that institutions based on force are replaced by an organisation of social relations that is bound only to communication free from domination. This does not occur directly through productive activity but through the revolutionary activity of struggling classes (including the critical activity of reflective sciences) (1972: p.53).

Habermas is implying here the necessity of critique both as a preface to revolution and as a continuing feature of revolutionary society. For while the repression by 'external' nature is limited by developments of the forces of production, repression by internal nature (naturalized social codes) can live on.

At the heart of the project is Habermas's attempt to deny the validity of a model of *instrumental* action for all human activity. In this respect, his attempt to formulate a theory of communicative competence (discussed shortly) stands apart from the competence models which we have criticised earlier. Basic to this theory, and distinguishing Habermas's position from that of the 'modernists', is the separation of labour from interaction:

1   *Labour* is purposive-rational action (Weber's *Zweck-rationalität*). It is concerned with the appropriation of outer nature

through techniques and theories based on truth claims. Consequently, the rationalization of labour signifies the growth of productive forces and the extension of technological control.
2   *Interaction* is communicative action or social interaction. It is
concerned with the appropriation of internal nature through norms
and practical insights that need to be legitimated in discourse.
Rationalization here means the extension of communication free
from domination.

'Modernism', via the competence model, reduces the practices of
both observer and observed to the category of labour. As exemplified in Weber's method, it constitutes both as technicians seeking
to control nature. A model of interaction, however, recognizes the
critical potential of discourse and emphasizes the establishment of
norms in dialogue. The distinction between interaction and labour
and the recognition of the degree of their autonomy also serves to
emphasize Habermas's rejection of another form of reductivism
which reduces everything to an expression of the 'contradictions' of
the 'system'. He writes: 'We can speak of the "fundamental contradiction" of a social formation when, and only when, its organis-
ational principle necessitates that individuals and groups repeatedly
confront one another with claims and intentions that are in the long
run incompatible' (1976: p.27).
    The two main threads of Habermas's critical theory of language
now become clearer. First, such a theory prepares for an attack on
'systematically distorted' communication in both scientific and
everyday discourse. In science, it reasserts the inseparability of
accepted dichotomies (fact and value, theory and practice, mental
and manual labour). In science and everyday life, it highlights the
relations of power surreptitiously incorporated into the symbolic
structures of speech and action, and reveals the blockages to
communication which conceal these relations.
    The second thread of the theory provides the essential platform
for the first. It seeks to establish a version of an 'ideal speech
situation', freed from all constraints of domination arising from
ideologies or neuroses, and to ground this version on the very
structure of communication itself.
    Habermas stresses that his analysis of speech will be concerned
with the nature of *communicative* rather than *linguistic* competence.
He argues (1970: p.138) that general semantics cannot be
developed from the narrow basis of the asocial linguistic competence proposed by Chomsky, for: 'The situation . . . in which
speech . . . becomes possible depends upon a structure of intersubjectivity which, in turn, is linguistic.' This 'structure of intersubjec-

tivity' acts as the silent guarantee of Chomsky's examples of presumed asocial linguistic competences. The examples are only plaus-
ible because they express modern Western cultures. Hence what is
needed is an analysis of what is involved in the command of speech
and symbolic interaction. And this implies an analysis of communicative rather than linguistic competence.

To this end, Habermas (1970) aims at the construction of a
'universal pragmatics', consonant with culturally and historically
changing worldviews (*Weltbilder*). Following Austin and Searle
(see Chapter 9), he argues that the 'illocutionary force' of an
utterance depends upon the culturally defined form of intersubjectivity. This intersubjectivity is expressed in what Habermas calls
'Dialogue Constitutive Universals' (DCU's) which are implicit in
the speech process. These DCU's define an ideal-speech situation
characterized by a system of personal pronouns, a set of expressions
regarding space and time, and a set of *performatives* focused on the
realities portrayed in the discourse and on the act of speaking itself:
'The DCU's at the same time generate and describe the form of
intersubjectivity which makes mutuality of understanding possible.
Communicative competence is defined by the ideal speaker's mastery of the DCU's irrespective of the actual restrictions under
empirical conditions' (1970: pp.140–1). So communicative competence, Habermas argues, presupposes 'mutuality of understanding'
irrespective of the distortions that may actually ensue. In order to
describe the deformations of pure intersubjectivity which arise in
the way in which the DCU's are applied (145), we need an
empirically-applicable statement of the pure form. In a most precise
formulation, Habermas writes:

> Pure intersubjectivity is determined by a symmetrical relation
> between I and You (We and You), I and He (We and They). An
> unlimited interchangeability of dialogue roles demands that no
> side be privileged in the performance of these roles: pure inter-
> subjectivity exists only when there is complete symmetry in the
> distribution of assertion and disputation, revelation and hiding,
> prescription and following, among the partners of communica-
> tion (143).

This kind of statement offers the opportunity to move on from a
critical *theory* of language to an examination of the critical linguistic
practices present in actual conversation. In this regard, Habermas's
position does not offer so much a critique of the competence model
of language but an attempt to shift the debate on to an altogether
more fruitful plane. It remains to be seen whether his formulation
can stand up when confronted by our clinic materials.

Critical practice

It will be recalled that we discovered evidence in the clinic talk of a practical challenge to Foucault's formulation of 'mode of discourse'. We also tried to imply that this discovery need not involve a return to that interpretive practice that he calls 'commentary'. Rather than reduce the talk to preconceived cultural stereotypes of medical encounters, populated by puppet figures, we must approach the worlds and selves set into play by the talk itself. In making this approach, we recall that one of Habermas's DCU's was a system of personal pronouns which enabled speakers to move between different voices. Following previous chapters, we can now turn to the talk to examine the voices that inhabit it and, by implication, the worlds they theorize.

For the moment, let us stick to D's utterances. D inhabits the voice of an 'I' which affirms its theorizing capacity – it 'thinks' and 'means'. The world that 'I' lives in is both natural and social, although the natural elements predominate.

This natural world is inhabited by a 'He' who is constituted by D as the possessor of various physical attributes ('he is well', 'he is missing part of the heart', 'he's not perfect'). 'He's' physical condition generates a 'situation' composed of possible courses of action, their consequences, and preferred responses. These are variously formulated by the impersonal pronouns 'It' and 'They' and by the 'there is/are' forms. Thus '*it* is probably extremely difficult', '*it* might be theoretically possible' and '*they*'re not going to give him a normal life'. The 'there' form crops up in 'there is no indication', 'there is no way of constructing that', and 'there are operations that can be done.' All these voices speak of a natural world and of possible responses to it determined by the facts of nature as interpreted by the voice of 'I'. Hence facts and responses are presented as non-negotiable features of a world to which only D has access.

However, the voice of 'I' does allow two references to a social world. In D's asterisked utterance, although 'He' is initially constituted as a natural object ('he's not perfect'), there is a subsequent switch to his social existence – 'He's leading a normal life'. This is the sole such reference made by D, and because it is occasioned by M's preceding utterance (also asterisked), we shall return to it later. The second appeal by D to a social world arises in the question: 'You know the situation long-term (   )?' So, like 'I', there is a 'You' who can think and hence 'know'. However the thinking/knowing of both is limited precisely to the natural world that 'I' theorizes.

In summary form, then, the world theorized by D contains the following four parties:

1 An 'I' who 'thinks' and 'means' with reference to the natural world.
2 A 'You' who 'knows' the natural world as constituted by 'I'.
3 A 'He' who is part of this natural world.
4 'It', 'They' and 'There' which describe the natural environment in which 'He' is placed.

From one-dimensional stereotypes of medical role-behaviour we have moved on to examine some of the complexities of linguistic practice. In doing so, we have found empirical referents for Habermas's formulations. 'Pure intersubjectivity' depends upon an 'unlimited interchangeability of dialogue roles and symmetry in the distribution of assertion and disputation . . . among the partners of communication' (Habermas, op.cit.). Yet here, D's attempts to limit the voice of 'I' to reflections on a purely natural world mean that no such interchangeability is offered. As long as D is the only (or most reliable) point of access to nature, then he must inhabit the voice of 'I', with M condemned to the listening and responding but not initiating role of 'You'. So the apparent dialogic rights extended by D's formulation of a 'You' are taken away as soon as they are offered. For only D is in a position to be the 'I' who can describe the natural world inhabited by 'He', 'It' and 'They' or to recognize what 'There is' of relevance in the environment. This further implies that D claims, in Habermas's terms, a fair degree of monopoly over the rights of assertion and disputation which are implied by performatives focused on the act of speaking.

However, the relation between society and nature is not given in the *topics* at which speech is directed. If this were the case, then medical encounters could only be natural phenomena. The issue turns instead on how this relation is *constituted* in speech. Where the sociality of linguistic practice is concealed or fixed in some apparently natural order, we have distorted communication. For here speech seems to be *labour*, determined by the forces of production, rather than *interaction* or communicative behaviour concerned to assert and dispute possible worlds.

No such assertion or disputation is allowed by D. The world of four parties that D theorizes is given the same unchallenged natural status as the physical condition that affects the child. D's utterances use a ploy common in practices that express a technical-cognitive interest. It is true that technical sciences quite properly recommend that their *topics* be recognized as natural facts. In paediatric medical encounters, such characterization of disease as natural is a basis on which parental feelings of 'guilt' can be contested. The point, then, is to dispute only the illegitimate naturalization of *social* processes, not to assert the social character of the truly natural.[4] Technical sciences, usually proceed, however, to reduce their *communicative behaviour* to the same status as their topics of study.

In much the same way, D here reduces discourse to the technical functions of providing information and reducing anxiety. What this establishes, as we shall shortly see, is a way of not listening to other ways of formulating discursive relations and topics. As Habermas shows, the rationalization of discourse involves emancipation from distorted communication *not* technical efficiency in satisfying pre-defined goals.

Viewed in this way, the conversational fragment that we have been considering seems to epitomize distorted communication. However, perhaps we have been too hasty in assuming that D's utterances preclude the emergence of any critical practice. In order to examine this possibility, we must turn to M's words.

In the asterisked utterance, M begins by formulating a 'He' who 'is noticing', 'says: "Look Mum" ', and 'is sort of catching on in his own way'. Unlike D, then, M locates the voice of 'He' firmly in the social world. M's 'He' *defines* his relation to nature; the 'He' of D is defined *by* his relation to nature. Equally, the 'I' in which M dwells affirms a theorizing capacity. ('I know'), but centred around what people do (the social) rather than what objective processes do to them (nature). Similarly, the dialogue-partner ('You') is constituted as a voice immersed in the social world, able to experience and respond to emotions ('you're angry with a child' and 'What's the matter with you?'). Finally, each responds to an environment in which 'there's something' which is mediated by his own theorizing ('There's something wrong with me. He's sort of catching on in his own way').

Using a summary form again, the world theorized by M contains the same four parties as that found in D's world. However, unlike D, all voices are accorded theorizing capacity, as follows:

1 An 'I' who 'knows' about the social world.
2 A 'You' who shares the same competence and hence can enter into dialogue.
3 A 'He' who experiences and can discuss the impact of nature.
4 A 'There' which is neither natural nor social but expresses the former mediated by the latter.

So M responds to D's utterances by challenging the discursive closure with which they operate. While D topicalizes nature and naturalizes the relations between the speaking parties, M topicalizes society and re-socializes the dialogue. While D formulates the reality of his practice as information-giving and reassurance, M affirms that its reality is to offer no discursive space to other voices. Rather than respond by 'interpreting' the appearance of what D says, M enters into it to transform it: In challenging the relation between appearance and reality formulated by D, M *interrupts* D's speech.

'The thing is . . . ', D responds. So M's utterance is reconstituted as the appearance of a pre-defined natural reality. While utterance 4 had resocialized the dialogue, utterance 5 offers a fresh discursive closure. 'He' becomes once again an object to be judged in terms of external definitions of 'perfection' and 'normality'. 'I' is the voice which speaks the reality to which 'You' only has access as a set of appearances.

The doctor immediately returns to his secure home-base of the natural environment in which 'there are operations' and 'They're not going to give him a normal heart.' The cue is taken by the mother who makes an observation now about an operation which does not challenge D's attempt to treat the child as data – 'They seem pleased with the shunt at H. Hospital'. Nonetheless, the 'They' she formulates belongs to people rather than to D's natural world and hence, for her, nature is still mediated by society (i.e. the issue is not the shunt in itself but that 'they' seem 'pleased' with it).

The last two utterances reassert the doctor's version of the reality of the speech as information-giving and the mother's acceptance of this reality, given her unsuccessful earlier challenge: 'Do you know what the shunt does?' 'Well not exactly. I would like to know.'

As an example of the success of critical practice, this fragment is not altogether satisfactory. Let us conclude this discussion, then, by briefly examining a conversation that occurred on a ward of the same hospital. The same doctor is speaking to a mother of a young child who, unfortunately, experienced a stroke after a diagnostic operation (catheterization). This relatively rare outcome, the doctor explains, now means that the child requires a further operation. Despite the mother's desire for an assessment of the extent of impairment caused by the stroke, the doctor advises that this operation should take place before the child is seen by a neurologist.

We will examine sequentially the conversation that then ensues:

1 D. What do you think about that?

A 'You' is formulated who 'thinks'. So a space is created for dialogue. The question remains: what kind of space?

2 M. Well I mean it's obvious he's got to have it done.
3 D. Um.

The answer to D's question constitutes a world with three parties. (1) a voice of 'I' which 'means'; (2) an 'It' which is a procedure determined by technical decision-making based on nature; and (3) a voice of 'He' who is the object of the decision. Both 'I' and 'He' are formulated as passive objects of natural processes. Natural facts define what 'I' can 'mean' and make 'He' a mere object. So 'I' hardly has room to move in a world where 'It' rules 'obviously'.

M here interprets rather than interrupts the relation between appearance and reality proposed by D's speech.

4 M. Um, I mean what more can I say?
5 D. Um.

We have to be careful with M's next utterance. It *appears* to express the resignation which was only implied by her previous comment. However, we know not to ask for the 'state of mind' indicated by an utterance but for its 'cash-value' (Austin). Viewed this way, another, contradictory voice of 'I' is being offered here. 'I' now 'means' and 'says' not as a passive object of nature but as the formulator of the social – whether located in discourse or the self. The claim is that the 'You' that I am offered gives no space to express this 'I' ('I mean what more can I say?'). But this 'I' claims the right to formulate the conversation and, thereby, to show the construction of nature in speech.

6 M. Probably I mean if things hadn't gone wrong when they did at the test I suppose I wouldn't be so apprehensive. I mean I can't help feeling that way.

Despite D's attempt to naturalize the world, this 'I' insists that nature is mediated by society ('if things hadn't gone wrong . . . I wouldn't be so apprehensive'). Similarly, inner nature, responding to the norms of communicative action and expressing personal sentiments, cannot be excluded by a discourse limited to outer nature ('I mean I can't help feeling that way').

7 M. He's got to have it done. You know it.

'He' has been placed in the natural realm. But this realm is also constituted in your speech – it is the space in which 'You' dwell ('You know it').

8 D. Yes.
9 M. There's no way round it. So . . . .
10 D. Would you like him to see the neurologist first? Would that put your mind at rest?

The world of nature in which 'There' is, has come to reign ('There's no way round it'). So nature has to be given its due but challenged when ever it illegitimately extends into social relations. Responding to M, D now reformulates the voice of 'You'. No longer is it implied that 'You' can only dwell among natural objects and processes. Instead, D constitutes a 'You' not unlike that proposed by the other mother. This 'You' has 'likes' and a 'mind' which can be in different states. It is a 'You' whose discourse can refer to inner nature – the norms expressed in interaction. Consequently, 'You' is able to hold a dialogue with an 'I' which, despite a special competence in the workings of the natural world, shares a *common* discursive existence with 'You'. Linguistic practice has challenged and overcome the attempt to reduce discursive space to 'clinical discourse'.

Here, then, is an interruption which succeeds. The doctor concedes in practice that the relation between nature and society is ordered in speech.[5] So we encounter critical theory in practice: the practical overcoming of Culler's 'circle of culture' and Foucault's 'modes of discourse'. Freed from a technical version of rational speech, a dialogue can proceed in which social, as well as natural, constraints can be challenged.

Notes

1 This material is drawn from a research study funded by The Social Science Research Council. The analysis has been aided by discussions with Robert Hilliard, Mary Kirk and Geoff Rayner.

2 There seem to be two different positions maintained by Foucault about the nature of unities and contradictions. At one point, he reduces contradictions to the character of a discursive formation, which is 'a space of multiple dissensions; a set of different oppositions whose levels and roles must be described' (1972: p.155). This seems in line with his discussion of the systemic character of such a formation, directed at 'what systematizes things said by men from the outset' (1973: p.xix). Yet, a little later, system seems to give way to practice: his purpose, he writes is 'to map, in a particular discursive practice, the point at which . . . (oppositions and contradictions) are constituted, to define the form that they assume, the relations that they have with each other, and the domain that they govern' (1972: pp.155–6).

3 Despite the inability of the concept of 'clinical discourse', as presented here, to account for challenge *internal* to a discourse, Foucault maintains elsewhere a concern with changes in practices. He attempts 'to show that a change in the order of discourse does not presuppose "new ideas", a little invention and creativity, a different mentality, but transformations in a practice, perhaps also in neighbouring practices, and in their common articulation. I have not denied – far from it – the possibility of changing discourse: I have deprived the sovereignty of the subject of the

exclusive and instantaneous right to it' (1972: p.209). This is an inspiring programme. We share the aim to uncover transformations in a practice not located in an individual subject. But Foucault's discussions of such changes are limited to historical changes in a whole discursive formation – such as the move from one clinical discourse to another.

4 In doctor-patient talk the natural order of He/It/There plays precisely the role of extraordinary external reality that the social order voice of We plays in the talk of schoolteachers (cf. Torode: 1976).

5 In *theory*, the doctor's utterance introduces a curious link between neurology and mind.

Bibliography

Chomsky, Noam (1965), *Aspects of a Theory of Syntax*, Massachusetts Institute of Technology Press.

Cicourel, Aaron (1973), *Cognitive Sociology*, Penguin: Harmondsworth.

Culler, Jonathan (1975), *Structuralist Poetics*, Routledge & Kegan Paul: London.

Foucault, Michel (1972), *The Archaeology of Knowledge*, Tavistock: London.

Foucault, Michel (1973), *The Birth of the Clinic*, Tavistock: London.

Habermas, Jürgen (1970), 'Towards a Theory of Communicative Competence', in H. P. Dreitzel, ed., *Patterns of Communicative Behavior*, Macmillan: New York.

Popper, Karl (1972), *Objective Knowledge*, Clarendon Press: Oxford.

Strawson, Peter (1972), *The Bounds of Sense*, Methuen: London.

Torode, Brian (1976), 'Teachers' Talk and Classroom Discipline', in M. W. Stubbs and S. Delamont, eds, *Explorations in Classroom Observation*, Wiley: London.

Turner, Roy (1974), ed., *Ethnomethodology*, Penguin: Harmondsworth.

Winch, Peter (1958), *The Idea of a Social Science*, Routledge & Kegan Paul: London.

Name index

Subject index

As an aid to the reader, an asterisk appears against page references which define the more important technical terms used in the text. The relevant terms appear in bold print.